CHRIST
THE KING
LORD OF HISTORY

CHRIST THE KING
LORD OF HISTORY

By
Anne W. Carroll

THIRD EDITION

*"Pilate therefore said to him: Art thou a king then?
Jesus answered: Thou sayest that I am a king. For this
was I born, and for this came I into the world."*
—John 18:37

TAN BOOKS AND PUBLISHERS, INC.
Rockford, Illinois 61105

ISBN: 0-89555-503-4

Library of Congress Control No.: 93-61594

Cover illustration: The Coronation of Charlemagne (as Holy Roman Emperor by Pope Leo III in Rome on Christmas Day, 800 A.D.), by von Kaulbach. Collection of the Stiftung Maximilianeum, Munich.

Printed and bound in the United States of America.

TAN BOOKS AND PUBLISHERS, INC.
P.O. Box 424
Rockford, Illinois 61105
1994

Dedicated
To My Husband

Table of Contents

Chapter One
What History Is All About

HISTORY IS THE JAPANESE DECISION to bomb Pearl Harbor, which brought the United States into World War II. History is Robert E. Lee's choice to command Confederate armies instead of Union armies in the Civil War, so that the Union had a much harder time winning the war. History is the settlement of New England by Pilgrims and Puritans, so that their ideas influenced the kind of government the United States eventually had. History is Christopher Columbus persuading the King and Queen of Spain to support his voyage in which he discovered the New World.

History is the record of events which have made a difference in the world.

You can easily see that not all events make history. When Robert E. Lee decided to command Confederate armies, he made history. His decision made a difference in the way the Civil War was fought and the results of that war. But not everything Robert E. Lee did in his life would be written in a history book. The book would be so long and dull that not even Mrs. Robert E. Lee would want to read it.

Historians are men who write history. They must make choices about the events to be included. They must decide which events have made a difference and should be recorded. Since every historian has his own ideas and views, each one will choose different events to put in his history. Nearly every historian of the Civil War will include Lee's decision for the Confederacy. But not all of these historians will think it is important to know whether or not Lee himself owned slaves. Some historians will emphasize one battle of the war, others a different battle. Some will give credit for the North's victory to President Lincoln, others to General Grant. There is no "perfect" history of the Civil War which includes every-

7

thing that everyone thinks is important. People have too many different ideas always to agree on what is and is not important.

It is the same with the history of any war or any country or any century. Each historian will write about the events he thinks are important and will give his own point of view on these events. If he did not, history would be a boring list of dates and events, nothing more.

The history in this book will cover events from about 4000 years ago up to the recent past. It obviously can't discuss everything or you would never finish the book. Therefore it must judge which events in the history of the world have made the most difference and have had the most influence on the most people.

Where can we begin in choosing these events? We can begin by asking ourselves this question: What is *the* most important event that has ever happened in the world, which has had the greatest impact on other events and has influenced the lives of the greatest number of people?

To answer this question, some people would choose the formation of one of the great empires of the world. An *empire* is a nation which rules other nations, and the greatest of these have certainly influenced history. Some of the great empires which you may know are Egypt, Babylon, Persia, Rome. But can they be *the* most important thing that has ever happened? They influenced many people at the time they existed, but nothing remains of them now but monuments that a tourist might visit. They all collapsed or were conquered and no longer influence history.

Other people might think of some great general or great ruler: Alexander the Great, who conquered an empire against greater odds than any other conqueror ever has; Augustus Caesar, who ruled the huge Roman Empire during a time of peace and prosperity; Napoleon of France, who dominated Europe for many years. Each of these men was very powerful and dominated the world while he was alive. Even after these men died, events were still influenced for a time by the things they had done. But where are any of them now? Their empires are gone and they no longer influence history.

Even when an individual influenced history after his life, we cannot find any evidence that he influenced history *before* he existed. Men and nations do not change the events that happened before them.

So to find the most important event in the history of the world, we must find an event that had a great influence at the time it occurred, that is still influencing history at the present time, and that even made a difference in history before it occurred.

There is only one event that meets all of these requirements. That event is what Christians call the Incarnation: the birth, life, death and Resurrection of Jesus Christ, who was both God and man.

You will probably think that any discussion of Jesus belongs in a religious book, not in a history book. But Jesus was not only a religious figure. He was a historical figure as well. The Roman historian Tacitus writes about Jesus in his history. The Jewish historian Josephus discusses what Jesus did.

But even more, we cannot really understand the history of the world unless we look at it from the standpoint of the Incarnation. Of all the nations that existed before the Incarnation, only one still exists today: the Jewish nation, the people who prepared the world for the coming of Jesus. Other nations which existed at that time have no effect on the way things are now.

After the Incarnation, the most influential events had to do with the establishment and spread of the Catholic Church. The Church was the only institution which survived the collapse of Roman civilization. The civilization in which we live, western civilization, could just as easily have been called Catholic civilization. Our world was shaped by Catholicism, the religion founded by Jesus Christ. At the present time, 2000 years after Christ, the Catholic Church is still the strongest and most influential institution in the world. Many of the problems which our world presently faces are caused by its rejection of the Church and its teachings. Even historians who do not believe Jesus was God acknowledge His historical importance.

This history book, therefore, will be based on the fact that the Incarnation is the central event in history and that everything else that has happened has meaning in relationship to this event. But this is not a study of religion under another name. We will find out what happened *in history*, why it happened, what its results were, and what difference it made afterwards. We will study the great people who have made history and their achievements. We will meet heroes and villains. In fact, we will cover most of the events other history books present.

But there will be one important difference. All history books have a point of view, as we have already seen. Some believe that money is the most important thing in the world; some emphasize wars; some believe trading and exploration explain everything. In this book we will say that Jesus Christ is the most important person who ever lived and that history makes sense only if we study it from that point of view.

If this method still seems strange, keep one fact in mind: there is only one event which has influenced every single person who ever lived—including every person reading this book. That event is the Incarnation of Jesus Christ.

The Where of History

History is the story of events and the people who made those events. We can't understand them fully unless we know *where* these events occurred. Geography can be confusing, but it is very important. It would make a big difference in your life if you were living in Africa or Asia or South America instead of the United States. The Civil War would make no sense to us if we thought it occurred in Sweden or Egypt or Japan instead of the United States. Different parts of the world have different characteristics, and these characteristics make a difference in the way things happen.

Most place names have changed in the course of history. The United States was not always called the United States. The countries of Europe used to have different names. Boundaries have shifted. Nations which used to exist don't exist now. Nevertheless, historians writing about any period of history usually locate events in relationship to the general areas of the world. So we will begin by reviewing these general areas. Then with each unit that we study, we will be able to place the events in their proper areas and find out the names given to the prominent places in that particular time.

As you already know, the globe is divided for convenience into hemispheres: sometimes we speak of the eastern and western hemispheres; other times of the northern and southern hemispheres. The great land masses of the world are the continents, of which there are seven. We will be concerned with only six, since the penguins of Antarctica have not yet made much history. Be sure that you can name and locate the six continents. You should also be able to name and locate the major oceans.

Since this is a survey of world history, we cannot study in detail all of the countries in the world. Therefore we must concentrate on the areas which have produced the greatest achievements and which have had the most effect on the rest of the world. That is why we will primarily study the history of Europe and the Middle East. This does not mean that nothing important happened anywhere else, but that we have to decide where the *most* important things happened.

Nor will we spend much time on American history, as significant as that is. The United States did not have a great influence on history until the 20th century. For most of the 4000 years of history that we will be studying, the United States didn't even exist. Even after our nation was founded, it was too small to make much of a difference in world events until about 1917.

Study a globe or map of the world until you can easily locate the following places: North Africa, Mediterranean Sea, Arabia, Egypt, Nile River, Russia, Middle East, Israel, Spain, Portugal, British Isles, Scandinavia, Greece, Italy, France, Germany, Asia Minor, Austria, Poland, Tigris and Euphrates Rivers, Indus River, Rhine River, Red Sea, India, China.

The When of History

Dates are the *when* of history. It is not always necessary to know the exact date of an event, but it is important to know approximately when it happened and whether it happened before or after related events. After all, it makes a big difference whether something happened in the 1900s, the 1600s, the 1200s or the 200s.

The most obvious point about the dating system which historians use is that it is divided into two parts: B.C. and A.D. B.C. stands for Before Christ; A.D. stands for *Anno Domini*, which is Latin for the "Year of Our Lord," referring to the years since the birth of Christ. Here is further evidence of our earlier conclusion that the most important historical event that has ever happened is the Incarnation; even our dating system is based on it.

Some non-Christian or anti-Christian historians today try to avoid using "Year of our Lord" and "Before Christ," by changing B.C. to B.C.E. (Before Common Era) and A.D. to C.E. (Common Era). But a change of designation does not change the reality that everyone in the Western world uses a dating system which counts down to and counts up from the birth of Jesus Christ.

You have also probably noticed that when we speak of centuries (100-year spans of time), the number of the century does not match the date. A person living in the 20th century would write dates beginning with 19. The reason is that the *first* century included the years from 1 A.D. to 100 A.D. The second century included the years from 101 A.D. until 200 A.D. and so on. So the century's number is always one number ahead of the actual dates that we write.

The years before Christ's birth, or the B.C. years, may be regarded as a kind of countdown to the birth of Christ. Therefore these numbers are the reverse of the A.D. numbers. The A.D. dates with the higher numbers occurred after the A.D. dates with lower numbers. The opposite is true of B.C. The higher numbers occurred earlier. The year 1900 A.D. is 100 years later than the year 1800 A.D. But the year 1900 B.C. is 100 years earlier than the year 1800 B.C. The last year dated B.C. is 1 B.C. That year was followed by 1 A.D. in our dating system.

We will begin our discussion of history around the year 2000 B.C.—two thousand years before Christ's birth—because this was the time that God began to act directly in history in preparation for the Incarnation. Before this time some events occurred of which we have records, but their influence didn't last and they have no significance to us now. Earlier than about 3000 B.C., we have no written historical records because writing had not been invented. The years before 3000 B.C. are known as *prehistoric* times and belong to the study of archeology rather than history.

The Bible Is History

One of the main reference books you will need is the Bible. The Bible is not solely history, but there is a great deal of history in it. Many people would not think of the Bible as history, but it records God's actions in history from the earliest days up to the founding of the Church.

There are also some people who say that the Bible contains very few historical facts but is mainly a collection of stories which didn't really happen. This argument was more common in the late nineteenth and early twentieth century, but it is still heard. There is little excuse for this argument, however, because archeological excavations in the Biblical lands and studies of the documents of nations which existed during Biblical times have confirmed the Bible at all important points.

The Bible was originally written in Hebrew and Greek. There are several different versions of the Bible based on different translations of the original languages. This means that the wording in the various passages is not identical in different versions, but the basic content is the same.

The Bible is divided into the Old Testament, written before the coming of Jesus Christ, and the New Testament, written after His Ascension into Heaven. The New Testament contains 27 books; the Old Testament contains 46 books. If you use an edition of the Bible commonly used by Protestants (such as the King James version or the Revised Standard Version), its Old Testament will have fewer books because it includes only those books originally written in Hebrew, whereas the Bible used by the Catholic Church includes the books written in both Hebrew and Greek. The names of the books also vary in different versions of the Bible.

Review Questions

1. Define history.
2. Why must history be written from a certain point of view?
3. Why do we say that the Incarnation was the most important event that ever happened?
4. What part of the world will we concentrate on in this book? Why?
5. Why will we spend less time on the U.S. than on some other countries?
6. What are the two divisions into which dates are placed? Why was this division made?
7. Why is the number of the century different from the number of the year? What is the difference between the way A.D. and B.C. dates are counted?
8. Where in history does this course begin? Why? What is prehistoric time?
9. Why may the Bible be used as a history book?
10. Why are some versions of the Bible different from others?

Projects

1. List what you think are the five most important events in U.S. history. Give reasons for your choices.
2. Of events that have occurred in the past year, which do you think most deserves to be recorded in history? Why?
3. Choose a recent newsworthy event about which people disagree. Write a short history of that event from one point of view. Then write another from the opposite point of view. How do the two histories differ? Why?
4. On an outline map of the world, locate the areas listed in the chapter.
5. Tape or paste together two sheets of paper. Down the center draw a line 20 inches long. Label the top end 2000 B.C. Label the bottom 2000 A.D. Mark off each half inch on the line. Each of these marks is to represent a century. Label them accordingly. (The first mark should be 1900 B.C., the second 1800 B.C., etc.) At the point where B.C. changes to A.D., write in "the Incarnation." Then choose any 20 events of history which you think important. Write them on your time line at the proper point. As you study history this year, add important events to

your time line.

6. Obtain a Bible and look through it to become familiar with the books
it contains.

Chapter Two
Abraham

FOR THOUSANDS OF YEARS—no one knows exactly how many—after the Creation and Fall of man, the descendants of Adam and Eve wandered the world, living on what they could hunt and kill or find growing wild, until eventually human beings were living in all parts of the habitable world. The way they lived remained essentially unchanged until the last Ice Age ended, when the climate became drier in many parts of the world, and men in search of a new food supply to replace the vanishing forest game began to gather wild grain and to domesticate wild sheep and goats. The transition from hunting and food-gathering to farming and stock-raising occurred first in the hill country of the Middle East, in the areas known to the ancient world as Mesopotamia and Palestine, and to the modern world as Iraq and Israel. This fundamental change in the way men lived is called the *Neolithic* or *agricultural revolution;* it dates, according to some calculations, back to the ninth millennium (9000-8000) before Christ.

The new food supplies made available by the Neolithic Revolution made possible a great increase in population and laid the foundations for civilization, which is distinguished from barbarism by the presence of true cities and the use of writing. The first civilizations grew up in river valleys, where the better soil and easy availability of water made farming easier. There were three: Mesopotamia (Iraq), Egypt, and Harappa (India).

The earliest civilization began in the fertile lands between the Tigris and Euphrates Rivers around 3000 B.C. and is called the Sumerian civilization after the name of its people. At first this civilization was made up of small, independent states, but they were eventually united under one supreme ruler, Sargon of Agade, in 2331 B.C. Sargon was a fierce warrior and the empire he ruled a mighty one, but as time went on and other rulers followed Sargon, uncivilized tribes (barbarians) were able to make inroads on Sumerian territory and overthrow the empire. These barbarians were themselves driven out, and a new king, Ur-Nammu, established his authority with a capital in the city of Ur. Finally, shortly after 1800 B.C., a king named Hammurabi was able to re-establish the empire, though with a smaller territory than Sargon had ruled. He established his capital at Babylon.

Each of the great cities of the Sumerian civilization—Agade, Ur, Babylon—was once a mighty center of government and trade, with large populations and many beautiful buildings. Today, if you were to visit Iraq and go to the sites of these cities, you would find practically nothing, except for the ruins of a temple near Ur where the people used to worship a moon goddess. The temple, called a ziggurat, is shaped like a stepped pyramid, and it is virtually all that remains of the first civilization in the world.

Egypt and Harappa

Only slightly later another civilization appeared, also in a river valley. This was the civilization of Egypt, which grew up along the Nile River in Africa.

Egypt is a narrow strip of fertile land surrounded by desert. Everyone in Egypt settled along the great river, whose yearly floods enriched the land, giving rise to great material prosperity. Every year the Nile would overflow, depositing rich soil, in which the people grew bountiful crops with very little effort.

Because the Nile River also gave easy communication with any part of the land, Egypt was from the beginning ruled as a dictatorship. From the time King Menes first united Egypt in 3100 B.C., the dictator—the pharaoh—was worshiped as a god.

The Egyptians learned to write from the Sumerians and made some discoveries of their own—particularly in mathematics—but extant records indicate that after the pyramids were built, around 2600 B.C., Egypt made no further contributions to civilization and settled into a routine. Daily life was little changed from one year to the next, no great works of art were produced, and no inventions or discoveries were made.

The strangest of the first three civilizations was that of Harappa. Civilization first grew up in India in the Indus Valley (northwestern part, now Pakistan) around 2500 B.C. The civilization had two great cities, Harappa (the name we give to the civilization) and Mohenjo-Daro. The inhabitants called their civilization Melukha (the only word of their language we know). We cannot read their language because we have too few written records from their civilization, only a few inscriptions.

The two great cities and most of the smaller ones which have been excavated are laid out according to rigid, identical plans of straight streets with right angle corners. There is no evidence of spontaneous growth. The houses are identical, made of mud brick. There is almost no evidence of any art or decoration. Each city had one and only one temple mound. There were huge collective granaries. The culture was apparently dominated by the priests, who ruled as dictators but with little need of force to impose their will. We have excavated no swords, and the spearheads would have crumpled at the first hard thrust. Perhaps the priests controlled the people through threats to cut off their food supply. The chief god was Siva, the many-armed god of death, and his consort was Kali, the goddess of death.

The Harappans were apparently uninterested in progress. Though Harappan traders reached Sumeria, where canal irrigation, deep plowing and well-made metal tools were in use, none of these improvements was ever adopted by Harappa.

Harappan civilization was destroyed in 1500 B.C. by Aryan invaders from the north. They were apparently horrified by what they found because they refused to inhabit any of the Harappan sites but built new cities of their own. After conquering the cities, they did not even linger to bury their dead.

When India was first opened to the West, many evils were found in it which had not been brought in by the Aryans or any of the other groups which conquered India. Apparently they originated in Harappa. Among them are the following:

The cult of Kali: A group called Thugs killed unsuspecting travelers as a sacrifice to Kali.

Suttee: The requirement that a wife throw herself on the funeral pyre of her husband. A number of barbaric tribes had this custom, but India was the only civilized culture known to have institutionalized enforced cremation.

Belief in reincarnation: The belief that man is doomed to keep coming back in different bodily forms to suffer the miseries of life forever.

Self-torture: A contempt for the body and for material creation. This led to self-torture, such as sleeping on beds of nails and walking on hot coals.

Caste System: Rigid social classes, with no way out. A person was born into his caste and couldn't rise out of it. It was apparently part of the Harappan priests' system for controlling society.

Denial of the reality of the objective universe and of the individual person: The Indian philosophy which has come down from Harappa denies that anything either is or isn't, and it has no concept of existence. Since the Indians did not believe in existence, they did not believe in a Supreme Creator. Because of the belief in reincarnation, they could not believe in the value of the individual human person.

The overall picture of the inhabitants of Harappa is of an oppressed people who have no concept of their individual worth or of a benevolent God or gods, who have nothing to look forward to except an endless cycle of misery.

God Calls Abraham

Hammurabi in his luxurious palace in Babylon was no doubt totally unaware that in the town of Haran, near the now-ruined city of Ur, there had recently lived a clan or tribe of people who looked to a man named Abram, whose name was later changed to Abraham, as their leader. There were many such family groups in the Middle East, wandering from place to place, fighting small battles with one another when conflicts arose, united by their blood relationship, their friendship, or their loyalty to one leader.

The records that we have of Abraham's life do not tell us much about his personality, but from the things he did we can draw some reliable conclusions. He must have been a man capable of inspiring great trust and loyalty, whose strength of character would persuade men to follow him into unknown perils. He must have been a man to do what he believed to be right no matter what the obstacles. He was a man who could commit everything he had to the accomplishment of a goal which went far beyond his own lifetime. There have been few men who have towered above history as this man has, who have made decisions and taken actions which influenced millions of people thousands of years after their death. For it was to Abraham that God chose to begin the revelation of the divine plan for the Redemption of men.

The Book of Genesis in the Old Testament tells us that the Lord said to Abraham: "Go forth out of thy country, and from thy kindred, and out of thy father's house, and come into the land which I shall show thee. And I will make of thee a great nation, and I will bless thee, and magnify thy name, and thou shalt be blessed. I will bless them that bless thee, and curse them that curse thee, and in thee shall all the kindred of the earth be blessed."

God made a covenant with Abraham. A *covenant* is a solemn agreement which binds the persons involved to each other; it was ratified by the shedding of blood in an animal sacrifice to show its seriousness. Abraham was to leave Haran and all that was familiar to him and go to a distant land which God had chosen for him, and he was to worship the one true God. In return, God would bless him and grant him the new land for his own and would give him many descendants who would make his name famous throughout the earth.

The Promised Land

The land to which God sent Abraham was Canaan. Other names for it are Promised Land, Palestine, Holy Land, and Israel. Why there?

Take a map or a globe of the world, and suppose that you have this problem: An event must occur, and truths must be taught, of supreme importance to every human being upon the earth. That event and those truths must be made known to as many men as possible, as rapidly as possible, and as soon as possible in man's history—they cannot wait until the progress of science has made transportation and communication very rapid. Therefore they must take place as near to as many centers of population as possible. This must be at a crossroads, from which knowledge and information can spread out rapidly. With these criteria in mind, we can see why God chose Canaan, for Canaan was the center of the world—the center of the human world, the point nearest to the great concentrations of population in the ancient world, a crossroads and a juncture among Europe, Asia and Africa. God sent Abraham to Canaan to establish there a people who would receive the necessary preparations for the coming of the Redeemer.

So Abraham took his family and his followers to Canaan—which they called the Promised Land—where they lived the life of other wandering tribes. They grew in numbers and in strength. At one point four powerful kings marched in battle against the cities on the southern edge of the Dead Sea. These kings (one of whom may have been Hammurabi himself) called upon Abraham and his tribe to help them fight a rear guard action, so we know that by this time his tribe was quite strong.

The Sacrifice of Isaac

But an important part of God's promise to Abraham had not been fulfilled. God had told Abraham that He would make him "a great nation," which meant that Abraham must have many descendants. Yet Abraham and his wife Sarah were childless and were already too old to have children.

Abraham and Sarah were living near Hebron, an oasis in the desolate, arid land. There God appeared to him as three men, with whom he spoke as one. Later it was to be revealed through Christ that God is Three in One; but no hint of this had been given to Abraham, who had first of all to understand that God is One rather than many, a wholly new idea in his time. So he could not have even suspected the significance of the appearance of his Divine Visitor as a trio; but that is what he saw.

The Visitor told Abraham that through the power of God Abraham and Sarah would have a son in their old age. Sarah, who was eavesdropping at the entrance of the tent, laughed, because she did not believe. But God speaks only truth, and "Sarah conceived and bore a son to Abraham in his old age, at the time God had promised. Abraham named the son born to him Isaac," a name which means "laughter."

But this was not the end of the story of Abraham. In order for him to receive the great reward which God had prepared for him, Abraham must prove his fidelity and trust in the Lord beyond any shadow of a doubt. So there came a day when God told Abraham to take his son Isaac, his long-awaited heir by Sarah who had been thought barren, to Mount Moriah and there to offer him as a sacrifice to God. Thus was Abraham called to place total trust in God, to believe that no matter how impossible it seemed from the words of God's command, his son would be restored to him and the promise of many descendants would be kept.

Genesis tells us this story, passed down over the centuries, the original words of which probably came directly from Abraham himself, told in a trembling voice to his son and his followers seated around him:

> After these things, God tempted Abraham and said to him: Abraham, Abraham. And he answered: Here I am. He said to him: Take thy only begotten son Isaac, whom thou lovest, and go into the land of vision: and there thou shalt offer him for an holocaust upon one of the mountains which I will show thee. So Abraham rising up in the night, saddled his ass; and took with him two young men, and Isaac his son: and when he had cut wood for the holocaust he went his way to the place which God had commanded him.
>
> And on the third day, lifting up his eyes, he saw the place afar off. And he said to his young men: Stay you here with the ass: I and the boy will go with speed as far as yonder, and after we have worshiped, will return to you. And he took the wood for the holo-

caust, and laid it upon Isaac his son: and he himself carried in his hands fire and a sword. And as they two went on together, Isaac said to his father: My father. And he answered: What wilt thou, son? Behold, saith he, fire and wood; where is the victim for the holocaust? And Abraham said: God will provide himself a victim for an holocaust, my son. So they went on together.

And they came to the place where God had shown him, where he built an altar, and laid the wood in order upon it: and when he had bound Isaac his son, he laid him on the altar upon the pile of wood. And he put forth his hand and took the sword, to sacrifice his son. And behold an angel of the Lord from heaven called to him, saying: Abraham, Abraham. And he answered: here I am. And he said to him: Lay not thy hand upon the boy, neither do thou any thing to him: now I know that thou fearest God, and hast not spared thy only begotten son for my sake. Abraham lifted up his eyes, and saw behind his back a ram amongst the briers sticking fast by the horns, which he took and offered for a holocaust instead of his son....

And the angel of the Lord called to Abraham a second time from heaven, saying: by my own self have I sworn, saith the Lord: because thou hast done this thing, and has not spared thy only begotten son for my sake: I will bless thee, and I will multiply thy seed as the stars of heaven, and as the sand that is by the sea shore: thy seed shall possess the gates of their enemies. And in thy seed shall all the nations of the earth be blessed, because thou has obeyed my voice.

Thus we see that Abraham went instantly to do God's will. And we see that his faith in God was complete: he told his young men that "I *and* the boy ... after we have worshiped, will return to you." He believed that somehow both he and Isaac would return. And so they did.

Abraham had kept his part of the bargain. He was now fully prepared to teach his people the truth that there is one God who is to be worshiped above all—and to teach it in such a way that it would be indelibly burned into their hearts and minds. And the Lord eventually fulfilled His promise of many descendants in a way beyond Abraham's wildest dreams. At our own moment in history, three religions call Abraham their spiritual father: Christian, Moslem and Jewish. They number one and a half *billion* living human beings. Still more persons, now dead, have honored Abraham as their father in faith over the four thousand years since he died. Not the mightiest monarch or conqueror who ever lived so much as dreamed of such a heritage as this. Abraham was promised descendants to match the stars in the sky and the grains of sand on the sea shore. That promise was kept.

And the sacrifice on Mount Moriah had another significance as well. In a day far in the future, another descendant of Abraham would carry wood—this time a cross—up to the top of a mountain, this time named Calvary. There he would be sacrificed, and he too would return—three days later, gloriously risen from the dead.

Abraham died and was buried in a tomb in Hebron, the location of which is marked today by a mosque (what the Moslem religion uses as a church), and which is honored by the three religions which call Abraham their father. Abraham's son Isaac married a woman named Rebecca and had two sons, Jacob and Esau. Jacob himself had twelve sons, each of whom was to become the founder of one of the twelve tribes which all together would make up the nation of Israel, also known as the Hebrew or Jewish people. One of those sons was named Joseph, who was sold by his brothers to wandering slave traders, who brought him into the land of Egypt, probably between the years 1700-1650 B.C. Thus began a new episode in the history of the Hebrew people and of the world.

The Empire on the Nile

Shortly before Joseph arrived, Egypt had been conquered by foreigners, the Hyksos, a people distantly related to the Jews. Because of his talents and ability to interpret dreams, Joseph rose to a high place in the Hyksos government.

When a famine struck the surrounding lands, Joseph's prudent advice spared Egypt the effects of the famine, and he invited his relatives from Palestine, who were suffering from the famine, to come to Egypt where there was food in plenty. The twelve tribes thus took up residence in Egypt. For a time all went well, but then Joseph died, and not long thereafter (1567 B.C.), the Hyksos were overthrown by the Egyptians.

The Egyptians had hated the Hyksos and everything associated with them. Therefore the new Egyptian rulers very quickly came to hate the Hebrews, who were growing in numbers and strength. The new pharaoh ordered the Israelites enslaved and set them to work building cities in the desert.

The new pharaohs also began a policy of invasion and conquest. Pharaohs in war chariots won victories throughout Palestine, Syria and Lebanon. Egypt became the greatest power in the world, all but irresistible. And Egypt returned to its days of absolute dictatorship, worshiping the god-king.

Only one pharaoh in all of Egypt's long history tried to break away from the established pattern: Akhenaten, who was king of Egypt in the second quarter of the 14th century (1375-1350) B.C. Akhenaten moved his capital to a wholly new city; refused to attack his neighbors or even to defend the territory in Asia conquered by his predecessors; encouraged beauty in art rather than the unreal, one-dimensional paintings, which we usually associate with Egypt; and above all rejected the many strange gods which Egypt had worshiped and which had been represented by weird and unnatural-looking animals. Akhenaten proclaimed that there was only one god—Aten—symbolized by the sun.

Akhenaten wrote a beautiful hymn to Aten, which resembles the 104th Psalm in the Bible. It seems likely that there was a link of some kind between Akhenaten and the Israelites, who at this time were living as slaves in Egypt. We have no way of knowing for sure, but it is possible that somehow Akhenaten heard of the faith of the Israelites, who worshiped only one God, and through this was led to his own religion.

But in spite of his grasp of the truth, Akhenaten was unable to bring his countrymen to share his belief. He apparently tried to force his new religion on the people, which would surely have angered the priests of the old gods. Akhenaten made too many enemies. Gradually abandoned by all those he had trusted most, including his own family whom he dearly loved, Akhenaten died a mysterious death and underwent a secret burial. After a few years of turmoil the old system was re-established almost unchanged. The pharaohs ruled as dictators and were worshiped as gods, and the Israelites were enslaved.

Review Questions

1. What was the Neolithic revolution? Why was it important? Where and when did it occur?
2. How is a civilization distinguished from barbarism?
3. What were the three earliest civilizations? Where did each grow up?
4. What were the main characteristics of Egyptian civilization?
5. What were the main characteristics of Harappan civilization? What archeological evidence is there for these characteristics?
6. List the evils that remained after Harappa was destroyed.
7. Where did Abraham live?
8. What is a covenant? How was the covenant between God and Abraham ratified?
9. What were the two things God asked Abraham to do and what did He promise him?

10. Where did Abraham take his people? Why did God send him there?
11. Why did God ask Abraham to sacrifice Isaac? How did Abraham show his faith during this episode?
12. Why is it true to say that God made Abraham a great nation?
13. When did Joseph go to Egypt? What did he do there?
14. Why did the Jews go to Egypt? What happened to them there and why?
15. What did Akhenaten attempt to do? Why did he fail?

Projects

1. Choose one of the patriarchs: Abraham, Isaac, Jacob, Joseph. Read of his life in the book of Genesis and write a biography of him.
2. Write an imaginary story explaining how Akhenaten came to believe in one God.
3. Do further research on one of the following civilizations: Sumerian, Babylonian, Egyptian. Prepare an illustrated report, including the following: dates of the civilization, location, important people, religion, accomplishments, art, architecture.
4. Prepare a map of the Middle East, including the areas discussed in this chapter. Mark the locations of the important events.

Chapter Three
Moses

AFTER THE PHARAOH AKHENATEN had died his mysterious death and undergone his secret burial, and the reigns of the successors of his own household had run their brief course, General Horemheb took Egypt and restored the god-king's empire. The old gods were worshiped and every effort made to blot out even the memory of Akhenaten—his name was removed from all records and everyone was forced to leave his capital city. After Horemheb a new *dynasty* (ruling family) began, the 19th in Egypt's long history, which—for the first time since the Hyksos kings three centuries earlier—moved the capital to the delta of the Nile in northern Egypt, near Palestine. The pharaohs Seti I and Rameses II built new cities upon which the Israelite slaves labored. This brings us to the first quarter of the 13th century B.C.

Rameses II reigned for 67 years. Few rulers in all history have approached him in splendor, prosperity, power and length of reign. His colossal statues of himself still tower over the Nile. Hieroglyphic inscriptions describing his military achievements cover acres of stone. By the world's standards, he was a successful king in every way. He died at the age of nearly 90, still an imposing figure as we can tell from his mummy which has been preserved to our own day. During his reign Rameses II was the most powerful man in the world. Yet he would be defeated by a man born a slave.

We know from the Book of Exodus in the Bible that Moses had been brought up in the Egyptian court. Upon learning of his Hebrew ancestry, he had attempted to defend his people and been forced to flee Egypt. What transformed this son of slaves, this fugitive in the desert, into a towering historical figure, the liberator of his people from the domination of the most powerful ruler of the times? The same power that brought Abraham out of Haran and into the Promised Land: Moses, like Abraham, heard the voice of God.

Let My People Go

In the Sinai peninsula, located between Egypt and Palestine, rock peaks rear more than a mile and a half above the level of the sea. Since the Ice Age Sinai has always been a wilderness, as it remains today—hot and parched and silent under a blistering sun. At the foot of a mountain in Sinai, out of a bush that burned but was not consumed, God said to Moses:

"I Am Who I Am. This," he added, "is what you must say to the sons of Israel: *I Am* has sent me to you." And God also said to Moses, "You are to say to the sons of Israel: Yahweh, the God of your fathers, the God of Abraham, the God of Isaac, and the God of Jacob, has sent me to you."

God had given Himself a name, the name *Yahweh*, which means *I Am.* Abraham had received instructions from God, but he had not been told His name. Now the people of Israel were ready to learn more about their God. Through Moses they would learn what philosophers would struggle over for centuries: that God was a self-existent being, that He owed His existence to no one or nothing else. All else in the universe is *contingent* being—at one time it did not exist; therefore it did not *have* to exist. Everything else in the universe is therefore totally dependent on God for its existence. God *is* existence itself; His name is I Am.

This revelation was surely no easier for the Israelites to understand than it is for us. But it was important that they learn God's absolute majesty, that He was above everything else, that He was totally independent while everything else was dependent upon Him. Otherwise they would not have been willing to do the things He asked of them.

To begin with, they had to put their trust in Moses as sent by God to lead them out of the land of Egypt. True, they were slaves there, but they were also secure and needn't worry where their next meal was coming from. True, they had to labor on Rameses' huge cities, but at least they needn't fear attack from invaders. Moses had to prove to them as well as to the pharaoh that they must leave Egypt and return to Palestine, to the land of the Promise.

The method chosen by God to convince both the people and the pharaoh to heed Moses was to bring about a series of catastrophes in the land of Egypt, the ten plagues. Each of these plagues, except the last, was in itself a natural occurrence at one time or another in Egypt. But this time they came in quick succession and with great severity, in direct response to the warning and the command of Moses, speaking in the name of the God Who Is.

By using natural phenomena to bring about the liberation of His people, God demonstrated to Israelites and Egyptians alike that He was the Lord of nature. In addition, each plague was directed against the Egyptian religion. The blood-red Nile was, of course, an attack on the worship of the Nile. The frogs which were driven out of the Nile symbolized the frog-headed goddess, Hecate. The gnats and flies which would have used the dead frogs for breeding grounds symbolized the scarab beetle and the god Beelzebul. The diseases contracted by cattle and men attacked the bull-god Apis and the magicians. The plague of locusts mocked the goddess Serapis, who was supposed to protect against locusts; the hailstorm destroyed trees and plants, which were used in pagan worship; and the thick darkness blotted out the sun, the symbol of the god Re or Aten.

Yet Rameses II would still not part with his valuable slaves. The world's most powerful monarch was not easily terrified. He refused to let Israel go.

It was full moon in the first month of spring, late March or early April by our calendar, probably sometime near the year 1275 B.C. Through Moses, God had told the people to be ready to march. They must eat their final meal dressed for a journey. They must kill a lamb and eat all of it because they would be leaving the next day. The bread that they were to bake must be unleavened. They must put the blood of the lamb on their doorposts as a sign to the angel of death that they were to be spared. And so God's people did as He commanded, and on this night, the Bible tells us, all the first-born males in Egypt died. But this last and most terrible of the plagues passed over the Israelites, protected by the blood of the lamb, and did not touch them. So forever after the Israelite people would yearly celebrate this night which they call the Passover—celebrate it with the same feast, which would recall how God had freed them from the slavery of Egypt. And though the Israelites did not know it, the feast would have a significance for men of all times, because it would foreshadow the day when God would free all men from the slavery of sin, through the blood of His own Son, who was called the Lamb of God.

And so they marched out—men, women and children—and Rameses II made no immediate move to stop them. In those times only two ways out of Egypt toward Palestine were open to men on foot. One was the coastal route, along the shore of the Mediterranean, but this was under

Pharaoh's constant watch and tight control. So they chose the other route, through Sinai. They were guided in their journey by a pillar of cloud by day and a pillar of fire by night, signs in the Scriptures of the presence of God. But when they camped near the Red Sea, they learned that Pharaoh was pursuing them. Frightened, the people complained to Moses, but he told them that they must put their trust in God. At God's command, Moses raised his staff over the water. The Lord swept the sea with a strong east wind throughout the night, driving the waters aside so that the people could cross in safety.

When Pharaoh tried to pursue the Israelites, the chariot wheels became mired in the mud. Then Moses raised his hand again, the sea flowed back to its normal depth, and the Egyptians were destroyed. Moses and the Israelites sang a song of triumph, proclaiming the greatness of God who had saved them from their enemies.

God would continue to work miracles for them as they proceeded on their journey, changing bitter water to sweet, providing manna and quail for food, producing water from a rock, and helping them defeat an enemy tribe. At each crisis, the people would complain, but God would not cease providing them overwhelming evidence of His loving providence.

The Ten Commandments

Moses led the people from one oasis and well to another across the thornbush wilderness of the Sinai desert to camp before the mountain where he had seen the bush that burned but was not consumed. There, in the shadow of peaks rising to 8500 feet, was a plain providing space and water for a long encampment. The Israelites stayed for nearly a year, from July to May.

There on the mountain God spoke again to Moses in smoke and thunder, making a new covenant, the Sinai Covenant, with the Israelites. For His part of the contract, God promised that "you of all the nations shall be My very own, for all the earth is Mine. I will count you a kingdom of priests, a consecrated nation."

For their part of the contract, the Israelites received from God, through Moses, a code of law, the Ten Commandments. Of Moses and his people, God demanded obedience to a specific and rigorous code of righteousness.

We are all familiar with these Commandments, but to the people of that time, over 3000 years ago, they were a shocking departure from established behavior. It is no wonder that God chose to deliver them with a volley of lightning bolts, lighting a fire on the mountain to signify the momentousness of the occasion. God commanded His people to worship one God alone, to reject the man-made idols which other nations worshiped, to refrain from murder, from theft, from perjury, even from coveting that which belonged to others. No law code of the time resembles the Ten Commandments, the demands were great—yet the Israelites were so awed by what they had seen that they promised, "We will observe all the commands that Yahweh has decreed." They then ratified the covenant with a blood sacrifice.

But the people did not long keep their part of the agreement. When Moses returned to the mountain for forty days, the people began to complain of his absence and finally broke their promise, setting up a golden calf to worship instead of the one true God. When he returned and saw the *idolatry* (worship of idols), Moses was appalled. In anger and desperation he broke the Tablets of the Law and ground them to powder. This man, who had stood so close to the fire on Sinai, knew far better than anyone else what a fearful thing it was to offend God.

By prayer Moses turned away God's anger, and after a fierce struggle Israel again promised loyalty to God, beginning a pattern of sin-repentance-restoration which would be repeated many times in the years to come in the story of the covenant between God and the Israelites.

At God's command, Israel at length built a tent shrine or tabernacle for the Ark of the Covenant, a beautifully decorated box which held the tablets of the Ten Commandments, and, carrying it before them, set out through the wilderness.

Forty Years in the Desert

The Israelites marched on through Sinai to the Promised Land, now occupied by hostile tribes. Moses sent twelve spies to view the land. They reported that it was rich and fertile, "flowing with milk and honey," but also that it was possessed by enemies as big as giants, beside which the Israelites seemed as grasshoppers. The people panicked, refusing to trust in God to help them conquer these enemies as He had helped them escape Rameses II. To punish their lack of faith, God decreed that none of the Israelites twenty years old and older would be permitted to enter the Promised Land except for Joshua and Caleb, whose faith and courage had never failed. All the rest would be condemned to wander in the Sinai wilderness for forty years, until an entirely new generation had grown up, strong in faith and trained by Joshua for battle. Even Moses himself weakened at the oasis of Meribah in the desert, and he too was condemned never to enter the Promised Land, though he was permitted a glimpse of it from a mountain top before he died.

The Israelites had to face enemies even in the Sinai wilderness. So long as they kept their part of the Sinai covenant, they would be victorious. Whenever they fell into idolatry, they were defeated. Finally, Moses came to the end of his long life. He completed the dictation of the Pentateuch, the first five books of the Bible, of which he is the chief human author. In his farewell speech, he reminded the people of all that God had done for them, admonished them to love God above all things, warned them against any acceptance of the customs and beliefs of the Canaanite tribes now occupying the Holy Land, and prophesied the coming of a great Prophet, whom we know to be Jesus Christ.

Moses died and was buried no one knows where. The leadership of Israel passed to Joshua, the great military commander chosen to win the victories that Israel required so that she could enter the Promised Land and become a great nation.

Review Questions

1. Who was Rameses II? When did he reign? Characterize his rule.
2. Describe Moses' early life.
3. Where did God speak to Moses? How did God identify Himself to Moses? What is the significance of that name?
4. What was the purpose of the ten plagues? List them.
5. How were the Israelites saved from the last plague? What is the significance of this for a Christian?
6. What was the first danger to face the Hebrews after leaving Egypt? How did they escape? Where did it happen?
7. What was the covenant between God and the Israelites on Sinai?
8. How were the Ten Commandments a unique law code for their time?
9. How did the Israelites break the covenant? What happened afterwards?
10. Why did the Israelites have to remain in the wilderness for 40 years? Who succeeded Moses as leader of the Israelites?

Projects

1. Read the story of Moses in the Book of Exodus and write a biography of him in your own words.
2. There are no records in Egypt of the events of the Exodus. Is this a

good reason for believing that they never happened? Why or why not?

3. Research the Passover Meal and present a report to the class on what the Jewish people today do on this holiday, showing especially the connections with the events of the Exodus.

4. Draw an illustration of the Ark of the Covenant, including a description of its parts. (See chapter 25 in Exodus.)

5. Act out a debate between Moses and the other Israelite leaders, in which Moses tries to persuade the others that they should follow him out of Egypt.

Chapter Four
The Kingdom of Israel

ABRAHAM WAS THE FATHER of the Chosen People, Moses their liberator and lawgiver, Joshua their general. When their years of preparation and training were over, Joshua led his people across the Jordan River into Canaan, the land which God had given to Abraham and his descendants. In a series of brilliant victories, Joshua defeated the enemy Canaanites. So the twelve tribes of Israel settled in their Promised Land.

Before he died, Joshua warned the people to choose no earthly king to rule over them. Instead, they were to rely on God alone as their king. In time of emergency one or another individual would be called by God to unite Israel briefly and lead the armies until the emergency was over. Those leaders were called Judges and were able to defeat the Canaanite uprisings and invaders from the desert.

Eventually, however, Israel had to meet its greatest threat up to that time: the Philistines, mighty warriors who had captured a part of the coast of Canaan while Joshua was conquering the hill country, had challenged Egypt at the Delta of the Nile itself, and were now pressing inland through Canaan. The land would soon be named for them: Palestine. The Israelites could not stand against these fierce warriors. They were soundly defeated and for 100 years were a conquered people, living under Philistine rule.

In desperation, the people began to beg for a king, turning to the holy Samuel, who had served as their Judge under Philistine oppression, and begged him to appoint a king over the land so that they could be like other nations. Samuel knew that the Israelites were not supposed to have an earthly king, and so he prayed to the Lord for guidance. God spoke to Samuel, telling him that He would send a king, so that the Jews could learn the lesson that earthly kings could never bring lasting peace and happiness to their land.

So in response to God's command, Samuel called Saul, a military leader, to be the first king of Israel. To show the sacred character of his kingship, Samuel anointed him in a religious ceremony, bestowing upon Saul not merely the authority to rule the people but the responsibility to rule in harmony with the will of God. So long as Saul was obedient to God, his armies were victorious, but Saul was too self-willed humbly to accept God's will. He wanted things his own way, not God's, and soon his army suffered reversals. He became fiercely jealous of the young David, who had defeated the mighty Philistine giant Goliath with a slingshot and who now was exceedingly popular with the people. He even tried to kill David, but David eluded capture, passing up an opportunity to kill Saul because he would not raise his hand against the Lord's anointed king.

Finally, in despair, Saul committed suicide. The people acclaimed David, and he was anointed king of all Israel at the age of only 30.

King David

Within two years David drove the Philistines from the land. By the year 1000 B.C., all of the Promised Land was under his rule, and he conquered Jerusalem, where he then established his capital city. He brought the Ark of the Covenant there, and Jerusalem has been ever since the holiest city in the world to the Jewish people.

David had proven himself a great leader and general, but like Israel's great leaders before him, he was also a worshiper of the one true God. God honored David by granting him a vision of a future King, one who would be descended from David himself, and who would establish an everlasting kingdom over all the earth. This king was called the *Messiah*, which means Anointed One. David wrote of his visions in the magnificent poems called the Psalms, which are one of the books of the Bible. Many of the Jews in later days would read these prophecies and think that they referred to an earthly king, who would once more bring to Israel the splendor of David's reign. But the more perceptive of the Israelites knew that the prophetic psalms referred to a throne more than earthly, to a King who would be more than a man.

David was the greatest of all the crowned kings of Israel, but he too was to be an example of the limitations of human kings. The temptations growing out of wealth and power began to work on him and he gave in.

Not satisfied with restoring Israel's rule of the Promised Land, he struck outward in quest of other lands to conquer, lands which had never been part of God's promise to Abraham. At one point his empire reached all the way to the Euphrates River. By his conquests David made Israel fully the equal of any power in the world of his time. It was in the course of these conquests that he fell in love with Bathsheba, the wife of a loyal soldier in his army, committed adultery with her, and ordered that her husband Uriah be placed at the head of his army in battle so that he would be killed. Thus David violated three of the Ten Commandments enshrined within the Ark of the Covenant that he had brought with such rejoicing to Jerusalem.

Nowadays when we hear of corruption in government, it is accompanied by success as often as by failure. But in the years before Christ, God was acting directly in history through the Israelites. David was an anointed king of Israel—this means that God Himself gave His blessing to his reign. David's rejection of God's laws, therefore, had swift and unmistakable consequences. His son Absalom murdered another son, Amnon; Absalom then rose in rebellion against his father and was slain by Joab, David's general. The king, who had given strict orders against this, cried out in grief. He suffered one bitter personal tragedy after another, until finally, old and feeble, he abdicated in favor of his son Solomon in order to prevent another son, Adonijah, from seizing the throne he had become powerless to defend—whereupon Solomon had Adonijah murdered and General Joab struck down as he clung to the tabernacle that housed the Ark of the Covenant.

David had gone from unknown shepherd boy to the greatest king in the world so long as he was faithful to God. But when he used his power to do evil, he saw his world crumble. Yet God had still another lesson to teach: that He can use weak and even sinful men to accomplish His aims. Thus David's sins did not wipe out the prophecy that one of David's descendants would be the King who would save not only Israel but all mankind.

Solomon

Having disposed of all major rivals and inherited a large and flourishing kingdom, Solomon settled down to enjoy his position as the equal of any king in the world. One of the first things he did was to order the building of the Temple of Yahweh in Jerusalem.

Solomon's Temple—the first of three that were to stand in Jerusalem—

was under construction for seven years and was dedicated in the eleventh year of his reign, about 950 B.C. This magnificent building of stone and cedar wood was decorated with precious metals and jewels; even some of the nails were gold. Solomon erected two huge statues of cherubim (mighty angels), whose wings stretched from wall to wall, to "guard" the holy place. The Temple's purpose was to house in a fitting manner the Ark of the Covenant, where the Israelites believed that God dwelt in a special way. To the Israelites, the Temple was Solomon's greatest accomplishment.

Solomon reigned about forty years, a period of prosperity for Israel unequalled in ancient times. The blessings of peace and unity marked most of these years, so that men remembered it as the age of "Solomon in all his glory." Solomon's fame spread to other lands; and Israelite trade extended from southwestern Arabia to tropical Africa, through the great Phoenician city of Tyre (in what is now Lebanon) across the Mediterranean perhaps as far as Spain. The Chosen People had achieved their highest point in earthly prosperity and earthly power. But one of the lessons of history is that earthly power and success do not bring real and lasting happiness.

This lesson was very hard for the Israelites to learn, though Solomon's reign alone should have been enough to teach the lesson. As glorious as his kingdom was during its middle years, Solomon eventually became too attached to wealth and personal prestige. He became a dictator, levying crushing taxes and enslaving large numbers of his people to work on huge building projects, not that much different from the kind of forced labor the Hebrews had known in Egypt. A small group of people—those close to the king and a few others—became very rich and powerful while everyone else became poorer.

When Solomon died in 922 B.C., his son Rehoboam—whom the Bible calls "the folly of the nation"—was not able to hold the kingdom together. It split into two parts—a northern kingdom called Israel and a southern kingdom called Judah. The southern kingdom consisted of the tribe of Judah and a small part of the tribe of Benjamin and kept Jerusalem for its capital. The northern kingdom consisted of the remaining tribes. Now that Israel was weakened by having split in two, other nations began to attack both kingdoms, and the territories outside the Promised Land which David had conquered were gradually lost.

Elias

Around the year 850 B.C., Achab became king of the northern kingdom of Israel. His wife was Jezebel, the daughter of the king of Tyre (Phoenicia), with whom Israel had concluded a treaty. It is very common for a wife from a different country to bring some of the customs of her land to the land of her husband. But Jezebel brought a particularly ugly custom with her: the worship of the pagan god Baal and the pagan goddess Astarte, worship which included immorality and the killing of children as sacrifices to the gods. Jezebel set about enforcing the worship of her gods throughout Israel, killing those officials who would not go along. Faithful Israelites had to hide in caves, living on bread and water. Achab was at a disadvantage. Not only was Jezebel a stronger personality than her husband, but Tyre was stronger than Israel. Therefore Achab did nothing to stop his strong-willed wife from having her way. To punish Israel for its treason, God sent the prophet Elias who caused it not to rain for three and a half years. Four hundred and fifty priests of Baal gathered on the top of Mount Carmel, facing the Mediterranean Sea, to pray for rain.

Then, suddenly, they were joined by Elias, an uninvited guest. He was a wild-looking figure, dressed only in a hair cloak and a leather loincloth. He had lived a lonely life, trying to persuade the Israelites to abandon their worship of the devilish Phoenician gods and to return to the one true God. He had come alone to the top of Mt. Carmel to challenge his 450 enemies.

The first reaction of the priests might have been to laugh. But there was something about his eyes—a strange fire burned in them—which frightened rather than amused them. Men whose religion demanded that they kill innocent babies were not very brave.

In a loud voice, Elias issued a challenge: "I only remain a prophet of the Lord: but the prophets of Baal are four hundred and fifty men. Let two bullocks be given us, and let them choose one bullock for themselves, and cut it in pieces and lay it upon wood, but put no fire under. And I will dress the other bullock, and lay it on wood, and put no fire under it. Call ye on the names of your gods, and I will call on the name of my Lord: and the God that shall answer by fire, let him be God."

The priests accepted the challenge—what else could they do? To refuse would be to admit that their god was a fraud. The wood was piled up, the bulls laid upon it. The priests began their incantations: "O Baal, hear us. O Baal, hear us!" Nothing happened. They called from morning until noon, but nothing happened.

Elias laughed. "Cry with a louder voice," he said, "for he is a god, and perhaps he is talking, or is in an inn, or on a journey, or perhaps he is asleep, and must be awaked." The priests cut themselves with knives until they were covered with blood, but all was quiet on the pile of wood.

Then Elias stepped forward. He called for buckets of water, twelve altogether, and ordered them dumped on the wood and the bull. He had a trench dug around his altar and had *that* filled with water. Elias knew it was no more difficult for God to set fire to wet wood than to dry. But the more difficult he made it appear, the greater the effect on his audience, and he wanted to lose no opportunity to mock the powerlessness of Baal.

Then he stepped back and prayed: "O Lord God of Abraham, and Isaac, and Israel, show this day that Thou art the God of Israel, and I Thy servant, and that according to Thy commandment I have done all these things. Hear me, O Lord, hear me, that this people may learn that Thou art the Lord God, and that Thou hast turned their heart again." Then the fire of the Lord fell and consumed the bull and wood and licked up the water in the trench. When all the people saw this, they cried, "The Lord, he is God, the Lord, he is God." Then Elias prayed for rain, and a small cloud rose out over the sea that developed into a mighty rainstorm, and the rains came and fell in torrents upon thirsty Israel.

The priests of Baal, who had done so much evil in the name of a god who did not exist, were slain. Jezebel ordered Elias' arrest. He fled to Sinai, where God spoke to him in a gentle breeze and sent him back to anoint a new king and a new prophet. The new king, Jehu, massacred Jezebel's whole court, and she herself was thrown to her death from a window. Shortly thereafter Elias was taken up to heaven in a fiery chariot, having completed his work.

Destruction

Elias had brought the northern kingdom back to the true God, but they had not yet learned their lesson about the dangers and insufficiencies of earthly prosperity. The kingdom tore itself to pieces in civil war; in fourteen years there were six kings, five of them dying by assassination. In 721 B.C., the Assyrians, a brutal people from northern Mesopotamia, conquered Israel after a three-year siege of Samaria, the capital city. Over 25,000 of its people were forcibly removed from their homes and resettled in other parts of the Assyrian Empire, to be replaced by refugees from other conquered lands. The refugees who were settled in Israel intermarried with the Israelites who were left. They adopted the Israelite religion but with misunderstandings and errors. The Jews had believed that sacrifice was to be offered only in the Temple in Jerusalem, but the people in the north—named Samaritans, after the capital city—also offered sacrifices. The Jews in the south resented the Samaritans, and this is the origin of the strong hatred between Jews and Samaritans at the time of Christ.

The destruction of the southern kingdom, Judah, took a little longer. Here were Jerusalem and the Temple, and God gave the Jews every chance to repent of their sins and worship Him alone. He sent holy men called *prophets* to Judah. The prophets had two tasks: first, pointing out again and again the sins of the people; and secondly, foretelling the disasters that would come upon the people because of their sins.

The year was 735 B.C., in the southern kingdom. A young man named Isaias was praying in the great Temple. Like Abraham and Moses before him, he received a personal visitation from God. He saw God sitting upon a throne, being worshiped by seraphim—the mightiest and most glorious of all the angels. The seraphim sang, "Holy, holy, holy, the Lord God of Hosts, all the earth is full of His glory."

Isaias was overwhelmed by his vision. He was very much aware of his own sinfulness, contrasted to the holiness of God. His first reaction upon seeing this majestic vision was that he would surely die, because of the enormity of his sins. But God had a mission for this young man. An angel came to Isaias, carrying a burning coal. He touched Isaias' lips with the coal and Isaias welcomed the pain as a sign that his sins were forgiven. But the Lord would not give Isaias His message until Isaias expressed a willingness to do His will. Never does God force a mission upon anyone, but instead He always requires our cooperation. So the Lord called Isaias: "Whom shall I send? Who will be our messenger?" And Isaias answered: "Here I am, send me." Like Abraham, Isaias accepted his mission immediately and totally, without doubt or reservation, and with all of his being.

His mission was a terrifying one: to tell his people of the destruction that would come upon them because they had not fulfilled the Sinai covenant. He must tell them in all the frightening detail so that when the destruction did come, they would know that it was the result of their sins. The people had sought earthly glory; they had turned to false gods. Therefore they must be punished so that they would realize there was one God alone.

Isaias' mission was to last about 55 years. During that time he would be an adviser to kings, he would denounce the sins of his people, he would predict the punishment for those sins. But the rulers of Judah refused to listen to Isaias. The king entered into alliance with Assyria, receiving protection from Assyria in exchange for allowing Assyria to control Judah's affairs. This is called *vassalage* and required Judah to honor the Assyrian gods. The king erected a new bronze altar in honor of Ashur, the Assyrian god, in the Temple in Jerusalem, and before long the First Commandment was being violated continually. The king himself seems to have sacrificed one of his own sons. Eventually Isaias was probably killed because he continued his denunciations of this idolatry.

But before he died he received his greatest prophecies from God. He had earlier prophesied the destruction of Judah and the deportation of its citizens—just as the citizens of the northern kingdom of Israel had been deported. Now he prophesied their eventual return under the Persian king Cyrus, who at this time had not even been born. And he looked even farther into the future to prophesy the sufferings, death and eventual resurrection of Christ, in words that are so exact a description of the Passion that they could only have come to Isaias from God Himself.

Idolatry, paganism, even child sacrifice—these evils persisted in Judah, in spite of Isaias and the other prophets. A new enemy appeared, the Babylonians, who had defeated Assyria and put Judah into vassalage. Finally they laid siege to Jerusalem, surrounding it with their armies so that no food could go in and no people get out. In 587 B.C., the city fell and the Babylonians had no mercy. They reduced Jerusalem to rubble and slaughtered countless people. Most of the rest were transported into captivity in Babylon. This is known as the Exile or as the Babylonian Captivity. The Temple was destroyed and the Ark of the Covenant disappeared.

The prophecies were thus fulfilled, but thanks to the prophets, the tragedy which had befallen the Chosen People did not destroy their faith. By explaining the calamity in advance in terms of a just punishment for breaking the Sinai Covenant, the prophets helped the people to realize that they must renew their commitment to the Covenant, that they must turn back to God to give Him the worship and love that were due to Him alone.

Restoration

While the Chosen People were in exile in Babylon, their first main prophet was Ezechiel, who kept them united and prepared them for their eventual return. Then came Daniel, who had been raised in the Babylonian court and had a Babylonian name. Like Joseph in Egypt, he rose to a position of power because he could interpret dreams. On the night of Cyrus' approach to Babylon (a story also told in the works of the Greek historian Herodotus), the crown prince Baltazar held a great feast. Mysterious handwriting appeared on the wall. Daniel was called to interpret the handwriting, which was a prediction of the fall of Babylon. The prediction came true immediately, as Cyrus, king of the Persians, had no difficulty defeating the Babylonians. In October, 539 B.C., Cyrus issued the following proclamation: "I am Cyrus, king of the world, great king, legitimate king, king of Babylon, king of Sumer and Akkad, king of the four rims of the world." Though like all others before it, Persian power would eventually be destroyed, for a time Cyrus was the most powerful man in the world.

But Cyrus was not cruel or arbitrary like other ancient conquerors. He used no terror tactics, massacres or deportations. Some historians believe that he was influenced by Zoroaster, a famous pre-Christian religious founder from Persia (modern Iran). Zoroaster in turn may have been influenced by Israelites dispersed after the destruction of the northern kingdom. Zoroaster was probably from Rhages in Persia, a town specifically mentioned in the Book of Tobias as an Israelite colony. Many of Zoroaster's beliefs were similar to those of the Israelites: an all-powerful Creator-God who is also addressed as intimate friend, God's love of right and abhorrence of wrong, His rewards and punishments for good and evil, the existence of angels and demons. Zoroaster also believed in a second great power, the source of all evil, only slightly inferior to the creator of good. These two powers warred for the universe, with all men involved in the struggle on one side or the other. Zoroastrianism is thus the first great dualistic religion. We do not know for certain that Cyrus was a Zoroastrian, but if he were that would explain his high moral code and the benevolence of his rule.

A good example of the justice of his rule is that he permitted exiles to return to their homelands. Among these exiles were the Chosen People, who recalled the prophecies of Isaias and hailed Cyrus as a deliverer. Cyrus himself may have heard these prophecies, and perhaps that is why the Jews were one of the first groups of people allowed to return home. Not only that, but Cyrus gave them money to help rebuild their Temple in Jerusalem.

The Jews, of course, rejoiced at the prospect of returning home. They would not be independent, because Persia would rule their homeland. But they would be living once again in the Promised Land, and they would soon be able to worship in their Temple in the Holy City. Once again the people would have a real sense of being united under God's protection. They would know that they were the Chosen People, for whom God had planned a special purpose in the history of the world. As the other nations rose and fell around them, the Jews alone remained.

Review Questions

1. What did Joshua do for the Israelites?
2. Who were the Judges?
3. Who was the first king of Israel? What is the significance of the fact that he was anointed king?
4. Who was the second king of Israel? When did he reign? What was his capital?
5. What were the psalms? What was prophesied in the psalms?
6. How did David break God's laws?
7. How was he punished?
8. Who was the third king of Israel? What was his greatest accomplishment? How did he sin? What were the results of his sin?
9. Who were Baal and Astarte? How did they come to be worshiped in Israel? How did Elias combat them?
10. Who conquered Israel? What happened to the inhabitants of Israel? What happened to the country itself?
11. What is a prophet? What was Isaias' mission? What were his most important prophecies?
12. How was Judah destroyed? What year did this happen? What was done to the inhabitants of Judah?
13. Who were the two main prophets of the Exile? What did each prophesy?
14. How did Cyrus differ from other kings of the time? What is a probable explanation for this difference?
15. What did Cyrus do for the Jews?

Projects

1. Read one of the following incidents from the Bible and write a newspaper account of it: Joshua conquers Jericho, David defeats Goliath, the Ark of the Covenant is brought to Jerusalem, the Babylonian conquest of Jerusalem, Isaias becomes a prophet, Elias and the priests of Baal.
2. Prepare an illustrated report on Solomon's Temple.
3. Prepare a report on one of the following civilizations: Phoenician, Assyrian, Babylonian, Persian. Include government, art and architec-

ture, leaders, accomplishments, religion.
4. Prepare a map for this chapter, locating the most important events.

Chapter Five
The Achievement of Greece

THE GREAT CYRUS had died in battle, to be succeeded by his son Cambyses. In 522 B.C. word came to Persepolis (capital of Persia) that Cambyses had died on campaign. His spear bearer, Darius, took over the government. Darius was challenged by Bardiya, Cyrus' younger son. Darius then accused Bardiya of being an imposter, whom he called "the lie." Darius organized an assassination team which murdered Bardiya and then was immortalized in stone sculptures along the grand staircase in Darius' palace as their reward for destroying "the lie." Darius had an inscription in three languages carved on the Behistun Cliff justifying his assassination of "the lie." Darius' need to justify himself is a reflection of the influence of the moral code of Zoroaster. As a Zoroastrian, Darius had to prove himself on the side of light and goodness. In contrast, no other pagan king felt it necessary to justify assassination. The trilingual inscription on the cliff, as it happened, was the key that made it possible for linguists to learn how to read Old Persian. By 500 B.C., the whole civilized world west of central India, except Greece and Carthage, was controlled by Darius the Great. His lands included all three original homelands of civilization.

The Persian Wars

But Darius was not satisfied with this huge empire. In 490 B.C. he attacked the cities of Asia Minor (what is now Turkey) where colonists from the land of Greece had settled. The cities in Greece from which these colonists had come sent soldiers to help them fight off the Persian forces. The Persians were victorious, but Darius was so angered by the action of the Greeks that he ordered his army to march into Greece itself.

His army first attacked some of the islands off the coast of Greece, where they met little resistance. Then the general in charge, Datis, crossed to the mainland, known in those days as Attica. They landed on the plain of Marathon, which looked ideal to the Persians because it was a large flat plain well-suited to their cavalry forces. Greece at this time was divided into *city-states*. It was not one united country but a series of independent cities which ruled the territory surrounding them. The most important city-state was Athens (which is the capital of modern Greece), and it was up to the Athenians to meet the Persian threat. The Athenians marched to Marathon and prepared to do battle: the soldiers of one small city-state in one small country against the forces of the mighty Persian Empire.

The commander of the Athenian forces was Miltiades, and he had devised a plan to deal with his foe. When the Persians began to march, he sent his men forward. The Persians had put their strongest troops in the center, but Miltiades made the center of his line its weakest point, with his best troops on either end or wing of the line. The Persians broke through the Athenian center, but suddenly found themselves surrounded by the troops from the two wings. When the fighting was over, 6400 Persians were found dead, as compared to only 192 Athenians, and the Persians had to retreat from Greece.

Darius was succeeded by his son Xerxes, who was determined to avenge the defeat at Marathon and again sent troops to Greece. Athens at this time was under the authority of Themistocles, who ordered the city evacuated. He had earlier supervised the building of a fleet of warships, believing that the best way to defeat the Persians would be on the sea.

Xerxes came personally to Greece, with an army of around 200,000 men. He led his huge force into Greece from the north, and along the way most of the city states surrendered. The Athenians appealed to Sparta, the second most important city state in Greece. The Spartans were military people—they had little culture or learning but devoted their time and energy to preparing for war. The Spartans sent a small army, commanded by Leonidas, which established itself at Thermopylae, north of Athens, in an attempt to stop the Persian advance.

Thermopylae was a mountain pass, and Leonidas set his troops in position to hold the pass. But they were greatly outnumbered. For two full days the Persians came at them, each time to be turned back but killing many Spartans before they retreated. Leonidas expected reinforcements from Sparta, but the needed troops never came. Finally, a traitor revealed to Xerxes a hidden path over the mountain. In a secret night march,

Xerxes sent his forces along this path.

The Spartan army appeared doomed, and if they were lost, then all of Greece might well fall to the invader. Leonidas appealed to his men: would a small force of volunteers remain behind to hold off the Persians as long as possible, giving the main body of the army the chance to escape? Three hundred men came forward. They fought an heroic rear-guard action, giving their lives to the last man. But seven thousand Spartans made a successful retreat, joining the other Greek forces to carry on the war against Persia.

The Persians marched on the evacuated city of Athens and burned it to the ground. Then the forces of the emperor turned toward the coast, where the Greek fleet waited near the Salamis Strait (a strait is a narrow stretch of water between two bodies of land). Themistocles tricked the Persians by a false message that his fleet was afraid and running away. The Persian galleys (ships propelled by oars) pursued what they thought were the retreating Athenian ships into the Strait. Then suddenly the Athenians closed their ships in a semi-circle, trapping the Persian ships in a noose which closed around them. Soldiers from the ships fought in hand-to-hand combat, until finally most of the Persian fleet was forced to surrender. Then the Greek land forces, reinforced by the Spartans, defeated the Persian army.

Xerxes had been decisively defeated. He was far from home and now realized that simply outnumbering his enemy would not bring victory. He turned his armies homeward, and never again did a Persian force march onto Greek soil.

Just as God had used the Israelites to provide a direct preparation for the coming of Christ, so did He use the pagans to provide an indirect preparation. The Persian Wars were important because they stopped the expansion of Persia and marked the beginning of the West as a historical reality. It was in the West that Christian civilization would be built, as the lands penetrated by Greek culture became Christian.

Athens' Golden Age

By its role in the Persian Wars, Athens solidified its position as leader of the city states. Its government was unique among ancient civilizations in being a *pure democracy*, a government in which all citizens met periodically to make the laws and set policy for the city, selecting one of their number to carry out the policies decided upon until the next assembly. Though only about one-fifth of the population were citizens (one-fourth to one-third were slaves, and women had no rights at all), this system worked well for a time, helping to create a society with a great patriotic spirit and love of the city.

This spirit, coupled with the confidence and optimism growing out of the victory over Persia, led to a time of great artistic and cultural achievements. This time, during which Pericles ruled Athens (457-429 B.C.), is known as the *Golden Age*. A beautiful temple called the Parthenon was built on the Acropolis in Athens, and a sculptor named Phidias carved a frieze (wide band) around the top, depicting amazingly lifelike people and animals participating in a parade to honor the goddess Athena. Many plays were written during this time, so powerful and realistic that they are still acted today. The most famous Greek playwrights were Aeschylus, Euripides and Sophocles. Greek scientists were also active, for example Euclid in geometry and Hippocrates in medicine. Greek sculptors carved lifelike statues, becoming the first artists on record to depict human beings realistically.

Among the greatest of the Greek achievements was the development of *philosophy,* the use of reason and logic to study the great questions of the universe: what is reality, is there a God and if so what is his nature, what is the nature of man, what constitutes ideal behavior, and so on.

The Greek Parmenides, who lived in the sixth century B.C., was the founder of *metaphysics,* the study of existence. He asked the question: "Why is there anything, rather than nothing?" He reasoned that if ever there had been nothing once, there would be nothing still. He concluded that Being could have no beginning and no end. His analysis was incomplete because he did not reason to the existence of a Person who simply was Being itself and the source of all other being. He therefore knew less than did the Israelites who had learned that God was Being itself through Moses and the Sinai revelation. Nevertheless his philosophy was a monumental achievement and the foundation of all metaphysics in the West.

He was followed by Socrates, who led his students to truth through the Socratic method of questions and answers. Socrates' pupil was Plato, who taught that everything on earth is an imperfect copy of an ideal form, that material reality as we see it does not really exist in the true meaning of existence. Finally came the greatest Greek philosopher, Aristotle, who reasoned to the concept of an eternal God, or Uncaused Cause. Aristotle, however, did not believe that his God took any interest in mankind. Thus, he fell far short of what the Israelites, despite all their tribulations, knew to be the case: God loved man.

The Greek philosophers taught us how to think logically about questions and problems, using our minds to find answers and solutions, rather than relying on guesswork, emotions or superstition. This ability to think rationally was handed down from the Greeks to the Romans and then to our own civilization. No other civilization in the world discovered reason, and that is why Western civilization (the civilization based in Europe and of which we are a part) was able to accomplish much more than civilizations of the East. Western civilization, for example, was much more advanced in science and medicine than was the East because the Greeks had taught the necessity of looking for rational answers to problems, of thinking through the evidence and drawing logical conclusions.

Greek philosophy was also very important in God's plan for the world. Christianity is a rational religion. The existence of God can be proved by logic. The doctrines of the Church can be defended rationally and better understood through the use of reason. When controversies arose in the Church over what exactly was the nature of Christ, these controversies were resolved with the help of philosophy. Philosophy, reason and logic aided the Church in explaining her teachings clearly and defining them precisely so that no one could be mistaken about what the teachings of Christianity really were.

Therefore the work of the Greek philosophers was important to the carrying out of God's plan. God used these brilliant men—who would never know Christ in this life—to make it possible for Christ's Church to teach and to grow.

Alexander the Great

In 431 Athens and Sparta went to war with each other, in a struggle for power in Greece known as the Peloponnesian War (because the peninsula on which Sparta was located was called the Peloponnese). In 404 the war ended in the total defeat of Athens. Since Athens had been the obvious leader of Greece before this war, the defeat meant that the Greek city states would never be united by themselves.

But to the north of the city states, a new nation was slowly growing in power: Macedon, under the rule of Philip the Great. Philip was skilled at politics. He took advantage of the division among the Greek cities and finally defeated them at the Battle of Chaeronea in 338 B.C., where his son Alexander played a key role as commander of a wing of cavalry. Philip became the ruler of all Greece, but he was assassinated only two years later. Alexander became the king of Macedon and Greece at the age of 20.

Alexander, though young, was ambitious and eager for great accomplishments. Within two years of assuming power, Alexander made up his mind to invade Persia and eliminate that threat once and for all. But this defeat of Persia was not all that he intended. Alexander had been tutored by Aristotle. This great genius had turned Alexander's thoughts toward more than simple conquest. Alexander decided that he wanted to march to the end of the world: to take his army beyond Persia until he reached the Eastern Ocean, which educated men of that time believed marked an end of the habitable world. No one had ever been there before. Alexander was determined to go. His men regarded Alexander as godlike; Alexander himself felt that some divine power was urging him onward. In fact it may well have been God Himself, because He would use Alexander's work to prepare for the Incarnation.

In the spring of 334 B.C., with an army of some 35,000 men, Alexander crossed into Asia. He struck the first Persian army to challenge him at the river Granicus, meeting its commanders and their guards head-on in person in a clash at the center of the battle line. Barely escaping death, he broke the Persian line, captured thousands of their Greek mercenaries, and was master of Asia Minor.

Behind Alexander was the Phoenician fleet of the Persian empire, some 400 warships, outnumbering his navy more than two to one. Alexander proceeded to capture all the Mediterranean ports of the Persian empire, leaving the hostile fleet no base. Then in 333, already far from home, his men confronted the massive army of Darius III, the Persian Emperor, at the city of Issus. Alexander's main formation was the phalanx, in which soldiers marched eight deep, so that it was almost impossible for an enemy to break through their ranks. Along with the phalanx, Alexander had his Companions, the best of his cavalry troops.

The phalanx drove deep into the Persian lines, opening a path among the enemy soldiers. Into that opening came the Companions, smashing through to the rear of the enemy. Darius, riding in a war chariot, was terrified. He quickly mounted a fast horse and fled. The Persian troops, without their emperor, broke ranks, and the battle turned into a rout.

Then Alexander captured the island city of Tyre by building a mole from the mainland to within 100 yards of the island, easy artillery range. So well did he build the mole that it remained permanently, joining the island unbreakably to the mainland. Alexander marched to Egypt, where he was welcomed as pharaoh without a battle fought and founded Alexandria, the first of the many cities he would establish. Then he turned back to Persia, where at Gaugamela on October 1, 331 B.C., he faced Darius III and his army of 45,000 cavalry and 200,000 infantry.

The Persians also had a new weapon: the deadly scythe chariot. But Alexander had a strategy. He ordered his phalanx to open their lines so that the chariots could ride harmlessly through. Then the lines closed to meet the Persian center. He sent the Companions on a charge to the right, broke the Persian line there, then turned and shattered the Persian center. The Persian army was cut to pieces. Darius once again fled in panic, now an almost defenseless fugitive.

Alexander marched to Babylon, Susa, Persepolis and Ecbatana, the four major cities of the Persian empire, taking each one easily in turn. He left behind some of his men to take over the government and to begin colonization. But he did not oppress the native people or deny them their customs. Instead he tried to create a harmonious blend of east and west, of Persian and Greek. In the main he succeeded.

In the spring of 330, Alexander pursued the still fleeing Darius III, who was now in the lands bordering the Caspian Sea. Finally, a Macedonian soldier found the king, stabbed in a chariot by his own men.

By this time, many of his men thought that they would soon return to Greece. But Alexander still had his dream of marching to the end of the world. On they went: subduing the barbarian tribes of central Iran, crossing the two-mile-high Hindu Kush (Killer) Mountains in March 329, onward almost to the borders of China, where Alexander founded a city which he called Alexandria-the-Farthest.

Hearing that the Sogdians had rebelled against him, he marched his men 180 miles in three days through the broiling summer. To complete the conquest of the Sogdians, Macedonian volunteers had to scale the rock fortress called the Sogdian Rock, which its defenders had boasted could be conquered only by "soldiers with wings." Though one in ten of the volunteers fell to their deaths, they took the fortress and the Sogdians surrendered. Alexander married Roxana, daughter of the commander.

Back across the Hindu Kush, Alexander led his men toward India. He took his men across the Indus River, then the Jhelum, where King Porus stood with a great army including 200 war elephants. Somehow Alexander managed to get 15,000 men across the river and into battle order for an attack on Porus. His cavalry defeated that of Porus; then he sent the phalanx to challenge the elephants. His men maddened the elephants with spear wounds until they ran wild and began to trample their own troops. Porus' line broke, the king himself was taken captive, and Alexander's great horse Bucephalus died of exhaustion. (Alexander named the city he founded on this site, Bucephalia.)

But Alexander was not finished yet. Across two more rivers and to the third. Alexander was only three months' march from the end of India. But the men had been eight years away from home. They were tired, many were wounded, and they had had enough of killer mountains, steamy jungles, and charging elephants. For the first time in all those thousands of miles, his men refused to go on. Alexander waited in his tent for three days, thinking they would change their minds, but they did not. Alexander had met his first defeat. He turned his men around and marched them west.

On the way back through India, Alexander paused to storm a rebellious fort. The Greeks took the fort, but Alexander took a yard-long arrow in his chest. But he would not rest. By the summer of 325 he had reached the Arabian Sea. He divided his army into thirds, personally leading one of the segments across the Gedrosian Desert. No other army in history has ever marched across the Gedrosian. Even Alexander could bring only one half of his men safely through.

Alexander himself never returned to Macedon. He died in Babylon in 323—only 32 years old—worn out in mind and body from the pursuit of his great dream and from the disappointment of having to turn back. After his death a civil war raged throughout his empire, resulting in its eventual division into five parts: Macedon and Greece, ruled by one of his relatives; Egypt (including the Holy Land), ruled by General Ptolemy; Syria and Persia, ruled by General Seleucus; and two smaller kingdoms in Asia Minor. Macedon, Ptolemaic Egypt and Seleucid Syria were the three great powers in the world.

Alexander's great feat is awesome in itself, but it had consequences the young Macedonian could never have imagined. Until Alexander's conquest, the Middle East and Europe were separated, with nothing in common. But since Palestine (east) was to be the site of the Incarnation and Rome (west) the eventual center of the Church, these two areas had to be brought together. Through his conquests and the colonizations which followed, Alexander united East and West, so that Greek language and culture spread throughout the Middle East and opened up lines of communication and transportation. All of these things helped the Catholic Church to spread throughout the known world. Thus the success which the early Christian missionaries achieved was owed in part to the young Macedonian king, known to the world as Alexander the Great, who wanted to march to the end of the world.

Review Questions

1. How did Darius the Great come to the throne of Persia?
2. Briefly describe these battles: Marathon, Thermopylae, Salamis.
3. What is the significance of the Persian Wars?
4. Describe Athenian government.
5. List the achievements of the Golden Age of Athens.
6. Summarize the chief philosophical teachings of Parmenides, Socrates, Plato and Aristotle.
7. Why is the Greek discovery of philosophy important?
8. Who won the Peloponnesian War? What was the significance of this victory?
9. What was the significance of the Battle of Chaeronea?
10. Why did Alexander want to march east?
11. Describe the steps in Alexander's conquest of Persia.
12. List the achievements in the remainder of Alexander's march.
13. Why did Alexander turn back? What happened on the march back to Babylon?
14. How did Alexander rule the lands he conquered? What happened to them after his death?
15. What is Alexander's most important significance to history?

Projects

1. Prepare a series of newspaper accounts describing the progress of the war between Persia and Greece.
2. Write a biography of one of the important persons in this chapter.
3. Imagine that you are a Macedonian soldier marching with Alexander and that you are keeping a diary of your march. Write the diary, giving impressions of the important events.
4. Choose one area of accomplishment during the Golden Age (e.g., art, sculpture, architecture, medicine, science, mathematics, drama, philosophy). Prepare a report on the accomplishments in that area.

Chapter Six
The Achievement of Rome

AFTER ALEXANDER'S EMPIRE SPLIT into five parts, these nations shared world power among themselves—first one was stronger, then another. Then, shortly before 280 B.C., King Pyrrhus of Epirus (ruler of Greece-Macedon) began looking for territory to conquer. He had trained a strong army; he even had some elephants, given to him by the ruler of the Seleucid Empire. Unfortunately for him, the territory to the east had already been conquered by Alexander—unless Pyrrhus chose to march all the way to India, which he had no particular desire to do.

Then the opportunity Pyrrhus had been waiting for appeared. An ambassador from some Greek colonists in Italy arrived, asking for help against the "barbarians" who were menacing them. Pyrrhus was delighted. If Alexander had conquered the East, why could not he—a distant relative of the great Macedonian general—conquer the West? In the spring of 280 B.C. he sailed to Italy, with 20,000 infantry, 3,000 cavalry, 2,000 archers, 500 slingers and 20 elephants. He had a phalanx like Alexander's and an elite cavalry corps similar to Alexander's Companions. He marched to Heraclea at the river Liris, then rode forward to observe the camp of the enemy on the opposite shore.

He saw a well built fort, guards posted, and muscular men with good armor and helmets. But he didn't have much time to watch. As soon as the enemy sighted his approach, they surged forward to attack.

They fought in a totally new way—not in disorganized masses, nor in the solid block of the phalanx. They fought in small groups (called maniples) which formed checkerboard fashion. These groups were very quick—they could strike at a weak point and get away before counterattack was possible. Pyrrhus would have lost the battle had he not brought his elephants. His opponents had never seen such animals before, and at last were forced to retreat from the battlefield. But Pyrrhus had lost 4,000 men and had been unable to take the enemy camp or drive the enemy from their position.

Then Pyrrhus sent an ambassador to the capital city of his enemy to try to negotiate a treaty. The ambassador came back with a message: "Rome never negotiates with an enemy in arms. Lay down your arms, and then we can discuss a treaty." Pyrrhus knew then that he was dealing with no ordinary enemy. This young nation—Rome—had an unconquerable spirit which prevented her from ever admitting defeat. This spirit and the skill and courage of the fighting men who had almost defeated Pyrrhus would one day make Rome the most powerful nation in the world.

Pyrrhus attacked again in 278 B.C. at Asculum, with similar results. He won the battle because of the elephants, but the Romans kept their camp and inflicted heavy losses on Pyrrhus. After the battle, Pyrrhus said, "One more such victory and I am completely undone," the origin of the phrase *Pyrrhic victory,* a victory in which one suffers so many losses that it might as well have been a defeat.

Then Pyrrhus and Rome met again—in 275 B.C. at Beneventum—for the conclusive battle. This time the Romans had found a general who was almost as good as his troops, which had not been the case before. His name was Manius Curius, and he finally thought of a way to defeat the elephants. He kept hidden a reserve force of legionaries (a Roman fighting unit was called a *legion*). Then at a key moment he sent them out to drive off the cavalry and force the elephants into a wooded ravine where two were killed and the remaining eight were captured. Three years later Pyrrhus was killed in street fighting by a tile thrown from a housetop by a woman. Rome soon controlled all of Italy, granting Roman citizenship to all conquered people, thereby winning their allegiance.

The Roman Republic

Rome was probably founded around 800 B.C., but it first appears in history in 510, when the Romans overthrew the Etruscans, who had been ruling over them. When they became independent, the Romans set up a *republic,* a government ruled by elected officials. Rome then had neither king nor emperor. It had five classes of ruling *magistrates* (men in authority), each independent of the others. The two most important were the consuls and the tribunes.

There were two consuls, each elected for a one-year term by the patricians (noblemen) of Rome. The consuls conducted foreign policy, raised armies and kept peace and order within Rome. Each consul could veto the actions of the other. The tribunes were elected by all citizens (free adult males). They could prosecute any other magistrate and veto any proposed bill to prevent its becoming law. Their veto could not be overridden. Any man who laid violent hands upon a tribune could be executed without a trial by any citizen. The main purpose of tribunes was to protect the plebeians (common people) from oppressive laws and actions by other magistrates. Their veto power meant that the only laws which could be enacted were those regarded as necessary by practically everyone.

Rome also had a Senate, composed of all ex-magistrates, which advised the magistrates in office; and three assemblies composed of citizens from all classes, which made the laws. For times of military emergency, the Roman constitution provided for a dictator: one man who would assume all powers of the government, but with a strict six-month time limit, after which he would resign and the government would return to its normal structure.

This governmental structure helped to protect the freedom of the people. Though no structure is perfect, because any system can be used well or badly, the Roman system had many safeguards for the liberties of the people, leaving the average citizen free to pursue his business as he chose.

The Romans had another strong point as well: their religion. Though they had not been blessed with revelation and were therefore still pagans, the Romans through natural reason had developed a fairly sane and sensible religion. Their gods were friendly gods: of field and farm, of hearth and home, of family and community. They had a moral code based on *natural law:* those moral principles which can be determined through natural reason, through thinking about life, human nature, and the way men should behave toward one another. The Romans possessed a good deal of natural virtue: honor and honesty and courage and justice.

The War of the Gods and the Demons

Not so the nation which faced Rome across the Mediterranean Sea. Carthage (in North Africa, near modern-day Tunis) had been settled by colonists from Phoenicia, and they had brought with them the gods they worshiped. In Carthage the chief god was known as Moloch, and he was fed by human blood, by the sacrifices of thousands of innocent children, thrown into a fiery furnace.

Carthage was a commercial and military rival of Rome, but more than that as well. Rome saw Carthage as an enemy, as evil, as utterly alien. In the war that would soon break out between the two nations, Rome's motto would be *Delenda est Carthago*: Carthage must be destroyed.

These wars were known as the Punic Wars (from the Latin word for Phoenician), and the first began in 264 B.C. Both Rome and Carthage wanted control of the island of Sicily as a naval base. Carthage confidently expected to win the war. They were fighting for an island, so the battles would be at sea, and Carthage had been a great naval power for 300 years. Rome, on the other hand, at the beginning of the First Punic War had not a single ship.

So Rome built a navy from scratch. And when on three separate occasions they lost more than 150 ships to storms at sea, they rebuilt it. They built and rebuilt and fought so well that they defeated the world's premier naval power, took control of Sicily and now dominated the Mediterranean.

But the Carthaginians too saw this as a war of more than minor significance. Their leading family, the Barcids, landed in Spain and gained more than had been lost in Sicily, establishing an outpost at the end of the Mediterranean and making allies of the barbarians in Iberia (Spain) and Gaul (France). And to impress on the younger members of the family the deadly seriousness of this conflict, young Hannibal Barca was made to swear eternal hatred of Rome at the age of nine.

In 218 B.C. Hannibal was ready to launch the Second Punic War. The most direct way for Hannibal to attack Rome was across the Mediterranean, but that was no longer possible since Rome controlled it. Hannibal had to attack overland, but he decided on a bold strategy. Hannibal would come from Spain, over the Pyrenees, over the Alps, into Rome from a direction least expected, bypassing the Roman frontier armies and catching the Republic by surprise.

His army was well-trained and well-equipped. He brought elephants with him, perhaps counting on the surprise and fear that elephants could inspire in an army not used to fighting the huge beasts. But the mountains are no place for elephants, especially not such mountains as those over which Hannibal led his men. Many of them died along the way; all but one of the rest died soon after arrival on Roman soil. But Hannibal did not after all need the elephants. He had his men and his genius, and that, at first, was enough.

He first encountered the Roman legions at Lake Trebia in December. He destroyed two-thirds of the Roman army. The next year he ambushed two legions at Lake Trasimene and cut them to pieces. Rome now appointed a dictator to deal with this military emergency. He is known to history as Fabius the Delayer because he tried to avoid battle with Hannibal. Hannibal seemed almost contemptuous of Fabius. When the dictator finally did seek battle, Hannibal played a monumental joke on him, sending two thousand oxen with torches tied to their horns through his camp at night, creating a diversion and avoiding the battle altogether.

Now it was 216 B.C. and the Romans called up a force of 50,000 men and sent them to Cannae. Hannibal was outnumbered but he was not outsmarted. In the center of his line, the Gauls and Iberians yielded but did not break. The Roman infantry crowded into the center, raising shouts of victory. But the shouts were premature. On the wings, Hannibal's infantry and cavalry stood fast, then swung around behind the Roman line, overlapping each other in a rear encircling movement. The Romans were caught in a double envelopment, outflanked from both sides at once. The legionaries were routed, and Hannibal won a smashing victory, the strategy of which is still studied in military colleges. The Romans lost 35,000, Hannibal only 5,700.

Rome appeared to be finished. The Italian cities now began to defect to Hannibal. Any other government would have given up. But Rome was fighting the devil god and they would not give up. The remnants of the Roman army straggled to Canusium, hardly in any condition to carry on a war. Twenty-year-old Scipio (known as Scipio the Younger, to distinguish him from his father, also a Roman general), came into the camp. He pulled out his sword and called upon every man there to swear on his blade that he would never desert Rome. Every one of them did.

The Senate called for a supreme effort. The people who had three times replaced a fleet destroyed by storm now replaced the army destroyed at Cannae. By 212 B.C., the Romans had 25 legions in the field.

Hannibal had not expected the Romans to keep fighting. But fight they did, and the longer the war went on, the greater were Hannibal's difficulties. The Romans were fighting on home ground; Hannibal was far from home. He couldn't get supplies and reinforcements by sea because of the Roman navy. He couldn't get them overland because Scipio the Elder blocked the way for five crucial years, 216-211.

During that time, the tide began to turn. By 211 Hannibal was isolated in southeastern Italy. He still had not lost a battle, but he was very slowly losing the war. His only hope was his brother Hasdrubal, who arrived in Italy in 208 B.C., after eluding Scipio the Younger in Spain. The Barcids were not ready to quit, either.

By 207 B.C., two Roman armies faced two Carthaginian armies. Claudius Nero held Hannibal with six legions; Livius Salinator held Hasdrubal with four. Claudius Nero took 7,000 picked men in a forced march along the Adriatic coast: forty miles a day for six days. Then he attacked. He outflanked Hasdrubal's elephants, his Gauls, and his Carthaginians. Attacking from the rear, he won a total victory. Hasdrubal was killed. Claudius Nero cut off his head and marched back to his army. He flung Hasdrubal's head into Hannibal's camp, serving notice that Rome's motto in the war still held: Carthage must be destroyed.

Meanwhile, Scipio took all of Spain; in 204 he landed in Africa. The next year he took Tunis, within sight of Carthage itself. Aware that they could not carry on, Carthage asked Scipio for peace terms, which were sent to the Roman Senate for ratification. The message came back from the Senate: Rome never negotiates with an enemy in arms upon her territory. So long as Hannibal and his army remained on Roman soil, there would be no treaty.

Hannibal had no choice now but to return after sixteen years in Italy to try to save Carthage itself. In 202 B.C. Scipio and Hannibal faced each other at last, at Zama. The armies were equal in numbers. But Hannibal had very few left of the veterans who had gone into Italy with him. He had to rely on emergency draftees from Carthage and on barbarian mercenaries. Suddenly, in the middle of the battle, the Spanish and Berber mercenaries in the front line turned against the Carthaginians in the second line. Instead of fighting the Romans, they were fighting each other. Hannibal's veterans held the center for a time, but at last were overwhelmed. Hannibal had suffered his first defeat.

The Third Punic War was a brief flare-up from 149-146 B.C., easily won by Rome. Afterwards, Rome leveled Carthage and sowed salt in the earth so that no one would ever inhabit the city again.

The men who honored home and family and farm had destroyed the men who worshiped the devil god. Never again would massive human sacrifice be known in the European or Mediterranean world. And when Christian missionaries would come to that world, they would find fertile ground. Carthage had been destroyed.

The Maccabees

While Rome was fighting its war to the death against the dark gods of Carthage, God's Chosen People were under the rule of the Seleucid

Empire, one of the successor states of Alexander the Great's empire. In 168 B.C. the ambitious Seleucid emperor, Antiochus IV Epiphanes, invaded Egypt and besieged its capital city Alexandria. The Egyptians looked for help to Rome, fresh from its magnificent victory in the Second Punic War.

The Romans sent the elderly ex-consul Popillius, who ordered Antiochus to leave Egypt immediately. Antiochus, standing in the desert sand outside Alexandria, asked Popillius for time to deliberate, to consult advisers. Popillius was only an ex-consul, Antiochus an emperor, but above all Popillius was a Roman. He gave Antiochus a scornful look, then with his walking stick drew a circle in the sand around Antiochus. "Deliberate here!" he said, insisting on an answer before the emperor stepped from the circle.

Antiochus knew enough about Rome to know that he must submit. He withdrew his army from Egypt. But fury seethed inside of him. To make up for the humiliation he had just suffered, he decided to impose his will elsewhere. He marched his army to Jerusalem, and began the first religious persecution in the history of the Greco-Roman world.

Antiochus seized the Temple and set up an idol there, dedicating it on December 25, 167 B.C., with the sacrifice of a pig, thus mocking the Jews, who believed the pig to be unclean and therefore never to be used in sacrifice.

Antiochus' soldiers went throughout the Holy Land, setting up altars and idols in even the smallest towns and villages, sacrificing pigs upon them. In each town, the people were ordered to participate in the sacrifices and to eat the pig's flesh. The death penalty was imposed on those who observed the Sabbath or were found to possess copies of the Scriptures. The pagans set out to destroy the faith of the Jewish people, to transform them from monotheists (worshipers of the one true God) into polytheists (worshipers of the many false gods of the Greeks). Those who wished to preserve their faith had to go into hiding. Many Jews were martyred. Other Jews apostatized (abandoned their faith), and it appeared that the mighty Seleucid Empire would easily crush the resistance of the remaining faithful Jews, who had no army, no weapons, no leadership.

In the spring of 166 B.C., a Greek army patrol came to the village of Modein to set up an altar and to sacrifice a pig. The people of Modein were ordered to the village square. The leading family of the town was the family of Mathathias, a priest, who had five sons: John, Simon, Judas, Eleazar and Jonathan. Judas had been nicknamed Machabeus—the hammer —so the five brothers were known as the Machabees.

The soldiers believed that the people would more readily cooperate if the town's most important citizen would be the first to sacrifice, and so they called Mathathias forward. But Mathathias refused, proclaiming his loyalty to the one true God. Surprised at this resistance by an aged and feeble man, the soldiers at first didn't know what to do. But then out of the crowd came the voice of another villager; he offered to perform the sacrifice in place of Mathathias.

But Mathathias could not allow this blasphemy to take place. He attacked the apostate villager and then turned on the commander of the patrol. Inspired by his example, the villagers rose up and killed the entire patrol.

The idolatrous worship had been prevented, but the people didn't know what to do next. Eventually word would get back to Jerusalem of what had happened, and they would be punished. But the Machabee brothers were now ready to lead the resistance. They called upon all those willing to fight. They would build up an army, and with the help of God drive the aliens from their land.

Judas Machabeus took the leadership. He knew that the Jews would have no hope of besting the Greeks in an open field battle, so he resolved on guerrilla warfare: hit and run raids, ambushes, sabotage, destruction of the pagan altars. Gradually they would build up and train an army and equip it with weapons seized from the enemy.

The plan worked, and the Greeks came to realize that this was no rag tag collection of military amateurs, but a disciplined force that would never surrender so long as their God was dishonored.

So in 165 B.C., a large Seleucid force marched south from Samaria. The force, about 2,000 men, could easily have overwhelmed the Machabees if they had met in open battle. But Judas had no intention of letting that happen. He ambushed the Seleucids in a narrow pass where the larger force could not maneuver. The Greeks were taken by surprise and their triumphal march turned into a disgraceful rout.

Judas used the same strategy against a force of 4,000, ambushing it at the pass of Beth-Horon near Jerusalem. In fury, the Greeks amassed an army of 20,000 and ordered it to stay out of the mountain passes. But the over-confident Greek generals divided their force into two parts. Judas attacked and defeated the first, then turned and defeated the other as well.

By December 164 B.C., the Machabees had control of the entire Holy Land, except for the fortress of Akra in Jerusalem. They cleansed and re-consecrated the Temple. On December 25 the Jews resumed the sacrifices commanded by the law of Moses. In commemoration of this great occasion, they designated that an eight-day celebration called Hanukkah would take place every year at that time. The worship of the one true God once again reigned supreme in the Holy Land.

But the Greeks still controlled the fortress Akra, and a new army marched on Jerusalem. This time the Seleucids had 32 war elephants. The Jews were frightened and confused by the beasts, and for the first time battle turned against them. Attempting to rally his men, Eleazar rushed into the enemy army, actually under the largest elephant. He thrust upward with his sword, killing the animal, but as it died it fell upon him, and he was crushed beneath it. The Jewish army retreated and disintegrated. Judas tried to rally his few remaining men, but in April of 160 his army was overwhelmed and he died in battle.

Though a third brother, John, was also killed shortly thereafter, Jonathan rebuilt his army. After winning a major battle, Jonathan was invited to a peace conference. But the Greeks betrayed him, massacring his men and holding him prisoner. The last remaining Machabee brother, Simon, took up the cause, demanding his brother's release. The Greeks promised to let him go for 100 silver talents. Simon sent the money. The Greeks took it, and then murdered Jonathan.

But Simon refused to surrender, so long as the pagans controlled any part of the Holy Land. In 141 B.C., Akra at long last surrendered to the Jews. At a great assembly in Jerusalem the following year, the priests and people proclaimed Simon their leader and high priest.

For the first time since the fall of Jerusalem to the Babylonians in 587 B.C., the Jews were independent. Though their independence would again be lost in 63 B.C. when the Romans took control of the Holy Land, the Jews would never forget the heroism of the Machabees, who would remain a symbol for the Jews, and indeed for all men, of the importance of religious freedom and the willingness, if necessary, to give one's life for that cause.

Julius Caesar

After its magnificent victory over Carthage, Rome had gradually expanded the territory it ruled, until it stood powerfully astride the Mediterranean. But the growing wealth and power that came to Rome as its rule extended brought with it great temptations. In the next to last century before Christ, we see Roman officials eagerly accepting bribes, unjust tax laws making the tax collectors wealthy, Roman senators buying up land

and driving the small farmers out of business. Murder became a political weapon; and two political parties were formed, each standing for something of value but each corrupt and willing to use violence against the opposition. The optimates sought to restore the old constitution and its checks on individual power with a minimum of change, while the populares wanted to carry out changes to check the concentration of wealth and power which the old constitution seemed unable to prevent, while opening the door to new seekers of wealth and power. Around 130 B.C. a time of civic disorder began in Rome, climaxed by the Social War of 91-88 B.C. in which the Romans fought the other Italians they ruled.

In the midst of the strife, a foreign enemy attacked, Mithridates of Pontus. Marius, leader of the populares, and Sulla of the optimates quarreled over who was to take command. Seemingly ignoring Mithridates, Sulla rallied his troops and captured Rome itself, exiling Marius. But when at last he turned toward the foreign enemy, the Roman legions rose to the occasion and won a smashing victory in 86 B.C. The war flared up again from time to time, and the civil strife in Rome continued without a pause. Spartacus led a slave rebellion in 73 B.C.; it was crushed, and 6,000 captives were crucified.

In 63 B.C., as part of the continuing Mithridatic Wars, General Pompey marched into Palestine and annexed it to the Roman Empire, ending the brief independence the Chosen People had known after the Maccabean victories. Thus did the Romans become rulers of the Jews.

Meanwhile, away from the corruption of Rome among the barbarians of Iberia, a young general was winning battle after battle and bringing these hitherto uncivilized lands into the Roman orbit. His name was Julius Caesar. He was an excellent strategist and beloved by his men. But Caesar had higher ambitions. On the strength of his western victories, he joined with Pompey, conqueror in the east, and Crassus, one of the wealthiest men in Rome, to form the First Triumvirate (rule of three). It quickly became obvious to all in Rome that Caesar had the intelligence, the courage, the determination and the popular support to rise to supreme power over all who stood in his way.

To get him out of the way, the Senate voted him a five-year command in Gaul. Caesar had the vision to see what no one else had yet seen: that Rome need not confine itself to the Mediterranean and those lands which bordered it, that Roman civilization and culture could be brought to these wild barbarians. Within a year he had made allies of the barbarians within Gaul itself. He fought off the barbarians from outside who tried to drive out the Romans. He put down rebellions within Gaul. He even led expeditions across the Channel to Britain in 55 and 54, winning battles there as well.

Back in Rome, the temporary peace won by the establishment of the First Triumvirate was too fragile to endure. Rival gangs of populares and optimates battled in the streets. Crassus was killed when he attempted to lead an army against Parthian horse archers. A Gallic chieftain named Vercingetorix organized a general rebellion of central Gaul against Caesar, believing that Rome was in such a state now that he could drive the invader from Gaul and rule the land himself.

But Caesar launched a counterattack and besieged Vercingetorix and his best troops in a fortress city. Then he had to fight two battles at once—sallies from within by Vercingetorix and attacks from without by a relieving force. He won them both, and the war, and forced Vercingetorix to surrender. Gaul remained in the Roman orbit.

Now Caesar turned once again to Rome. His command in Gaul was drawing to its legal close. He wished to return to Rome with his army and become consul. But Pompey had grown to like power too much and no longer intended to share it. He knew that Caesar was much more talented than he was, that he would quickly be eclipsed by the more brilliant man, so in January 49 B.C., he pressured the Senate into passing a declaration of war against Caesar if he crossed the boundaries of the territory of his military command.

That boundary was the Rubicon River in northern Italy. If he crossed the river, Caesar would be fighting for his life and would plunge Rome anew into civil war. Uttering the now famous phrase, "The die is cast," he crossed the Rubicon.

Pompey was no match for Caesar militarily. And he was no match for Caesar with the people, the majority of whom supported the victorious general from Gaul. Within 60 days after crossing the Rubicon, Caesar controlled all of Italy, and Pompey had fled to Greece. Caesar pursued him there and won a total victory at Pharsalus in the summer of 48 B.C.

Pompey escaped to Egypt where he joined forces with the boy king Ptolemy XII. For three months Caesar fought, and at the end Caesar won. He was greatly aided by an army from Jerusalem, and Caesar rewarded the Jews by extending the special protection of Roman law to Jews throughout the Empire. He also met and married the ambitious Egyptian princess, Cleopatra.

Caesar returned to Rome and had himself proclaimed dictator for

life. Though he was still enormously popular with the people, the optimates, led by the former consul and great natural law philosopher Cicero,
denounced him as a tyrant. They plotted against him. Finally, on March 15,
44 B.C. (the Ides of March), their opportunity came, and he was assassinated by Brutus and Cassius and their friends of the old aristocracy.

But they could not destroy the work he had done. He had made Gaul
Roman, so that soon it would have Roman laws, Roman language, Roman
transportation and communication systems. When Christian missionaries arrived, they would find a congenial environment for preaching the Gospel
of Jesus Christ.

Caesar Augustus

Caesar's assassins did not achieve their goal of restoring the old republic. Rome had moved too far beyond that. A new triumvirate was
formed: Marcus Lepidus (who was insignificant), Mark Antony (a friend
and supporter of Caesar) and Octavian (Caesar's nephew and heir). They
killed 2,000 enemies of their regime, including Cicero, and pursued Brutus
and Cassius to Greece. Octavian and Antony defeated the two assassins at
the Battle of Philippi, whereupon both of them committed suicide. The
victors returned to Rome, squeezed out Lepidus, and divided the world:
Antony took the East, Octavian the West.

Part of Antony's territory was Egypt. Having failed in her dream of
ruling the world with Caesar, Cleopatra then turned her charms on
Antony. He promptly forgot his wife in Rome and married the Egyptian
beauty. The Romans were disgusted with Antony's behavior, and Octavian
persuaded the Senate to declare war on him.

The decisive battle was fought in 31 B.C., a naval battle at Actium,
near Greece. At a crucial moment, three of Antony's squadrons deserted
him. Cleopatra, present at the battle in her purple-sailed ship, panicked and
fled. Antony, his mind preoccupied with Cleopatra, forgot the battle and
went in pursuit of her. The rest of his fleet was destroyed or surrendered.
Antony and Cleopatra escaped to Alexandria, with Octavian in pursuit.

When Antony's troops deserted to Octavian and Antony heard a
false rumor that Cleopatra was dead, he committed suicide. Thereupon
Cleopatra tried a third time to win over a Roman ruler. But Octavian was
made of sterner stuff than either of his predecessors. He told Cleopatra
that he was taking her back to Rome to display her to the people in a triumph (victory parade). Not being able to bear the thought of such a humiliation, Cleopatra committed suicide. This was the end of Egypt's semi-

independence, as Egypt became the last of Alexander's successor states to come under Roman rule.

Octavian declared himself *princeps* (first citizen), but this humble title did not disguise the fact that he was an emperor, ruling more territory than any man before him. He soon exchanged that title for a new one: *Augustus*, which meant god-like. He is therefore known to history as Caesar Augustus.

Augustus was such a strong and able ruler that he was able to settle the turmoil in Rome, ushering in a period of peace and prosperity. It is true that he had complete power and the people did not have as much freedom as in the old days of the republic. But the mass of people had so sickened of the turmoil of the preceding 100 years that they welcomed Augustus as a bringer of order. Furthermore, his immense power did not corrupt him or drive him insane, as it later did lesser men. He ruled well for 43 years of peace, and was finally succeeded by his stepson Tiberius in 14 A.D.

Rome's Contribution to the World

In terms of God's plan for the redemption of the human race, the Romans had a very important role to play. Their significance can be summed up under four main headings.

1. *The defeat of Carthage.* If Carthage had defeated Rome and become ruler of a great empire, Christianity would have had a much more difficult time spreading throughout the civilized world. Although the Romans were pagans, they had many values in common with Christians. Therefore the Romans would be more likely to accept Christianity than would the Carthaginians, with their wholly evil god, Moloch, who demanded child sacrifice. The defeat of Carthage and elimination of child sacrifice provided Christianity with a much friendlier environment in which to begin and grow.

2. *Natural Law Philosophy.* The development of natural law philosophy also provided Christianity with a favorable environment. Christianity taught that behavior should be governed by unchanging laws, which were handed down by God Himself. The Romans already accepted many of these laws and therefore were better prepared to listen to the teaching of the Apostles and the first missionaries.

3. *The spread of civilization into western and northern Europe.* The spread of Roman law and culture north and west from the area of the Mediterranean and the Middle East—especially through Caesar's conquest

of Gaul—gave Christianity a much wider field for missionary activity. This meant that the missionaries were able to go into civilized instead of barbarian lands, thereby giving the Church a much firmer foundation.

4. *A period of peace and order.* Augustus brought an end to disorder, establishing peace and the rule of law throughout the known world. This cultural unity, lasting hundreds of years, made it much easier for Christianity to spread. If early missionaries had been forced to travel through lands torn by war and strife, their task would have been more difficult.

God could, of course, have worked a miracle to achieve all these same goals. Instead He worked through human beings, allowing them to cooperate—whether knowingly or not—with His plan for the Redemption of all men.

Review Questions

1. Why did Pyrrhus win the first two battles against Rome? Why did Rome win the third?
2. What is a republic? What was the role of the consuls and the tribunes?
3. Describe Roman religion.
4. What were the events and results of the First Punic War?
5. What was Rome's motto in the Punic Wars? Why?
6. Summarize Hannibal's accomplishments. Why was he unable to win the war in Italy?
7. Describe the Battle of Zama.
8. What were the results of the Punic Wars?
9. Why did Antiochus Epiphanes persecute the Jews? Describe the persecution.
10. How did the Maccabee revolt begin? Summarize the Maccabee successes.
11. What does Hannukah commemorate?
12. How did the Maccabees win the final victory? What were the results of their victory?
13. Why did peace and order break down in Rome?
14. What happened in the Mithridatic Wars?
15. Summarize the accomplishments of Julius Caesar as general.
16. How did Julius Caesar come to complete power?
17. Who assassinated Julius Caesar and why? What happened to the assassins?
18. How did Octavian come to complete power?
19. What kind of ruler was Octavian? Why did the people welcome his

rule?

20. What were the four ways the Romans contributed to the spread of Christianity?

Projects

1. Write a biography of one of the following: Hannibal, Julius Caesar, Cicero, Octavian, Cleopatra.
2. Find pictures of Roman ruins which exist today and present them to the class, explaining what they are.
3. Act out a session of the Roman Senate debating what to do about Hannibal and Carthage.
4. Prepare a report on Roman religion.

Chapter Seven
The Most Important Event
in History

IN THE FIRST CHAPTER of this book we discussed the dating system which all historians use—dividing all dates into B.C. and A.D. The division point is the birth of Christ—the Incarnation. The use of this event as a measuring point for determining all dates indicates that the Incarnation is the most important event in history. Although most people nowadays don't think of it, whenever anyone writes a date, he is saying in a way that the Incarnation is the central point of history because the year that he writes is counted up from the birth of Christ.

From another point of view, God's becoming a man, dying and then rising from the dead are unique events. Nothing else even remotely like them has ever occurred. Emperors and empires have come and gone, wars have been fought again and again—but only once did God become a man.

Therefore a history book which is concerned with the truly important events of history must discuss the Incarnation. A religious book studies what the coming of the Messiah meant to each of us, that Christ was both God and man, that He made up for our sins and made it possible for us to receive sanctifying grace and enter heaven. But it is the purpose of history to examine the historical evidence that this event really happened and the facts of how it happened. Any history book which does not give these facts is presenting a false and incomplete picture of the story of the human race.

The Gospels Are Historical Documents

The primary source of our information about Christ as an historical figure comes from the New Testament. Christians are often challenged with the claim that the Gospels are not historical documents and therefore cannot be relied upon to give factual information about Jesus Christ. But the historical facts of the life of Christ are as well or better attested than those of many events which we take for granted.

The first test of a historical document is its closeness in time to the events it describes. The earliest New Testament document we have is probably the Epistle to the Corinthians by St. Paul, written in 55 A.D., only 25 years after the Resurrection. The three synoptic Gospel accounts (Matthew, Mark and Luke) were written at least by 70 A.D., because they make no mention of the destruction of the Temple, which occurred in that year. Many Scripture scholars now tend to put the Gospels earlier, perhaps even as early as the 40s A.D. Thus the New Testament accounts are closer to the events they were describing than most ancient sources to their events, for example the Greek historian Herodotus and the Battle of Marathon.

Here are other tests for historical reliability and the extent to which the New Testament measures up.

Were the documents based on eyewitness accounts? Matthew and John were Apostles, present at most of the events described. Mark was a disciple of St. Peter, and Luke specifically says at the beginning of his Gospel that it is based on the accounts of eyewitnesses, one of whom had to be Mary, the Mother of God, because he includes information that only she could have known.

Is there corroboration by external, independent testimony? Josephus, a Romanized Jewish historian, has the following passage in his book, *The Jewish War*:

"It was at this time [when Pontius Pilate was procurator of Judea] that a man appeared—if 'man' is the right word—who had all the attributes of a man but seemed to be something greater. His actions, certainly, were superhuman, for he worked such wonderful and amazing miracles that I for one cannot regard him as a man; yet in view of his likeness to ourselves I cannot regard him as an angel either. Everything that some hidden power enabled him to do he did by an authoritative word....

"In the days of our pious fathers this curtain [in the Temple] was intact, but in our generation it was a sorry sight, for it had been suddenly rent from top to bottom at the time when by bribery they had secured the execution of the benefactor of men—the one who by his actions proved that he was no mere man. Many other awe-inspiring 'signs' happened at the same moment. It is also stated that after his execution and entombment he disappeared entirely. Some people actually assert that he had risen; others retort that his friends stole him away. I for one cannot decide where the truth lies."

Did the authors have anything to gain from deception? The authors of the Gospels and the other books of the New Testament were all martyred or threatened with martyrdom. If their accounts had been deceptions, surely at least one of them would have confessed in order to save his life.

Were the accounts contradicted by anyone at the time? The Gospels refer by name to many people who were still alive or were known to those who were, such as Joseph of Arimathea, but none of these people appeared to contest the data. We have no record that any of the Jewish leaders presented evidence proving the Gospels false. If there were any such evidence, they certainly would have produced it because of the inroads Christianity was making among the Jews. Instead they kept silence.

Thus we can regard the Gospels as sound historical documents.

The Last Days before Christ Came

In the last century before Christ, the Jews could hardly have been in worse condition in earthly terms. Since 63 B.C. they had been under the rule of the mighty Roman empire. The Romans were hated by most of the Jews, who believed them usurpers of the rightful destiny of the Chosen People. The Jews were rebellious and unruly, not an easy province to rule.

The man whom Augustus had appointed to rule Israel as a Client King (under Rome's ultimate authority) was Herod the Great. Herod's people, the Idumeans, had not been born Jews but had been forced to accept Judaism. Herod himself cared more for power and prestige than for religion. The Jews knew that and had no love or respect for Herod.

To try to win their support, Herod lavished a great deal of expenditure on building projects in the Holy Land, especially the rebuilding of the Temple in Jerusalem, restoring it to its days of glory at the time of Solomon. But these new buildings could not hide Herod's essential cruelty. He executed his wife Marianne because he wrongly believed that she had been unfaithful to him, and then executed his two sons by her because he feared that the people might try to put one of them on the throne instead of him. Though known as Herod the Great to the outside world because of his building projects, he was known as Herod the Terrible to the Jews.

The Jews were not united but quarreled among themselves. The chief sects (divisions) of the Jews were the Pharisees, the Saducees, the Essenes and the Zealots. The Pharisees were regarded as custodians of the law which Moses had given to the people, but they had piled interpretations and elaborations upon it so that the people were constantly perplexed and confused as to what the law really meant. The Sadducees were chiefly interested in worldly power and cooperated closely with Herod and the Romans. The Essenes believed that almost the whole Jewish people had forsaken the one faith and allegiance to the one true God, so they had gone to the desert around the Dead Sea to await the coming of the Messiah. The Zealots urged violent opposition to Roman rule. All the Jews still felt very strongly that they were the Chosen People and they looked eagerly for the coming of the Messiah, whom they hoped would free them from Roman domination and restore their independence.

In 6 B.C. the whole world was at peace, for the first time in recorded history. Communication was faster and transportation more convenient than at any earlier time in the history of the world. The language of the Romans (Latin) was known throughout the empire so that messages could be understood everywhere. Every major city west of India had Jews in it. It was an ideal time for the Messiah to appear.

The Years of the Infancy and Hidden Life

The story of the birth of Christ is told in the first chapters of the Gospels of Luke and Matthew, known as the Infancy Narratives. These accounts are sometimes attacked as mere picturesque stories or legends. But the Infancy Narratives can be confirmed by external evidence at several important points:

The census: Mary and Joseph went to Bethlehem to be enrolled in a census. We know that censuses were taken throughout the Roman Empire around this time.

The site of Christ's birth: Christ was born in a cave used as a stable. The exact spot was shown to visitors to Bethlehem as early as 155 A.D. Bethlehem became a Christian town almost immediately after the Ascension and is still a Christian town today.

The Magi: In the Persian Empire, there were wise men who studied the heavens because they believed that events on earth and events in the heavens were related. Because Jews lived in the Persian Empire, these wise men would have been aware of the prophecies concerning the Messiah and would have come to Jerusalem to find Him.

The massacre of the Holy Innocents: We have no specific historical record of Herod's order of the slaughter of all baby boys in Bethlehem.

But we know from Herod's character that he was more than capable of giving such an order. He had killed his own sons to prevent their taking his throne; he would certainly not have hesitated to kill the sons of strangers for fear that one of them would become "king of the Jews" in his place.

The flight to Egypt: Egypt was the nearest place free from Herod's control where there was a large colony of Jews. It is therefore reasonable that Mary and Joseph would have taken the Christ Child there to escape the slaughter of the baby boys.

After Herod's death, shortly after the birth of Jesus, his kingdom was divided among his sons. Archelaeus became Client King of Judea (which included Jerusalem), Samaria and Idumea. Herod Antipas ruled Galilee, and Philip ruled east of the Jordan River. Archelaeus proved to be every bit as cruel as his father. Riots and revolts broke out, and the Sadducees appealed to Augustus. He deposed Archelaeus and made Judea a Roman province under a Roman governor called a procurator. The most famous of these procurators was Pontius Pilate, appointed in 26 A.D.

While Jesus was growing up in Galilee, Augustus died in 14 A.D. His stepson Tiberius succeeded to the throne, but he was far from happy. He once said that as emperor, he felt like a man holding a wolf by the ears. If he let go (resigned his office), he would be immediately killed, but remaining in office was almost as dangerous. His personal life was also unhappy. Augustus had forced him to divorce his beloved wife to marry Augustus' daughter Julia. Julia and Tiberius couldn't stand each other. It is said that Julia starved herself rather than live under Tiberius. Her daughter Agrippina worked against Tiberius. He had to organize a secret police because of her and his other enemies. In 26 A.D. he went to live on the island of Capri, where he was alone, afraid and unhappy.

Not long after, a new prophet appeared in the Holy Land, a man named John the Baptist. Some people thought he might be the long-awaited Messiah, but John refused to claim that title for himself. Instead, he urged the people to repent of their sins in preparation for the appearance of the true Messiah, which would be soon.

The Father and I Are One

One day when John was preaching by the Jordan River, a young man suddenly appeared and asked John to baptize Him. John immediately began telling all his followers: "Behold the Lamb of God, who takes away the sins of the world." This man, John was saying, is the Messiah. The man's name was Jesus. He was a young carpenter from Nazareth, whose life up to this point had been insignificant, so much so that the people from His home town would refuse right until the end to believe that Jesus could be the Messiah.

But shortly after His appearance at the Jordan, Jesus began to preach, to teach and to work miracles. Was He another prophet, the people asked, or could He be the Messiah? Jesus Himself, at first, did not directly answer their questions. Instead, He began to make an even greater claim for Himself. He began to exercise, on His own authority, three powers which the Jews thought belonged to God alone: the power to forgive sins, the power to give and to change the Law, and the power to judge.

In his Gospel, St. Luke tells us that Jesus once said to a paralyzed man at Capharnaum: "My friend, your sins are forgiven you." When He did this, the Scribes and Pharisees whispered among themselves that this was blasphemy (claiming to be the equal of God): "Who can forgive sins but God alone?" Christ knew their thoughts, and replied: "To prove to you that the Son of Man has authority on earth to forgive sins," He turned to the paralyzed man and said, "I order you to get up, and pick up your stretcher and go home." Immediately the man rose and went home, praising God.

Christ's assumption of the divine power to give and modify the Law was one of the greatest sources of controversy between Jesus and the Pharisees. In Matthew's Gospel, for example, Christ's disciples, with His permission, were performing forbidden work on the Sabbath. When the Pharisees objected, Christ said: "The Son of Man is master of the Sabbath."

The Jews believed that eventually God would judge all men. Christ specifically stated that *He* would be that Judge: that He, on His own authority, would determine the eternal disposition of all men.

Jesus, therefore, claimed divine powers and rights. But the people might still have thought of Jesus as the *representative* of God, possessing some superhuman powers but certainly not being God Himself. Gradually Jesus contradicted this idea, explicitly claiming to be equal to God. Here are some of these incidents:

Matthew (11:25-27) tells us that on one occasion Christ said: "Everything has been entrusted to me by my Father; and no one knows the Son except the Father, just as no one knows the Father except the Son and those to whom the Son chooses to reveal him."

In the Gospel of John (10:22-39), Christ says: "The Father and I are one." The Jews picked up stones to throw at him because "you are only man and you claim to be God." Stoning was the traditional penalty for blasphemy.

One of the most dramatic of all these incidents is described for us by John (8:31-59). Jesus had been preaching to a hostile crowd. He told them that if they refused to hear His words, then they were not God's children. The people angrily accused Him of being a devil. Christ only added that those who hear His words "will never see death." The people whispered among themselves: Surely He knows that Abraham and the prophets had died? How can He claim to preserve anyone from death? Jesus spoke up again: Their honored father Abraham *rejoiced* to see His coming.

The people would have broken out in laughter: This man is stupid to say such a thing and expect us to believe it. He isn't even 50 years old. Abraham died over a thousand years ago. How could He have seen Abraham? Jesus must have stood very quietly until the noise lessened and gradually stopped. Then in the Temple courtyard, into the stillness, the words thundered: "I tell you most solemnly, before Abraham ever was, *I Am*."

This was a claim to eternal existence. It was more. The words "I Am" were the traditional Hebrew name for God.

Jesus did not make this earth-shattering revelation at the beginning of His ministry. Nor did He shout it from the housetops with no explanation. He couldn't have done so. The revelation had to be gradual because the main distinguishing characteristic of the Jews had been their belief in one God. First the people had to come to trust Him because of His teachings and His love for them; then they could gradually be told the overwhelming truth: Jesus was God. At His trial before His death, all doubts were laid at rest; and Jesus—knowing it meant the death penalty—claimed in a court of law to be divine.

Some people writing today claim that Jesus was simply a good and holy man who wanted to help people be better. But Jesus clearly claimed to be much more than that: He claimed to be God Himself.

The Miracles

It certainly wasn't enough just to make such a claim. Jesus also presented clear evidence that He was God. This evidence was His miracles. A miracle is an act which can only be performed through the power of God. If Christ could perform miracles, then He must be telling the truth. Therefore opponents of Christianity have tried to argue that the miracles were not miracles at all. They argue that Christ did not cure real diseases, because these illnesses were simply in people's minds—were psychologically caused and cured. They also seek naturalistic explanations for the other miracles. For example, they say that the miracle of the loaves and fishes was probably a result of mass hypnotism.

These theories could explain some of the miracles; some of the illnesses cured by Christ could very well have been psychologically caused. But most of them could not. A withered hand cannot be psychologically caused nor psychologically cured, yet Christ cured a withered hand, instantly. Blindness may be hysterical (caused by emotional problems), but a man who has been blind since birth could not have brought his blindness upon himself; and Christ cured a man blind since birth. The son of the official in Capharnaum was cured at the instant Christ announced the cure, twenty miles away. Conceivably a crowd of 5,000 could be convinced by hypnotism that they had eaten, but hypnotism cannot produce twelve baskets of fragments left over from the banquet.

But the most important answer to the doubters is this: dead men do not return to life from psychological pressure. On three separate occasions, Christ raised the dead to life: the son of the widow of Naim, the daughter of Jairus, and Lazarus. The raising of Lazarus is the most significant, because he had already been four days in the tomb. There could be no doubt that he was really dead and that he really came back to life. Even Jesus' enemies, the Pharisees, knew this. "Here is this man working all these signs," they said, after Lazarus came back to life. "If we let him go on in this way, everybody will believe in him..." If the miracle hadn't really happened, all the Pharisees would have had to do was show the people that Lazarus was still dead. Instead, they believed they had only one course of action: they would kill Jesus.

The Body That Disappeared

They achieved their goal. On a Friday following the Passover celebration (probably in April in the year 33 A.D.), Jesus Christ was condemned to death by the Jewish Sanhedrin (court) and by the Roman procurator Pontius Pilate, cruelly tortured, and crucified. He was hastily buried in a borrowed tomb, because the Jewish Sabbath was approaching and no one could prepare a body for burial on the Sabbath. The chief priests and the Pharisees, remembering Christ's prophecies and fearful of a plot by the Apostles, had a guard set by the tomb.

Sometime early Easter Sunday morning, there was a tremendous physical disturbance, something like an earthquake, which knocked out the guards. By the time they recovered their senses, the stone had been rolled back and the tomb was empty. The guards went to the Pharisees, fearful of punishment because of neglect of duty. Instead they were given money and told to spread a story that the Apostles had stolen the body while the soldiers were asleep. This they proceeded to do. We can see the comedy of the situation. Instead of being punished for failing in their duty, the soldiers were given money to broadcast that they had failed even more spectacularly than they actually had: to tell the world that they were such sound sleepers that the Apostles had been able to remove the heavy stone and steal the body without the soldiers even waking up.

Very early that same morning, several of the women who had loved and followed Jesus when He was alive (Mary Magdalene, Mary the mother of James, and Salome are mentioned by name in the Gospels) came to the tomb with spices to complete the enbalming of the body. Mary Magdalene probably arrived first, saw that the tomb was empty and immediately went to tell the disciples, thinking that some enemy had stolen the body.

The other women then arrived and were greeted by an angel who gave them the message that Jesus had risen, instructing them to report this news to the disciples. At first the women were too bewildered and frightened to deliver any message. But shortly thereafter Christ appeared to them Himself, assuring them that He had risen and repeating the message of the angel.

When Mary Magdalene brought what she thought was terrible news to the Apostles, John and Peter immediately went to the tomb. There John saw the shroud in which Christ had been buried. It was neatly folded, which no thief would have done. John therefore realized that something unusual had happened.

In the meantime, Mary Magdalene wandered sadly away. She saw a man she thought might be the gardener and asked him where Christ's body was. But it was not a gardener—it was the Lord Himself. Mary was filled with joy and rushed off to tell the Apostles.

The Apostles were stubborn men who refused to believe the women. But that night, when they were in the upper room with the doors locked, Jesus suddenly appeared in their midst. To prove that He had truly returned to life and was not a ghost, He sat down and ate with them. Thomas was absent from that meeting and refused to be convinced until he personally saw Christ's wounds. But the following Sunday Christ appeared again and spoke to Thomas directly. Thomas fell on his knees with an affirmation of faith in the divinity of Christ: "My Lord and my God."

The Resurrection Happened

Those who try to explain away the evidence of the Resurrection advance three main theories to disprove it. As Christians we should be aware of these theories and how weak they really are.

The first is that the Apostles and other followers of Jesus conspired to steal Christ's body and then to pretend that they had seen the risen Christ. But the Apostles at the time were not the type of men to plan and carry out such a daring plan. They were cowering in their rooms, afraid to go out, full of despair at the death of their leader. Secondly, they could not really have rolled back the heavy stone at the entrance to the tomb without awakening the guards. Thirdly, they had nothing to gain, neither wealth nor power. Instead, ultimately, they gained only martyrdom. When the time came that they were faced with death for their beliefs, surely—if it had been a plot—at least one of them would have admitted it to save his life. None of them did. Fourthly, Roman soldiers were the best in the world. The normal complement of a Roman guard was sixteen men, with four on duty at all times. It is impossible that they would have been guilty of such a dereliction of duty as all to be asleep at the same time. Finally, St. Paul tells us that the risen Christ appeared to 500 people, many of whom were still alive at the time he was writing. If we accept the conspiracy theory, we have to assume that 500 people were in the conspiracy, and that none of them ever confessed.

The second explanation is that Christ only pretended death and then left the tomb to appear to His Apostles, convincing them that He had truly risen. The primary argument against this theory is that after the torture He had undergone, it is impossible to believe that Christ had the strength to roll away the stone, elude the guards and then appear to His Apostles in such a way as to convince them that He had gloriously risen. Furthermore, the Roman soldiers who crucified Christ knew their business—they weren't in a habit of allowing men still alive to be removed from the cross, and in fact pierced Christ's heart with a lance to prove that He was certainly dead.

The third theory is that the Apostles were seeing visions or hallucinations. But the hallucination theory includes no explanation for the empty tomb. If there had been no empty tomb, Christ's enemies could easily have discredited the Resurrection by producing His body. But they never did. Secondly, the material reality of Christ's appearances dispels doubt that they were imaginary. Surely this is why Christ ate and drank and encouraged the Apostles to touch His body. Then we have the 500 witnesses St. Paul mentioned and the number and variety of other appearances. To account for these, we have to assume that many people at different times were seeing the same hallucination, which is not likely. In addition, there is the nature of hallucinations themselves. It is a psychological fact that people usually see hallucinations of things they expect or fear or hope for. None of this applies to the disciples. None of them expected or even hoped for Christ's resurrection. The fact that the women planned to anoint the body showed that they expected that there would be a body to anoint. Furthermore, people prone to hallucination are usually mentally unstable, highly imaginative and sensitive. No description could be more unlike the Apostles. They were hard-headed, practical men—fishermen, a tax collector, etc.

We Christians living now should be grateful that the Apostles were difficult to convince. This makes their testimony that much more believable. First they had to be persuaded that the tomb really was empty and that Christ was appearing to men. Then they had to be convinced that it was the same Christ, soul and body, and not a vision. But once they were convinced, they were willing to lay down their lives for their faith.

The Holy Shroud

One of the most striking pieces of historical evidence outside the Gospels on the passion, death and Resurrection of Christ is the Holy Shroud. According to Jewish burial customs, Christ's body was placed on a long piece of linen, which was then folded lengthwise over His body. Then the linen-shrouded body was placed in the tomb. After the Resurrection the Shroud was found neatly folded. For centuries, all that could be seen on the Shroud was faint markings and bloodstains. But now, with the advent of modern scientific techniques, the Shroud has been minutely examined and found to contain so complete a record of the passion and death of Christ that it is virtually impossible that it could be a forgery or be the burial cloth of anyone else.

Among the facts related in the Gospels which are confirmed by the Shroud are the following: bruises on the face, caused by the servants of the High Priest striking Christ; the scourging, which was by two men, one taller than the other, and which covered the entire body; the crown of thorns, which was a cap, not a circlet; the lance wound in the heart and the emission of a watery fluid as well as blood; the nail wounds, which were in the wrists, not the palms, and which severed the median nerves, causing the thumbs to be jammed against the palms, so that the thumbs are invisible on the Shroud; the carrying of the cross, which rubbed against the shoulders and produced a large abrasion; the falls, attested by wounds on the knees and traces of dirt; the crucifixion itself, attested by differing patterns of blood flow caused by the crucified man's raising and lowering of his body in order to breathe. The Shroud image also slows that two coins were placed over the eyes, as was customary in Jewish burials. By high magnification it can be seen that these coins were ones minted only by Pontius Pilate in Palestine between October 28 A.D. and October 31 A.D. The image of the Shroud can also be reproduced in three-dimensions by a special machine called a VP-8. No ordinary painting or photograph can produce such an image.

The Shroud even provides indirect confirmation of the Resurrection. If the body in the Shroud had decayed in the normal way, or even remained in the Shroud for more than a few days, the Shroud would have been discolored and eventually itself have decayed. If the body had been stolen or removed by other natural means from the Shroud, large portions of the Shroud would have adhered to the body, as any cloth would adhere to open wounds, and been torn off. In both cases, any image would have been destroyed. But if the body in the Shroud miraculously passed out of it, the Shroud and any image on it would have been undisturbed.

In 1988 the often unreliable Carbon 14 tests dated the Shroud to the 14th century, conclusive proof, many said, that the Shroud was a medieval forgery. But when only one piece of evidence (and that very shaky, at best) presents a conclusion contradictory to all other evidence, it is logical to seek an explanation for that one item, rather than denying all the evidence on the other side.

There are several possible explanations for the Carbon 14 results. First, the Shroud was touched by many people and articles over the centuries; this contamination could have distorted the test results. Second, in 1532 there was a fire in the Chambery church housing the Shroud. The heat was intense enough to melt the silver tube holding the Shroud, yet the Shroud did not catch on fire. Therefore, the tube must have been air-tight. Both the air-tight tube and the intense heat could have altered the test results. Third, the very event which probably produced the image, the Resurrection, could have had an impact on the test.

It is sometimes argued that the Holy Shroud cannot be accepted as authentic because much of its history is unknown. In later chapters of this book, however, we will present a reconstruction of the Shroud's history which is based on solid historical evidence.

There remains but one plausible explanation for the image on the Shroud, namely the one presented by the Gospels: He was crucified, died, and was buried. On the third day, He rose again from the dead.

Review Questions

1. Summarize the reasons why the Gospels are reliable historical documents.
2. How was the Holy Land governed at the time of Christ's birth? What was the attitude of the majority of the people to this government? What were the four sects of the Jews and what did each believe?
3. List the ways in which the infancy narratives are supported by external evidence.
4. What happened to the Holy Land after Herod the Great's death?
5. Who was emperor at the time of Christ's public life? Why was he an unhappy man?
6. Describe and give examples of the three ways in which Christ claimed to have powers which belong to God alone.
7. Point out incidents in the Gospels where Christ claimed to be God. How did the Jews react to these claims? Why did Christ reveal His true nature only gradually?
8. Give evidence showing that when Christ healed people these were genuine miracles, which could not be explained away.
9. Summarize the events of Easter Sunday morning.
10. Explain each of the three theories used to deny the Resurrection. Refute each theory.
11. Summarize how the Holy Shroud confirms the Gospel accounts of the Passion. How is the Holy Shroud indirect evidence of the Resurrection?

Projects

1. Read the Gospel accounts of the Resurrection and write a narrative explaining the events beginning Holy Saturday night and going up to Christ's first appearance to all His Apostles in the upper room on Easter Sunday evening.
2. Do research and give a detailed report on the scientific investigations of the Holy Shroud.
3. Write an imaginary account of the conversation between the soldiers and the Pharisees after Christ had risen from the dead.
4. Read the Gospel accounts of one of the following and report on it to the class: the raising of Lazarus, the healing of the man born blind, Jesus' trial before the Sanhedrin, Jesus' appearance to the disciples going to Emmaus.

Chapter Eight
The Apostolic Age

SHORTLY BEFORE HIS ASCENSION into Heaven, probably in May, 30 A.D., Christ had told His Apostles to wait in Jerusalem for the coming of the Holy Spirit. For nine days, the Apostles, the Blessed Mother and other followers of Jesus prayed together in the room known as the Cenacle or the Upper Room, which had been the site of the Last Supper and of several of Christ's appearances after His Resurrection. On the tenth day, a Sunday, a sound like a great wind was heard in the room. Then a ball of fire miraculously appeared, separating into individual flames which hovered over the head of each person there. This was a visible manifestation of the Holy Spirit (just as the burning bush had been a visible manifestation of God), who had come to the Apostles to help them to understand the truths which Christ had taught and to give them the courage and love they needed to take this message out into the world.

This day is known as Pentecost Sunday and is celebrated as the birthday of the Church, because from that moment the Apostles were transformed from fearful, confused men into strong, courageous missionaries. Their first missionary effort was to preach to the crowd who had assembled outside the Cenacle, attracted by the strange sounds which they had heard. The Apostles preached so persuasively that 3,000 persons accepted Christianity on that day.

The man who led the Apostles in preaching to the crowds was a former fisherman, an outspoken, hasty man, whose tendency to act before he thought had more than once gotten him into trouble. His name had originally been Simon, but Jesus had changed it to Peter—which means Rock—because He intended Peter to be a foundation stone on which the Church would be built (Matthew 16). In spite of his many weaknesses—on the night before Christ died, Peter even denied that he knew Him—Christ made this man the leader of the Apostles and the first head of the Church (what we now call the Pope). Strengthened by the Holy Spirit, Peter overcame his weaknesses and gave the Church the strong leadership it needed during its difficult first years.

Under Peter's leadership, the Apostles and other followers of Jesus brought the message of Christianity first to the Jews. These were the people who had safeguarded the belief in one God and the expectation of a Messiah for almost two thousand years. But though many of them accepted Christianity, many more refused to believe that Jesus was truly the promised Redeemer. Probably the main reason for this refusal was selfishness; the Jews had been the Chosen People for so long that they did not want to admit that now *all* men were to be Chosen, that their special rituals and practices were to be replaced by Christianity.

Whatever the reason, the leaders of Judaism despised the followers of Christ, and in the year 37 A.D., when Judea was temporarily without a Roman governor during the interval between Pilate's removal and the appointment of a new procurator, the Pharisees launched a persecution. St. Stephen became the first Christian martyr, stoned to death for blasphemy.

Present at this martyrdom was a brilliant young Pharisee named Saul. Although he possessed Roman citizenship, a rare thing among Jews, he believed in interpreting the Law strictly and in observing Jewish rituals exactly. Saul regarded Christians as evil destroyers of Judaism; and after the death of Stephen, he prepared for a journey to Damascus, Syria, where he intended to launch a persecution of the Christian community which had grown up there. Together with some friends, he set off for Damascus on horseback.

But God did not allow him a peaceful journey. In fact, a great light blinded Saul and he was knocked from his horse by a mysterious force. Saul was not easily frightened, but he must have been frightened then. A voice came from Heaven: "Saul, Saul, why do you persecute Me?" Saul trembled. "Who are you, Lord?" he asked. "I am Jesus of Nazareth, whom you persecute." Imagine Saul's reaction. As a devout Jew, he knew that God sometimes spoke to men. He also knew that when God did speak, it was wise to listen. So Saul listened, and realized that Jesus of Nazareth was not the enemy of the Chosen People, but their Redeemer.

God's special mission for Saul was to be the Apostle to the Gentiles, the non-Jews who were now to be called into the one true Church. Saul changed his name to Paul—a Gentile, not a Jewish name—and spent several years in prayer and preparation for his mission.

The Dispersion of the Apostles

In 42 A.D., King Herod Agrippa, who had been appointed ruler of Judea by Emperor Claudius, launched a second persecution of the Christians. During this persecution Peter was imprisoned, miraculously escaping with the help of an angel. Peter decided that it was now time for the Apostles to begin their mission of carrying the Gospel to all men, and he ordered the dispersion of the Apostles throughout the known world.

There is good reason to believe that by the Passover of 42 all of the Apostles had departed from Jerusalem except James the Greater, James the Lesser and Peter. That same year James the Greater was beheaded, the first of the Apostles to suffer martyrdom for Christ. James the Lesser became Bishop of Jerusalem and remained in the Holy Land to minister to the Christians there. Peter went to Rome. It was inevitable and necessary that the leader of the Church come to the leading city of the world. The decisions made in Rome affected the lives of people throughout the civilized world. Everyone looked to Rome for leadership. Therefore it was essential that the headquarters of the Church be located in Rome. At first the men in power in Rome paid no attention to Peter. As far as they were concerned—if they thought of him at all—he was just another Jew. But he began to preach and teach among the Jews living in Rome, gradually building up a Christian community.

The following list represents the most reliable traditions as to where the other Apostles went: John, with the Blessed Mother, went to Ephesus in Asia Minor; Andrew went to Ukraine and perhaps Greece; Bartholomew went to south Arabia and perhaps India: Matthew went to Egypt and Ethiopia; Philip went to Asia Minor; Simon went to Iran; Matthias is entirely unknown; Jude went to Mesopotamia; Thomas went to India. The most striking fact about this list is that half of the Apostles went beyond the boundaries of the Roman Empire. Thus the Apostles took Christ's words about carrying His Gospel to the ends of the world quite seriously. We know more details about Thomas and Jude than we do about any of the others who went outside the Empire, and their stories bear repeating.

When the dispersion of the Apostles came, Thomas' assignment was India. To the land of the denial of reality was sent the Apostle who insisted on physical evidence for the Resurrection. He went by caravan to Taxila in northern India and worked as a carpenter in the court of King Gundofarr. Thomas remained at Taxila for several years, winning some converts. But after he departed, barbarians invaded Taxila and Thomas' Christian community was wiped out.

There is evidence that Thomas returned to Jerusalem at the time of the death and Assumption of the Blessed Mother and to attend the Council of Jerusalem (discussed below). Then he returned to India, this time by the recently discovered southern monsoon route directly across the Arabian Sea to south India. He arrived on the Malabar (southwestern) coast of India probably in the year 52. Christian tradition tells of cures of hundreds and the baptism of thousands.

Thomas worked for seventeen years on the Malabar coast, then moved across the peninsula to the opposite coast. He came eventually to Mylapore near the city of Madras. Nearby was a temple of Kali, the goddess of death. One day in 72 A.D., Thomas was praying in a cave on a hill. Priests from the temple of Kali attacked him, piercing his heart with a lance. He was buried at Mylapore, where ever since Indian Christians have venerated his tomb. The Christian community he founded at Malabar survived for over a thousand years until India was opened up to the West. Their descendants are still known as the Thomas Christians.

The story of the Apostle Jude is tied in with the history of the most important relic in Christendom, the Holy Shroud. Some years before Thomas left India for the first time, in the city of Edessa in northwestern Mesopotamia, about 350 miles north of Galilee, King Abgar had been stricken by a dread disease, probably leprosy. He had heard of Jesus and His healing miracles. He sent a message to Jesus, begging for a cure.

When the message arrived, Jesus had already ascended into Heaven. So the Apostles decided to send instead the Apostle Jude with the Holy Shroud. But it could not be brought and shown as a shroud, for all people have a natural revulsion toward objects which have been in close contact with the dead. Therefore, before being brought to King Abgar, the cloth seems to have been folded and decorated so that it showed only the portrait-like image of the Holy Face of Jesus.

Jude brought the Shroud to Edessa. Abgar was cured and baptized, and Jude established Christianity in Edessa. The Shroud remained there. But in 57 A.D. a persecution of Christians broke out. The portrait-like Shroud was hidden away for safekeeping in a hollow place in one of the city gates, so well-hidden that the very knowledge of its whereabouts was soon lost. It was not rediscovered until the sixth century, when an earthquake damaged the walls and revealed the hiding place. By this time, Edessa was once again Christian, and the Shroud was enshrined in its main church.

Peter and Paul

Around the year 45 A.D., Paul began his great missionary journeys, carrying the Gospel to the Gentiles. He made roughly three journeys: one to the Middle East, one to Greece and one to Asia Minor. These journeys are recounted in the Acts of the Apostles in the Bible, written by St. Luke, one of the evangelists and Paul's companion on some of his missions. Everywhere he went he founded Christian communities, to which he later sent letters to continue their instruction in Christian doctrine and to solve controversies. Paul frequently met with hostility and opposition and suffered scourgings, stonings and beatings. But he had given his life totally to Christ, saying, "Now I no longer live, but Christ lives in me."

Peter remained in Rome until 49, when Emperor Claudius banished all Jews from Rome, referring to "tumults" raised by "Chrestus." The Roman officials could not distinguish between Jews and Jewish Christians. All they knew was that there were great controversies in the Jewish community over the teachings of one whose name the Romans thought was "Chrestus."

Peter returned to Jerusalem and called the other Apostles together there for a general council in 50 A.D., the Church's first council. The main topic for discussion was whether Gentiles should be required to obey the Mosaic Law as a condition for becoming Christians. Paul argued persuasively that the Law would be too heavy a burden to bear, that Christ had come to bring freedom in the love of God. Peter, as head of the Church, made the final decision, that the Law had passed away and henceforth could not be a requirement for membership in the Kingdom of God. It was probably during this same year that the Blessed Mother died and was assumed into Heaven. By 54 A.D., Peter had returned to Rome.

In 58 A.D. Paul returned to Jerusalem. As a former Pharisee and now a leading Christian, his presence caused so much controversy that the Roman authorities arrested him. As a Roman citizen, he had the right to demand a trial in Rome, which he did, being brought to Rome in the year 60. On the way he suffered a shipwreck and was stranded on the island of Malta, where he converted the Roman governor and established a Christian community. In Rome, he was kept under house arrest for two years and then acquitted. Afterwards he continued missionary work, perhaps even going as far as Spain.

The Decline of Rome Begins

Power is dangerous, and total power can destroy those who possess it. The emperor of Rome possessed total power. Both Augustus and Tiberius were strong and good men and were thus able to use power without being destroyed by it—though Tiberius spent the last years of his life surrounded by bodyguards on the island of Capri because he feared assassination. When he died in 37, he was succeeded by Caligula, who was insane: He once said that he wished the whole world had one neck so he could cut it off. He was assassinated in 41 and followed by Claudius who ruled fairly well. But in 54, Claudius was fed poison in a dish of mushrooms by his wife Agrippina, whose son by a previous marriage, Nero, consequently became emperor and later killed his murderous mother.

Nero possessed enormous pride. Added to his enormous power, it drove him insane. He was a brutal dictator, demanding that he be granted every conceivable honor. He had a 120-foot statue of himself erected in the imperial palace, entered athletic contests in which all the other contenders had to let him win and then held huge parties in celebration of his "victories," and commanded the Roman nobility to attend his musical performances to praise his singing.

Nero is sometimes remembered as the emperor who "fiddled while Rome burned." He may in fact have played his harp and sung a poem which he had written while the great fire of July 18, 64, was taking place. But after the fire had finally burned itself out, leaving large parts of the city in ashes and thousands of people homeless, the citizens of Rome began to blame Nero for the fire. He was already extremely unpopular because he had murdered his lovely wife Octavia so that he could marry a woman named Poppaea. In addition, the people had heard rumors that Nero wanted to build a new and larger palace for himself. Perhaps he had made space for the palace by burning down half the city.

Nero realized that he must find someone to blame for the fire, else the people might revolt and overthrow him. The city was in such a state of confusion and disorder that almost any rumor would be believed. Who better to blame than a group of people professing a new and strange religion—the Christians? The word went out to arrest Christians and bring them to Nero's Circus, a horseshoe-shaped stadium where the emperor staged entertainments. Now he had a new entertainment to delight his friends: the brutal torturing and killing of Christians.

Christians were fed to wild beasts; forced to act the role of characters who were murdered in plays, but the murders were not make-believe;

soaked with oil, tied to posts and then set on fire to serve as torches for the emperor's evening parties. The moral decay of Rome since the days of the republic was nowhere more evident than in the popular approval given to these hideous spectacles.

Of course Nero's soldiers would have been ordered to seek out the leader of the hated Christians and bring him to the Circus. Peter was arrested in 67 A.D. and condemned to death by crucifixion—a fulfillment of Christ's prophecy that Peter would one day stretch out his arms and be led away. But Peter did not feel himself worthy to die the same way that Jesus did, and the soldiers granted his request that he be crucified upside down. Now, the most important church in the world, St. Peter's Basilica, is on the site of Nero's Circus; underneath the Basilica is the tomb of the first Pope.

Peter was succeeded by the second pope, Linus. We know only a few facts about Linus: He was born a slave, he had been ordained by Peter, and he had attended Paul. He served as Pope from 67-79. But the most important fact about him is that his succession as Pope shows that the Church could not be destroyed by killing its leader.

Paul was also arrested about the same time. He was martyred in the same year by beheading, the method of death for Roman citizens. His tomb is in the Church of St. Paul outside the Walls in Rome, on the site of his death.

After fourteen increasingly horrible years, Nero's insane rule was brought to an end by the Praetorian Guard (a special division of the Roman army). With a troop of their horsemen about to overtake and kill him and a new emperor (Galba) already proclaimed, Nero committed suicide whispering: "What an artist dies in me!"

Then came 69 A.D., known as the "year of the four emperors." Galba was murdered on January 15; Otho committed suicide after being defeated in battle on April 19; Vitellius was slain in the streets of Rome on December 20. Finally came Vespasian, who was the only Roman emperor between 37 and 96 A.D. known for certain to have died a natural death. A practical man who was not greedy for power, he ruled well for ten years and did not persecute Christians.

The Conquest of Jerusalem

The most important event during Vespasian's rule occurred in the Holy Land. Two successive procurators in Jerusalem had been brutal and greedy, driving the Zealots to revolt. In 68, a Zealot army entered Jerusalem and slaughtered everyone suspected of Roman sympathies; some

8,500 died, and Jerusalem was in a state of terror.

Vespasian sent his son Titus as commander of a Roman army to put down the revolt and restore order. The Zealots were defeated in Galilee and retreated to Jerusalem, where Titus besieged the city and settled down to starve the people out in the spring of 70 A.D. For five months the people of Jerusalem lived in horror as food supplies ran out. Roman catapults bombarded the walls with 100-pound stones. Battering rams crashed against the gates. A new machine was used which could fling many lead balls at once.

Finally on August 9 the Roman soldiers breached (broke through) the first wall surrounding the city, then the second. The bloodthirsty John of Gischala, the Zealot general, and his starved soldiers retreated to Mount Moriah, the hill on which stood the Temple. The Roman soldiers came up the hill, but the Jews forced them to fight for every inch. Finally, a few made it to the top.

One soldier found himself standing in front of an open window of the Temple. Frustrated and angry because of the bitter fighting, he picked up a lighted torch and threw it inside. The Temple went up in flames. The Roman army showed no mercy. They went through the city, killing and looting. They rounded up those Jews still alive, sending 97,000 prisoners to the arenas. They took Temple treasures back to Rome: the seven-branched candlestick known as a menorah, made of silver and weighing more than a ton; an altar; the curtain which had surrounded the Holy of Holies. The Temple was demolished, thus fulfilling Christ's prophecy that "not one stone would be left upon another." All that was left was the foundation of the west wall. This became known as the Wailing Wall, because of a law which existed for a time that no Jew could enter Jerusalem under pain of death—except once every four years, on the anniversary of the destruction of the Temple, when Jews might go to this wall and weep.

One group of Zealots—960, including women and children—escaped to the mountain fortress of Masada. With ample supplies of food and water, they hoped that they could outwait the Roman legion camped in the desert at the foot of the cliff. But the Romans used Jewish slaves to build an earthen ramp and assaulted the fortress with a huge wooden tower pushed up the ramp. Realizing that they were doomed, the last Zealot force committed mass suicide, every man, woman and child dying.

The Church and the Empire

In 79 Titus succeeded his father as emperor. In that same year Pope

Linus died, possibly martyred though we do not know for sure, to be succeeded by Pope Cletus. In 86 Titus was succeeded by his brother Domitian. Domitian at first seemed to be a reasonably good ruler, but the vast power he possessed drove him into paranoia, so that he believed that he was surrounded by enemies. He established a reign of terror through the use of informers, drove all philosophers from Italy, ordered all citizens to swear by and sacrifice to the divine genius of himself, and persecuted Christians. During this persecution an attempt was made to martyr the Apostle John, the only Apostle still alive. The attempt was miraculously foiled, so instead John was exiled to the island of Patmos in the Mediterranean. There he wrote the last book of the Bible, the Book of Revelation or the Apocalypse.

Pope Cletus was martyred in 92. He was succeeded by Clement, who reigned from 92-101. From Clement we have one document: a letter written to the Church in Corinth, Greece, to settle a dispute there. This letter is important historically because it clearly shows that the Pope in Rome was regarded as having authority over the whole Church, with the power to settle disputes wherever they might arise. This evidence contradicts the enemies of the Church who have said that the Pope was not regarded as anyone special until several centuries after Christ.

History and the First Century, A.D.

In the first century A.D., we note three important themes:

1) *The growth and spread of the Church.* During the first century the Church took firm root, proving that it could survive persecutions which killed many members, including its two greatest leaders. The location of the Church's headquarters in Rome meant that Christianity could spread throughout the civilized world.

2) *The decline of Rome.* Rome was proving again that great power and wealth tempt men to terrible sins. The Romans, for all the virtues they had once possessed, could not resist these temptations. Eventually the great empire would weaken and break up, although not before countless people had suffered.

3) *The destruction of the Temple.* The Jewish religion as it had existed for two thousand years had come to an end. The religion would continue—but now it would be a religion of the Pharisees' law code, not a religion of the Temple, sacrifices and the hope for the Messiah. The Jewish people had refused to accept the Messiah. Therefore they would no longer have their divinely appointed role in world history. Instead the Church would reach out to

all men of all races.

Review Questions

1. Why is Pentecost Sunday called the birthday of the Church?
2. Why did Jesus give Peter his new name?
3. Who launched the first persecution of the Christians? Who was the first martyr?
4. Describe the conversion of Paul. What was his mission?
5. Who launched the second persecution of the Christians? Who was the first Apostle to be martyred?
6. List the area where each Apostle went at the time of the Dispersion.
7. Summarize Thomas's mission to India.
8. Summarize Jude's mission to Edessa and what happened to the Holy Shroud afterwards.
9. Where did Paul go on his missionary journeys? What were his main activities?
10. Why did Peter return to Jerusalem? What happened at the Council of Jerusalem?
11. What other event happened about this time?
12. Why was Paul taken to Rome? What happened there?
13. Describe Nero's rule over Rome.
14. Why did Nero persecute Christians? Describe the martyrdoms of Peter and Paul. Who was the second Pope?
15. What happened to Nero?
16. What happened during the Year of Four Emperors?
17. How and why was the Temple in Jerusalem destroyed?
18. What historical document do we possess from the fourth Pope? What is its significance?
19. What happened during the reign of Domitian?
20. Explain the significance of the three historical themes of the first century A.D.

Projects

1. Write a biography of one of the characters in this chapter.
2. Imagine that you are a Christian in Rome in 64 A.D. Write a diary of

the events that are taking place, beginning with the great fire.

3. Imagine that you are a Jew in Jerusalem in 70 A.D. Write a diary of the events that are taking place.

4. Prepare a chart of Roman emperors from Augustus to Domitian. Give the dates, list important events, and tell what happened to each.

Chapter Nine
Empire Versus Church

THOUGH THE EVENTS of the first century A.D. showed that the Roman Empire could never again be the proud, healthy nation it had once been, Rome remained the strongest power in the world. Eventually Rome would come into direct conflict with the growing new religion called Christianity and would try to eliminate this religion from the empire. The contest at the beginning seemed unequal: the mighty Roman government with the power of life or death over its citizens, the Roman army, and the instruments of torture, against a small religious group which had no army, no wealth, nothing but faith. But like earlier contests in history—Moses against Rameses II, Elijah against the 450 priest of Baal—the outcome of the struggle would be far different from what anyone expected.

The Good Emperors

Around the year 96, a group of intelligent and brave Romans, most in their sixties and seventies, gathered together to try to bring an end to the stream of assassinations, insanities and horrors which had caused so much suffering. These men had grown up during the hideous reign of Nero and lived their middle age under the cruel rule of Domitian. They knew evil very well and resolved to protect themselves and others from as much of it as possible.

They planned and successfully carried out the assassination of Domitian in 96. They chose one of their number as emperor, the elderly senator Nerva. Nerva then chose his successor, a Spanish general named Trajan, whom he adopted as his son in order to avoid the struggles and bloodshed over who would be emperor. Trajan became emperor in 98.

The example set by Nerva was followed by the next three emperors. Each adopted as his son a talented man of similar political views. Each adopted son peacefully became emperor. The four emperors thus chosen—Trajan (98-117), Hadrian (117-138), Antoninus Pius (138-161) and Marcus Aurelius (161-180)—each ruled approximately twenty years. During the entire period of their rule the Roman people knew more peace and order than they had since the days of Tiberius.

As long as they reigned, these men—known as the Good Emperors—were able to stop the worst evils of the earlier emperors who had been concerned with wealth and power for themselves. But the Good Emperors could cure only some of the symptoms of Rome's sickness; they could not cure the disease. Though the assassinations of emperors were stopped, other evils continued.

One important symbol of the spiritual sickness of Rome was the Colosseum, a huge stadium built by Vespasian and still standing today, though in ruins. In the Colosseum were held the "games" which entertained the people of Rome. By the time of Marcus Aurelius, the games were held 135 days a year. These games were not the sports events which are held in our own stadiums. They were bloody spectacles involving death and destruction, which the people flocked to see and to cheer. Trajan celebrated his conquest of Dacia (Rumania) by 123 consecutive days of games during which 10,000 gladiators fought and 11,000 animals were killed. Captured prisoners of war fought to the death. These gladiators had no choice—it was kill or be killed—and the crowd cheered and screamed for blood.

In addition, the Good Emperors continued to persecute Christians. They saw Christianity as weakening the empire because Christians gave their first loyalty to what seemed to be a foreign god. Marcus Aurelius, especially, regarded Christians with suspicion. During his reign occurred the martyrdoms in Lyon, when the most horrible tortures since Nero were inflicted: the ninety-year-old bishop was beaten to death; several of the Christians were roasted in an iron chair; living bodies were torn to ribbons.

The moral standards of the people became lower and lower. They did less work while prices and taxes continually rose higher. Mystery religions, whose secret rituals involved mutilation and perhaps even cannibalism, gained in popularity. The population declined as people stopped having children or allowed the ones who were born to die.

Disaster hung over Rome like a huge, dark cloud. As long as Marcus Aurelius lived, he could hold it off. But Marcus Aurelius had a son, Commodus. The emperor loved him and named him to succeed him on the throne. Commodus was insane.

Years of Horror

The next 100 years were almost like a replay of the first century—only worse. The insane Commodus was emperor for thirteen years. His wild spending completed the bankruptcy of the treasury. But when he was finally strangled by his own chosen personal bodyguard (193) and replaced by a simple man of common sense, Publius Pertinax, the corrupt senate and governmental officials would have none of Pertinax's efforts to economize. He was murdered in three months by the Praetorian Guard (the emperor's personal army), which then literally auctioned off the empire to the highest bidder, one Didius Julianus. Didius paid the Praetorian Guard, but he was unable to buy the army in Africa. Its commander, Septimius Severus, marched on Italy and became ruler of the world in the spring of 193. In Rome he found the treasury empty.

So he increased taxation, driving people from their homes to become bandits. Immorality and lawlessness reigned, and the only solution anyone could think of was to keep trying new emperors. In the ninety years after the death of Commodus, there were twenty emperors. As the table below reveals, not one of them died a peaceful death:

Emperor	Died	Circumstances of Death
Septimius Severus	211	died on campaign against the barbarians
Caracalla	217	murdered by army officers
Macrimus	218	killed in battle with Elagabalus
Elagabalus	222	murdered by the Praetorian Guard
Alexander Severus	235	murdered by his army
Maximus Thrax	238	murdered by his army
Gordian	244	murdered by Philip the Arab
Philip the Arab	249	killed in battle with Decius
Decius	251	killed in battle with Gallus
Gallus	253	murdered by his army
Valerian	259	captured by Persians, died in captivity (his body stuffed and hung in a temple)
Gallienus	268	murdered by his army
Claudius Gothicus	270	died of plague
Aurelian	275	murdered by his army officers

Emperor	Died	Circumstances of Death
Claudius Tacitus	275	murdered by his army
Probus	281	murdered by his army
Carus	283	killed by a bolt of lightning

The efforts of the Good Emperors were as if they had never been. Corruption, horror and death dominated Rome.

The Church and the Popes

In one way only, Commodus was an improvement over his father: he did not persecute Christians. He stopped the martyrdoms and ordered the release of those Christians who had been sent to slave labor in the mines. One of those released was Calixtus, who was elected Pope in 217. But a man named Hippolytus was not impressed by Calixtus' sufferings for the faith. He declared that *he*, Hippolytus, was the real Pope. When a man sets himself up as Pope when a true Pope reigns, the false pope is called an *anti-pope*. Hippolytus was the Church's first anti-pope. Hippolytus said that Calixtus was too lenient toward sinners, that some sins could never be forgiven. Calixtus knew better; he knew that any repented sin could be forgiven. Finally Calixtus was martyred by a Roman mob. A new Pope, Urban I, was chosen, followed by Pontian in 230. Through it all Hippolytus continued as anti-pope.

In 235 the giant emperor Maximus Thrax ordered Pontian arrested and sent to the mines in Sardinia. Hearing about Hippolytus' claims, Maximus ordered him arrested too. And so the anti-pope and the true Pope were side by side in the mines. Pontian, knowing that he would certainly never return to Rome, resigned his office as Pope, the first to do so. Although no one can *depose* (force out of office) a Pope, because no one on earth has higher authority than the Vicar of Christ, a Pope can resign as Pontian did. Not long after, Pontian died from the suffering and hardships of the mines. Seeing Pontian's holy example, Hippolytus was shamed into admitting that his pride had been too strong. He realized that he was wrong; he repented. He sent a message to his followers, saying that he no longer claimed the title of Pope and urging them to obey the true Pope. Hippolytus also died in the mines and is the only anti-pope to be venerated as a saint.

Emperor Decius launched an even more vicious persecution, requiring for the first time that everyone in the empire sacrifice to the spirit of the emperor himself. The first person he ordered martyred was Pope Fabian, declaring afterwards that he would rather lose his throne than see the election of another Pope. The Roman clergy, who in those days were responsible for the election of the Pope, did not dare elect another man while Decius lived. So the papacy remained vacant for about a year, until Decius was killed in battle in 251.

In 257 Sixtus II was elected Pope. Emperor Valerian had a superstitious fear that the disasters befalling the Empire were due to the gods' anger at the Christians. He intensified the persecution, forbidding liturgical worship and access to the catacombs, where the Christians had gone to celebrate Mass secretly during times of persecution. Sixtus' consecration as Pope was held in secret. The next year, Valerian enacted a harsher law: bishops, priests and deacons could be executed without trial. But Sixtus was not afraid. He gathered his people for Mass at the chapel in the cemetery of St. Calixtus. Only the flickering of candles lightened the darkness of the small room. Only the rustling of bodies broke the silence.

Then Sixtus began the Mass. His voice was quiet but firm. Slowly, reverently, he spoke the prayers of the Mass. The people were caught up in their love for Christ, forgetting the anger that surrounded them. Suddenly they heard a crash at the door. It fell open. Torches blazed into the room. The tramping of boots, harsh voices and the clashing of spears destroyed the peaceful silence. The commander strode forward. "Give me your leaders," he ordered, "or we will kill you all." The doorway was blocked. No one could escape. Sixtus stepped forward. "I am the Bishop of Rome," he said in a calm voice. "Let the rest of these people go." His four deacons came to stand by his side. "We are deacons," they said. "We are also guilty of worshiping the true God."

"Get the rest of the people out of here," the captain shouted, while other soldiers laid harsh hands on the Pope and his deacons, though they had no intention of escaping. No time was wasted. The five holy men were forced to the ground. Sharp swords were withdrawn from scabbards. They were beheaded on the spot. Their bodies fell to the stone floor. But their souls went immediately to Heaven. They had given their lives for Christ and the Church.

Diocletian

After the bolt of lightning eliminated Carus, a struggle began for the imperial throne. In spite of all that had happened, men still craved power and the chance to get their hands on the money taken in by taxation. After several months of warfare, one man emerged out of the dust and blood as the most powerful man in the empire. He was Diocletian, who became emperor in 284. Though he had risen to power through violence, he disliked bloodshed, preferring persuasion to force. He loved Rome deeply and longed to see her return to her days of glory. Diocletian was no fool—he may have realized that such a goal was impossible to achieve. Nevertheless he determined to do everything he could to restore order and to bring a measure of peace to his unhappy homeland.

He began by staving off economic collapse by establishing a sound currency and compelling men to remain at their jobs. He eliminated all special privileges and appointed able and qualified men to positions of importance in local governments and the army.

Diocletian moved his capital from Rome to Nicomedia in Asia Minor in order to be closer to the wealthier half of the empire. And he developed a plan to eliminate the controversies over the succession to the throne. He divided the empire in half, appointing a man named Maximian to rule in the West while he ruled in the East, each with the title Augustus. Under each of the two Augusti was an associate, called a Caesar, who was to become emperor upon the death or retirement of the reigning emperor. Diocletian's Caesar was Galerius; Maximian's was Constantius. Through this plan Diocletian hoped to minimize the struggles for the throne and to reduce the temptations by reducing the power.

The Great Persecution

Diocletian wanted to do what was best for the empire and all its citizens. It is one of the strange facts of history that nine years after he came to the throne, he approved the beginning of the greatest persecution which Christians were ever to suffer.

Diocletian cannot be wholly blamed for the persecution. The greatest responsibility probably belongs not to anyone in power in the empire, but to a woman named Romula. Romula was a priestess of the mountain gods of Germany, possibly involved in mystery religions, and she hated Christianity and Christians. She taught this hatred to her son, who happened to be Galerius, Diocletian's Caesar.

Influenced and urged on by his mother, Galerius tried to persuade Diocletian to wipe out Christianity. Diocletian was reluctant. He had hoped to bring an end to bloodshed. Finally, under Galerius's urgings, he passed decrees stating that Christians could not hold office in the government or in the army, but this did not satisfy Galerius or his bloodthirsty mother.

For months the debate went on, Galerius calling for a general perse-cution of Christians, Diocletian holding back. But the one thing Diocletian feared more than anything else was a return to the civil wars which had raged earlier over who was to be the next emperor. He had to keep his chosen successor happy. At last—pushed into the decision by a fire in his palace which Galerius blamed on Christians but which was probably started under his orders—Diocletian, early in 303, signed decrees ordering the destruction of Christian books and churches and the imprisonment and torture of any Christian priests who would not sacrifice to pagan gods.

Then it appears that Diocletian underwent a psychological collapse, perhaps caused by guilt over having ordered the persecution. He shut him-self away in his palace at Nicomedia, allowing Galerius to rule the empire. Galerius is therefore almost certainly responsible for the order in the spring of 304 requiring all Christians to sacrifice to the pagan gods or die. Thus began the Great Persecution, the strongest effort in history to wipe out Christianity. The decree was enforced throughout the empire, except in Gaul and Britain, which were under the authority of Constantius, who may have moderated the persecution because of the influence of his first wife, Helena, a Christian.

From city to city, village to village, the imperial soldiers came. Citi-zens were called out of their homes and brought before judges. Each citi-zen was ordered to offer sacrifice to the pagan gods and to the emperor. Those who refused were usually tortured to force them to relent. If they still held firm, they were murdered. Christians were scourged, torn with iron hooks, roasted alive, hung by one limb from trees, stretched on the rack, pierced with arrows. Women and children as well as men underwent torture. Christians were forced to watch the sufferings of others as a means of weakening their own determination.

Some people did give in to torture, but many did not, holding firm in spite of the worst the imperial forces could do. They died heroically, often smiling or singing to show that they were happy to be going to their Lord as His witnesses. The word *martyr* means witness.

"In This Sign You Will Conquer"

In March of 305 Diocletian emerged from seclusion, but he was a sick man and unable to resist the pressure from Galerius to abdicate. According to the plan Diocletian had originally drawn up, Maximian would abdicate at the same time, leaving Galerius and Constantius as Augusti. Then Galerius appointed the new Caesars, Severus and Daia, two men of low morals who would be under his control. He thus left out of consideration a young man whom everyone had expected would be named as Constantius' successor: the son of Constantius and Helena, Constantine.

But there was more involved than simply the loss of a position. Constantine was in danger of losing his life as well. He was residing in the palace at Nicomedia, in the power of Galerius, sixteen hundred miles away from his father, who was old and sick. Galerius refused to give Constantine permission to leave.

Then, one evening, in the spring of 305, Galerius signed a pass permitting Constantine to leave the palace. The most likely reason for this surprising reversal was that Galerius was drunk and didn't realize what he was doing.

But Constantine knew exactly what he was doing. He was riding for his life and for the chance to rule the empire. All night long he rode west. At each post-station, he chose the best horse as a new mount and hamstrung all the rest to prevent pursuit. He reached the Bosporus at dawn and took the ferry across the waterway from Asia to Europe. Then he rode on. Galerius did not awake until noon, by which time Constantine had fifteen-hours' head start and there were no uninjured horses with which Galerius could pursue him.

On across Serbia, up the Danube, across Austria, Switzerland, the Rhine, into Gaul and past Paris, Constantine rode sixteen hundred miles to reach his father's side at the English Channel. When his father died the next year, the legions in Gaul proclaimed Constantine as Augustus, totally ignoring Severus.

Galerius was furious and continued the persecution. But the Christian God was stronger than the pagan emperor. Galerius came down with a horrible disease, his body being eaten away by an ulcer. He began to fear that his sufferings were a punishment inflicted by this strange god whose followers did not fear to die. He ordered an end to the persecution, in the superstitious hope that the Christian God would remove his torment.

When Galerius died in 311, Daia ordered a resumption of the persecution in the territories he controlled. Maxentius, the son of Diocletian's co-Augustus, Maximian, ruled Italy and Africa, without major persecution, but without morality or respect for law, either. Maxentius had a larger army than Constantine, and no one doubted that he wanted to rule the entire empire.

Constantine was militarily in a weak position and he knew it. His military advisers warned him not to march against Maxentius. His pagan soothsayers read the omens and issued the same warning. But an Authority far higher than these called to Constantine, and the young man listened. Some time in the year 312, he saw a vision in the sky, a cross with the Latin words, "In hoc signo vinces" ("In this sign you will conquer"). Constantine ordered a cross made, and on top of it the Greek letters Chi and Rho, the first two letters of Christ in Greek. This was to be the standard for his army. Then putting his trust in Christ and in His cross, he marched toward Italy.

In response to a dream the night before the decisive battle, he ordered his soldiers to paint the Chi Rho sign on their shields. The battle was fought on October 28, 312, the Battle of the Milvian Bridge or Saxa Rubra (Red Rocks), nine miles north of Rome on the banks of the Tiber River. The center of Maxentius' line was held by the *cataphracti*, heavily armed cavalry. But Constantine had trained a corps to deal with the cataphracti with heavy maces. He led it in person to the attack. The cataphracti broke, and Maxentius and his men were driven toward Rome. When they crossed the Tiber on the Milvian Bridge, it collapsed under their weight. Maxentius in his heavy armor sank into the mud and drowned.

The victorious general entered Rome in triumph. Constantine had conquered.

The Founding of Christendom

Upon taking power, Constantine did not order a slaughter of his enemies as was customary. He called the other powerful men in the Empire together for a meeting in Milan, Italy, where they worked on solutions to the major problems facing the Empire. They especially turned their attention to the question of religious freedom. The result of their deliberations was the Edict of Milan, also known as the Edict of Toleration. Issued in 313, the Edict declared: "We therefore ordain that anybody—including the Christians—may observe the faith of their sect and cult." The empire was now officially neutral toward religion. In the struggle between the Church and the empire, the Church had won.

Constantine, who was eventually baptized, modified the Roman laws to reflect Christian principles: Sunday became a festival day, the killing or torture of slaves was prohibited, gladiatorial fights were forbidden, orphans and widows were protected, crucifixion was abolished. Constantine thereby set up a society in which the laws reflected the laws of God and honored Christian principles. Another name for this kind of society is *Christendom*, and Constantine is thus honored as the Founder of Christendom.

Helena, Constantine's mother, surely deserves much of the credit for this official victory of Christianity. Constantine brought her to live in the royal palace, but she eventually went to the Holy Land, where she established Christian shrines and discovered the Cross on which Christ had died. She had suffered a great deal in her earlier life—Constantius had divorced her because he did not think her (the daughter of an innkeeper) sufficiently noble for the wife of an emperor. But her faith and patience were rewarded, both on earth and in Heaven, where she is now a saint.

Review Questions

1. List the Good Emperors. When did they begin to rule? What was their goal and how did they go about it?
2. How did things change for the better during the rule of the Good Emperors?
3. What evils existed during their reigns?
4. What brought the rule of the Good Emperors to an end?
5. What characterized the rule of Rome from the time of Commodus until the time of Diocletian?
6. Give the significance of Hippolytus and of Pontian.
7. Describe the martyrdom of Pope Sixtus II.
8. How was Diocletian different from the emperors who had preceded him? What did he try to do for the empire? What steps did he take to accomplish his goals?
9. Describe the steps leading up to the launching of the Great Persecution in full force.
10. Why was Constantine's life in danger? Describe Constantine's Ride.
11. How did Galerius die? What did he do just before his death?
12. What did Constantine see in his vision? What did he do the night before the battle?
13. Describe the Battle of the Milvian Bridge.
14. What was the Edict of Milan? Why is it important?
15. Why is Constantine called the Founder of Christendom?

Projects

1. Prepare an illustrated report on the Colosseum.
2. Marcus Aurelius was a Stoic. Prepare a report on the Stoics.

3. Write a series of newspaper accounts of Constantine's rise to power.
4. Prepare a report on the martyrdom of one or more martyrs during the Great Persecution.
5. Imagine that Romula and Helena had met. Write an account of the conversation they might have had.

Chapter Ten
The Great Heresies

SOON AFTER COMING TO POWER, Constantine made the decision to build a new capital city in Asia Minor. The city was first named New Rome and later called Constantinople in honor of its founder. The modern city is Istanbul, Turkey.

Constantine selected a magnificent location for his city: a beautiful natural harbor called the Golden Horn, with the water providing protection from attack. The location was a crossroads of all trade routes, both land and sea, and a bridge between Europe and the East. Constantinople was completed in 330 and until 1453 remained the most important city in the world. During that entire time, it was conquered only once.

The founding of Constantinople and the greater wealth in the East meant that the center of power now shifted from Rome to the East. Though retaining its primacy in spiritual matters as the seat of the Pope, Rome became less and less significant in secular matters. During the fifth century barbarian invasions began in the West (which we will discuss in the next chapter). As a result the Roman Empire became less Roman and more Greek or Hellenistic, being dominated by the areas which had been conquered by Alexander and culturally influenced by the Greeks. Greek was the official language and Greek culture was dominant. In fact, by the end of the fifth century it was no longer possible to speak of *the* Roman Empire. There was a western area being attacked by barbarians, and an eastern empire which was usually given the name Byzantium or Byzantine Empire (after a small town which had stood on the site of Constantinople). The two areas had very little in common.

The Arian Heresy

Having failed to destroy the Church from without by the Great Persecution, Satan then attempted to destroy the Church from within. The 300's, 400's, and 500's were the centuries of the Great Heresies, attempts to enforce false doctrine (heresy) on the Church. The first great heresy was Arianism, which attacked the very foundation of Christianity—the doctrine of the divinity of Christ. At one point it appeared that Arianism had triumphed, but the Holy Spirit was with the Church. Working through the Pope and a great saint, the Holy Spirit brought about the triumph of orthodoxy (true doctrine). The gates of hell did not prevail.

During the last years of the Great Persecution, a little red-haired boy was growing up in Alexandria, Egypt. Young Athanasius couldn't help but be familiar with the heroism of the martyrs, some of whom lived in his very city. When he was about 14, many of his neighbors, men, women and children, were led through the streets of Alexandria, all singing joyfully, to be tortured, scourged, racked and crucified. Knowing that these heroes and heroines preferred torture and death to denying the faith, even to the seemingly slight extent of burning a few grains of incense on the emperor's altar, had a profound effect on young Athanasius, who learned that the Catholic Faith was worth dying for.

The other great influence on him was Anthony of Egypt, the hermit saint who went into the desert so that he might be free of the temptations of worldly society. Athanasius served St. Anthony for a time, learning through this holy man the power of the love of Jesus and the reality of the God-man's presence in the world.

Athanasius became a priest and secretary to the bishop of Alexandria. Then in 321, a handsome deacon named Arius began publicly preaching in Alexandria the doctrine that the Son had not always existed, that He had been created by God, that there was a time when He was not. Arianism was popular with the Greeks of Alexandria and elsewhere because the Greeks had always been intolerant of mysteries; they wanted understandable explanations for everything. It was so much easier for these well-educated, proud people to accept a teaching that Christ was not really God than it was for them to bow humbly to the divine mystery. But the ordinary people, the poor and uneducated, did not like Arian notions. If Jesus is both God and man, then they felt close to God because His Son was a man like them. But if Jesus was not true God, then God could seem distant and unapproachable. The intellectuals preferred a distant God; the ordinary people wanted a God they could see and hear and touch.

The Church, of course, had always taught that Jesus was both God and man, but the precise way in which this could be possible had not been worked out. Now the controversy erupted, with Arius on one side and Athanasius on the other; before long the dispute came to the attention of the Emperor Constantine. Though not fully understanding the significance of the Arian denial of Christ's divinity, the Emperor was worried that the controversy would destroy the hard-won unity of his empire. He commanded the bishops of the Church to meet in a council at Nicaea in Turkey in 325.

From all over the empire came 318 bishops to hot, steamy Nicaea, including a Spanish bishop named Hosius, who was the official representative of the Pope and who was appointed chairman. All the main actors in the drama were present: Constantine in his royal robes; the handsome, impressive Arius, then 75 years old; and the stoop-shouldered, 27-year-old Athanasius.

The debate thundered through the meeting hall, with the arguments finally settling on one phrase (in Greek, only one word—*homoousion*); was Christ *one in being* with the Father? Athanasius pointed out from both Scripture and philosophical reasoning that Christ must be equal to God the Father. The Father had declared to Moses: "I Am Who Am." The Father is self-existent, the source of all being. If the Son is one in being with the Father, then His name as well is I Am; He is co-equal and co-eternal with the Father. And *I Am* is precisely the name Christ had given to Himself: "Before Abraham ever was, I Am."

Athanasius' arguments were devastating, and the Nicene Creed was drawn up—a summary of the most important teachings of Christianity, including a description of Christ as "begotten, not made, one in being with the Father." All but two of the bishops signed the Creed. Constantine gave a great banquet celebrating the happy conclusion of the Council, and the bishops returned to their dioceses with the controversy apparently settled. Within three years Athanasius had been made bishop of Alexandria, the almost unanimous choice of the Alexandrian clergy and the Egyptian bishops. It appeared that orthodoxy had triumphed.

But the Arians had not given up. Almost as soon as Athanasius became bishop, the Arians began plotting against him. They were led by a man named Eusebius, who trumped up charges against Athanasius and persuaded or bribed enough people to accept them that Athanasius was brought to trial for the murder of one Arsenius. Eusebius manipulated the trial so that the majority of the judges were Arians; and with confidence one of his cohorts stood up and solemnly accused Athanasius of the murder of Arsenius. As evidence he produced a withered hand, which he alleged Athanasius had cut off to use in a magic ritual. All eyes turned to Athanasius.

The red-haired bishop only smiled. He looked around the room and asked if any of those present had known Arsenius. "Oh, yes," answered many of them. Athanasius gestured to the back of the room. A man whose face had previously been hidden by a monk's cowl rose and threw back the hood. It was Arsenius, who not only was alive but possessed both of his hands intact. The Arians were furious, and only the quick intervention of Count Dionysius restored order and prevented the Arians from seizing Athanasius and killing him on the spot.

But Eusebius was not finished. He went directly to Constantine, now old and sick and not fully rational, and told him the lie that Athanasius had threatened to cut off Egypt's grain shipments to the imperial capital. This threat preyed on the sick man's mind, and he ordered Athanasius exiled to Trier, Germany, at the outer reaches of the civilized world. This is an example of *Caesaro-papism*, the attempt by the emperor to control the Church.

While Athanasius was unperturbedly accepting his exile, using the occasion to write letters to his flock in Egypt urging them to stand fast against Arianism, first Arius and then Constantine himself died. The Empire was divided among Constantine's three sons, all named after him: Constantine, Constantius, and Constans. Constantius took the eastern area, which included Egypt. Though an Arian, his first goal was to get control of the empire. He allowed Athanasius to return to Alexandria in the hopes that the people of Egypt—whose love for their bishop had never slackened—would support Constantius in his struggles. This indeed happened, and by 350 he was sole ruler of the Empire, the other two brothers having been killed.

Athanasius Against the World

Now Constantius showed his true colors. His emissaries pressured Pope Liberius to support Arianism. When he refused, he was seized in the middle of the night and eventually exiled and imprisoned. All orthodox bishops were ordered exiled. On February 8, 356, imperial troops surrounded the church where Athanasius was conducting services. Athanasius calmly ordered the deacons to chant a psalm. His congregation stood in the way as the troops broke through the doors, enabling Athanasius to get away to a hiding place in the desert. No one has ever discovered exactly where the hiding place was, but it was probably among the tombs. An Arian named George, a pork dealer who had made himself rich by fraud, was installed as bishop of Alexandria and proceeded to persecute orthodox Catholics. Athanasius stayed in hiding for six years. Keeping in touch with events in Alexandria through courageous friends, he sent back a constant stream of messages encouraging the people to hold fast to orthodoxy in spite of persecution.

Now it was truly Athanasius against the world, and the Church appeared in deadly peril. All orthodox bishops were exiled; Arian bishops were in control. Even Hosius of Cordova had been imprisoned and tortured and forced to sign a pro-Arian statement at the age of 101. Liberius, under torture, signed a condemnation of Athanasius and a document called the Third Formulary of Sirmium, which was unclear and could possibly be seen as an Arian document. But he added a "P.S." to the document stating that he was in no way approving any statement which declared the Son to be less than equal to the Father. And in spite of a year's pressure, he never signed the Second Formulary of Sirmium, which was clearly Arian. But the Pope was in no condition to fight for orthodoxy, and it was left to Athanasius to direct the battle from his hiding place among the dead.

And what a general he was. He wrote a memorable letter to the bishops of Egypt, denouncing Arianism and bidding them stand firm. He wrote *History of the Arians, On the Incarnation* which gloriously affirmed the divinity of Christ, and a moving *Life of St. Anthony*. He even made secret visits to his flock in Alexandria, slipping in and out under the very noses of the bishop George and his followers.

The Arians had won the palace, but thanks to Athanasius they could not win the people. Soon the corruption and greed for power of the Arians became obvious. Bishop George made himself so unpopular that he was first driven from the city by the people, and then—when he ventured back—was thrown into chains and lynched. Constantius died of a fever in 361, whereupon his cousin and rival Julian took the crown. Julian hated all Christians and wanted to restore paganism; hence he is known to history as Julian the Apostate. He refused to support either side in the Arian struggle and in fact persecuted both heretics and orthodox Christians. He allowed all bishops, including Athanasius, to return to their dioceses so that he could keep them under surveillance. Deprived of the support of the government, Arianism began to wither away.

But Athanasius' fearless public advancement of Christianity soon angered Julian, who had expected the bishop to be chastened by his six years in hiding. Julian ordered Athanasius out of Egypt at the end of 362. Athanasius promised his friends that he would soon be back and took a boat up the Nile, intending to hide until the storm blew over. Some distance up the river he learned that the imperial soldiers were in pursuit. "Turn around and go downstream," he commanded his rowers. Soon they neared the imperial boat, rowing furiously upstream. "We are looking for the Bishop Athanasius," shouted one of the officers. "Have you seen him?"

"Keep right on going," replied Athanasius. "He is not far off." Athanasius escaped, hiding in an Egyptian monastery, until word of Julian's death reached him and he returned to Alexandria.

Before his death, Julian attempted to rebuild the Temple in Jerusalem as a means of proving Christianity false. But so many mysterious happenings intervened—lightning out of a clear sky, earthquakes, visions—that workers refused to continue. Julian was forced to abandon his plan, and Christ's prophecy that not one stone would remain upon another remained fulfilled. To this day, the Temple has never been rebuilt; it is no longer needed because of the existence of the new and eternal Sacrifice, the Mass, in the Catholic Church. Julian was forced to admit his powerlessness as he lay dying. Referring to Christ, he said, "Pale Galilean, You have conquered."

Athanasius had to hide one last time. The empire was divided, Valentinian ruling the West and Valens the East. Valens was an Arian and ordered Athanasius into exile. For the fifth time in his life, Athanasius went into hiding, this time for four months. When Valens became occupied with other matters, Athanasius came back to Alexandria and resumed his see.

Athanasius lived the last seven years of his life in peace, seeing the Church strong and united once again and Arianism reduced to a dead letter. He died on May 2, 373, and was welcomed into the arms of the God-Man whose divinity he had so successfully defended.

Thus did the Pope, the ordinary people and one bishop standing firm for orthodoxy defeat the combined power of the intellectuals, the wealthy, the powerful and the government of the Roman Empire. Of course the two sides in the struggle were not quite evenly balanced. The forces of orthodoxy had—as they will always have—the Holy Spirit on their side.

The Fathers of the Church

The second half of the fourth century was an age of giants, as the Fathers of the Church built on the foundations of the Apostolic teaching a towering theological structure in which the Church finds nourishment to this day. St. Jerome (342-420) rose to heights of genius in his Latin translation of the Bible, much of it done on the spot in Bethlehem, where he died. There was St. John Chrysostom (347-407), whose sermons as archbishop of Constantinople earned him the title "golden-mouthed" as he preached against abuses in church and palace. St. Augustine (354-430) gave the Church theological writings which are still mined for their riches.

One of the greatest of the theologians among the Fathers was St. Augustine's teacher, St. Ambrose of Milan. Ambrose was born in 334 in Gaul, probably in Trier, where Athanasius had spent some time during one of his exiles. His aristocratic family was probably part of Trier's flourishing Christian community. Ambrose grew up during the Arian heresy and the reign of Julian the Apostate. He couldn't help but be aware of the problems caused when the state tried to dictate Church doctrine, as in the Arian controversy, or set itself higher than the Church, as in the reign of Julian the Apostate.

Nevertheless, Ambrose's first inclination was to enter the imperial service, following in the footsteps of his father. He was first a lawyer and then in 370 was appointed governor of the province of Milan. The first few years were calm enough; then in 374 the see of Milan became vacant and a furious conflict erupted between Arian and orthodox factions in the city over who was to be the new bishop. The two groups met in noisy debate in the cathedral to hold the episcopal election; Ambrose, worried about this threat to the public peace, entered the cathedral to restore order. Though only five feet, four inches tall, he was nevertheless an imposing figure, having earned the respect and homage of all the people. They quieted to hear what he had to say. As he was addressing the crowd, the voice of a child rose in the back: "Ambrose bishop!" The cry raced through the crowd; Ambrose seemed the logical choice. The only Milanese, in fact, who was unhappy with the choice was Ambrose himself. He had a successful life as governor; why give it all up for the controversies facing a bishop? Moreover, though believing in Christian doctrine, Ambrose had not yet been baptized. He tried to hide, but to no avail. He had to make a choice. Ambrose chose Christ and was baptized. On December 7 he was consecrated bishop, almost immediately handing over all his wealth to the Church.

His commitment was total. He transformed the comfortable life of an imperial officer to a penitential life centering on prayer and study, totally devoted to the welfare of his flock.

He was an active, pastoral bishop. His first concern was to bring the people closer to Christ by encouraging them to be less dependent on worldly things. He educated his subjects in penance, not only through writings and sermons but through his example. He encouraged women to live as consecrated virgins, thereby gaining the dignity which women had not been granted by pagan society.

Ambrose also had to struggle against paganism, which, though in its death throes, had found a new vigor. Here Ambrose enlisted the help of the emperor in the West, Gratian, who in 382, under Ambrose's tutelage, deprived paganism of its resources and confiscated the goods of the temples, thereby firmly separating paganism from any state sanction. The pagan aristocracy reacted. Ambrose met them head-on in a vigorous debate in 384 before the emperor. Ambrose carried the day, and paganism went into a final, fatal decline.

It was also in 384 that a young rhetorician (teacher of public speaking and debate) named Augustine came to Milan. He was hired by the pagan aristocracy in a last desperate attempt to undermine Ambrose's position. The rhetorician was a Manichean—believing that a principle of good and a principle of evil, equally powerful, warred within the universe. By denying the existence of an infinite, all-good Creator, the Manicheans were allies of the pagans. Because of Ambrose's stature, the young teacher paid a courtesy call on Milan's bishop; he left the audience deeply impressed, not only by the bishop's learning but because he was "a man who was kind to me." Augustine, though steadfastly denying any allegiance to Christianity, began attending all of Ambrose's sermons; for the first time in his life he saw that Christianity was intellectually unassailable. The intellectual barriers to his acceptance of Christianity were thus swept away by the eloquence of Ambrose.

But conversions, once the barriers are down, must come through grace. Grace came to Augustine through his mother Monica, who had never ceased praying that her wayward son would accept Christ. In a garden in Milan in July 386, Augustine cried in anguish: "How long? How long shall this be? It is always tomorrow and tomorrow. Why not this hour an end to all my meanness?" As he spoke a child close by was singing a refrain: "Take up and read." Augustine reached for a book—St. Paul's Epistles. Opening it at random he read, "Put on the Lord Jesus Christ and make no provision for the flesh to fulfill the lusts thereof." Augustine's soul was flooded with a peace such as he had never known. He henceforth belonged to Christ. At the Easter vigil on April 24, 387, Ambrose baptized Augustine; the alleluias reverberated in Heaven itself.

Confrontation in Milan

It was during the time of Ambrose's instruction of Augustine that Theodosius, emperor of the eastern half of the empire, entered Milan as a conqueror and sole master of the empire. For the last time, the empire would be ruled by one prince, and the man possessing this great political power would come into direct conflict with his spiritual master.

The two men first met in 388 and each had a favorable impression of the other. Theodosius was an orthodox Catholic who continued Gratian's opposition to paganism. Ambrose impressed Theodosius as a man of talent and dedication. But soon problems arose. Theodosius was used to the flattering attentions of the bishops in the East, far too many of whom were more concerned with political advancement than with spiritual. One day at Mass, Theodosius took a place in the sanctuary near the altar among the priests. Ambrose had to send a deacon to ask the emperor to go down among the people, reminding him: "The emperor is in the Church, not over it."

When Ambrose condemned an action by Theodosius, the latter began to show deference and regard to the pagan nobility, visiting them in their homes and thereby strengthening their position against the Church. He enacted laws to harm the Church and forbade his advisers so much as to speak to the bishop.

The crisis came in the spring of 390. A serious revolt broke out in Thessalonica, the capital city of Macedonia, eventually resulting in a riot in which the commander of the imperial troops was stoned to death. Soon word of the uprising reached Milan, and rumors quickly spread that Theodosius planned a fearful revenge. Though he was out of favor, Ambrose managed to gain an audience with the emperor, pleading with him to show mercy, condemning the idea of any vengeance on innocent people as an atrocious crime. Theodosius gave Ambrose some vague reassurance and dismissed the bishop.

Shortly thereafter, word again reached Milan of events in Thessalonica. Theodosius had sent word that the people were to be invited to the stadium. Expecting the start of the races, they were set upon by imperial troops. After three hours of slaughter, the death toll stood at 7000 defenseless men, women and children.

Theodosius himself seemed shocked by his appalling crime against innocent life. He had even sent an order countermanding the massacre order. But it arrived too late. Ambrose wrote the emperor a confidential letter in his own hand, not even using a secretary because he wanted no one but Theodosius to see this heart-to-heart plea of a bishop to one of his flock who had grievously sinned. "I write with my own hands what I wish to be read by yourself alone," wrote Ambrose, who went on to remind Theodosius of King David, who had also sinned grievously but had repented. The letter was tactful, merciful, loving, but also firm; by his public crime, Theodosius was excommunicated until he did public penance: "I dare not offer the sacrifice, if you determine to attend. For can it possibly be right, after the slaughter of so many, to do what may not be done after the blood of only one innocent person has been shed?"

Theodosius sent no reply, but his conscience gnawed. He did not force a confrontation by going to the basilica; he issued a new law in August that 30 days must elapse between a condemnation and an execution. But though he personally regretted his actions, he was not yet ready to make a public act of submission to ecclesiastical authority, not yet ready to acknowledge that the moral authority of the Church was higher than any other authority on earth, including that of the Augustus of Rome. Ambrose agreed to shorten the period of public penance, but insisted that public penance be done before Theodosius could again receive the Eucharist.

Finally in October the emperor came to the door of the basilica. He laid aside his imperial ornaments, to acknowledge that he was now simply Theodosius, repentant sinner seeking the mercy of his Lord. He knelt and publicly confessed his sin, tearfully asking the pardon of the Church. His amazed subjects wept with him. On Christmas Day the period of penance ended and Theodosius received the Body and Blood of Christ, now fully reconciled with the Church.

Afterwards Theodosius said: "I know of no one except Ambrose who deserves the name of bishop," because Ambrose was not subservient to the state but upheld the Church's rightful role as moral judge of society and of the kings and princes who governed it.

This would not be the last time that Church and State would face each other in fierce combat. But through his courage, determination and total dedication to Christ's law, Ambrose had made it clear that even Caesar must render to God the things that are God's.

The Nestorian Heresy

On Christmas day of the year 428, the brash and impetuous new bishop of Constantinople, Nestorius, stepped into the pulpit of his cathedral to deliver a sermon against Mary's motherhood of the Incarnate God. "Mary did not bear God," he proclaimed. "The creature did not bear the Creator, but the man . . . He who was formed in the womb of Mary was not God Himself but God assumed him." In the congregation was the lawyer Eusebius, who loved the Blessed Mother. He stood up and challenged the bishop.

But despite this public opposition, Nestorius continued to develop his theme in a series of sermons, saying, "How could she be the mother of Him who is of a different nature from herself?" He argued that Christ's humanity is merely "a garment" which God puts on, and Mary conceived and bore only that fleshly garment.

Word of the Nestorian heresy spread rapidly. The next year, Bishop Cyril of Alexandria defended the teaching of the Church by asking the key question: "Is her son God, or is He not?" Both Nestorius and Cyril sent their views of the controversy to Pope Celestine. In 430 Celestine pronounced Nestorius heretical.

But Nestorius wouldn't change his views and the controversy waxed hotter. So the Emperor Theodosius II called for an ecumenical council, which was approved by Pope Celestine. The Council was convened in Ephesus (modern-day Turkey) on June 22, 431, in the church dedicated to Our Lady, near the spot where she had actually lived.

Cyril of Alexandria was chairman of the council. Never one to waste time or put up with pointless argument, he concluded all of the council's business in a single day. Nestorius and his teachings were anathematized (condemned); he was deposed as bishop of Constantinople. Mary was indeed the Mother of God, because Jesus Christ was one divine Person with two natures, human and divine. A mother is the mother of a person, not of a nature alone. Mary was the mother of a divine Person; therefore she deserves the title Mother of God.

It was night when the council finished its tremendous day's work, but the people of Ephesus were still waiting outside to hear what the bishops had decided. Receiving the news with joyous shouts of "Theotokos! Theotokos!" (Greek for Mother of God), men and women formed torchlight processions to escort the bishops to their residences.

The Nestorian heresy was to be revived in later years in the Persian Empire and farther east. But it quickly disappeared throughout almost all the Roman world because it never had a large following. And from this point on, Marian devotion rapidly spread and grew, until wherever the Catholic Church was found, there also was the Mother of God honored and loved.

The Monophysite Heresy

In reaction to Nestorianism, a new heresy arose. Nestorians had downplayed the divinity of Christ. This new heresy, monophysitism (which means "one nature"), denied His humanity. The monophysites said that Christ was not truly a man, but had only the appearance of a human body—rather like the angels who had appeared to men.

A council was called for August 449, again to be held in Ephesus. Pope Leo the Great prepared a document, the Tome of Leo, which stated the doctrine that Christ was one divine Person possessing two complete and perfect natures, divine and human. The chairman of the council was Dioscorus, who tended toward monophysitism. He wouldn't recognize the papal legates (Pope's representatives), Julius and Hilary, arguing that since they had dined with Flavian, who was anti-monophysite, they were therefore prejudiced. When an orthodox statement was read, Dioscorus led the monophysites in shouting it down. Dioscorus then proclaimed that monophysitism had been approved.

Pandemonium broke out. Hilary and Flavian were beaten, Flavian dying from his injuries. Hilary somehow escaped, alone, picking his way across country. He reached Kusadasi on the coast, found a small boat, went to the nearby island of Samos and then onto Rome. After hearing Hilary's report, Pope Leo condemned the council as *latrodinium*, a robber council, and it is known to history as the Robber Council of Ephesus.

In 451 a second council, the Council of Chalcedon, was held. Eusebius (the lawyer who had spoken out against Nestorius) presented the full case against Dioscorus. When the account of the Robber Council was read, the bishops who had been present there were ashamed that they had let it happen. Then the Tome of Leo was read and enthusiastically accepted by the council: "Peter has spoken through Leo."

But as with Arianism, the heretics did not give up easily. They went about the empire claiming that the Pope was trying to dictate to the East. They rejected his authority, saying that Byzantium was far superior to the

West and therefore its position should dominate. In this, they found allies in the Byzantine Emperor Justinian and especially in his wife Theodora.

Theodora had not been born to royalty. She was a former circus dancer. Once when the circus had fallen on hard times, she had been out of work and hungry in Egypt. Monks in a monastery had offered her hospitality. They had also offered her their monophysite doctrines. She eagerly accepted both.

Later she married Justinian, a talented soldier who rose rapidly through the ranks and became emperor. Though he was orthodox, he was primarily interested in his dream of re-establishing the Roman Empire and more or less let Theodora take care of religious matters. The primary religious matter she wanted to take care of was to establish a monophysite heretic as patriarch (chief bishop) of Constantinople.

Meanwhile in Rome, the papal election process had become strongly influenced by political leaders. The Roman clergy, who had the authority to elect the Pope, were subject to pressures from wealthy and powerful Roman families. Therefore Pope Felix III (526-530) decided to change the papal selection procedures, announcing that he would name his own successor. He chose the holy Boniface II, who came to the papacy in 530. Boniface, too, decided to name his successor, and chose a clever and ambitious deacon, Vigilius. But opposition arose. Some didn't like the procedure of a Pope's picking his own successor; others didn't like Vigilius, who seemed more interested in his own advancement than in the good of the Church. So Boniface reversed his decision and announced that the clergy would once again elect the next Pope. He died in 532, and John II, a humble and simple man, came to the throne of Peter.

Vigilius was furious. His greatest dream, the papacy, had been within his grasp and then snatched away and given to a candidate much less worthy (in the eyes of Vigilius). John reigned only three years, dying in 535. The holy and wise Agapetus was elected as next Pope. Again Vigilius was passed over, and again he was frustrated and seething with anger.

That same year Theodora made her move in Constantinople. A monophysite, Anthimius, was installed as patriarch. At the same time, Agapetus went to Constantinople to ask Justinian not to attack Italy, which his general Belisarius was about to do as part of the emperor's campaign to re-establish the united Roman Empire. Vigilius was in the party accompanying the Holy Father to the eastern capital.

Pope Agapetus arrived in Constantinople in February 536. He met Anthimius, realized he was a heretic, and instantly removed him from office. Almost as instantly, Agapetus mysteriously died. Before returning to Rome, Vigilius met with Theodora, and received from her 700 pounds of gold and the promise of the papacy if he would cooperate with her heretical schemes. Though there is no conclusive proof, it seems likely that the two main people behind the death of Pope Agapetus were Vigilius and Theodora.

In June 536 Silverius was elected as successor to Agapetus. He soon received a letter from Theodora demanding the restoration of Anthimius. The Pope of course refused. Theodora wrote then to Belisarius: "Find some occasion against Silverius and depose him, or at least send him to us. Herewith you have our most dear deacon Vigilius, who has promised to recall the Patriarch Anthimius." Belisarius ordered Silverius seized, stripped of his pallium (symbol of office), and sent off to exile.

The clergy of Rome under pressure from the Byzantine army proclaimed Vigilius Pope, though Silverius still lived and had not resigned. Thus Vigilius was an anti-pope. But by June 20, 538 Silverius was dead of starvation on the island of Palmyria, a painful and lingering death arranged by "our dear deacon": Vigilius.

Vigilius was recognized as Pope, because the clergy of Rome feared that anyone else would meet the same fate as had Agapetus and Silverius. Thus Vigilius became the validly elected Pope. Theodora must have breathed a sigh of relief in her palace on the Golden Horn. Her will had prevailed. The Church was hers.

But something strange happened to Vigilius, the man who had been for sale, the man who had agreed to support heresy to become Pope, the man who had collaborated in the murders of his two predecessors. He wrote to Theodora, vowing to stand by orthodox doctrine. Theodora was shocked by his words: "Far be it from me, Lady Augusta. Formerly I spoke wrongly and foolishly; now I assuredly refuse to restore a man who is a heretic [Anthimius]. Though unworthy, I am Vicar of Blessed Peter the Apostle, as were my predecessors, the holy Agapetus and Silverius."

Theodora exploded. In November 545, Vigilius was arrested while saying Mass. He was taken to Constantinople and put under constant pressure to give in. But he would not. Theodora finally died in 548, but Justinian kept up the harassment, putting Vigilius under close confinement. He escaped and ran to a church, throwing his arms around the altar and begging the people to protect him. Another time he escaped by lowering himself out of a window on a rope. Later he was kept in confinement on bread and water. But he never gave in. He was finally sent home after ten years of exile, but died on the way.

The Holy Spirit had worked through this very unlikely man, in what is probably the most persuasive piece of historical evidence for the infallibility of the Pope. Monophysitism was rejected by the Catholic Church, east and west, and orthodoxy reigned triumphant.

Review Questions

1. Where did Constantine build his new capital? Why did the two parts of the empire become less and less similar?
2. What is Arianism? Why did it become popular? Why did the ordinary people reject it?
3. What were the two influences on the formation of Athanasius?
4. What happened at the Council of Nicaea? What did the Nicene Creed decree?
5. What did Constantine do to Athanasius?
6. What did Constantius do?
7. What happened to Pope Liberius and what did he do?
8. What factors caused Arianism to decline?
9. Who was Julian the Apostate? What did he do to Athanasius?
10. Why did he try to rebuild the Temple? What happened?
11. What was the significance of St. Jerome and St. John Chrysostom?
12. How did Ambrose come to be bishop?
13. Describe the way that St. Augustine came to be converted.
14. How did Ambrose and Theodosius come into conflict? What were the results of the conflict?
15. What was the Nestorian heresy? How was it defeated?
16. What is monophysitism?
17. What happened to Pope Agapetus? To Pope Silverius?
18. How did Vigilius come to be Pope?
19. What did Vigilius do when he became Pope?
20. How is his papacy evidence for papal infallibility?

Projects

1. Imagine that you are Vigilius. Write a diary, beginning with the time that Theodora asked you if you wanted to be Pope, and covering the

most important events, up through the time that you were arrested.

2. Imagine that you are Athanasius. Write a diary covering the most important events of your life from the time that Arius began preaching until Arianism lost its influence.
3. Write a report on one of the Fathers of the Church.
4. Write a report on devotion to Mary.

Chapter Eleven
The Barbarians and the Church

WE HAVE SEEN in earlier chapters the decay and corruption which too much wealth and power had brought to the Roman Empire. Rome had lost its earlier virtues, and both ordinary people and rulers had brought much suffering upon themselves. The ultimate solution to Rome's problems was Christianity, but Christianity could not change Rome overnight. Weakness and corruption remained, and Rome's still existing wealth was a powerful temptation to groups of people outside the empire, who would not hesitate to take advantage of Rome's weaknesses.

The Barbarians Invade

The enemies of the empire would be the uncivilized barbarian tribes, who had previously lived outside the empire, kept under control by Rome's mighty armies. But the strength of the armies, along with everything else in the empire, was slowly decaying. Roman citizens had lost their ability to fight, so that the Roman emperors had been forced to recruit soldiers from the barbarians themselves. Most of the good officers had more in common with their fellow tribesmen across the frontier than with the corrupt Romans.

The first permanent breach of Rome's frontier came in 378, when the Goths won the Battle of Adrianople, defeating and killing Emperor Valens. A peace treaty was concluded, allowing the Goths to settle in the empire. Then on December 31, 406, the Rhine River—Rome's northwestern frontier—froze. Tribe after tribe of barbarians swarmed across the border and into the empire—led by the savage Vandals. The Visigoths (Western Goths) swept through Gaul and on into Spain, while the Vandals continued all the way to North Africa, which they conquered. In 410 the

118

Goths, under Alaric, invaded Rome and sacked it, only the second time in its long history that the city of Rome had been conquered. Alaric died soon afterwards, and the Goths withdrew from the city; but the myth of Rome's invincibility had been forever shattered, and the emperor in the West was virtually powerless, forced to do the bidding of whatever barbarian chieftain held power at the moment.

Even though the barbarians came as conquerors, at least they were not totally strange to the Romans, having lived on their borders for many years. But in the 450's, a tribe of Orientals from central Asia swept across Europe. These were the Huns, who had been driven out of China by the Chinese emperor and were now pushing toward Rome. They were led by Attila, who wanted to establish an Asiatic empire in Europe to replace the Roman Empire. In August 452 they swept through northern Italy, causing whole populations to scatter, a seemingly unstoppable advance. The people and the rulers panicked.

Then, on the very day Attila was preparing to attack the city of Rome, he saw a strange procession marching slowly toward him: priests, monks and deacons bearing crosses and banners. From the entire column the rhythmical responses of hymns and psalms were heard. In the midst of the procession rode an old man with a white beard, praying as he rode. The Hun galloped toward the river, urged his horse into it, and halted on a sandy islet, within hailing distance of the strangers. "What is your name?" Attila shouted to the old man. Came the answer: "I am Leo, the Pope." Attila hesitated, then urged his horse to the far bank. The Pope came forward to meet him.

No one knows exactly what the two men said. A few hours later Leo returned to Rome. All he would say to Emperor Valentinian III was, "Let us give thanks to God, for He has delivered us from great danger." Attila ordered his Huns to retreat; Rome was safe. With Attila's sudden death the following year, the Hunnish host broke up.

Rome was spared the devastation which a Hunnish conquest would have brought, but the barbarians kept coming. In 455 the Vandals menaced the city. Emperor Petronius made no effort to stop them. When he tried to flee the city he was slain by the enraged people. So there was no emperor, no army; only Pope Leo the Great again stood between the people and the barbarians. The Pope won a promise from the barbarians that there would be no torture, no massacre, no burning, no sacking of the largest churches. Again Rome was spared the worst of a barbarian attack, thanks to the intervention of the Pope, and the evidence was becoming ever stronger that though the Roman Empire was dying, the Church was very much alive.

Then in 476 the last Roman emperor in the West—a young boy with the grand title of Romulus Augustus—was deposed by the barbarian leader Odovacar. Henceforth the western Roman Empire ceased to exist. It was replaced by barbarian kingdoms, whose boundaries were constantly shifting and whose rulers could not keep order and did not even attempt to administer a just law. The chief kingdoms were the following: Visigoths in Spain, Vandals in North Africa, Franks in France, Ostrogoths and then Lombards in Italy, Angles and Saxons in England.

Because of its greater wealth and the virtually unconquerable location of Constantinople, the Byzantine Empire in the East was never subdued by barbarians. But its emperors nevertheless were almost constantly fighting, could not expand into new territories and did not come to the aid of the West. Except for Justinian, who tried and failed to re-establish the empire, the Byzantines withdrew within themselves, content to preserve what civilization they could behind their massive walls and the waters of the Golden Horn.

Europe now entered into the time which historians call the Dark Ages, lasting approximately from 450-1050. Barbarism had overwhelmed civilization, and the barbarian chieftains had nothing to replace the order, culture and learning of the Roman Empire, corrupt as it was, which they had destroyed. Throughout the length and breadth of what had once been the mightiest empire in the world—where Roman law had been justly administered, where Roman legions had kept the peace so that commerce and learning could flourish, where Roman roads had provided easy, efficient transportation and communication—there was no law but the sword, no justice but what the stronger could extract from the weaker, no order, no commerce, no learning. Night had fallen on the world.

The Light from Ireland

Europeans caught in the Dark Ages had little idea that at the very moment they were suffering the deprivations of barbarian conquest, civilization was flourishing in far-off Ireland. So far removed from the civilized world that the Romans had not conquered or colonized it, Ireland gloried in its Golden Age. From Ireland would come missionaries to rekindle the light of Christianity and civilization in Europe, just as God would many times use the least expected persons, places and things as channels of grace.

Ireland had never been part of the Roman Empire. Most of the contact across the Irish Sea came from raids of Irish pirates and slave raiders. In an Irish slave raid somewhere on the west coast of Britain, probably about the year 415, a sixteen-year-old boy named Patrick was seized and carried off to the shores of Killala Bay in County Mayo, where he was put to work tending sheep. There, he tells us, "the love of God and His fear came to me more and more, and my faith was strengthened." After six years he escaped, and took ship probably to the coast of Scotland, whence he made his way back home.

A few years after his return, he had a dream in which he heard the Irish calling him to return. Soon afterwards, Patrick was ordained deacon and asked to be sent to Ireland as a missionary. After a period of training, probably in Gaul and Italy, he returned to Ireland as a bishop.

The pagan Druid priests were violently hostile to Patrick and his religion, but Patrick was not deterred from his mission. Legend has it that on Easter Eve, 432, he violated the Druid command that only they could kindle fire, by lighting the Paschal candle on the Hill of Slane. He was nearly condemned to death for his audacity, but King Laoghaire was so impressed by Patrick's miraculous powers that the king permitted him to evangelize Ireland and may even himself have accepted baptism.

Within ten to fifteen years he had preached all through the northern half of the island, baptizing thousands, ordaining priests, accepting the vows of religious to a consecrated life, and finally setting up his episcopal headquarters at Armagh in Ulster (Ireland's northern province). The conversion of Ireland was unusually rapid, unusually thorough, and, above all, peaceful. The Druids opposed it, but were helpless to stop it. Within twenty-five years of his coming, all of Ireland was Catholic. Patrick built more than 700 churches and encouraged the establishment of monasteries, which would become the focal point of Irish Catholic life. Patrick continued to live and work in Ireland for sixty years, until his death around the year 493. Patrick established Christianity so firmly that the worst persecutions could not destroy it. One writer has said that before Patrick came, "at every grass blade in Ireland was a devil," but after Patrick's death, "at every grass blade was an angel."

Patrick's Successors

Patrick not only gave the Irish the Faith but he inspired many of them to the monastic vocation. The Irish seemed especially drawn to consecrate their lives totally to God. One of the earliest of these saints was Bridget (450-525). Her mother was a slave; hence Bridget was born into bondage, somewhere near Kildare. Her father was her mother's master, and Bridget was so attractive and talented that he wished to arrange a match for her with a man of the higher classes. Bridget, however, wished to dedicate her life to Christ as a consecrated virgin. The legend goes that as the arranged wedding day neared, she prayed to God for help. Just before the wedding she somehow became so ugly that the prospective bridegroom lost all interest in her. She was then permitted to make her vow of virginity before the bishop. At this point her beauty was miraculously restored. She and some companions settled in Kildare. Bridget and the other women lived a life of community prayer and penance. The women had a little farm and were self-supporting, soon becoming known for hospitality and almsgiving. Bridget had medical skill and was constantly on call to serve the sick in the neighborhood. Her travels in charity throughout the countryside helped bring the Faith to those who had not yet heard of it or fully accepted it. One of the most famous stories concerns her nursing a dying pagan chieftain. As she sat beside his bed, she idly plaited rushes into a cross. When he asked her what she was doing, she explained to him the meaning of the cross. Her story of Christ's love for mankind so impressed the chieftain that he requested baptism before he died. Sometimes known as Mary of the Gael because she so closely followed the example of the Blessed Mother, Bridget is regarded as the leader and patron of all the consecrated virgins of Ireland down through the years. Her true holiness is summarized in the words that conclude her life in the Book of Lismore: "She was abstinent, she was innocent, she was prayerful, she was patient, she was glad in God's commandments. She was firm, she was humble, she was forgiving, she was loving. She was a consecrated casket for keeping Christ's Body and His Blood. She was a temple of God. Her heart and her mind were a throne of rest for the Holy Spirit."

Following St. Bridget was St. Colmcille (521-597), also known as St. Columba. Colmcille's great-grandfather was Conall, a disciple and helper of Patrick, who founded the Tirconnail clan, which 1000 years later led the Catholics in battle against Queen Elizabeth. His father was the King of Tirconnail, but Colmcille was called early to the monastic life rather than the royal. While still in his youth he received an apparition of an angel who said, "Choose now the gifts and virtues thou wouldst have from Him." Colmcille answered, "I choose purity and wisdom." He consecrated his life to God and studied in various monasteries, including his favorite, that in the bleak and penitential Aran Isles. As he was nearing the end of his studies in one monastery, a pestilence broke out and he was sent home. As he came to the river marking the border of the Tirconnail lands, he blessed the river and prayed that the pestilence would not cross. It didn't. Having finished his studies with distinction and holiness, he was chosen to be abbot in Derry. He was sent to be ordained, but Ireland was still so rural that Colmcille had to wait until the bishop finished plowing his fields to receive Holy Orders.

While visiting a neighboring monastery, Colmcille was impressed with the beautiful copy of the Gospels in the monastery's possession. He asked the abbot if he might borrow it to make a copy for his own monastery's use. The abbot refused, jealous of the rare book. Furious, Colmcille surreptitiously began copying the book at night. The abbot discovered him, and the two had a ferocious quarrel. Finally they decided to refer the dispute to Diarmuid, the High King over all of Ireland. He knew of no precedent regarding the copying of a book, so he fell back on the only rule of law he thought applicable: "To every cow belongs its calf; so to every book belongs its copy," thereby ruling against Colmcille. Colmcille's anger increased when the king arrested a fugitive to whom Colmcille had given sanctuary. Enraged, Colmcille's royal blood and fighting spirit came to the fore. He went home to Tirconnail and encouraged his clan chieftain to launch the "War of the Book" against Diarmuid. When Tirconnail won, the clan offered Colmcille the high kingship. It was Colmcille's supreme temptation. But God flooded Colmcille's soul with repentance for his worldliness. He rejected the offer. To make amends for causing the war between Tirconnail and Diarmuid, he vowed to convert as many pagans as the number of Christians who had died in the battle. Ireland, however, was so thoroughly Catholic that Colmcille could find no pagans to convert. So he chose to exile himself from his home to travel to pagan lands, thus beginning his great missionary effort.

He went first to Iona, off the coast of Scotland, a bleak island reminding him of his beloved Aran Isles. He established a monastery there, where his monks practiced what they called white martyrdom—a life of penance to make up for their lack of martyrdom of blood. Iona was Colmcille's base for a missionary effort in Scotland. He first had to get permission from the barbarian king of the Picts to evangelize Scotland. The king ordered his men to refuse admission to the gaunt monk, but Colmcille's commanding personality won the day, and he was admitted to see the king. He soon established monasteries all over Scotland, which became the base for later missionary journeys into England. He became so respected and loved that he was chosen to crown King Aidan as the first Christian king of Scotland. Aidan united Scotland and founded the royal line which lasted through the Stuart kings. Colmcille died peacefully in 597.

Another interesting Irish saint of the Golden Age is St. Brendan. St. Brendan was a holy monk with a missionary bent. His writings spoke of amazing voyages in a leather boat to lands west. Most scholars tended to discount his writings as exaggerations, but recent studies have tended to confirm them. A group of Irishmen built a duplicate of Brendan's boat and sailed it from Ireland to Newfoundland. They found not only that a voyage such as Brendan described was feasible, but that many of the places and things he described, such as a pillar of crystal (iceberg), a paradise of birds (islands off the coast of Scotland), and an island of fire (Iceland, with its volcanoes and geysers) really existed. So the voyages of Brendan the Bold are yet another achievement of Ireland's Golden Age.

Ireland's Golden Age was truly an age of saints. Throughout the island, holy men would attract disciples, leading to the foundation of schools. Men came from England and the continent of Europe to study in these schools, because there were none back home. They studied grammar, geography, history, theology, law, mathematics, astronomy, philosophy, logic, music, art and metalwork, preserving knowledge which had already been forgotten in the lands conquered by the barbarians.

This was a time not only of learning and study, but of artistic achievement. Great high crosses were erected, carved with stories from the Bible. Exquisite work was done in metal and jewels. Books were *illuminated*—decorated with paintings and drawings. Printing presses had not been invented, so all books were copied by hand, and monks and scholars worked to make their printing itself a work of art.

And Ireland did not keep its achievements to itself. Thousands of missionaries went out to Europe—from Germany in the north to Africa in the south, from Iceland in the west to Palestine in the east—bringing the message of Christ back to the lands which had lost it and keeping learning and culture alive in the process.

The Monasteries Preserve Civilization

The primary way in which civilization was preserved during the Dark Ages was through the *monasteries*—enclosed areas where monks (men who have dedicated their lives to God) live an ordered life of prayer, study and work. Monasteries had existed in the East, primarily as places of penance and protection from the corruptions of Roman civilization. But the monastic movement in the West had a far greater effect on history. The founder of this movement is the man who has earned the title "Father of Western Monasticism": St. Benedict.

Born into a wealthy family in Rome, Benedict had received a good education before the worst of the barbarian invasions. He saw first hand the collapse of society around him. The days of peaceful rides through the Italian hills, of study in the libraries, of quiet conversations along the banks of the Tiber were gone, apparently never to return. Benedict's first reaction was to become a hermit—to try to escape the collapse of society by living by himself and devoting his time to prayer and penance. But he felt called to help others as well as himself. In 520 he led a small group of men to a towering hill eighty-five miles southeast of Rome—Monte Cassino. Benedict destroyed the pagan temples he found on the summit and established a monastery.

Between the years 530 and 540 Benedict wrote his famous *Benedictine Rule*, which established a pattern followed by monasteries to this day. In Benedict's Rule, the elected abbot had full authority over the other monks. The men who entered the monastery promised to remain in the monastery (enclosure), to obey the abbot (a vow of obedience), to share all things with the other monks rather than owning anything personally (a vow of poverty), to remain celibate (a vow of chastity), to recite the Divine Office (a selection of prayers to be recited during different parts of each day), to work on the monastery lands and to study. The Rule was strict yet compassionate toward the weak, and its purpose was "that in all things God shall be glorified." Benedict emphasized many virtues which were totally different from the confused, dangerous life outside the monastery: simplicity, regularity, discipline, charity, prayer and self-control. Benedict's monasteries were self-contained and self-supporting, growing or making everything needed, preserving knowledge of craftsmanship and agriculture which would otherwise have been lost. These monasteries were a gleam of light in the Dark Ages, preserving what was best from the old Roman civilization and providing small centers of peace and beauty.

In addition to Benedictine monasticism, the other great monastic influence in Europe of the Dark Ages was Irish monasticism. One of the most important contributions the Irish missionaries made to Europe was the spread of Irish monasticism to the continent. Perhaps the best known Irish missionary-monk was St. Columbanus. Born in 543, he was so handsome when he grew up that all the local girls were in love with him. But he left home to study at a monastery in Bangor, where he was ordained a priest and became a teacher.

He wanted to do even more for Christ so he left Ireland and went to Luxeuil in France, where he established a monastery and school. This was so popular that he had to found a larger one at Fontaine. But Queen Brunehilde and her grandson Theodoric became angry with Columbanus because he condemned their evil lives, and they ordered him to leave Europe.

He boarded a boat for Ireland, but when it was driven ashore by a storm the captain was sure that this was a sign from God that Columbanus was not to leave France. He could not return to Fontaine, so with a few disciples he traveled through various barbarian kingdoms in France, then up the Rhine River to Germany, through Switzerland, and finally into Italy, settling down at last in the town of Bobbio. All along the way he founded new monasteries, bringing Christianity to the people. In addition, his disciples, followers and students went on to places that he couldn't visit, establishing still more monasteries as centers of religion and learning.

The monasteries founded by Columbanus and other Irish missionaries lived according to a strict rule, which provided a healthy and needed contrast to life outside the monastery. Columbanus insisted on absolute obedience, poverty, silence, abstinence and chastity. Like the Benedictine monasteries, Irish monasteries were an oasis of peace, brotherhood and self-discipline, in the midst of the wars, hatred and selfishness outside, and helped make it possible for civilization to be reborn.

The Light of Christianity

The light which shone most brightly in Ireland's Golden Age glowed elsewhere in Europe: in England with a Christian king, in France with a king who became a Christian, and in Spain with a king who became orthodox.

The Christian king in England was King Arthur, known to most people as a legendary figure only. But King Arthur really existed; though the later legends are fanciful embroiderings, the embroidery covers a real historical figure in England's history. His exact date is uncertain, probably the first half of the 500's. The Roman army had been withdrawn from Britain to meet threats closer to home; the savage Saxons (nicknamed the Sea Wolves) swooped down from Germany onto unprotected Britain. Arthur united what was left of Roman civilization with the original Britons whom the Romans had conquered. He forged a fighting force which stood against the Saxons and held them off, preserving a bit of civilization for almost a century. His most important battle was the Battle of Mt. Badon, in which, according to the Annals of Wales, "Arthur bore the cross of Our Lord Jesus Christ on his shoulders for three days and three nights, and the Britons were the victors." We don't know for sure what the chronicler meant by "cross of our Lord Jesus Christ," but it is clear that Arthur was fighting for Christian as well as Roman civilization. Arthur's exploits were so heroic that they endured in memory down through the Dark Ages which finally descended on Britain and provided a ready foundation for the mythic tales which the Middle Ages built. Arthur was said to be buried in Glastonbury, where a Christian monastery stood from the earliest years of Christianity in England. His grave was despoiled during the Protestant Revolt, in the same manner that the graves of England's saints were desecrated, again clearly showing that Arthur lived in men's memories as a *Catholic* king.

The king who became a Christian was King Clovis of the Franks, and the credit for his conversion belongs to his wife, St. Clotilde. Clotilde was born in 474 in the city of Lyon. Her mother was a Christian and raised her daughter under the inspiration of the Martyrs of Lyon. When Clotilde's father died in 490, the family moved to Geneva. It was there that she was courted by the triumphant young king of the Franks, Clovis. He had many reasons for wanting to marry her: she was beautiful; he wanted the Burgundians (her people) for an ally; and though Clovis himself was a pagan, he felt that a Christian wife would bind his Roman subjects more closely to him. Her guardians accepted the marriage suit because they wanted the protection of Clovis against other tribes. So at the age of 17, knowing little of her future husband, Clotilde left Geneva to become queen of the Franks.

During the first year of marriage, a son was born, but he died immediately after baptism. Enraged, Clovis accused Clotilde: "It is your God who is the cause of our child's death. If he had been consecrated to mine, he would have been alive now." Her husband's wrath, added to the loss of her first-born, was a heavy cross for Clotilde to bear, but her faith and trust in God were unshaken: "I give thanks to Almighty God that He had not considered me unworthy to be the mother of a child admitted into the celestial kingdom. Having quitted the world in the white robe of his innocence, he will rejoice in the presence of God through all eternity." The next year a second son, Clodomir, was born. He too became ill shortly after his baptism, but this time God answered Clotilde's prayers by his recovery.

Clotilde's exemplary life and her constant prayers began to have their effect on Clovis. In 496 he was at war against the fierce Allemani. During the crucial battle, his Franks were having the worst of it. Desperate, Clovis prayed: "Jesus Christ, Thou who art, according to Clotilde, the Son of the Living God, help me in my distress, and if Thou givest me victory, I will believe in Thee and will be baptized in Thy name." Clovis's soldiers recovered and attacked, so fiercely that the Allemani flung away their arms and begged for mercy. Clovis gave them mercy and then made ready to fulfill his promise.

The baptismal ceremony took place on Christmas Day 496 in the city of Rheims. The whole city was decorated. Dressed in white garments, Clovis, his personal bodyguard, and 3,000 Franks marched in solemn procession to the cathedral to be baptized by the bishop, St. Remi. It was Clotilde's proudest moment, and the people in the church witnessed the birth of the first Christian nation, France, known thereafter as the "Eldest Daughter of the Church."

The king who became orthodox was the Visigothic king of Spain. The conversion of the Visigoths in Spain, like the conversion of the Franks in France, can be credited largely to the influence of a Catholic queen.

The Visigoths had been converted to Arianism, but not to orthodox Christianity. In 579 King Leovigild arranged a marriage between the elder of his two sons, Hermenigild, and Ingunthis, a Frankish princess, only 12 years old. On her way to Spain for her wedding, she spoke with Bishop Phronimius about what her religious duties in Spain would now be. He told her she must guard herself carefully against "the poison of Arianism"; she must maintain her faith even in an anti-Catholic court. With Clotilde's blood flowing in her veins, she could do nothing less.

Leovigild's wife Goswintha was jealous of the beautiful, intelligent and pious Ingunthis. Right after the wedding, Goswintha demanded that Ingunthis be rebaptized as Arian. Ingunthis replied that "it was enough to have been once washed clean of original sin in the regenerating waters of baptism" and that she "confessed the Holy Trinity in undivided equality." Goswintha leaped on her, pulled her hair, struck her until she bled, and threw her into a fish pond.

To avoid more violence Leovigild sent the young couple off to Seville. It was there that Leander, Bishop of Seville, met the prince and princess. Ingunthis and Leander worked together for the conversion of Hermenigild. Before the end of the year, he was fully instructed and confirmed as a Catholic.

Leovigild was not at all pleased with this news. He demanded that his son return to Arianism. Inspired by Ingunthis' example, the prince refused. Leovigild then proclaimed his son a rebel, sent an army against him and his

Catholic supporters, began a persecution of Catholics, and expelled Phronimius.

Seville and its region declared for Hermenigild and acclaimed him king; by 582 there was all-out war. Hermenigild sent Ingunthis and their little son into Byzantine territory in Spain for safe-keeping. When Seville fell, Hermenigild went to Cordoba, and was captured there when it too fell, early in 584.

Again his father demanded that he apostatize. Again he refused. He was kept in close confinement for a year. Then in April 585 Hermenigild was killed with his father's approval.

Leovigild himself died the next year. He was succeeded by his second son, Reccared. Influenced no doubt by the example of his brother and sister-in-law, Reccared had gone to St. Leander for instructions in orthodox doctrine. In 587 he convened an assembly of the bishops of his realm to announce his own conversion to the Catholic Church. Then at the Third Council of Toledo in 589, Reccared personally addressed the delegates to explain why he had converted. Arianism was condemned and the Nicene Creed ordered to be recited at all Sunday Masses. Spain was Catholic and would remain so.

Meanwhile, little Ingunthis had died about the time her husband was martyred. She lived only 18 years, but her firm adherence to the Faith had brought first her husband and then his country into the one true Church.

Pope Gregory the Great

One of the greatest Popes of the Dark Ages had never even wanted the office. His name was Gregory (he reigned from 590-604), and he had been born into a wealthy Roman family. He had held an important position in the Roman government, but he retired to a monastery, where he hoped to spend the rest of his life in prayer and contemplation. But Pope Pelagius called him out of the monastery to serve the Church. When Pelagius died, Gregory was chosen to be the new Pope, though he wrote to a friend, "With a sick heart I undertook the burden of this honor."

Gregory was elected in February. The winter had been brutal to Rome. The Tiber flooded, destroying the grain stores on which the city depended. Weakened by hunger, the people fell victim to a plague which raged through the city. Pelagius himself had died of the plague. Immediately Gregory was faced with the problem of the sick and suffering city. He turned to the mercy of Christ. He organized pilgrimages through the city, calling all those well enough to walk to join him in prayer. During one of these pilgrimages a vision was seen of St. Michael the Archangel, above the spot where the Castel Sant'Angelo (Castle of the Holy Angel) was later built. The plague suddenly ceased.

Though the plague ended, the problems facing Gregory still seemed overwhelming. Because of the barbarian raids, half the population of Rome had fled or died. Buildings crumbled. Grass grew in the streets. Crime went unpunished. The people turned in desperation to the Church, to Gregory. Gregory did not let them down.

The people were hungry. The Church owned much land because no one else could care for it. Gregory ordered that the surplus crops grown on the land be brought to Rome to feed the hungry people. We still have copies of some of the letters he wrote and so we know that Gregory had to think of everything. He had to tell the overseers what to do with the cows who were too old to have calves. He had to tell them what to do with extra tools. He had to make sure that the peasants who lived on the land were treated fairly. If any of them had a complaint, Gregory took care of it himself.

The barbarian Lombards attacked the city. Gregory had to organize a force of armed men and had to show them where to set up their defenses. Then, knowing that his small army could hold off the Lombards only temporarily, he had to negotiate with the barbarian leaders to persuade them to live peacefully with the Romans. Under Gregory's influence, the Lombard prince Adalwald became a Catholic, thus beginning the conversion of the Lombards.

Gregory was also responsible for the conversion of the barbarians in England. Around 595, Gregory received word that Saxons and Angles in England wanted to be baptized. Since King Ethelbert of Kent had married Bertha, a Frankish Christian princess who had brought a bishop to England with her, Gregory decided to take advantage of the opportunity and send missionaries to the distant isle. He chose Augustine, a monk of the Monastery of St. Andrew, which had been erected by Gregory, sending him and forty monks on the way to Britain. They left June 596 but soon began to hear stories of the wildness of the English barbarians. The monks wavered, asking Augustine to go back to Rome to present their difficulties to Gregory. But Gregory did not waver and the monks continued their journey.

They reached England in the spring of 597. King Ethelbert met them, standing under an oak tree for protection against any magic spells these strange men might utter. They simply told him of the Gospel and of their desire to preach it. The king was impressed and gave them permission to preach throughout his lands. Augustine set up his headquarters at Canterbury (so he is known as St. Augustine of Canterbury—also as St. Austin). The king was baptized at Pentecost, and 10,000 more Angles were received into the Church at Christmas. Thus came true Gregory's prophecy upon seeing Angles in the slave markets of Rome: "Not Angles, but angels."

Because of the confusion and disorder in Rome, the bishop in Constantinople, which was now the wealthiest city in the empire, decided that he should have more authority than the Bishop of Rome. He started signing himself with the title, Universal Bishop. Gregory had to take time from all his other problems to tell this bishop and his supporters that only the successor of Peter was bishop for the universal Church. Gregory gave himself a more humble title, which summed up his whole life: Servant of the Servants of God.

The barbarians had destroyed the old Roman civilization, but they had nothing to put in its place—neither a culture nor moral standards. But the Catholic Church, through its Popes, monks, missionaries and devoted laypeople, preserved what was best in Roman civilization, converted the barbarians, brought Christ to the ordinary people so that they could have hope for the future in the midst of the sufferings of the present, and laid the foundations for the building of a Christian civilization.

Review Questions

1. What happened at the Battle of Adrianople? What happened in December 406? What happened to Rome in 410?
2. List all of the major barbarian tribes and tell in what country they settled.
3. Why were the Huns especially feared? Who was their leader? How were they stopped from invading Rome?
4. Why was it necessary for Pope Leo to take the lead in stopping the barbarians? What agreement did he make with the Vandals?
5. What date is given for the fall of the Roman Empire in the West? What event happened in that year?
6. Summarize the early life of St. Patrick, up to the time he became a bishop. What part of Ireland did he evangelize first?
7. Describe the incident of the Easter candle and the druids. How long was St. Patrick's mission in Ireland?
8. Summarize the life and achievements of St. Bridget.

9. Summarize the life and achievements of St. Colmcille.
10. Why is St. Benedict called the Father of Western Monasticism? List the main elements of his rule.
11. Summarize the life and achievements of St. Columbanus.
12. What is the historical significance of the monastic movement?
13. What are the known historical facts about King Arthur? What is his historical significance?
14. How was Clovis converted? Why is France called the Eldest Daughter of the Church?
15. Describe the conversion of Spain to orthodox Christianity.
16. List the accomplishments of St. Gregory the Great.
17. Describe the mission of St. Augustine of Canterbury to England.

Projects

1. Imagine that you lived during the Dark Ages. Write an account of what your life might have been like, including what you might have thought and did when some Irish missionaries came to your village.
2. Imagine that you are an Irish missionary in France. Write a letter to your family in Ireland telling them of your experiences.
3. Write an imaginary account of the conversation between Attila and Pope Leo, or act out their meeting.
4. Choose one of the following topics for a report: St. Brendan, St. Scholastica, the art of the Golden Age in Ireland, the island of Iona as a missionary center, an Irish saint not mentioned in this chapter, the details of St. Benedict's rule.

Chapter Twelve
The Prophet and the Emperor

THE WESTERN ROMAN EMPIRE had fallen, but the Eastern Empire still survived behind its mighty walls on the Golden Horn. In 572 the Persian Empire began a war to conquer Byzantium, which the Byzantines only feebly resisted. Under Emperor Phocas, a cruel and incompetent ruler, the Persians were unchecked. By 622 they had conquered Syria, Turkey, the Holy Land, Sinai and Egypt. In Jerusalem, the Persians butchered 60,000 people and enslaved 35,000 more. They demolished churches and carried the relics of the True Cross to Ctesiphon, their capital on the Tigris River. (The only church they spared was the Church of the Nativity in Bethlehem, because of the mosaic of Persian Magi on the wall.)

But in 610 Phocas was overthrown and slain, and Heraclius I took the throne. Heraclius was an able, courageous ruler; he was also a committed Christian. Supported by the people, he raised a new army and took the offensive against the Persians in 622. In the Battle of Nineveh (627), he won a decisive victory and marched on Ctesiphon. The Persians sued for peace. All the Persian conquests were returned, and Heraclius was hailed as the savior of Christian civilization. In 629 he marched into Jerusalem to restore the relics of the True Cross. To this day, the date—September 14—is celebrated by the Church as the feast of the Triumph of the Cross.

Persia was defeated and Byzantium was exhausted. Neither was prepared to face a new and surprising enemy. Yet they had been forewarned. In the midst of Heraclius' victorious campaign, envoys had arrived at both the Persian and Byzantine courts, from an unknown Arabian town called Medina, demanding the acknowledgement of Mohammed as the living apostle of the Lord. The envoys had been dismissed, but the followers of

Mohammed were not to stay dismissed.

The Prophet's Message

No one in the civilized world at this time paid much attention to the warring and disunited tribes of the deserts of Arabia. But in the town of Mecca lived a man named Mohammed. He was a merchant in the caravan trade, was married to a wealthy widow, and spent much of his time thinking about religious questions. The people of the area were pagans—they worshiped a black stone (called the Black Stone of the Kaaba) and had many gods. But Mohammed had heard snatches of the teachings of Judaism and Christianity. He had unfortunately never heard the total Christian message because the many heresies in the Middle East had left non-Christians confused as to what Christianity really was. Nevertheless, Mohammed was impressed with the idea of one supreme God, so much so that he rejected all idea of the Trinity and Incarnation, proclaiming that there was one God ("Allah" in his language), who was only one person.

Mohammed believed that he had been instructed by Allah to write his ideas in a book, which he called the *Koran*. He preached six essential doctrines: one God; angels; three prophets—Abraham, Jesus and Mohammed, of whom Mohammed was the greatest; belief in the Koran; the rising on the Last Day; and a rejection of free will. His religion had six essential duties: recitation of the profession of faith; accepting the formula "there is no God but Allah and Mohammed is His Prophet"; prayers five times daily; the fast in the month of Ramadhan; the pilgrimage to Mecca (to be made once in each person's life); and the Holy War against infidels (non-Moslems). His religion was simple and adapted itself to the moral standards of the Arabs; it praised war, teaching that anyone who died fighting infidels would go immediately to paradise; it permitted revenge, an important part of the life of the desert tribes; and it promised a paradise filled with material pleasures.

The people of Mecca were not impressed by Mohammed at first; after four years he had made only fifty converts. So he fled to the city of Medina, whose citizens had shown more interest in his teachings. His flight is called the *Hegira*, and the year it took place—622—is the year 1 in the Moslem calendar. (A follower of Mohammed is called a Moslem; his religion is called Islam.)

Gradually Mohammed's influence spread, largely through fear of the growing strength of his army. Eventually even the people of Mecca came to accept him, after he declared that the Black Stone of the Kaaba should still be honored. From the beginning Mohammed was looked upon as a political leader as well as a religious prophet and gradually a feeling of Arab unity came to replace the old divisions and hatreds among tribes. Thus Mohammed was largely responsible for the formation of a new nation.

The Whirlwind from the Desert

When Mohammed died in 632, many of the Moslems began to lose interest in their religion, since they had adopted it only to avoid attack by Mohammed's raiders. The new religion might have died then, if it had not been for a policy adopted by Mohammed's successor, Abu Bakr, who took the title of Caliph (which means Successor). Abu Bakr declared that anyone who apostatized from Islam would suffer the death penalty. He went from village to village, ruthlessly enforcing his decree. Before long the apostates were all back and new apostasies ceased. This policy was enforced for centuries; and though it is rarely invoked today, anyone who considers leaving Islam faces total rejection by other Moslems, to such an extent that apostasy is still very rare.

Abu Bakr's successor was the Caliph Omar, who reigned from 634-644. Under him began the great Arab conquests. Omar himself was a holy man according to the standards of Islam; he lived a simple life, even after he became a wealthy and powerful ruler. He would sit barefoot in the dusty plaza of his capital city, while riches from conquered countries were laid before him. But though much in Omar can be admired, the guiding principle in his life brought destruction and suffering over most of the civilized world. Said Omar: "It behooves us to devour the Christians and our sons to devour their descendants, so long as any of them remain on the earth." This bloodthirsty order was unflinchingly obeyed by the Moslem armies, as they rode like a whirlwind out of the desert.

The first major victory by the Moslems was on August 20, 636, against the Byzantines at the Battle of Yarmuk River in Syria. They were fighting in the hottest month of the year in one of the hottest places on earth. The battle took place during a thick storm of dust. The Arabs were protected by their burnooses, but the Byzantines panicked. Heraclius abandoned the field and made no further effort to protect Syria. The Moslems then besieged Jerusalem, which continued to fight under the urging of the Patriarch Sophronius, even though Heraclius had left. The siege lasted four months before the desperate residents finally surrendered.

In the summer of 637, the Arabs attacked the Persians at Kadisiya.

The battle raged for three days, as the Persian elephants were able to stop the Moslem cavalry. But on the morning of the third day, a raging sandstorm turned the air dark. A small band of dedicated Moslems fought their way to the Persian command post and toppled their leader from his throne. Wounded, he reached the baggage train and was about to drive away with the treasure when he was seized and killed. The Persian army dissolved in panic.

In 640 Egypt fell after Alexandria was taken with the help of a traitor. Then the Arabs marched on Ctesiphon. At the emperor's White Palace, the royal throne rested on a carpet of emeralds and pearls, a crown of solid gold set with jewels hung from a chain on the roof, and beside the throne stood a golden horse with teeth of emeralds and a mane of rubies. The emperor, fearing assassination, fled with the imperial treasury, as 600 Arabs hurled their horses across a raging river, surprised the garrison, and took the city.

Soon four Moslem armies were on the march: to India, where they took the northern half of the country, the old Harappan civilization, and set up the Mogul Empire, which endured until the eighteenth century; to China, where they came up to the very gates of the ancient empire and established enduring Moslem rule in what is now Afghanistan and parts of Russia; to Byzantium, where they besieged the city; to the West, roaring across North Africa and into Spain. Except for one country (Spain), all the lands conquered by the Moslems then remain Moslem still.

The Only Moslem Defeats

Only three times during the great Arab conquests were the Moslems stopped. The first was at Constantinople itself in 718. The Byzantines held their capital city because of its superb defensive location and enormous walls and because of the invention of Greek fire. This was a compound including oil, which burned on water and was virtually inextinguishable. The Moslems were never able to learn how to put it out.

The second is the dramatic stand by the Spaniards at Covadonga. The Moslems had swept across Spain. The Visigothic king, Roderic, was dead. The few remaining noblemen retreated to the Asturias Mountains and elected Pelayo as their king. They gathered in 718; the battle would be fought at Covadonga in 722. As the Moslems prepared their attack, Bishop Oppas came to Pelayo to persuade him to surrender to avoid further bloodshed: "You know how all the armies of the Goths united were not able to resist the pressure of the Saracens [Moslems]; how then can you hold out in this mountain? Hear my counsel, give up your undertaking and you will gain much benefit by the side of the Moors [Moslems]."

But Pelayo replied: "Have you not read in Holy Scripture that the Church of the Lord is like a grain of mustard seed which, small as it is, through the loving kindness of God grows more than any other seed?" The bishop answered: "Truly, so it is written." And Pelayo said: "Our hope is in Christ; this little mountain will be the salvation of Spain and of the Gothic people; the loving kindness of Christ will free us from the multitude."

The Moslems attacked; Pelayo and his Spaniards resisted. The Christians won the Battle of Covadonga, and the Moslems turned away. The Moslem general dismissed the Spaniards with the contemptuous words: "What are thirty barbarians perched on a rock? They will inevitably die." His words can be contrasted to Pelayo's: "This little mountain will be the salvation of Spain and of the Gothic people; the mercy of Christ will liberate us from this multitude." Who was right? At present there are something like 300,000,000 Hispanic Catholics in the world; Spain was the only country once conquered by the Moslems which was eventually restored to Christianity. The "thirty barbarians perched on a rock" were indeed the beginning of the "salvation of Spain"; Christ's mercy did indeed liberate His people.

After bypassing the Asturias, the Arab forces pushed into central France as far as Tours. In 732 they met the forces of the Franks, led by Charles Martel—whose last name meant "the Hammer." The Moslems tried their usual tactic of hurling their cavalry in wild charges at the enemy. But the Franks were not the Persians or the Byzantines. Charles' men stood firm against the enemy arrows. Any Moslem who came within reach of the Franks' weapons was lost. When evening came, the battle ceased. During the night the Moslems retreated, so hastily that they left their tents behind, causing the Franks to believe that they were still there. The Battle of Tours marked the farthest Moslem penetration into the West; and for centuries afterwards the Moslem word for all westerners was "Franks" in tribute to the enemy they could not defeat.

But this was one of the few defeats the Moslems suffered. By 732, only 100 years after the death of the Prophet, the wild tribesmen from Arabia controlled most of the civilized world and were without a doubt the strongest power in the world. The conquered people converted to Islam, thereby firmly entrenching the Moslems in the conquered areas so that they remain in most of them to this day.

The reasons for the Moslem success can be summarized thusly: 1) The

Arabs were fired with religious zeal, especially since they believed that death in battle brought instant entrance into paradise. 2) They had fine cavalry troops which could attack at any point in the enemy formation and then dash away. These constant skirmishes soon wore down the less mobile forces arrayed against them. 3) The people ruled by the Byzantines and Persians were dissatisfied. Since many of these people were of the same race as the Arabs (Semites), they looked upon the Moslems as liberators. 4) Islam offered inducements to the people to convert. Non-Moslems had none of the rights of citizenship and were forced to pay heavy taxes. It was easy to become a Moslem, and Islam offered a simple faith to replace the confused mixture of heresies and Cesaro-Papism which the people in these areas had suffered. 5) The death penalty for apostasy meant that almost no one would leave Islam. Thus Islam gradually gained converts, while losing no one.

The Moslem conquests had three main effects on later history. 1) Christianity now had a new and powerful enemy. 2) A religion was established which is still strong today. 3) The East and West—after having been united by Alexander and Rome—were now alien again, divided between the Moslem East and the Christian West.

The Pope Looks West

Charles Martel's victory at Tours showed that the Franks were the West's only hope for peace, order and culture. The Spaniards could hold the mountains of the Asturias but were not strong enough to aid the rest of Europe. Furthermore, the West could no longer look to Byzantium for help. The Byzantines were constantly harassed by the Moslems, torn by heresies, and afflicted by warfare over the throne.

The only unifying force in the West was the Church. The leader of the Church, the Pope, made a deliberate decision to renounce his dependence on the old and dying Eastern Roman Empire and turn to the West—barbarian still, but strong and alive. This decision freed the Church from the corruptions and confusions of Byzantium. Because of this decision, the Church was a powerful force in the building of the new civilization in the West.

The Pope first looked to the Franks when King Aistulf of the Lombards swore to cut off the heads of all the Romans with a single sword unless they submitted to him. Pope Stephen II journeyed to the Frankish capital to meet with King Pepin (Charles Martel's son). In 754 Pope Stephen anointed Pepin as king of the Franks. This was the first time that a barbarian king had been anointed by the Pope. This act greatly strengthened Pepin's authority over his unruly people. In return he promised to keep peace with the Church, suppress injustice, and defend Rome against the Lombards. Pepin was declared "King by the grace of God"—signifying that he drew all his authority from God through the Church in the person of the Pope.

Pepin's Franks decisively defeated the Lombards, King Aistulf barely escaping with his life by sliding down a rocky slope. Two years later the Lombards attacked again but this time Pepin drove them out of southern Italy for good. He gave their land to the Pope, a gift known as the Donation of Pepin, which was the foundation of the later Papal States.

Charlemagne

Before Pepin died in 768, he divided his kingdom between his two sons, Charles and Carloman. The two didn't get along, but in 771 Carloman died, leaving Charles ruler of all the Frankish lands: roughly modern day France, Belgium, Netherlands, West Germany, and Switzerland. The first enemy he had to face was the Saxons of northeastern Germany. The Saxons were pagans, worshiping Woden and Thor and including in their worship occasional human sacrifice and ritual cannibalism. They made constant raids into Charles' territory. In 772 Charles dealt the Saxons a severe defeat.

Next he faced the Lombards, who were once again menacing the papal lands. Charles drove them out of northern Italy, taking over their territory. He made a triumphal march into Rome, where it is recorded that he went sightseeing as would any modern tourist. He bore now the title King of Franks and Lombards.

The Saxons had taken advantage of Charles' absence to raid deep into his territory. While he crossed the Alps with the main body of his troops, he sent a small contingent ahead on a forced march. They caught the Saxons by surprise and drove them out. Charles believed that only their conversion would cause the Saxons to live peacefully. Unfortunately he thought that the only way to convert them was by threat of force. Many Saxons were baptized, but their conversions were often insincere.

Next Charles turned toward Spain to counter the Moslem threat. His invasion was not well enough prepared and he was unsuccessful in a series of minor battles. Finally he decided to return to his own lands. He appointed the nobleman Roland to command the rear guard and to signal for help with his horn if he were attacked. Roland was a proud man, with too great a confidence in his own abilities. He neglected to take proper scouting precautions and was attacked at Roncesvalles, but his pride kept him from blowing his horn until it was too late. His men fought and died to the last man. The episode is immortalized in the epic poem, *Chanson de Roland* (*Song of Roland*).

The incident at Roncesvalles sobered Charles, and he turned his attention to peaceful pursuits, becoming a patron of the arts and encouraging education. Because his lands were at peace, protecting from external and internal disorders, a Golden Age flourished in France during the last quarter of the eighth century, known in his honor as the Carolingian Age. Painters, silversmiths, goldsmiths, ivory carvers, manuscript illuminators, sculptors, and scholars all received Charles' support. The most famous scholar was the monk Alcuin, who was Charles' minister of education and established schools all over his dominion. He also encouraged Charles to take a more lenient attitude toward the Saxons, converting them by persuasion rather than force. Charles built good roads, the first since Roman days. He established just government, listening to and acting on complaints against local officials.

But in 782 the Saxons rebelled. Charles put down this rebellion but soon a Saxon force was across his borders. Charles had to keep his armies in the field both winter and summer for three years. Both sides were exhausted. Finally Charles offered terms. He promised to withdraw his army from Saxony if the Saxon king would be baptized. King Witikind agreed. After the baptism, Charles loaded his former enemy with gifts and requested Pope Hadrian to order three days of feasting and thanksgiving throughout Christendom.

In 788 the Avars, Asiatic barbarians, attacked. Charles sent his son Pepin, who successfully countered the attack. Conversions were voluntary this time, and Charles treated them with mildness.

In 794 Charles established a permanent capital at Aachen. A great wooden bridge was erected over the Rhine; he built a magnificent palace and an octagonal chapel, which still stands today. Charles summoned Church councils to fight heresy and cooperated with the Pope in reforming the Frankish clergy. When Pope Hadrian died in 795, Charles wept.

The new Pope was Leo III. Vatican intriguers who wanted one of their party as Pope kidnapped Leo, pulled him from his horse and beat him, held him a prisoner, and even attempted to blind him. He was eventually rescued by being lowered over a wall with a rope. Concerned for the Pope, Charles invited him to a conference. When the Pope returned to

Rome, Charles sent his own troops with him for protection.

In March 800, Charles travelled around his dominions to put everything in order. He erected watchtowers to guard against a new barbarian threat, the Vikings. In August he set out for Rome with a large army and wagonloads of gold and silver ornaments for churches. On Christmas day 800, Romans, Franks, Bavarians, Lombards, Goths, Basques, Anglo-Saxons and Greeks crowded into St. Peter's. Close to the altar were Charles' daughters and sons and Charles himself. During Mass, Pope Leo lifted a crown from the altar and crowned Charles emperor, the first in the West since 476. Truly Charles was now Charlemagne (Charles the Great). He was the Roman Emperor, but his empire was based firmly on Christianity. Hence his new title was *Holy* Roman Emperor. The crowd roared: "Long life and victory to Charles Augustus, crowned by God the great and pacific Emperor of the Romans."

As emperor, Charlemagne believed himself responsible for Christians everywhere. He exchanged embassies with the Moslem sultan and held negotiations to protect the right of pilgrims to visit the Holy Land. He enforced justice and protected the poor, widows and orphans. Some of his decrees sound more like sermons. Towns sprang up and trade increased because of peace within his empire. Charlemagne had wrested civilization from the Dark Ages. He died in 813, but his fame lived on and grew to epic proportions as it became clear that no one else could even preserve what he had built.

The Holy Roman Empire

The idea of a Holy Roman Emperor was very important in history for three reasons. First, it gave the Church a special protector. The Pope and the Church would not be at the mercy of whatever barbarian or war-like tribe would attack it. It would have a temporal power to fight its battles and preserve its independence. The notion of the Holy Roman Emperor as the particular protector of the Pope and the Faith in Europe endured until the 20th century.

Secondly, all the Christian peoples were united by spiritual bonds and looked to one spiritual head, the Pope, and the temporal head, the Emperor. This union did not mean that local differences were wiped out, but that men realized that something was bigger and more important than any local differences. They regarded Christianity as more important than anything else in their lives. This unity was a further development of the idea of *Christendom.* Just as Constantine may be called the Founder of Christendom, so Charlemagne may be called the Builder of Christendom. The unity which the concept of Christendom brought about made possible the eventual rebuilding of civilization in the West.

Thirdly, men realized that a higher authority existed than that which any particular king or ruler might exercise. Charlemagne acknowledged that his power must have come from Christ and therefore must be exercised in accord with Christ's commandments. This provided limits on the king's powers. We have already seen how the Roman Republic limited government through many classes of magistrates who could prevent abuses by other classes. But this system depended on the good will of the magistrates. Now rulers had a more important motivation against tyranny: they were responsible to Christ Himself for their actions. This was to produce one of the freest and most just societies the world has ever seen.

Review Questions

1. Summarize the Persian-Byzantine wars of the early seventh century. What was their main consequence?
2. Where did Mohammed come from? What influences caused him to develop his religion?
3. Summarize the chief duties and doctrines of Islam. What was the Koran? What are the followers of Mohammed called?
4. What was the Hegira? What year did it occur? Why was it important?
5. Who was Mohammed's successor? How did he strengthen Islam?
6. Who was Omar? What was his guiding principle?
7. List the territories conquered by the Moslems.
8. Why did the Moslems fail to conquer Constantinople?
9. Who resisted the Moslems in Spain? What was his motivation? What were the results of his resistance?
10. Who defeated the Moslems in France? Name and describe the battle.
11. Why did the Pope turn to the West? What is the significance of the anointing of Pepin as King of the Franks?
12. Summarize the military accomplishments of Charles the Great.
13. Summarize his non-military accomplishments.
14. Summarize the circumstances of his crowning as Holy Roman Emperor.
15. What is the historical significance of the Holy Roman Empire?

Projects

1. Do a report on the achievements of the Carolingian Age.

2. Do a report on Islam today.
3. Imagine that you are a Spanish Christian fighting with Pelayo. Write an account of your experiences.
4. Prepare a map showing the Arab conquests.
5. Prepare a map of Charlemagne's empire.

Chapter Thirteen
The Foundation of a New Civilization

In THIS CHAPTER we will study the events from the death of Charlemagne in 814 until about 1050, the date commonly used to mark the end of the Dark Ages and the beginning of the High Middle Ages—a time of the rebirth of civilization, learning and culture, and of the re-establishment of peace and order. Obviously the second date cannot be exact—men did not wake up on January 1 in the year 1051 and announce to each other that it was time to end the Dark Ages and begin the High Middle Ages. But it is a convenient point at which to divide the two historical periods. Before 1050 the average person was more likely than not to be uneducated and familiar with nothing beyond how to scratch out a living; he had no surplus wealth or property but just barely enough to survive; he lived in constant fear of bandits and war. From 1050 on, more and more people could be more confident of dying a natural death rather than being killed by bandits or raiding tribes; had some leisure time to think about art and architecture and learning and to celebrate with festivals; and might have some surplus property or possessions to trade with their neighbors.

During this period of time, we will see four main themes: first, the decline and then reappearance of the Holy Roman Emperor; second, a new wave of barbarian invasions; third, the development of feudalism as a means of protection; fourth, the difficulties of the papacy and the Church, which were eventually brought to an end by reform movements led by the Cluny saints.

The Eclipse of the Empire

By establishing the Holy Roman Empire, Charlemagne had established peace and order throughout Western Europe. This in turn made possible a temporary revival of learning and of culture. But conditions in Europe were still unsettled, and the Franks and other peoples were still close to the days when they were invading barbarian tribes. Therefore the benefits brought by the Empire—and the Empire itself—could last only as long as a strong leader could hold the Empire together.

Charlemagne was succeeded by his son, Louis the Pious—so called because of his devotion to religion. But unlike his father, his religious faith was not accompanied by a commanding personality which could inspire loyalty. He was crowned Holy Roman Emperor and managed to hold the Empire together until his death, but already the different sections were becoming more independent.

When Louis died, his sons (Lothair, Louis the German, and Charles the Bald) fought over who was to dominate the Empire. Their quarrels were brought to an end in 843 by the *Treaty of Verdun*, which divided the Empire into three parts: France in the west, Germany in the east and Lotharingia in the middle. Lotharingia included northern Italy, Holland and Belgium (all countries which exist today) and Alsace, Lorraine and Burgundy (which today are part of France).

The Treaty of Verdun is an important historical landmark. By setting up France and Germany as independent kingdoms, it marked the beginning of the modern idea of nations, an idea which was almost totally new. The area of Lotharingia became a constant battleground as France and Germany fought over various parts of it. They were still fighting over it as late as World War II. A third significance is that the division of the Empire almost fatally weakened it.

Lothair took the title of Holy Roman Emperor, but he was in fact the weakest of the three and had no real authority or power over the others. Thus most of the advantages of the Holy Roman Empire melted away. Lothair was succeeded by his son, Louis II, who ruled from 855-875. Louis did his duty as best he could, fighting off the Moslems and the Vikings, but he had effective rule only over Lombardy (northern Italy). Louis II had only a daughter, Ermengarde. The crown therefore passed to his uncle, Charles the Bald, who was Emperor from 875-877 but did nothing imperial. Charles the Bald died without heirs and a struggle for the throne ensued, led by Ermengarde's husband, Boso. The struggles ended when Louis the German's son, Charles the Fat, finally established himself on the throne in 881. But, as we shall soon see, he was unworthy to wear Charlemagne's crown and was deposed in 887. Quarreling and chaos afflicted the Empire as several ineffectual men passed the crown among themselves. By 901, the Carolingian line had died out, and it appeared as if the Holy Roman Empire had died too, as no one remained to carry on Charlemagne's great dream. It was as if a protective wall had been demolished, so that the evils of the tenth century—chaos, fear, lawlessness, ignorance—could come rushing in to engulf Europe once more.

The Vikings

These evils were given a big boost by a new wave of barbarian invasions. Bands of blonde and red-haired sea pirates sailed down from Scandinavia—from Norway, Sweden, Denmark. Known as *Vikings* or *Norsemen,* they at first raided coastal towns only. Eventually they became bolder and swept inland, sailing their narrow ships with the dragon-prows up rivers and even carrying the ships on their backs when the rivers became too shallow. They burned villages and farms, destroyed churches and monasteries, carried off valuables, kidnapped innocent people to serve as slaves. The earlier barbarians who had invaded the Roman Empire had been whole tribes—men, women and children—who settled down and thereby left themselves open to being civilized. The Viking raiding parties consisted of warriors only, who returned to their homes in the north after taking what they could and destroying what they didn't want. They struck such fear into the souls of the people that a new prayer was added to the Church's litany: "From the fury of the Norsemen, O Lord, deliver us!"

Because of the breakdown in the Holy Roman Empire, no strong force existed to stop the Viking raids. But on three separate occasions, heroes rose up to resist the Vikings.

Alfred the Great. The year was 878. The Norsemen from Denmark—the Danes—had overrun most of England. Only one man remained undefeated: King Alfred of the Saxons, a people who had conquered Britain after the Romans withdrew their forces and had become Christian. Alfred, refusing to despair in spite of what seemed to be overwhelming odds, led a group of trusted and talented men into the marshes in the early spring, where they hid themselves and planned their strategy. In May he marched out, and all the Saxon warriors in the surrounding countryside came to meet him, eager to fight under his banner.

He met the Danes near a town called Ethandune, and—an historian of the times tells us—"closed his ranks, shield locked with shield, and fought fiercely against the entire heathen host in long and stubborn stand.

At last by God's will he won his victory, slew very many, and pursued the rest to their place of refuge, striking as he went." Alfred besieged the Danes in their fort until they surrendered. The Danish leader, Guthrum, became a Christian, and the Norsemen withdrew their forces from a considerable part of England.

This victory over the Danes at Ethandune marks the beginning of England as a nation, a nation which would be Christian, with its own culture—the culture eventually established in English colonies, including our own land. Alfred established a just rule, wrote a Christian law code and encouraged art and education. Because of his accomplishments, he is known to history as Alfred the Great.

The Siege of Paris. As the Carolingian dynasty died out, a new family emerged to provide strength and leadership to the Franks. The founder of this family was Robert the Strong-armed, who had fallen fighting the Norse in 866. His son, Count of Paris Eudes, was the leader of Paris as the Vikings came to attack in November 885. Paris at this time was mostly limited to the island in the Seine, connected to the mainland by two bridges, the Great Bridge and the Little Bridge. Both bridges were fortified. When the Vikings arrived, their ships so covered the water of the river that no glint of light could be seen reflecting off the Seine. They had 300 warships and 30,000 men. The Norsemen besieged the city, cutting off all food supplies, and bombarded the city with their siege engines. On February 6, the Little Bridge was destroyed by the winter floods. The Parisians who had been in the bridge's fortified tower were trapped. The Vikings offered the men amnesty if they would surrender. They did surrender but were immediately killed.

In May Count Eudes was able to slip out to go for help. He persuaded one of Charles the Fat's men, Count Henry, to send aid. But Henry delayed, and so Eudes, though he was now safe, decided that he must rejoin his people. On his return journey, Viking scouts saw him. Only the speed of his horse and his swordsmanship enabled him to re-enter the city. Finally, in August Count Henry arrived. But the Vikings were expecting him and dug traps which they had carefully covered over. Henry and his men fell into the traps, Henry being killed.

The situation within Paris was grim, but the people would not even consider surrender. In September Charles the Fat arrived. But instead of fighting the Vikings, he began negotiating with them. He concluded an agreement by which the siege was lifted, but the Norsemen received Burgundy to pillage. This was the virtual end of any authority Charles the Fat had over the Parisians. Eventually the Carolingian line was totally ignored and the descendants of Eudes became kings of France, a dynasty known as the Capetians (after Eudes' descendant, Hugh Capet), which lasted until the 16th century.

Brian Boru

Ireland had never been politically united. Various clans controlled the different parts of the country, often warring with each other. There was also an office of High King, which was sometimes hereditary, sometimes taken by force, sometimes held in great respect by the clan kings, sometimes not. By the tenth century, Ireland was divided into its four historical provinces—Connaught in the west, Ulster in the north, Munster in the southwest, Leinster in the southeast. In the second century Munster had been divided between two sons, producing the Desmond line and the Thomond line. The royal residence of Cashel and the title of King of Munster was to be alternately held by their descendants, which resulted in much quarreling.

In 951 the Thomond king, Kennedy, was slain by the Danes in one of their frequent raids on the Irish countryside. The oldest son Mahon became King of Thomond. Mahon lacked the stamina to challenge the Danes, so made peace with them. His younger brother Brian, who came to be known as Brian Boru, refused to accept the peace. He took a few followers (sometimes their number was as low as 15) and waged guerrilla warfare against the Vikings. His men endured great sufferings, but Brian's inspired leadership and his total willingness to share all the hardships with them kept them in the field. Finally he shamed Mahon into resuming the war. He allied himself with the Desmond line, and with Brian's men as the spearhead of the attack won a number of battles. In 964 he entered Cashel in triumph.

Ivar of Limerick was head of the Munster Danes. He was allied with Molloy of Desmond, who was jealous of Mahon. In 968 Brian attacked them at the Battle of Sulcoit. The Irish had learned to use Danish battle-axes, so the Danes' chain mail did not help them. Brian pursued the Danes to Limerick and sacked the city. Ivar and his remnant force fled to Scattery Island, and Munster had eight years of peace.

Mahon was killed through Desmond treachery, making Molloy King of Munster. Brian first went after the Danes, defeating them in 977 and slaying Ivar. Then he turned to his Irish enemies, defeating the Desmonds and ruling Munster uncontested. He was head of a well-trained, well-disciplined army which was totally devoted to him. Leinster thought it prudent to give homage to Brian and to take no chances on arousing his wrath against them.

Next Brian returned to the field against the Danes. He subdued the Limerick and Waterford Danes. Maelmorra, King of Leinster, now chafed under Brian's dominating position and allied himself with the Dublin Danes. Brian sent his men in a rapid forced march so that they would meet the Danes in the narrow valley of Glenmama, where the Danish cavalry would be no advantage. The strategy was successful, and Brian crushed the combined forces. The year was 1000. In 1002 Brian was crowned High King. The next year Connaught and Ulster gave their allegiance to Brian, who became the first ruler of a united Ireland.

Brian proceeded to make the time of peace a new golden age for Ireland. He built roads, bridges, harbors, fortresses. He endowed monasteries and churches, schools and colleges. The remaining Danes paid tribute. He established such complete peace and order within the country that it was said that a richly dressed girl, wearing a ring of solid gold, had walked unmolested the whole length of Ireland.

Peace lasted for ten years. Then Maelmorra began to be restless, partly motivated by the envious realization that Brian was so much the better man. He stirred up the Ireland Danes to rebel against Brian and gained allies from Norsemen in Norway, Denmark and England. Brian summoned men from all over Ireland, putting an army of 20,000 into the field. By Palm Sunday 1014, the whole surface of Dublin Bay was covered with Viking ships. The Danes decided to attack on Good Friday, April 23, and moved onto the field at Clontarf.

In spite of being 73 years old, Brian wished to lead his army in person, but his advisers persuaded him to retire to a tent, putting the command under his son. Before the battle, Brian mounted his horse, and, with a golden hilted sword in one hand and a crucifix in the other, urged his men to meet the enemy with courage and strength. He gave his son the place of honor, leading the men from his home clan who had fought with him from the beginning. The battle raged all day. Brian prayed in his tent as the Irishmen fought valiantly. Maelmorra was slain; Brian's son fell to a Norwegian chief. After 6:00 P.M., Danish ships were carried out to sea by the tide so that the Danes couldn't reach them. Many Vikings perished in the sea or were pounced upon by Brian's reserves, which cut off the Danish retreat.

As reports came into Brian in his tent, he allowed his bodyguard, eager for action, to join in the final pursuit of the Danes. He returned to his prayers. Suddenly he heard a sound behind him. Thinking it was his priest, he welcomed the visitor. Then he turned and saw that it was Brodir, Viking chieftain. The Viking fell on the unarmed Brian and stabbed him to death.

Though Brian's dream of a united Ireland did not outlive him, his victory over the Danes drove the intruders from the country and preserved Christian Ireland. And the memory of the great High King remained ever after in Irish hearts.

Feudalism

Despite the efforts of such heroes as Alfred the Great and Brian Boru, the Vikings were able to devastate Europe. As we have seen in the case of Charles the Fat, the kings were generally too weak to provide much protection. Therefore the people needed some other means of safeguarding their lives and what little property they had, not only from the Vikings but from bandits and other criminals as well. The system that developed was *feudalism.*

Imagine that you are living in France or Germany or England during the 900's. Money is worthless because nothing is being made for anyone to buy. Only land is valuable because with land a man can produce enough food to feed his family. You had once owned some land. You had planted fields and built a small but warm house. Then the Viking raiders came. They burned your house and fields to the ground. They drove off your animals and kidnapped your sons and daughters. What can you do?

You know that not far away lives a man who had fought the Vikings. He is wealthy enough to own a horse and armor and to hire men to fight with him. He had driven the Vikings away and they had not destroyed his house, which he had built on a hill for protection. You also know that he controls much land but does not have time to work it himself because he must be ever on the watch for the Norsemen.

You go to this man and make an agreement. You and your family promise to spend the rest of your life working on his land, in return for keeping enough of what you produce yourself to feed your family and—most importantly—in return for his protection. You exchange labor for protection. This exchange is called feudalism. The men who provided the protection were called *knights* or *barons,* and the land they owned was called a *fief.* The laborers were the *serfs.* Feudalism has been criticized because the serfs had little freedom—they could not leave the land and had to turn over much of what they produced to the landlord. But this criticism overlooks the fact that without the feudal system, the serfs might not have been alive at all.

The wealthy landlords, in turn, were often pledged to serve still more powerful noblemen. Those pledged to service were known as *vassals*. They would fight for the noblemen, who would provide protection when the forces of the raiders became too powerful for one man to resist. These powerful noblemen, known as *overlords*, in turn served the king. The feudal system was like a pyramid, with each level swearing *fealty* (loyalty and service) to the higher level, which provided protection for those lower down. The system was based on trust and honesty and therefore encouraged a higher standard of morality than had been present earlier in the Dark Ages. In order to emphasize the importance of keeping one's promises, the vassal would swear fealty at a special ceremony, solemnly declaring to the overlord: "I become your man. I shall keep faith with you against all others." The lord showed his acceptance of the oath by handing the vassal a special object such as a ring, a stalk of grain or a piece of turf (symbols of the fief).

The system worked well, helping Europe recover from the Viking raids. Gradually enough surplus would be produced on the land so that trade and commerce could again be possible; men had less need to spend all their time on warfare and could turn to learning and culture, thereby enabling civilization to be reborn.

Otto the Great

By the middle of the tenth century, no strong central authority had existed in Europe since Charlemagne, 150 years earlier. But because it was less easily reached by the Viking raiders, Germany was spared the worst effects of the Viking invasions. Gradually the German kingdom of Saxony grew to be the strongest force in Europe.

In 936 the Saxon barons elected 24-year-old Otto as king. He was crowned on August 7 in Aachen, Charlemagne's capital. Otto was a great admirer of Charlemagne. He had many of Charlemagne's strengths and would be the one to restore the Holy Roman Empire. He faced attacks from the Slavs in the northeast, the Magyars in the east, and rebels in his own kingdom. First he established authority over the barons, calling upon them to swear fealty to him, and appointed churchmen as the chief administrative officers of his kingdom in order to reduce the barons' power and unite the kingdom.

Then in 951 a call came from Italy. Young Queen Adelaide had been left a widow at 19. The ruthless nobleman Berengar wanted Adelaide for his wife and her kingdom for his own. When she refused him, he imprisoned her. Her friends turned to Otto for help. Otto marched on Italy. Such was his reputation that Berengar fled without giving battle. Otto rescued the lovely young queen, and then married her himself. Their marriage was deeply happy.

Next came attacks from the fierce pagan Magyars, who had raided as far as Italy, Burgundy and even Spain. On August 8, 955, the Magyars attacked Augsburg, and the frightened citizens within the city walls were sure their city would soon fall. Ulrich, Bishop of Augsburg, rallied the people and urged them to stand firm. They were barely able to fend off the Magyars as night fell, but they were so exhausted that surely the next day would bring defeat. Ulrich spent the night in prayer, lying prostrate on the cathedral floor, beseeching the Virgin Mary to protect his people. As the next day dawned, the anxious townspeople watched in amazement as the Magyars retreated: they had received word that Otto was on his way with a large force.

On August 10, the feast of St. Lawrence, Otto's Germans and the Magyars met at the Battle of Lechfeld. That morning at Mass, Otto vowed that if he won he would endow a diocese in thanksgiving. He went into battle behind a banner of St. Michael the Archangel. Soon after the battle began, he received word that a large force of Magyars had crossed the river and circled behind his men. The eighth, seventh and sixth legions had already broken and were running. Otto immediately called on the fourth legion to ride to the rescue. He put in command Conrad (his son by his first wife, who had died), greatly to everyone's surprise since Conrad had earlier rebelled against his father. But Otto had confidence in Conrad, and Conrad came through. He drove off the Magyars and pulled the frightened men back into order. Then the royal legion with Otto at the head rushed against the main host in a determined and persistent drive. The Magyars fled as Otto won a decisive victory.

At the end of the exhausting and bloody battle, on a battlefield littered with corpses and discarded weapons, Otto's cheering troops proclaimed him emperor. Otto's power was now secure. In 962, the Pope solemnly crowned him, and the Holy Roman Empire was re-established—this time with a German rather than a French base—to endure until 1806.

Next the Slavs made trouble. Otto camped in the woods and marshes of the River Recknitz in Mecklenburg. First he tried a conciliatory message to the Slav king, telling him that if he surrendered he would find in Otto a friend. But the king scornfully refused the gesture of friendship, thinking that he would he would have an easy victory. But in the night Otto moved his men across the river. In the morning he launched an attack, defeating the Slavs, ending their military threat, and opening them to Christianity.

Otto had Charlemagne's broad vision, accepting spiritual responsibilities as well as temporal. He offered protection to the Pope, restored order in Italy, and encouraged missionary activity among the barbarians. The peace and order he established throughout his lands guaranteed that civilization could continue to grow. Adelaide played an active part in these pursuits and lived such a holy life that eventually she was canonized a saint.

The Magyars, meanwhile, retreated into Hungary, where they established a kingdom. In 955 the Magyar king Stephen married a German princess and was baptized. In the year 1000 he received a royal crown and papal blessing from Pope Sylvester II. Stephen brought his whole country into the Church, and the Hungarian kingdom survived until World War II, for much of that time united with the Holy Roman Empire as the defender of Christianity.

Night upon the Pope

In his poem "Ballad of the White Horse," about Alfred the Great's victory at Ethandune, G. K. Chesterton describes conditions in Europe as Alfred prepared to do battle: "And there was death upon the Emperor and night upon the Pope." The century preceding the coronation of Otto the Great as Holy Roman Emperor was the darkest period in the history of the papacy. Some Popes were immoral, others were incompetent, and political factions fought for control of the papacy.

In 891, for example, the aged but ambitious Formosus was elected Pope though he was strongly opposed by the Duke of Spoleto and his supporters. Formosus died in 896, but his opponents were not content to let him rest in peace. Stephen VII, the candidate of the Duke of Spoleto, elected in 896, had the body of Formosus dug up from the grave, seated on a chair, and judged by an assembly—known as the Synod of the Corpse—over which Stephen presided. All of Formosus' misdeeds, real and imagined, were recalled and he was judged guilty—not surprisingly, since he could hardly defend himself. The papal robes were torn off and the corpse was thrown into the river. Stephen annulled all of Pope Formosus' acts, but was himself imprisoned and killed.

Among the successors of Stephen, we have the following: Leo V, who died in prison under unknown circumstances; Sergius III, who took Rome by force; John X, who was imprisoned and murdered; John XII, who gave moral scandal; Benedict IX, who resigned to get married and then tried to regain the papacy later as an anti-pope.

Besides the problems of the papacy, there were other grave problems in the Church. Church offices were bought and sold, bishops took orders (and bribes) from noblemen, monasteries were taken over by greedy men who wanted the wealth their lands could produce. It appeared that Christianity was dying and that it would soon go the way of all earthly institutions.

But this was not the first time the Church appeared to be dying. It had survived persecution; it had survived heresy; now it would survive the Dark Ages. Even at the Church's lowest point, a reform movement was beginning.

In 910 the Duke of Aquitaine founded a monastery at Cluny in France, headed by an abbot named Berno, later a saint. Unlike most monasteries of the time, Cluny was not forced to submit to the authority of anyone except the Pope. Therefore Berno, and his successor, St. Odo, were able to establish a spiritual, holy rule of life for the monks, rather than an earthly, greedy one. Odo went out from Cluny to other monasteries throughout Europe to reform them as well. His efforts were not always welcome. Once he was met by armed monks ready to resist him. But his theme was "I come peacefully—to hurt no one, injure no one, but that I may correct those who are not living according to [the Benedictine] Rule." And he did. Gradually, one after another, corrupt, worldly monasteries returned to the spiritual ideal of earlier saints.

St. Odo's successors, many of them also saints, spread the reform throughout Germany, Italy, Spain and even as far as England. Eventually 1500 Cluniac monasteries had been established in Europe. The reform of the monasteries led to a reform of the priesthood, of bishops and priests, and of the papacy, when the German Emperors—working for the good of the Church—brought about the election of Cluny monks as Popes. The most important was Sylvester II, from 999-1003, who even as Pope lived a simple, holy life and began the process of reforming the Church as the Cluny saints had reformed the monasteries.

And though the Church greatly suffered from the evils that afflicted it during the ninth and tenth centuries, even during those dark times missionaries were going out to bring Christ to the barbarian lands in the East and the North.

Sts. Cyril and Methodius: Cyril and Methodius were brothers who were apostles to the Slavs of Moravia (parts of present-day Hungary, Bohemia and Poland). St. Cyril (827-869) was a Byzantine monk who knew the Slavic language and customs. He devised a Slavonic alphabet and translated the liturgy and Scriptures into Slavonic. With Methodius he arrived in Moravia in 863. The Germans at first objected to their efforts, arguing that the liturgy should be said only in Latin, Hebrew or Greek, not in Slavonic. But Cyril and Methodius received papal authorization for their work. Cyril died in Rome in 869, and Methodius carried on the work until his own death in 885. Methodius was also the main apostle to the Bulgars. Prince Boris I wanted to make his wild tribe into a Christian nation. His appeal for missionaries was answered by Methodius in 863, who expounded Christianity to the Bulgars by a picture of the Last Judgment. Boris was baptized and the rest of his nation soon followed his example.

Russia: Olga, a Russian Slavic princess, had come into contact with Christians who had been evangelized by St. Cyril. In Constantinople she was baptized, but few Russians imitated her. When her son Vladimir became ruler of Russia, he made a marriage alliance with the Byzantines, who insisted on his conversion to Christianity. He was baptized and then set out to convert his entire nation. He traveled throughout the country destroying pagan shrines and urging his people to accept Christ, thereby bringing Russia into the Christian orbit.

Denmark: The first Christian king of Denmark was King Harold Blue Tooth (936-985). His son, Sweyn Fork Beard (985-1014) relapsed into paganism, and Christianity was forced underground. But a younger son, Canute the Great, came to the throne in 1018. He was an ardent champion of Christian religion and culture, advancing Christianity in Denmark and in all of Scandinavia.

Norway: King Harold Fine Hair (875-930) allowed his younger son Haakon the Good to be educated by Christians in England. When Haakon came to the throne in 936, he was unable to convert the rest of the country. Finally came King St. Olaf II (1015-1030), who had been baptized in England. He brought in missionaries from England and vigorously fought paganism. He is Norway's national patron saint and hero.

Thus we see that Christ's promise that the gates of hell will not prevail against the Church applies even when the Pope himself falls victim to the evils of the day. The promise of papal infallibility refers specifically to the teaching of faith and morals. Popes can be and have been great sinners. But during the entire dark night of the papacy, there is not even a hint that one single Pope taught heresy. And even during the worst of times, reform movements were beginning within the Church, and the missionaries were bringing Christ to new nations.

The Holy Shroud

After the Holy Shroud was recovered from the wall in Edessa, it was enshrined in the church there. Edessa was in the territory conquered by the Moslems, but the Arabs had not harmed the Shroud since they honored Jesus as one of their prophets. The Shroud was still regarded as a miraculous portrait and not known to be the burial cloth of Christ.

In the year 943, the Byzantine Emperor Romanus Lecapenus wanted to climax his relatively peaceful, prosperous reign by bringing the miraculous portrait to Constantinople. He sent his most able general, John Curcuas, who waged a series of brilliant campaigns through Moslem territory, penetrating to cities that had not seen a Christian for 300 years. In the spring the Byzantine army camped outside the Edessan walls.

Curcuas offered the Moslem emir (leader) the following agreement: the city would be spared, 200 high-ranking Moslem prisoners would be released, 12,000 silver crowns would be paid, and Edessa would be guaranteed perpetual immunity from attack, in exchange for the portrait. The emir was perplexed. If he agreed, the Christian inhabitants would be furious; in addition he would lose the lucrative trade from pilgrims who came to see the portrait. Finally he told the Christian clergy to surrender the portrait.

The clergy had no desire to see their portrait leave the city so they tried to fool the Byzantines with first one counterfeit and then a second. But Curcuas was not fooled. Finally the portrait was surrendered and the Byzantine army brought it triumphantly to Constantinople. This event was most providential. Two centuries later, Edessa was sacked by the Turks. They would surely have destroyed the Shroud if it had still been there.

The portrait was installed in the royal chapel, but was never shown to the general public. At some point, however, someone finally unfolded the cloth and realized that it was a Shroud and not just a portrait. We know this happened because there was a dramatic change in representations of Jesus' burial, showing the Shroud and showing His body as it appears on the Shroud. So at last the true nature of this cloth was known. The Shroud remained in Constantinople, honored and revered, especially on Easter Sunday, when it was used in a ceremony representing Christ's Resurrection from the dead.

If you had lived around the year 1000, you would have feared the Vikings, looked to a feudal lord for protection, been dismayed at the evils in the Church. But you would also have had hope: peace and order were slowly being re-established through the efforts of the German Holy Roman Emperors and feudalism, and the Church was reforming itself. You would be encouraged by the bravery of the men fighting the Vikings and the local bandits, and you would have rejoiced to see the Holy Spirit purifying the Church.

Amid the evils of the ninth and tenth centuries, seeds of a new civilization were being planted, seeds which would eventually burst into bloom in that great and glorious time known as the High Middle Ages.

Review Questions

1. What is the significance of the year 1050?
2. Why was the Holy Roman Empire weakened after Charlemagne's death?
3. When was the Treaty of Verdun signed? What were its provisions? What is its significance to history?
4. Who were the Vikings? What effect did they have on history?
5. How did Alfred the Great resist the Vikings? What is the long-term significance of his victory?
6. How did the people of Paris resist the Vikings? What ruling family replaced the Carolingians as a result?
7. How did Brian Boru resist the Vikings? What else did he do for Ireland?
8. Why did feudalism develop? How did it work? What did it accomplish?
9. How did Otto the Great revive the Holy Roman Empire? What were his other accomplishments?
10. Summarize the evils in the papacy and the Church in the century preceding the coronation of Otto the Great.
11. How was the Church reformed? What is the significance of the fact that the Church reformed itself?
12. Briefly summarize the conversions of Hungary, the Slavs, Russia, Den-

mark and Norway.

13. What happened to the Shroud in the tenth century?

Projects

1. Prepare a chart of the system of feudalism, showing the relationships among the various classes of society and what each did for the other.
2. Imagine that you were a participant in Alfred the Great's battle with the Danes, in the siege of Paris or in the Battle of Clontarf. (You can be on either side.) Write a first-hand account of your experiences.
3. Give a report on the Cluny saints and the Cluniac reforms.
4. Give a report on Romanesque architecture.

Chapter Fourteen
The High Middle Ages

THE YEARS FROM about 1050 to 1450 are known as the High Middle Ages. The name "middle" was bestowed upon this period by later historians, who regarded these years as a kind of low point between the ancient world and the modern world. Some people still believe that everything from the time of the fall of Rome to about the sixteenth century (when Greek and Roman art, architecture, and literature became very popular) was unimportant. But the people who actually lived during these 400 years certainly didn't think of themselves as a low point or the middle of anything. Their art, architecture, literature and music reveal a real joy in living; the structure of their society provided freedom for all as well as protection and help for the weak and the poor; and they made great progress in a variety of fields.

The Dark Ages were brought to an end by the reform of the Church, the revival of the Holy Roman Empire, and the peace and economic revival resulting from the feudal system. The Church gradually brought every single European people into its fold, completing the work of conversion with the Lithuanians in the fourteenth century. By the year 1400 virtually every European was a baptized Catholic. And Catholic Europe of the High Middle Ages built a Christian civilization rich and glorious, reaching an artistic summit in the cathedral at Chartres, an intellectual summit in the *Summa Theologiae* of St. Thomas Aquinas, and a summit of holiness in the life of St. Francis of Assisi.

Pope Leo IX

The first Pope of the High Middle Ages was St. Leo IX (1049-1054).

He was related to the Holy Roman Emperor Conrad and had served in his court. Leo administered the Diocese of Toul so well that Conrad's successor, Henry III, said that Leo should be Pope when Pope Damasus died. Personal ambition was far from Leo's mind, and he did not want to be a creature of the Emperor. He said that he would accept the office only if freely acclaimed by the people of Rome. So he came to Rome in pilgrim's guise and barefoot, asking the people to accept him as the Servant of the Servants of God, rather than as the "Emperor's man." The people welcomed him with enthusiasm.

Now Leo was ready to proceed with the great work of reform. As his chief assistant and adviser he had Cardinal Hildebrand, later to be Pope Gregory VII, the dominant figure of the eleventh century. They traveled throughout Europe and held synods, reforming the local dioceses. The chief evils combatted by Leo and Hildebrand were *simony* (buying and selling of Church offices and other holy things) and the violation of the law of priestly celibacy.

Another problem faced by Leo was that the Normans (descendants of the Norsemen who had settled in France) were ravaging southern Italy. Leo tried to persuade the Holy Roman Emperor to come to the aid of the Italian coastal towns, but the Emperor refused. Leo then personally led a papal army and fought the Normans in the Battle of Civitella. Although Leo's army lost, the Norman leaders were so impressed by the Pope that they moderated their attacks.

A third major issue in Leo's reign was the controversy with the Patriarch of Constantinople. Patriarch Michael Cerularius attacked the Pope, declaring that the Church in Constantinople should receive equal honor with the Church of Rome and should not be subordinate to it. Leo sent two cardinals to Constantinople to mediate. Imprudently, the cardinals excommunicated Cerularius, whereupon he excommunicated Leo, taking the Greek Church into schism. This schism is known as the Greek Schism, and involved the Church in all that was formerly the Byzantine Empire, as well as the Church in Russia. The descendants of these schismatic churches are the Russian Orthodox Church and the Greek Orthodox Church of today. The key issue was obedience to the Pope. Because the Eastern Roman Empire still survived in reduced form, the patriarchs in the East tended to feel superior to the Church in the West. They did not wish to accept the authority of the Pope. Today, the Orthodox churches teach basically the same doctrines as the Catholic Church and have valid sacraments, but still do not accept the authority of the Holy Father. The date of the schism is 1054, the year that Leo died.

Church reforms continued under Leo's successors, Victor II, Stephen X, and Nicholas II, as did problems with the Holy Roman Emperors over papal election procedures. The Emperors continued to believe that they should have a deciding voice in the papal elections. Finally, Nicholas set up the College of Cardinals as the body which would elect the Pope, the same system as exists today. The Emperor challenged this system at the time of the election of the next Pope, Alexander II, but Alexander and Hildebrand held firm and won out.

During Alexander's reign, William Duke of Normandy, who had only a slight claim to the English throne, invaded England and fought Harold, who had no real claim at all, at the Battle of Hastings in 1066. Harold was killed and William took the throne in what is known as the Norman Conquest. Because William had substantial holdings in France in vassalage to the French king, the affairs of England and France would become intertwined. In addition, William established the Plantagenet dynasty in England, which provided many able rulers of England and, through marriage, to other countries of Europe.

Pope St. Gregory VII

Gregory VII, who reigned as Pope from 1073-1085, was born in Tuscany of a humble family. He was educated in a Cluny monastery and became a Benedictine. He came to Rome with Leo IX and played important roles under Leo's successors. He was the dominant figure in Rome for twenty years before his election. Gregory lived a virtuous, penitential life and was popular with the people.

Gregory knew that the work of reform must go on. He wrote: "I find everywhere bishops who have obtained their office in an irregular way, whose lives and conversations are strangely at variance with their sacred calling, who go through their duties not for the love of Christ but from motives of worldly gains." He continued to work against simony and clerical incontinency, issuing new decrees. These decrees were met by a storm, especially in Germany, where there were many married priests. The Archbishop of Rouen, while endeavoring to enforce the law of celibacy, was stoned and had to flee for his life. The Abbot of Pontoise was imprisoned and threatened with death. Gregory sent out legates empowered to depose all simoniacal and incontinent clergy. But he was at loggerheads with Emperor Henry IV, who was using the process of *investiture* to put his own men in office. During the Dark Ages many bishops had come to be large landholders. Thus as temporal lords they were under the authority of the king or Emperor and received from him (were invested by him) with the symbols of their temporal authority. Henry had expanded the investiture process to include the bestowal of symbols of spiritual authority as well. The controversy between Henry and Gregory is therefore known as the Investiture Controversy.

In response to Henry's refusal to cooperate, Gregory ordered Henry to Rome. Henry refused to come, instead holding a Diet (meeting) at Worms in January 1076. Henry ordered the bishops of Germany to declare the Pope deposed, threatening to take away their lands if they did not go along with him. Henry sent the declaration of deposition and an insulting personal letter to Gregory. Henry and the German bishops had refused to face the truth that no power on earth can possibly have authority over the Vicar of Christ, who holds the keys of the Kingdom of Heaven, given him directly by Christ.

Gregory had no intention of letting Henry get away with his high-handed action. Gregory issued a solemn proclamation that Henry and his ecclesiastical supporters were excommunicated and that Henry's subjects were absolved from their allegiance to him. Henry was furious, but the bishops abandoned him. Henry's Saxon subjects demanded a new king, and the German lords declared his crown as Emperor forfeited if he was not reconciled to the Pope within a year.

The Pope was spending the winter in Canossa in northern Italy. Secretly Henry traveled from Germany to Canossa, with only one servant, his wife, and his son, crossing the Alps in the depths of one of the severest winters on record. He arrived in January 1077. He took off his royal robes and dressed himself in sackcloth, a rough material worn as a sign of penance. He stood barefoot in the snow outside the castle gates. Some of Gregory's advisers may have warned him that Henry could not be trusted. But Gregory was above all a priest, and when a sinner comes to a priest, doing penance, asking to be forgiven, the priest must give him absolution. Gregory absolved Henry, revoked the excommunication and restored him to his throne.

Later, Henry once again turned on Gregory and in 1080 he was excommunicated again. For the rest of his life Gregory would be at odds with the willful German Emperor. In 1084 Henry forced his way into Rome and set up an anti-pope. But Robert Guiscard, Duke of Normandy, in alliance with the Pope, marched on the city and forced Henry and his army to flee. Unfortunately, the Normans' excesses caused Gregory to withdraw to Salerno, where he died, saying, "I have loved justice and hated iniquity; therefore I die in exile."

But in a larger sense Gregory had won the victory. He had shown that not even the Emperor could depose a Pope. He had shown that the Pope had spiritual authority over temporal rulers. After all, it was Henry who walked barefoot in the snow, not Gregory.

Gregory was followed by Blessed Victor III (1086-1087). He had been the abbot of Monte Cassino and didn't want to be Pope. In fact, the Holy See was vacant for a year before he could be prevailed upon to accept. Though he reigned only a short time, he sent an army in August 1087 to capture the town of El Mahadia under the banner of St. Peter, forcing the Moslem ruler of Tunis to promise tribute to the Holy See and to free all Christian slaves. Thus Victor was in a sense the first crusading Pope.

Pope Blessed Urban II and the First Crusade

Urban had been a Cluny monk and an assistant to Pope Gregory. For a time, he had been a prisoner of Henry IV. When Urban was elected, Rome was held by the imperial anti-pope. Urban spent the first three years of his reign in south Italy, but he held councils and improved ecclesiastical discipline. Finally the forces of Countess Matilda of Tuscany, who had supported Gregory against Henry all along, defeated Henry at Canossa. Urban entered Rome, but the anti-pope still held the strong places. Urban didn't sit on the Papal throne until six years after his election.

Urban's main achievement was convoking the Council of Clermont, November 1095, which called the First Crusade. The Byzantine Emperor, Alexius Commenus, had sent a desperate appeal to Urban for armed knights to defend Christianity against the Moslem enemy. When the Pope laid the Emperor's pleas before the knights in Clermont, the main concern of the noblemen there was not so much the defense of Byzantium as the rescue of the Holy Land from Moslem domination. Palestine had been under Moslem control since the days of the Caliph Omar, but at least the Arab Moslems had allowed Christian pilgrims to visit the places made sacred by the life of Christ. The Seljuk Turks, now the dominant Moslem power, had, on the other hand, closed off the Holy Land.

Thus the Pope concluded his speech to the council with these words: "Men of God, men chosen and blessed among all, combine your forces! Take the road to the Holy Sepulcher assured of the imperishable glory that awaits you in God's kingdom. Let each one deny himself and take the

Cross!" With a shout—"God wills it!"—the Assembly rose. They adopted a red cross as their emblem, and within a few hours no more red material remained in the town because the knights had cut it all up into crosses to be sewn on their sleeves. Because of their emblem (*crux* is the Latin word for cross) they were given the name Crusaders.

It is important to understand that the Crusades were a just war. The Church is frequently attacked on the question of the Crusades, sometimes on the grounds that the Christian nations of Europe were the aggressors and encouraged to be so by the Popes, sometimes on the grounds that this kind of war was inappropriate for Christians to fight, and sometimes on the grounds that immoral things happened on the Crusades. Each of these objections can be countered, showing that the Crusades were a just war.

First, the Christian nations of Europe were definitely not the aggressors. As we have seen in earlier chapters, the Moslems had been aggressors against the Christians since the seventh century. Their attacks on Christian countries were still going on in the eleventh century. In 1071 the Turks had attacked and virtually annihilated the Byzantine army at Manzikert. It was this defeat that led the Byzantine Emperor to appeal to the Pope for aid against the Moslems. The Christian countries of Europe were clearly justified in defending themselves against Moslem attacks and also in going on the offensive in order to prevent future attacks. At no point did the Crusaders attack the Moslem homeland, Arabia, but only those originally Christian territories that the Moslems had conquered.

Second, it certainly was and is appropriate for Christians to defend themselves and the innocent and helpless against attacks, which is exactly what the Crusaders were doing. It is also appropriate for Christians to try to regain lands which their enemy had conquered, as was the case with the Holy Land. The religious significance of the Holy Land makes it even better that Christians try to regain it, rather than worse, since Christians had every right to govern the lands where Christ had walked and to protect them from desecration.

Finally, there were certainly abuses during the Crusades, most notably the Sack of Jerusalem and the Sack of Constantinople, both of which are discussed below. But an immoral action during a war does not detract from the justice of the cause of the war. The immoral action should be condemned, as Godfrey de Bouillon condemned the Sack of Jerusalem and Simon de Montfort condemned the Sack of Constantinople, but the war itself remains just.

On to Jerusalem

In the summer of 1096 the various contingents of Crusaders began making their way to the Holy Land. There was no one overall leader. Henry IV, the Holy Roman Emperor, certainly could not be trusted with such a responsibility, nor was any other ruler in Europe in a position to assume leadership. So knights from the different areas followed their own overlords. The Pope appointed Bishop Adhemar as his personal representative, with the responsibility of keeping the lords working in as much harmony as possible to achieve their mission. As the Crusade progressed, the dominant figures would be Bohemond, leader of the Normans of Italy; Godfrey de Bouillon, leading the contingent from Lorraine and the Low Countries; and Raymond of Toulouse, with knights from southern France. The contingent under Raymond was the largest, and of all the leaders he was the one most committed to the crusading ideal: the restoration of Jerusalem to Christian control.

The lack of a unified command was only one of the reasons why, from a purely worldly standpoint, the Crusade seemed unlikely of success. The Crusaders would be fighting far from home, whereas the Moslems would be on familiar ground. The economy of Europe was just beginning to grow so that commerce and trade could flourish and surplus wealth be produced. The Moslems, on the other hand, were living off a long-standing economy. But these Moslem advantages paled beside the devotion and enthusiasm which motivated the majority of those who sewed the red crosses on their sleeves, leaving home and family to fight for Christ against His enemies.

The main Crusader contingents arrived in Constantinople by April 1097, and in June took nearby Nicea from the Moslems. A week later, they began marching east, through arid wastelands under a blistering sun. The local Moslem commander thought these foolish knights could be easily conquered, the more so as they had divided their forces into two columns. On July 1 he attacked at Dorylaeum.

Bohemond and his men bore the first onslaught. He exhorted his men to stand firm and sent messengers for help. The Normans held until Raymond's men arrived and then a contingent led by Bishop Adhemar. The Turks fled, having suffered five times as many casualties as the Christians.

On they went, through the midsummer heat, finally reaching fertile lands in August. After a rest they were on the march again, reaching the important city of Antioch in October. The siege of the city was long and difficult. Some of the less dedicated leaders weakened and returned home.

But Raymond, Godfrey and Bohemond held firm, inspiring their men, leading charges, resisting enemy attacks. Finally Bohemond, with the help of a traitor inside Antioch, broke into the city and opened the gates to the rest of the Crusading army. Antioch fell to the Christians, but they soon found themselves in turn besieged by a Moslem relief army. Conditions looked grim, but on June 28, Bohemond called forth the entire Christian army. After a final hand-to-hand struggle, the Moslem army was routed, and Antioch was secure.

The leaders let their army rest and recuperate until November 1. In August Bishop Adhemar died, leaving no successor. Without his steadying hand, the leaders quarreled among themselves. Bohemond considered that Antioch was his personal possession and seemed to have lost interest in Jerusalem. Raymond, whose commitment to the conquest of Jerusalem never wavered, insisted that they march on. Reports of their quarrel reached the men. The soldiers had no doubts as to what they wanted to do. They demanded that the army march to Jerusalem at once or they would tear down the walls of Antioch. The leaders promised to go, but there were more delays. Once more the men had to deliver an ultimatum.

Finally, on January 13, 1099 Raymond led the Crusaders on the final march to Jerusalem. They won a series of fairly easy victories and on June 7 arrived within sight of Jerusalem for the first time, viewing it from a mountain which pilgrims had long before named Mountjoy. Said one man writing at the time, "When they heard the name of Jerusalem, they could not restrain their tears. Falling upon their knees, they gave thanks to God for having enabled them to reach the goal of their pilgrimage, the Holy City where our Lord had chosen to save the world."

But the siege of Jerusalem was even more difficult than the siege of Antioch. The sun shone pitilessly and the wind from the desert drained moisture from the flesh. The Moslems had poisoned the wells near the city, and men would lick dew from the grass or dig into the ground to find moist earth. But then one of the priests with the Crusaders reported that he had seen a vision of Bishop Adhemar, who had asked that the army fast and then walk barefoot around the walls of Jerusalem begging God's help. If they would do so, victory would be theirs.

The men had loved Bishop Adhemar and they all responded to this request. The Crusaders had renewed confidence and courage, and on July 15 the final assault was launched. Godfrey led it, from a wooden siege tower, at one point even holding up a cracked beam with his own back. His men flung open the Gate of St. Stephen. Through it came the Normans and then the main force under Raymond. Jerusalem was taken.

As the men entered the city, all their pent-up frustration erupted. They went wild, looting the city and killing many innocent people. This behavior was totally against the promises these men had made at knighthood, and marred what would otherwise have been a splendid victory. Neither Godfrey nor Raymond, however, participated in or in any way approved of the Sack of Jerusalem.

The Crusaders now offered the crown of Jerusalem to Raymond. He refused it, declaring that he would not wear a crown of gold where his Savior had worn a crown of thorns. Godfrey was then offered the crown, and he too refused it with the same words. But he agreed to take responsibility for Jerusalem's defense, under the title Defender of the Holy Sepulcher. At last Christians could freely travel in the Holy Land and worship at the holy places.

Soon after the conquest of Jerusalem, a new religious community was organized, called the Knights of St. John, or the Hospitallers. The Knights of St. John took vows to dedicate their lives to God as did the monks in Europe. They also had a charitable purpose—care of the sick (hence the name Hospitallers)—as did some monks in Europe. But besides all this, the Knights regarded themselves as a military organization, which would fight whenever necessary in the service of the Church or to protect the innocent. They were, for example, entrusted with the protection of the Holy Sepulcher. The Knights provided the Latin kingdom of Jerusalem with a permanent army which represented the best of the spirit of the Crusades.

St. Bernard and the Second Crusade

Pope Paschal II (1099-1118) followed Urban and encouraged the crusading spirit. He had investiture troubles with Henry IV's son, Henry V. The next Pope, Gelasius II (1118-1119), had a dramatic confrontation with Henry. When news spread of Gelasius' election without the Emperor's consultation, imperialists seized Gelasius, cast him to the ground, stomped on him, dragged him by the hair, and threw him chained into a dungeon. The Roman people were incensed. They freed Gelasius so that he could be crowned. Angry, Henry marched into Rome, forcing Gelasius to flee down the Tiber, pelted by stones and arrows. He fled to France, where he remained during the rest of his short pontificate. His successor, Calixtus II (1119-1124), was on good terms with the Emperor and worked out a solution to the investiture controversy. Henceforth, the Emperor would invest the bishop or abbot with the symbols of his temporal authority only, while the Pope's representative would invest him with the symbols of his spiritual authority.

But the dominant figure in the twelfth century was St. Bernard of Clairvaux (1090-1153). Born into a noble family of Burgundy, he was devoted in his youth to the Scriptures and to the Blessed Mother. He triumphed over severe temptations and knew he had a religious vocation.

In 1098, St. Robert, Abbot of Molesmes, had founded a new, reformed monastery at Citeaux, where he restored the full Rule of St. Benedict. The regimen was severe and attracted few, Citeaux remaining small and obscure. But in 1113, Bernard determined to enter at Citeaux and brought with him thirty young Burgundians, including his uncle and brothers. Bernard's family was at first horrified, since Citeaux had no prestige and no wealth. But Bernard persevered, choosing Citeaux because he knew that his passionate nature needed strong medicine. Three years after joining, Bernard was chosen by the new abbot, St. Stephen Harding, to head a band of twelve monks in the foundation of a daughter house at Clairvaux. The beginnings were trying and painful, as the monks at Clairvaux lacked nearly everything. So austere was their life that Bernard's health was impaired. But he attracted many disciples, and soon new daughter foundations were established. The new order, now known as Cistercians (after Citeaux), had established a reputation as one of the holiest of orders. Some of the old Cluny foundations that had become lax were critical of Bernard, but his spirited defense of his order resulted in the Cluny foundations' reform.

Bernard would have preferred to devote his life to prayer and penance but the Church needed his services. Besides assisting in the reforms of older orders, he traced the outlines of the Rule of the Knights Templars, who soon became the ideal of the French nobility; he defended Innocent II against incursions of the Emperor; he made peace in France and Italy, reconciling obstinate rulers to the Church. Finally he received permission to retire to the cloister in 1135, where he devoted his time to composing the doctrinal works which resulted in his later being named a Doctor of the Church. His special devotion was to the Blessed Mother, and he wrote the beautiful and popular prayer, the Memorare.

In 1145, Eugenius III, a monk from one of Bernard's monasteries, was elected Pope. On his election, Bernard sent an instruction: reform of the Church must begin with sanctity of the Pope; prayer must precede action; temporal matters are only accessories to the spiritual. Eugenius took the advice to heart, continuing to wear his coarse Cistercian habit underneath his Papal robes and leading a life of sanctity. (He was later declared Blessed.)

Soon after his election, Eugenius received word that Jerusalem and Antioch were threatened anew by the Turks. He commissioned Bernard to preach the Second Crusade. King Louis VII of France and his wife Eleanor of Aquitaine (who had substantial land holdings of her own in southern France) prostrated themselves at the feet of Bernard in Vezelay in 1134, pledging themselves and their vassals to go on the crusade. Bernard went on to Germany where the Holy Roman Emperor Conrad and his nephew Frederick Barbarossa received the cross from Bernard.

The Crusade, though inspired by a saint, had problems from the beginning. Though Eleanor's knights swelled the total, she caused more problems than she solved. She insisted on coming along, with her ladies-in-waiting and all their baggage. Furthermore, when the crusade reached the Holy Land, Eleanor began intriguing with her uncle, the Prince of Antioch, against Louis, as dissension split the crusading forces. The German troops were undisciplined and overconfident. And the Christian nobles of Syria betrayed the crusaders, preventing the capture of Damascus. The French and German crusaders accomplished nothing, and a permanent breach developed between Louis and Eleanor, so that when they returned home, he succeeded in having his marriage to her declared invalid.

Meanwhile, however, one good result came from the Second Crusade. A group of English knights had taken the cross. On their way to the Holy Land, they stopped off in Portugal and freed Lisbon from the Moslems.

St. Thomas Becket

Thomas Becket was born December 21, 1118, the son of a Londoner. He was well educated, studying for a time in Paris. In 1142 he was taken into Archbishop Theobald's household, gradually becoming Theobald's most trusted adviser. He met many great men and developed skills as a diplomat and a speechwriter. He was ordained a deacon. William the Conqueror had enforced a good deal of state control over the Church in England, and Thomas moved back and forth between the political and ecclesiastical worlds.

Thomas became close friends with the heir to the throne, who was crowned King Henry II in 1154, though he did not get along as well with Henry's wife, who was none other than Eleanor of Aquitaine, who had married the English prince after the annulment of her marriage to Louis. Henry appointed Thomas Lord High Chancellor, the highest office in

England next to the king himself, and the two were practically inseparable. Because of his high position, Thomas had a household of 700 knights, and he once personally led them in battle in France.

In 1162 the Archbishop of Canterbury died. Henry pressed Thomas to take the appointment as new archbishop. Thomas had serious doubts. Though he was quite worldly, he also had a sensitive conscience. He knew that the close ties between Church and state in England could lead to serious problems, and he did not wish to come into conflict with his close friend. Finally he agreed, providing he could resign as Chancellor. He was ordained June 2 and consecrated archbishop on June 10.

Almost immediately a change came over Thomas as the graces of the office had a profound effect on him. He became less worldly, more prayerful. He wore a hair shirt and used the discipline (a small whip). He would say that he had been transformed from "a patron of actors and a follower of hounds to a shepherd of souls." Before dawn each morning he would call thirteen poor men into his private rooms. Thomas would personally wash their feet and serve breakfast to them, giving each four silver coins. He doubled the amount of alms his predecessor had given to the poor, using money he had formerly spent on luxuries.

Thomas's new moral concerns led him inevitably to a clash with Henry. Their first quarrel arose over a financial matter. Henry decided to keep for himself a tax formerly collected by sheriffs. Thomas opposed the move, arguing that it was a mistake to deprive the men on whom Henry depended for honest and efficient government of an important source of income: it would encourage them to get more money unjustly. Thomas ordered his bishops to refuse to pay this tax on Church lands to Henry. Henry then retaliated by abolishing the privilege of ecclesiastical courts to try all clerics of any crime, but Thomas would not back down. Henry, who was never known for his even temper, was furious. He seized Thomas's land and castles and removed his young son from Thomas's tutelage. At a meeting with Thomas, the king accused the archbishop of ingratitude. Thomas assured Henry that his friendship was still strong, but that "we must obey God rather than men." Others tried to persuade Thomas to give in; after all, the issue was not a major point. But Thomas knew that the controversy was larger than the single point of which courts should try clerics accused of secular crimes. He knew that the issue was the same that Gregory VII had confronted with Henry IV: would the Church be able to exercise its moral authority over secular rulers, or would the government come to control the Church?

The two men met again at Clarendon. Henry presented Thomas with decrees which would have taken away many of the Church's rights. Thomas refused to sign them, but Henry proceeded to enforce them anyway.

Finally in 1164 Henry had Thomas brought to trial. He rigged the court so that Thomas was found guilty of treason. When the verdict was announced, Thomas simply stalked out of the courtroom. No one dared lay a hand on him, because the common people were totally on his side. Henry soon sent troops after Thomas, but the archbishop escaped on a stormy night. On November 2, he sailed to Flanders in a small boat over a rough sea, taking refuge in a Cistercian monastery.

Again Henry retaliated, sending everyone associated with Thomas, including their families, into exile and seizing their possessions. He also threatened the Cistercians with the seizure of their lands in England if they continued to harbor Thomas. The abbot urged Thomas to stay, but Thomas did not want to jeopardize the whole order. He went on to the Benedictine Abbey of Sens, which was under the protection of King Louis VIII, who cared for Henry about as little as he cared for Henry's queen. A friend said to Thomas: "As for the king, he seems to want nothing but your head on a platter."

Finally, in 1169 the king was in France to meet with Louis. Thomas threw himself at Henry's feet, so moving Henry that he raised him and embraced him. Thomas said: "I throw myself on your mercy and your pleasure, *saving the honor of God.*" At this last phrase, Henry exploded, accusing Thomas of pride, vanity, ingratitude, and ambition. Henry left, unreconciled.

Pope Alexander III then entered the controversy, threatening England with an interdict if Henry did not permit Thomas to return home. In a country under interdict, all public worship is forbidden. Henry knew that the people would be furious with him if the Pope issued an interdict. Furthermore, conditions in England were deteriorating as Henry's high-handed policies alienated the people. Henry went to Thomas and gave him the Kiss of Peace, permitting him to return home. Thomas arrived back in England on December 1, 1170. He returned to find that justice had declined in his absence, with the royal officials hostile and insulting.

Meanwhile three of Thomas' enemies went to Henry, who was still in France. They told him that crowds were cheering Thomas, and that the archbishop was forming a party against Henry. One of them, Roger of York, said to Henry: "I assure you, my lord, while Thomas lives you will have no good days, nor quiet times, nor a tranquil kingdom." Henry's temper again got the best of him: "The man ate my bread and mocks my favors. He tramples on the whole royal family. What disloyal cowards do I have in my court that not one will free me of this lowborn priest?" Henry probably did not mean his words to be taken literally, but the barons were looking for just such an excuse to kill Thomas. They immediately returned to England, arriving on December 28.

Thomas, meanwhile, was in his cathedral at Canterbury. On the evening of December 29, he was officiating at vespers at the high altar. The armed knights arrived in Canterbury, pretending to be on Henry's orders to arrest Thomas. They entered the cathedral, violating the rule that no weapons could be brought into the sacred premises. Thomas made no attempt to defend himself. He was brutally struck down before the altar.

Almost immediately Canterbury cathedral became a pilgrimage site. Upon hearing of Thomas's death, Henry grieved, repenting of his impetuosity. His repentance led to a real reform, as he restored to the Church every right for which Becket had fought. Once again, as with Gregory and Henry IV, a tyrannical monarch had been checked by a spiritual authority who stood up for the rights of Christ and His Church.

Baldwin, the Leper King

Though Raymond of Toulouse had refused to wear a crown of gold, Christian kingdoms were soon set up by other noblemen throughout the Holy Land. Unfortunately, many of these noblemen were more interested in power and wealth for themselves than in defending Christendom. But in 1161 was born an heir to the crown of Jerusalem who would set a shining example of Christian heroism: Baldwin IV, the King of Jerusalem, known as Baldwin, the Leper King. According to a chronicle of the time: "One day when Baldwin was playing with the sons of the nobles of Jerusalem, it was discovered that his limbs had no feeling. The other little children shouted when they were wounded; Baldwin, however, didn't say a single word. This happened many times, so much so that the Archdeacon William became alarmed. . . . Then, addressing him, he asked him why he suffered those wounds without complaining. The little one responded that the children were not wounding him and that he didn't feel anything of their scratches. Then, the teacher examined his arm and his hands and verified that they were asleep. It was the evident sign of leprosy." From then on, "all of his life was nothing more than a struggle against the irreversible evil. And, more yet, much more, it was a testimony to the powers of a man over himself and of the amazing incarnation of his highest obligations."

In 1174, Saladin, the Turkish Sultan of Damascus, besieged the Catholic city of Aleppo. Baldwin, though only 13 and already suffering from his disease, counterattacked at Damascus and forced Saladin to raise the siege. In 1176 Saladin attacked again. Once more, Baldwin counterattacked at Damascus and Andujar and drove off the Moslem assault. In all the battles, Baldwin rode in the forefront, never using his illness as an excuse for removing himself from the post of greatest danger.

In 1177 Saladin invaded South Syria, intending to besiege Ascalon. Baldwin immediately marched on the beleaguered city with his army of only 500 men, all he had time to assemble. He arrived in Ascalon just before the besieging army invested the city. Saladin quickly concluded that Jerusalem had been left undefended. Since he had a huge army, he decided he could safely split it, leaving a portion at Ascalon and taking the rest to Jerusalem, planning to reconquer the city. It seemed that Jerusalem would fall, and with the city, the Christian kingdom. But Baldwin was equal to the challenge. He managed to send a message summoning the Knights Templars from Gaza. While they attacked the besieging army in the rear, Baldwin and his men broke out from Ascalon. Then Baldwin, the Templars, and a few additional barons rode hard after Saladin. They overtook the Egyptians near the castle of Montgisard outside Ramleh. The Christians were outnumbered and the men frightened. Baldwin prostrated himself before the wood of the True Cross which was carried by the Bishop of Bethlehem, begging God to aid him in battle. Then he held his men back until the Egyptians were just crossing a steep ravine. Baldwin ordered the charge while the Egyptians were disorganized. A vision of St. George was seen in the sky as the Christian army attacked. The Egyptians fled in panic. Saladin himself would have been captured if his bodyguard had not sacrificed themselves to delay his pursuers. The Battle of Ramleh was a brilliant tactical maneuver, showing Baldwin to be one of the finest cavalry commanders of all the crusading era.

In 1181 Saladin again marched on the Holy Land, invading by way of the south shore of the Sea of Galilee. Near the castle of Belvoir he met the army of Jerusalem and was forced to retreat. Then Saladin rushed toward Beirut, hoping to find it ungarrisoned. But King Baldwin hurried to the relief of the city, and once more the Moslems retreated.

Saladin spent the next year warring against Moslem rivals. Then in 1183 he assembled a large army and again turned toward Jerusalem. He besieged the Castle of Kerak while the nobles of the Kingdom were assembled for a great marriage feast. Baldwin marched the army of Jerusalem to the relief of the castle, though he himself was so ill that he had to be carried in a litter. Saladin was forced once again to retreat.

Finally Saladin himself fell ill, and Baldwin was able to spend the last two years of his life in peace. He died a holy death on March 16, 1185, an example of the best of the crusading spirit.

Richard the Lion-Heart and the Third Crusade

After the death of Baldwin, Saladin again threatened the Holy Land, re-occupying Jerusalem in 1187. By the end of 1187, only Tyre, Tripoli and Antioch were left in Christian hands. But a new Christian hero appeared in Europe to lead the Christian forces: Richard of England, known as Richard the Lion-Heart.

Richard was born in 1157, the son of King Henry II of England and Eleanor of Aquitaine, thereby receiving a heritage of stubbornness and strong will. In 1189 Henry died and Richard was crowned king of England.

Immediately he began preparing for the crusade to win back Jerusalem. On the way to the Holy Land, the ship carrying Richard's fiancee and his sister was captured by the Moslems on Cyprus. Richard attacked and easily conquered Cyprus, which became an important base for the Crusaders.

On June 8, 1191, Richard joined the Christian army which was besieging Acre. Richard's ships and siege machines (including a movable tower higher than the city walls) contributed to the fall of Acre on July 12, which led to the release of 1500 Christian prisoners in Saladin's custody.

Richard decided to march to Jaffa along the coast, then strike inland for Jerusalem. He marched with the sea on his right and infantry on the left to fight off the constant Turkish cavalry attacks. Saladin marched parallel to Richard, sending skirmishers to break the Christian ranks. Richard gave strict orders to keep ranks closed. The men struggled on through the intense heat. Finally, Saladin decided to launch a major attack on September 7 at Arsuf. Richard held his men in tight discipline to wear down the Turkish cavalry. The brunt of the attack was borne by the Knights of St. John in the rear. Finally the Knights broke ranks and charged, and it appeared as if the Turks would win in the confusion. But Richard personally led a series of charges with his Norman and English reserves, snatching victory out of defeat. His bravery in hand-to-hand combat inspired all present.

Richard entered Jaffa on September 10, but his forces were not strong enough to mount an attack on Jerusalem. He spent the next several months winning a series of minor battles and receiving reports that his brother John was making trouble in England. The closest he came to Jerusalem was in June 1192, when he climbed Montjoy for a view of the Holy City.

Richard then marched north toward Beirut. Saladin took advantage of his absence to re-take Jaffa. Richard rushed back, arriving late at night on July 31. On August 4, he fought the Battle of Jaffa. Richard found himself facing Saladin's seven thousand cavalrymen with just 54 knights, 15 horses, and two thousand foot soldiers. For more than half the day his infantrymen fought off the charging horsemen. By mid-afternoon, Richard was actually able to lead an offensive attack. Saladin was so impressed with Richard's bravery that when he saw Richard fall as his horse was killed under him, he sent a groom leading two fresh horses as a present from one king to another.

By evening, the Turks were in retreat, withdrawing to Jerusalem, which was strongly fortified. Richard became ill; both sides were eager for a truce. Saladin and Richard agreed to a three-year truce on September 2, giving pilgrims the right to visit Jerusalem in safety and leaving everything from Tyre to the Jaffa coast in Christian hands. On October 9 Richard set sail for home.

Richard's troubles still weren't over, as he was captured by forces of the Holy Roman Emperor and held for ransom. He was not released until February 4, 1194. When he at last returned home to England, he easily restored his authority there, then turned to France where nobles were rebelling. In March 1199 Richard was besieging Chalus-Chabrol, a vassal who had rebelled against him. The siege was going well, and on the evening of March 26, Richard rode out to observe the progress. He was hit in the left shoulder by a crossbowman. Gangrene set in, and he died April 7, forgiving the man who had killed him and receiving the Last Rites of the Church.

Innocent III and the Fourth Crusade

Innocent III reigned as Pope from 1198-1216. He immediately re-established papal authority in Rome and extended political power over the peninsula. When Henry VI's widow Constance was dying, she appointed Innocent as guardian of four-year-old Frederick II, heir to the crown of Holy Roman Emperor. Eventually Frederick II was elected Emperor (1211), but he would cause much trouble for Innocent's successors.

Innocent came into conflict with King John of England, the youngest son of Henry II and Eleanor of Aquitaine. Whereas Richard the Lionheart had seemed to inherit all the good qualities of his parents, John seemed to inherit all the bad. His high-handed rule included seizing Church property and treating the clergy with cruelty. Innocent placed an interdict on England which forced John to submit. Shortly afterwards the barons and bishops united in revolt against King John, forcing him to surrender to their demands at Runnymede in 1215, where he agreed to sign the *Magna Carta* (Great Charter), guaranteeing the rights of the noblemen against the king.

Innocent fully realized his responsibilities as the highest authority in Christendom. He prepared a crusade against the Moors in Spain which led to the Battle of Las Navas de Tolosa (see chapter 16); protected the people of Norway against a tyrannical king; mediated between the king of Hungary and his rebel brother; sent the royal crown to the king of Bulgaria; arbitrated the crown of Sweden; restored ecclesiastical discipline in Poland.

Early in his reign, Innocent called for still another crusade, the fourth. This was to lead to the worst moment of the Crusades. Genuine religious enthusiasm was dying down; the knights of Europe were tiring of this seemingly endless war against the Moslems. Nevertheless, a crusade was organized. But when the Crusaders reached Constantinople, they had no money to pay the Venetians for ships to take them to the Holy Land, and they were stranded there.

Then the leaders of the crusade received a visitor, a young man named Alexius, whose uncle had forcibly removed his father from the throne, then blinded and imprisoned him. Alexius had escaped, and now promised the Crusaders that he would pay the Venetians for their ships if they would help him gain the throne. Alexius also promised to reunite the Greek Orthodox Church with the Pope if he was successful. The Crusaders were further tempted by the great wealth which had accumulated in Constantinople in the many years it had remained unconquered.

The Crusaders succeeded in overthrowing Alexius' uncle, but then the new emperor had no money with which to keep his promises. So on April 13, 1204, with the help of a fire and of a traitor who opened the gates for them, the Crusaders broke into the city. For three days they looted, burned and killed. They even broke into some of the city's beautiful churches, destroying art work and committing acts of sacrilege (the destruction or insulting of holy things). In the chaos, the Holy Shroud disappeared from Constantinople. The sack of Constantinople produced such justifiable resentment in the minds of the Byzantines that any hope for re-union of the Greek Orthodox Church with Rome was destroyed.

One Christian knight refused to take any part in the Sack of Constantinople: Simon de Montfort, who returned to France to war on the Albigensians (see below). After the sack, Innocent excommunicated those responsible for the outrage.

The Albigensians and St. Dominic

The Albigensian heresy was a particularly powerful attack on Catholic life in the High Middle Ages. The Albigensians taught that there were two principles of existence in the universe. The evil principle created all material things and natural phenomena; the good principle created all spiritual things. The evil principle was responsible for all moral evil because matter caused sin. The evil principle imprisoned souls in the body after deceiving them into leaving the kingdom of light. Earth was a place of punishment; there was no hell. Since the body was evil and the soul imprisoned, suicide was commendable. For the same reasons, procreation and childbearing were to be avoided. There was no Resurrection of Jesus nor any resurrection of the body for human beings.

Two groups of people were attracted to this heresy. One group were those who thought themselves better than anyone else. They were known as the *perfecti* and lived a highly ascetic life. The others were attracted by the Albigensian teaching that sins of the flesh were not really sins since we were imprisoned in our bodies. These people used this teaching as a license to sin freely.

Large groups of people joined this movement, especially in southern France. The Albigensians came to control several towns and used force against those who would not accept their teaching. They had become a threat not just to Catholic doctrine but to the whole social order.

Simon de Montfort fought the Albigensians with his sword. The key battle was the Battle of Muret in 1213. Simon de Montfort, outnumbered forty to one, spent the night before the battle in prayer. His opposing general, Pedro of Aragon, spent the night carousing. The Catholic forces won an impressive victory and checked the political power of the Albigensians.

But those who had fallen into this heresy still had to be won back, a work which could not be entrusted to the sword. Instead it was entrusted to one of the greatest saints of the High Middle Ages, St. Dominic (1170-1221).

St. Dominic was born into the noble Spanish family of Guzman. Both his mother and his brother Manes have been beatified. He became a priest and lived quietly until he was 30, though charitably and austerely. King Alfonso IX of Spain wished his son Ferdinand to marry the daughter of a Scandinavian prince. Dominic was included in the delegation which was sent to ask for her hand. On the way, the group passed through southern France and stopped at Toulouse, where most of the principal men of the city were Albigensians. Dominic spent the night at an inn, arguing with the heretic innkeeper until dawn. By morning, the innkeeper was on his knees asking forgiveness. Dominic then went on his way to Scandinavia, but he had received his first exposure to what would be an important part of his life's work.

Later, Dominic was again in a delegation going to fetch the bride-to-be. But before they reached Scandinavia, they received word that the princess had died. So Dominic's bishop decided to detour to Rome and take Dominic along. There they met Innocent III and learned of the failures of previous missions to make headway against the Albigensians. The main reason seemed to be that the Catholic representatives had lived a luxurious life style which scandalized the austere Albigensians. In addition, the missionaries had not been well enough educated to counteract the heretic arguments.

With the blessing of Pope Innocent, Dominic determined to engage in spiritual combat with the Albigensians. First Dominic established an order of nuns, to counteract the influence of the heretics on women; later he established his Order of Preachers, more popularly known as Dominicans. He emphasized three things: asceticism (detachment from material things), learning, and devotion to the Blessed Mother. His friars carried their rosaries at their hips, like a sword. Soon he was reconverting heretics all over France. In addition, he was a close friend of Simon de Montfort, and Dominican prayers aided De Montfort's battles. In 1233 the Dominicans were put in charge of the Inquisition, a court used to try heretics. The Dominicans were chosen as judges because they were the most educated men in the Church. Later Dominic established his Third Order Dominicans for laypeople.

Dominic's methods were successful, and the Albigensian threat ended. His Dominicans remained one of the most important religious orders in the Church.

St. Francis of Assisi

One of the most popular of all the saints exemplifies the total and joyful dedication to God that is a chief characteristic of the High Middle Ages. St. Francis of Assisi was born in 1181 or 1182, his father a wealthy merchant in Assisi. Francis was not particularly studious, nor did he have an inclination to follow in his father's footsteps. He was pleasure-loving and sought glory on the battlefield in the many small wars that afflicted Italy at the time. But capture in battle, illnesses, and several strange dreams combined to turn his thoughts to more serious matters.

While praying before a crucifix, he heard a voice saying, "Go, Francis, and repair my house, which as you see is falling into ruin." Taking the words literally, he sold some of his father's cloth goods to buy building material to repair the ruined church of St. Damian. His father was furious, and Francis was forced to hide to avoid his wrath. Later, taken before the bishop by his father, Francis renounced his inheritance and even stripped off his clothes so that he would have no further association with his past life of luxury. He dressed in a beggar's brown robe tied with a cord, ever after the habit of the Franciscan order.

He proceeded to live a life of prayer, penance, poverty and service to others, especially the lepers. Though many regarded him as half-mad, others were drawn to him by his holiness. Gradually he attracted followers and formed them into the community which eventually became the Friars Minor (Little Brothers), popularly known as the Franciscans. Pope Innocent III approved his order and its rule.

During the Lent of 1212, Francis was sought out by the wealthy young heiress, Clare, who asked that she be allowed to embrace the same rule of poverty and penance as the Friars. Her parents strongly objected, and she had to sneak out of the house on the night following Palm Sunday. Francis received her submission by torchlight, then lodged her with Benedictine nuns. Other women soon joined her, and she eventually founded the Second Franciscan Order of Poor Ladies, now known as Poor Clares.

Francis preached throughout Italy, bringing souls back to Christ and truly repairing Christ's spiritual house. He also established a Third Order, in which those who remain in the world could live according to the Franciscan spirit.

In 1219 Francis achieved a long-cherished dream, journeying to North Africa with the intention of converting the Moslems or receiving the crown of martyrdom in the attempt. He was taken prisoner and actually had an audience with the sultan, who reportedly told him: "If all Christians were like you, I would indeed become a Christian." Francis achieved neither of his goals, but his Franciscans have ever since been the guardians of the Holy Places in the Holy Land.

During Christmastime of 1223, Francis reproduced in a church at Greccio the stable and manger of Bethlehem, and he is thus regarded as the founder of the custom of the Christmas crib or nativity scene. It is said that when he placed the figure of the Christ Child in the manger, the Holy Babe came alive in his arms.

In early August 1224 he retired to the mountain of Alverno so that he could meditate on the Passion of Christ, a devotion to which he was increasingly drawn. On or about the feast of the Triumph of the Cross (September 14), he saw a vision of a flaming seraphim in the sky. From the vision came beams of light, imprinting on his hands, feet and sides the five wounds of Christ, the holy stigmata. With the stigmata came great pain, as Francis was granted spiritually the martyrdom he had desired but not received physically.

Increasingly ill and almost blind, he paid a last visit to St. Clare and composed his "Canticle of the Creatures," in which he praised all that God had created. He continued preaching almost up to his death. But at last he had to be carried to the little Portiuncula chapel, the original home of his Friars Minor. He asked to be laid on the ground, and he was carried away by his "Sister Death," in whose honor he had just added a verse to the "Canticle of the Creatures." He died on October 3, 1226.

St. Francis of Assisi is a worthy patron for all those who seek to imitate the total consecration to Christ which is the hallmark of the High Middle Ages.

Review Questions

1. Where did the term "Middle Ages" originate? Why is it inaccurate?
2. Summarize the accomplishments of Pope Leo IX. Why did the Byzantine Church go into schism?
3. Why did Gregory and Henry come into conflict? What were the results of the conflict? How do the results of the conflict show the supremacy of the spiritual authority of the Church over the temporal authority of the emperor?
4. Why did Pope Urban call the First Crusade? Why were the Crusades a just war?
5. Summarize the accomplishments of the First Crusade. What was the Sack of Jerusalem? How did Godfrey come to rule Jerusalem?
6. Summarize the accomplishments of St. Bernard.

7. What happened on the Second Crusade? What was the only good result?
8. Why did Henry and Thomas Becket come into conflict? What were the main events of the controversy?
9. How did Thomas come to be martyred? What happened to Henry as a result?
10. Summarize the accomplishments of Baldwin the Leper King.
11. What was the background of Richard the Lion-Heart? What happened on the Third Crusade?
12. How did King John of England try to become tyrannical? How was he prevented from carrying out his plans?
13. What happened on the Fourth Crusade?
14. What did the Albigensians believe? How did Simon de Montfort combat them?
15. Summarize the accomplishments of St. Dominic.
16. Give specific examples from his life to show how St. Francis of Assisi exemplifies the High Middle Ages.

Projects

1. Prepare a detailed report on the Magna Carta.
2. Act out the confrontation between Henry II and Thomas Becket or between Gregory VII and Henry IV.
3. Prepare a map of the Holy Land, marking locations of events discussed in this chapter.
4. Write an account of one of the Crusades as if you were a participant.
5. Report on other incidents from the life of St. Francis of Assisi.

Chapter Fifteen
The Greatest of Centuries

THE THIRTEENTH CENTURY has been referred to as "the greatest of centuries." It was the summit of the High Middle Ages, the time of the glory of Christendom. Perhaps the greatest Catholic king of this greatest Catholic century was King St. Louis IX of France.

St. Louis

Born in 1215, Louis became king at only eleven years of age, when his father, Louis VIII, died. His Spanish mother, Queen Blanche of Castile, served as his regent until 1234, ruling well and instructing Louis in the duties and responsibilities of a Catholic monarch. She received the final submission of the rebellious Albigensian provinces, which were united to France in 1229.

Louis came to the throne in his own right when he was nineteen, the same year that he married Margaret of Provence, who eventually bore him eleven children. Margaret and Louis were deeply in love, and she was one of his most trusted advisers.

Louis consecrated his whole life to the glory of God and to the good of his people and of the Church. He took seriously his mother's words, "I would rather see you dead at my feet than guilty of a mortal sin." He spent long hours in prayer and penance, fed daily over one hundred poor, founded hospitals, and ministered to the lepers. He insisted on justice for all his people, poor as well as rich. He set up the *curia regis* (court of the king) and judicial commissions called *parlements* which provided local government for the people. He would travel through France, hearing grievances and administering justice. Perhaps the most famous case involved the lord of Courcy, who had killed three boys for trespassing on his property. King Louis ordered Courcy to appear before him, and when he refused had him imprisoned. The other barons objected, saying that it was none of the king's business. But Louis persisted, found Courcy guilty, and punished him severely.

In sharp contrast to Louis was the Holy Roman Emperor Frederick II (1194-1250). Elected Emperor in 1211, Frederick at first pretended to be loyal to the Pope and eager to fulfill his duties to the Church. But in reality Frederick was an exceedingly ambitious man who had rejected the Catholic faith. He regarded Italy as the heart of his empire and wanted the papal lands for his own. He was attracted by Islam and traveled with a harem and a collection of exotic animals. He despised Christian doctrine, and it is said that once he sealed a man in a barrel to kill him, in order to prove that when the barrel was opened no soul would fly up to heaven. He called himself *Divus Augustus* (Divine Emperor), *Sol Invictus* (Invincible Sun), *Stupor Mundi* (Wonder of the World). He spread violence and destruction wherever he went.

Finally in 1239 he was excommunicated by Pope Gregory IX because he had proclaimed himself supreme over the Pope. In retaliation he hanged all blood relatives of the Pope and destroyed villages loyal to the Pope. Then he marched on Rome. Gregory led a procession with relics of Sts. Peter and Paul, saying that the defense of Rome was in their hands. The people rallied around Gregory. Frederick decided that it would be wiser not to attack.

After Gregory died in 1241 there was a vacancy in the papacy for two years except for the two-weeks reign of the elderly and infirm Celestine IV. Finally Innocent IV was elected in June 1243. Innocent repeated the condemnation of Frederick, whereupon he planned to capture the Pope at the Council of Lyons in 1247. But Lyons was in France, and Louis would never permit such a crime on his territory. He prepared to defend the Pope, and Frederick was once again forced to withdraw.

With the Pope safe, Louis looked abroad and saw his duties as a Christian king toward the Holy Places in the Holy Land, since the Moslems had now won back nearly all the territory they had lost in the First Crusade. On August 25, 1247, the royal fleet of 38 vessels sailed toward the Middle East. St. Louis decided to attack Egypt first. His knights fought bravely, but the Moslem forces gradually wore them down. Finally Louis himself became very ill as did many members of his army. He decided to negotiate peace terms. But the Moslems put out a rumor that the king was a prisoner and that the only hope of saving his life was for every man to lay down his weapons. His followers loved Louis so much that they at once surrendered. The Moslems proceeded to kill all the sick. St. Louis was put in chains while lying helpless on his bed. To reduce the number of able-bodied prisoners, the sultan ordered 300 of them to be killed every day.

Finally Louis was able to negotiate a treaty. He would give the Moslems the town of Damietta, which he had conquered, and pay a ransom, so that his men could go free. In order for this bargain to work, the Christians had to hold the town of Damietta until the peace treaty was concluded. If the Moslems took it ahead of time, Louis would have nothing to trade. Since Louis was imprisoned, Queen Margaret organized the defense of Damietta. She rallied the knights and courageously directed the army, even though she gave birth to a baby during this time, a boy whom she named Tristan, which means Child of Sorrow.

At last the treaty was signed, the Moslems took Damietta, and Louis and his men were freed. Louis remained in the Holy Land four years, using diplomacy to keep the Moslems at bay. At the news of the death of his mother, who had been acting as regent, Louis returned to France.

Even while he was in the Holy Land, Louis had continued to support the Pope against the Emperor. He returned to the news that Frederick's Italian cities had revolted against him. The Emperor's power had gradually slipped away, until he died of illness on December 13, 1250, in the camp of his Moslem soldiers.

But Louis could think only of the crusade. In March of 1267, he and his three sons took the cross, resolving to land at Tunis in North Africa. The crusaders landed on July 17, 1270, but the plague broke out in their camp. On August 25, Louis succumbed to the disease. He received the Last Sacraments, repeating the verses of the psalms as the priest recited them. In his sufferings, he prayed to St. Denis and St. Genevieve, patrons of his country. Then he asked to be laid on a bed of ashes on the ground, where, with his hands folded peacefully upon his breast, he died. He never saw the earthly Jerusalem, the goal of so many of his efforts, but he entered gloriously into the heavenly Jerusalem, which he had always served.

St. Thomas Aquinas

The greatest intellectual genius of the Middle Ages and perhaps of all time was born in 1226, one of eight sons of the Aquinos, a wealthy and powerful Italian family. Thomas' brothers fought on the side of Emperor

Frederick II; when one of them went over to the Pope, he was caught and executed. The dominant figure in the family was Thomas' mother, who had great ambitions for her sons. It soon became obvious that Thomas was the quiet one of the family, more interested in thinking than in fighting. (His favorite question as a small child was "What is God?") So his parents sent him at the age of five to the great abbey of Monte Cassino, with the understanding that when he was old enough he would become abbot, a suitable office for a son of the Aquinos.

But when Frederick II attacked Monte Cassino (for the second time), the monastery had to be evacuated, and Thomas, now 15, was sent off to the University of Naples to study liberal arts. Thomas always loved to study, but he found that he loved even more the Dominican monastery nearby. The devotion of St. Dominic's friars made a profound impression on young Thomas, and he determined that he didn't want to be abbot of Monte Cassino or anywhere else. He wanted to be a Beggar, as the Dominicans were contemptuously called by those who did not think their poverty and penance were quite respectable.

If his family had been willing to see one of their sons an abbot instead of a general, they were certainly not willing to see him a beggar instead of an abbot. So when Thomas and four other friars were on their way to Paris, two of his brothers, accompanied by 30 armed men, kidnapped the young Dominican and carried him off to the family fortress at Rocca Secca. They locked him in his room and tore off his habit, no easy task since Thomas was tall and strong. But the imprisonment had no effect on him (after all, he could still think) nor did any of the arguments his mother and brothers tried.

So his brothers came up with the despicable idea of sending a beautiful girl into the room to tempt him to break his vow of chastity, believing that even their intellectual brother was flesh and blood like any other man. The girl came into the room, and Thomas instantly realized what was happening. He was indeed flesh and blood, but he also loved God above all things. He grabbed a burning brand from the fireplace and chased the terrified woman from the room. Then he slammed the door shut and burned into the wood a huge cross. Afterwards, he prayed for purity, and he saw a vision of two angels who tied a burning cord around his waist. He suffered an excruciating pain, but when it was over he was never again in all his life tempted against purity.

After a year or a little more, his family gave up, and he was allowed to escape and rejoin his Dominican brothers.

He went first to the University of Paris, in 1248, and then on to the University of Cologne. His chief teacher was the scholar and scientist, St. Albert the Great. When he heard the other students, noticing Thomas' huge size and customary silence, calling him a "dumb ox," Albert replied: "You call him Dumb Ox, but I tell you this Dumb Ox shall bellow so loud that his bellowing will fill the world."

His studies completed, Thomas returned to Paris to work on his first major book, the *Summa Contra Gentiles*, which would show the harmony of faith and reason, a task which would be Thomas' life work. He was sent to Rome in 1265, where he began his longest and most important work, the *Summa Theologica*, a summary and rational defense of all Catholic doctrine.

Thomas and Louis IX were great friends, and the king once gave a huge banquet to which Thomas was invited. Thomas at a king's banquet was like Thomas anywhere else, totally engrossed in his thoughts. His thoughts at this time were focused on the Albigensian heresy, also known as the Manichean heresy, which denied the goodness of creation, hating life and procreation. Deep in thought, Thomas hardly noticed anything around him. He didn't notice when the conversation was lively or when it died down. But at one of the moments when it had died down, he brought his huge fist crashing down on the table and shouted out, *"That* settles the Manichees!" Dishes rattled, and surely many of the knights and ladies there were sure Thomas' head would rattle too, as the king avenged this insult. But Thomas' host and fellow saint simply called for a scribe and sent him to the Dominican's side, to write down his argument to make sure he didn't forget it.

Thomas had settled the Manichees with the argument that only God is self-existent; therefore only God is the source of all being; therefore all being is good. There are no bad things, only bad wills. Material things, the body and procreation must be respected because they came from God and were hallowed by God's assuming a body at the Incarnation.

Never allowed to sit still for long, Thomas was sent back to Paris in 1269 to challenge Siger of Brabant and his "two truths" doctrine. Siger claimed that rational truth and religious truth were two separate truths, which could contradict each other. The individual was to keep each in a separate compartment of his brain, as it were, calling upon each as needed and not worrying about any contradictions. The "two truths" was in utter opposition to all that Thomas wrote and taught and he proceeded to de-molish Siger of Brabant's ideas. God is the source of all truth; He is in fact infinite truth. God reveals religious truths to us directly, and He permits us to determine natural truths through natural reason. But God is the source of both. Therefore contradictories cannot possibly both be true.

Remaining in Paris, he was asked to write the hymns for the liturgy of the new feast of Corpus Christi, just instituted by the Pope in honor of the Holy Eucharist. Most of the great Eucharistic hymns—"Tantum Ergo," "O Salutaris," "Lauda Sion"—come from the pen of Thomas Aquinas as he gave full expression to his love for the Blessed Sacrament.

In 1272 Thomas was back in Naples, working on that part of the *Summa* which dealt with the difficult doctrine of the Eucharist, the presence of the true Body and Blood of God under the appearances of bread and wine. Thomas developed the doctrine of Transubstantiation: the substance of bread and wine disappears, replaced by the substance of the Body and Blood of Christ, while the accidents (appearances) of bread and wine remain. Much effort and prayer went into the treatise, and when he finished, he went into the chapel, threw it down at the foot of the crucifix and knelt to pray. We are told that Christ came down off the crucifix and stood on the scroll, saying, "Thomas, thou hast written well concerning the Sacrament of My Body. What wouldst thou have as a reward?" Thomas' reply: "Only Thyself."

It was not long after this that Thomas ceased writing. When asked why, he replied, "I have seen things that make what I have written appear as so much straw." He was being blessed with mystical visions of God Himself. Compared to the reality, his explanations did indeed seem as straw.

Though his health was bad and he wanted nothing so much as to give himself totally to prayer, Thomas readily answered the Pope's request that he attend the General Council of Lyons in 1274. But he never reached Lyons. He became ill and had to stop at a Cistercian monastery. Father Reginald, his constant companion, heard his confession, then came running out to exclaim, "I have heard the sins of a five-year-old child." As he lay dying, Thomas asked the monks to read to him the Canticle of Canticles, the great Old Testament poem of love of God. With those words sounding in his ears, he went peacefully and joyfully to his beloved God.

The Cathedral at Chartres

The greatest artistic achievements of the greatest of centuries were the Gothic cathedrals, with spires soaring toward the sky all over Europe. Perhaps the greatest of these cathedrals was built in Chartres, France. Here is its story.

On June 11, 1194 the people of Chartres were in a turmoil. From all the surrounding countryside they had flocked into the town. No one was working. Everyone was standing as near as they could to what remained of their church. The day before, a great fire had almost destroyed their beloved church, leaving only the foundations, the towers and the west front. Most of the people milling around the town felt as they would if their own homes had burned down, perhaps worse. After all, it was not especially difficult to rebuild a small peasant's cottage. But the beautiful church—what could be done?

It so happened that a special representative from the Pope was visiting Chartres at the time of the great fire. He called a meeting of the bishop, the priests, the noblemen and representatives of the artisans and craftsmen. Everyone agreed that the church must be rebuilt, but more magnificent than ever before. "Let us make Our Lady's Church the most splendid in Christendom," said someone, and everyone else enthusiastically agreed. A nobleman who had traveled throughout France described the new church being built at the Abbey of St. Denis. "There are no pillars or inside supports. The ceiling is higher than any I've ever seen. They're filling the walls with windows. I can't imagine how it all stays up."

The Pope's representative, who had visited this church and others, replied: "I'm not an architect, but the master builder at Noyon has explained the principle. The weight is put on outside supports, called buttresses, which carry the stress of the building down to the earth. That means that the walls do not have to bear all the weight of the building and can be filled with glass." The bishop and the priests had been conferring. Now the bishop rose. "We must hire this master builder. We must have that kind of church. We will donate part of our income for the next three years to help pay for the building." He had scarcely finished speaking before the noblemen, too, pledged gold and silver toward the building of the new church. The craftsmen and artisans, each in their turn, promised to donate whatever work was needed. Suddenly the representative of the stonemasons jumped up. "If the church is to be filled with windows," he said, "the stonemasons will contribute the cost of one of the windows." Immediately each of the other groups of craftsmen—called *guilds*—promised to do the same. "Our window will tell the story of Joseph and his brothers," said the bankers guild. The coopers, carpenters and wheelwrights—all workers in wood—said that their window would be of Noah, who built an ark of wood. The furriers decided to erect a window in honor of the great Emperor Charlemagne. And so it went. All agreed that the finest artists in stained glass must be brought to Chartres—the windows must be perfect in form, color and realism.

The meeting broke up late at night, but by early morning everyone knew of the wonderful plan to rebuild the church. Those who had skills came to the priests to promise as much work as they could perform. Those who had money brought it to the site of the church. Those who had neither let it be known that they would keep the workers supplied with food and water during the long building process.

The Master Builder was hired and brought to Chartres. He put all his soul into the design of the church and the supervision of its construction. So little did he care for personal fame or wealth that people in later centuries could find no record of his name, even though he was one of the greatest architects of all time. Artists in stained glass began putting together the tiny pieces of colored glass to tell story after story in the tall windows called *lancets* and the circular windows called *roses*. Their goal was to fill the church with colored light whenever the sun shone through the windows and to tell the story of God's mercy to men—from the creation through the Redemption and up to Christ's coming in glory at the end of the world. At the same time, sculptors were creating the statues which would surround the outside of the church, telling the same story as the glass inside.

Perhaps the hardest workers were the craft guilds, especially the stonemasons, who were responsible for carrying out the plans of the Master Builder. The guilds were a unique feature of the Middle Ages. Each skill had its own guild, which trained new workers, called *apprentices*, until they became talented enough to work on their own as *journeymen*. Eventually they could earn the title *master*. The guilds made sure that working conditions were pleasant, that prices were fair, and that the quality of the work was high. Aged, sick and unemployed members were cared for by contributions from their fellow members. Probably never before or since have workingmen been so highly respected and well cared for.

Gradually the church began to take shape as the years went by. Boys who had first come to work on the church as apprentices had grown to adulthood and become masters, while the masters who had begun the church had died. The Master Builder himself grew very old, and may not have lived to see the completion of his masterpiece. But through it all, the people of Chartres—from the wealthiest to the poorest—had given all they had to the building of the church.

Then at last, in 1240, the people of Chartres once again gathered from far and near. Noblemen rubbed shoulders with peasant farmers, as the grand procession marched toward the church. Led by the bishop, followed by the priests and deacons, with the acolytes carrying lighted candles, the procession entered the church where a great High Mass was sung, dedicating the cathedral to the glory of God under the patronage of the Blessed Mother. The sun shone through the windows making rose, gold and violet patterns on the floor. The carefully cut and dressed stone of the church gleamed golden, and the statues seemed to have haloes.

When the Mass ended, and the bishops went to a feast prepared by one of the noblemen, some of the people remained in the church, sleeping the night there because they were so far from home. But they did not feel homesick because to them the church was a second home, especially since it seemed to them much like what Heaven must be—filled with light and music and beauty. After all, Heaven was their last and best home. Life on earth was just a way of getting ready for Heaven. And their beautiful new cathedral would remind them of Heaven and of what they must do to arrive there. They put themselves and their church under the care of their beloved Mary, and knew that nothing on earth could ever really harm them.

Achievements of the High Middle Ages

We have seen how the Church protected the people from tyrannical kings and emperors. The Church also played an important part in civilizing the knights and barons. During the Dark Ages these men had been forced to spend most of their time fighting. When the Viking attacks ceased, the feudal lords turned to fighting each other. To curb this violence, the Church instituted two customs, the *Peace of God* and the *Truce of God*. The Peace of God forbade the lords from attacking certain people and areas, such as monasteries. The Truce of God forbade warfare at certain times of the year, such as Lent and Advent. Gradually both the Peace and Truce of God were extended, until feudal warfare was greatly reduced.

The Church also worked to establish rules of warfare so that fighting became less brutal, and to encourage men to use their weapons only against the enemies of Christendom instead of against each other. Out of this effort grew the institution of *chivalry*, a code of Christian conduct for knights. In all things, the knight was expected to be honorable and courageous, to protect the weak, and to defend the rights of the Church.

Another great advance during the Middle Ages was the freeing of the serfs. New inventions made it possible for an individual man to work more land, so that more food could be produced by fewer men. Farmers had more free time and were not so closely tied to the land. The Church had always acted to protect the serfs from ill-treatment by their overlords; now she began freeing whatever serfs were still working on lands owned by abbeys and bishops. Gradually the nobles followed the Church's example, so that more and more men came to own their own land.

Education began to spread during this time, and parishes began to have their own schools. Although critics of the Church have said that she tried to keep people in ignorance so that they would not question the decisions of the bishops, the opposite is true. Without the Church, education would not have existed. At this time also, the great universities, such as those at which St. Thomas Aquinas taught, flourished.

Modern science had its beginnings during the High Middle Ages, especially through the efforts of St. Albert the Great and Roger Bacon, who learned to observe and experiment with nature. Bacon's book on *The Secrets of Art and Nature* contains predictions of such inventions as steamboats, balloons, cranes, submarines, microscopes, telescopes and gunpowder. Bacon formulated the laws of the reflection and refraction of light, and wrote a whole book to prove the absurdity of magic.

Art and literature reached new heights during the High Middle Ages. An Italian shepherd named Giotto became the founder of a new school of art which portrayed reality realistically and beautifully. Another Italian—a poet named Dante—wrote a great masterpiece, the *Divine Comedy*. In this poem, an imaginary journey by Dante through Hell, Purgatory and Heaven, Dante gives an overall picture of medieval life and faith.

The Church's Problems Begin

Though the thirteenth century was a time of glorious achievement, no century is perfect and no human society is perfect. Eventually serious problems would arise which would bring the High Middle Ages to an end. The first was that the growth in the prestige, wealth and authority of the Church during the Middle Ages resulted in corruption and power struggles. The first serious problem that afflicted the Church was the *Babylonian Captivity*.

In 1303 King Philip IV of France sent an official and some guards to Anagni, the Pope's residence. They broke into the Pope's bedroom, dragging him out of his bed and arresting him. The Pope, Boniface VIII, had angered Philip by issuing a decree called *Unam Sanctam*, which declared that the Pope had the right to judge all things, including the action of kings. Boniface died shortly after this outrage, and Rome fell into anarchy.

The next Pope reigned only a year before dying. The Pope succeeding him, Clement V, decided that it would be healthier to be on friendly terms with the French king and moved the entire papal court to Avignon, France. Avignon was owned by the papacy, but it was surrounded by French territory. By moving the papacy to Avignon, Clement was implying that the French king was more powerful than the Pope. For over sixty years, the papacy deserted Rome, which had been the Church's headquarters since the days of St. Peter. This is called the Babylonian Captivity, after the time when the Jews were forced to go to Babylon.

Seven Popes lived in Avignon, allowing Church policy to be more or less dictated by French leaders. The danger to Christendom was obvious: other nations might want their own private Church and Pope, thus splitting the Church into tiny pieces. But that didn't happen. The credit for ending the Babylonian Captivity belongs primarily to two women: St. Bridget of Sweden and St. Catherine of Siena.

Bridget had been a wife and mother of eight children. After her husband died, she devoted herself to prayer and good works. Eventually she went to Rome, where she worked tirelessly to persuade the Pope to leave Avignon. Finally Pope Urban V did return to Rome in 1367, but the temptations to return to France were too strong and he prepared to return to Avignon in 1370. Bridget prophesied that he would die within the year if he left Rome, but Urban refused to listen. Her words were no doubt on his mind, however, at the end of December, when he died exactly as she had prophesied.

That left it up to Catherine, the 25th child of an artisan—a dyer—from Siena, Italy. She wrote letter after letter to Urban's successor Gregory IX, urging him to return to Rome and to reform the Church. When her letters did not move him, she went to Avignon herself. Almost daily she visited Gregory. She argued, pleaded, insisted that he heed Christ's will.

But even more than her arguments, Catherine's presence was what Gregory needed. Somehow she gave him the strength of will to turn a deaf ear to the Frenchmen of Avignon. He stopped wavering and in September began the journey home. He arrived in January of 1377, ending the Babylonian Captivity.

But Gregory was spiritually and physically exhausted. He died only a little over a year later, as if the act of leaving the comforts of his French palace and coming to a strange land had consumed all his strength. Upon his death, the people of Rome made it clear to the cardinals who arrived to elect a successor that they wanted a Roman Pope. The cardinals were frightened and hastily elected and crowned an Italian (though not a Roman), Urban VI.

Almost all of the cardinals soon turned against Urban. They held their own papal election, setting up an anti-pope, who made his head-quarters in France. This situation, with a Pope and an anti-pope both claiming authority over the Church, was known as the *Great Schism.*

In 1409 some of the cardinals held the Council of Pisa to try to end the Schism. They elected a second anti-pope, leaving three men claiming authority over Christendom.

At last a second council, the Council of Constance, was convened in 1414 at the urging of the Holy Roman Emperor Sigismund, who was finally doing his job of looking out for the Church. Gregory XII, the valid Pope, agreed to resign in favor of a new Pope chosen by the Council. Cardinal Cossa, the conciliar anti-pope, also agreed to resign. That left only the anti-pope DeLuna, whom almost everyone now ignored. The new, validly elected Pope was Martin V. The Schism was healed.

Nevertheless, the whole situation had caused Christians to lose confidence in and respect for the papacy. Furthermore, reforms needed in the Church were not made because of the papal power struggles. The glories of the Church in the High Middle Ages were fast fading.

Nationalism and the Hundred Years War

Another factor causing the decline of the High Middle Ages was the rise of *nationalism.* Men during the Middle Ages gave their first loyalty to the Church, regarding their community and their country as part of a larger whole: Christendom. Men regarded each other as brothers in Christ, and checks and balances kept any one person or group from getting too much power. But gradually men began to give their first loyalty to the government of their nation, which was regarded as independent of the Church and having no obligation to respect the rights of people outside the nation.

Nations formed for many reasons: the economy became stronger so that it could support larger governments; improved transportation and communication made it easier to govern larger areas. These new nations were a temptation, encouraging the people of one nation to concentrate on the ways they were different from others and encouraging kings to increase their power at the expense of other nations.

An example of nationalism was the power struggle between England and France known as the *Hundred Years War.* During the years following the Norman Conquest, England gradually became stronger, while France became weaker. By the year 1337, England controlled about half of France, and the English king, Edward III, claimed the French throne. Thus began the Hundred Years War, so named because there was fighting off and on until 1453. The key issue was whether France would survive as a nation.

By 1429, France was in a sorry plight. The countryside had been almost ruined by battles and by English pillaging. After the English won the Battle of Agincourt in 1415, the French king Charles VI had promised that upon his death Henry V of England would become king of France. Still the French people fought on, though their cause seemed hopeless, in defense of their homeland and of the man who should be king, the Dauphin (prince) Charles, son of Charles VI. Yet the Dauphin was too afraid of the English to assert his right to the throne.

It was then that the totally unexpected happened. An eighteen-year-old peasant girl named Joan of Arc responded to voices from Heaven—the Archangel Michael, St. Margaret and St. Catherine—who told her: "Leave your village, daughter of God, and journey into France! Choose your flag and raise it boldly! You shall lead the Dauphin to Rheims, that he may there receive the crown and the anointing that are his by right! You shall deliver France from the English!"

The local commander provided Joan a military escort, and she traveled to Chinon, where she persuaded the Dauphin to give her command of the army. Joan's spirit gave the French new courage, new hope. She raised the siege of Orleans and then won a great open field victory at Patay. Timid Charles still wavered, but at last, on July 17, 1429, Charles was crowned king at Rheims, Joan standing proudly at his side. Though the final victory had not yet been won, Joan had turned the tide of war and saved France from English conquest.

The English had their revenge before leaving, bringing her to trial as a witch and burning her at the stake. But Joan died as she had lived, trusting in God and wanting nothing more than to do His will and glorify His name. And the result of her victory would be far greater than even she could have realized. By preserving France's independence, she was preserving its Catholicism, for in less than a hundred years after her death, England would reject the Catholic Church. If England had controlled France at the time, France too might have been lost to the Catholic Church. And how much more of Europe would have gone with it? But thanks to the young soldier girl, this was not to be.

Unfortunately, the spirit of nationalism which had led England to attempt to conquer France remained strong and spread throughout Europe.

The Black Death

A final factor which led to the end of the High Middle Ages was the bubonic plague, or Black Death, as the people of the time called it.

During the 1300's, trade with the Levant—Syria, the Holy Land, Lebanon—increased. The ships which traveled back and forth were infested with rats. The rats were flea-infested, and the fleas carried a bacillus which caused the deadly bubonic plague. By early 1348 the plague appeared in Sicily in the far south of Europe, and then it spread with devastating speed, reaching Scandinavia in the far north by December 1350. Italy was overwhelmed, every village suffering from the plague. Every village in the British Isles was afflicted likewise; London lost twenty to thirty thousand out of a population of seventy thousand. Overall, it is estimated that thirty percent of the population of Europe succumbed to the Black Death.

The plague spread so rapidly and the victims died so quickly that those who had not yet had the plague were terrified. Often they would flee their homes as soon as one member of the family became ill, abandoning him to his terrible death. To many, the plague seemed to be a punishment for the sins of men, and some did extreme penances to try to avert disaster. An example is the flagellant crusade in Germany, where participants went from town to town scourging themselves mercilessly.

The Black Death contributed to the decline of the High Middle Ages in two ways. First, its devastation produced in many a mood of despair and bitterness, rather than the optimism and trust in God of the High Middle Ages. Furthermore, the plague affected the quality of the clergy. The holiest and most dedicated priests would nurse the sick and bring them the Sacraments, with the result that many of them became ill and died themselves. The more corrupt and selfish clergy would flee to the countryside to escape the plague and avoid all contact with victims. Thus, once the plague had burned itself out, the clergy remaining tended to be of a much lower moral quality.

A few pockets were unaccountably spared: Bohemia, large sections of Poland, some tracts in the Pyrenees. But Europe as a whole was devastated, and the effects would be felt for years to come.

Moslems Attack and Are Repulsed

In 1291 the Crusaders lost their last foothold in Palestine and withdrew all their forces from the Middle East. The Knights of St. John, who still possessed the Crusading spirit, withdrew to Rhodes, hoping thereby to provide a line of defense against further Turkish raids into western Europe.

Meanwhile, the Ottoman Turks came to dominate the Moslem world. In 1453, they at long last took Constantinople, thanks to their possession of gunpowder. Thus the Roman Empire in the East finally fell. Under the rule of their leader, Mohammed the Conqueror, the Turks set up an empire throughout the Middle East, and then looked for new lands to conquer in the West.

Pope Nicholas V tried to rally Christian Europe against this new Moslem threat but was unsuccessful. Upon his death in March, 1455, the Cardinals turned to the Spaniard Alfonso Borgia, who had already shown a strong desire to stop the Moslem march. He took the name Calixtus III.

Almost immediately after his election he issued a solemn proclamation to all Christian lands calling for a new Crusade. He called into his office trusted Cardinals and bishops. "Go, you to the Holy Roman Emperor, you to the Duke of Burgundy, you to the King of France, you to the Duke of Naples. Tell them that we are launching a Crusade, that we must have gold to finance it, men to fight it, leaders to ride at the head of the army. Tell them that they must forget the disagreements they have with each other. They must unite in God's cause. During the past years we Christians have become weak. We care more for wealth than for honor. We fight each other instead of our common enemies. This Crusade can put an end to all of that. If Christian princes will unite around the Cross, we can make our people better Christians, we can become more holy, more devoted to Christ. This Crusade will not only rid us of an enemy; it will unite us as friends." Calixtus' voice was powerful. He summoned all the strength in his 80-year-old body to help these men who would be his representatives to see the Crusade as he saw it, so that they could persuade the Christian princes to join.

The messengers left on their missions, but Calixtus did not sit idly by. He began the construction of a papal fleet to lead the naval battle against the Turks. He ordered the selling of papal jewels and other valuable possessions to raise money for the Crusade. He sent letter after letter to all parts of Europe, explaining, pleading, encouraging Christian men to enlist in the Crusade. The previous Pope had been a lover of all forms of art; he had hired many craftsmen. Now Calixtus set the painters and embroiderers to making banners, the sculptors to making stone cannon balls.

The representatives returned. Replies came in to his letters. They made promises but the promises were not kept. They made excuses. They thought of reasons for delays. More messengers arrived with the alarming news that the Turks were preparing a huge attack on Hungary. Calixtus thundered: "Only cowards fear danger. The palm of glory grows nowhere but on the battlefield." But King Alonso of Naples, who had promised to lead the sea attack against the Moslems, instead led an attack against Genoa, a Christian state. The Duke of Burgundy, who had promised to lead the land attack, did not stir from his castle. The promised contributions did not arrive. The Pope sold the silverware from his table. One day gilt saltcellars appeared at a meal. Calixtus roared, "Away, away with these things. Take them for the Turks. Earthenware will do quite as well for me."

In June 1456, the Turkish drums were beating. Mohammed the Conqueror was leading an army of 150,000 men toward Hungary, the last Christian outpost before all of Europe would be laid bare to the Moslems. His army besieged Belgrade. Mohammed boasted that the city would surrender within two weeks.

The people in Belgrade were in despair. They felt abandoned. But they were not. Calixtus sent his trusted friend Cardinal John Carvajal to Belgrade. With him came John Capistrano (eventually to be canonized) and John Hunyadi. The three Johns knew what to do. The Hungarian king and his nobles had fled in terror of the Turks. But John Hunyadi raised an army of 7,000 men at his own expense. Cardinal Carvajal procured transport and provisions. John Capistrano preached in the towns and villages and gathered an army of poor citizens and peasants, monks, hermits, and students, armed with axes, pikes, flails, and pitchforks. In Rome, Calixtus appealed to divine aid, since humans had failed him. On the Feast of St. Peter and St. Paul (June 29), he called for "processions in every diocese in order to pray that the threatened Turkish invasion might be averted." Every priest was required to deliver the following prayer in every Mass: "Almighty, everlasting God, to whom all power belongs, and in whose hand are the rights of all nations, protect Thy Christian people and crush by Thy power the pagans who trust in their fierceness."

Belgrade sits on a rocky hill, with rivers on two sides. Mohammed had not only shut in the fortress completely on the land side, but had also sent a fleet of boats to cut off communication by river. Hunyadi and Carvajal collected 200 boats. They filled the boats with men, and on July 14, taking advantage of the current, bore down upon the Turkish ships. For five hours they fought, hand to hand, while John Capistrano stood on the shore and encouraged the warriors by holding up the crucifix which the Pope had sent. Then the Christians broke through the line. Victory was won.

Hunyadi and his men entered the fortress, with supplies and food for the people. Mohammed was furious. Night and day he sent up an unceasing artillery barrage. On the evening of July 21, he sent his best troops to assault the fortress. St. John again held up the Pope's Crucifix and prayed for divine aid. Hunyadi went where the fighting was heaviest. Then Hunyadi led a force out of the city to attack the Turkish encampment itself. The Sultan, wounded by an arrow and insane with rage, ordered a retreat. The whole of the Turkish camp fell into the hands of the Christians.

When word came to Rome, Calixtus rejoiced. He decreed that in thanksgiving for the victory the Feast of the Transfiguration was to be celebrated by the whole Church every year on August 6. Throughout Rome, church bells rang, processions of thanksgiving marched through the streets and bonfires were lit.

Though the leaders of Christian Europe never heeded the Pope's cry for a march on Constantinople, the Pope's determination and the courage of the three Johns had stopped the Turks for twenty years.

In the spring of 1458, the Pope became ill. Now 83, his strength was gone. On August 3, a burning fever took away the last hope that he would recover. He received the Last Sacraments. On the evening of August 6, the Feast of the Transfiguration, which he himself had instituted, God released him from his sufferings.

The Moslems next turned their attention to Rhodes. In June 1480 the mightiest power in the world attacked the small band of Knights of St. John who were holding the island. The Grand Master, Pierre D'Aubusson, estimated that 3,500 cannon balls were launched against the walls in a space of 38 days. The Turks sent a message: the Knights might remain on Rhodes if they would become the vassals of the sultan. D'Aubusson wrote back a furious reply: Never would the Knights swear fealty to a Moslem. "We worship Christ with complete and utter conviction, and for Him we shall fight and meet death before we ally ourselves with Mohammed as your promises suggest." The Turks resumed their bombardment.

Finally the Turks launched an all-out assault. D'Aubusson, in spite of four wounds which turned his armor red with blood, rallied the Knights.

They fought back, the Turks panicked, and the battle was won for the Christians. The red flag with its white cross of St. John still flew over the battered city.

1453, the fall of Constantinople, is often given as the date for the end of the High Middle Ages. But though the Turks had taken the Byzantine capital, they had not taken Christian Europe; and would not, so long as men like Pope Calixtus and the Knights of St. John remained to fight.

The Holy Shroud Reappears

Around 1356 the Holy Shroud reappeared in the possession of the DeCharney family in France. Its long disappearance has led some to doubt the authenticity of the Shroud. But historians have now been able to trace the probable story of the Shroud, which follows.

Eighty years before the fall of Constantinople, the Crusader Order of the Knights Templars was founded. By 1204, they were wealthy and powerful and possessed a series of fortresses, which served as useful storehouses for treasures. Many of their meetings and rituals were secret, and by 1300 rumors spread that they worshiped a mysterious "head."

This rumored idolatry gave Philip IV of France (the same king who had seized Pope Boniface VIII) the excuse he wanted to suppress the Knights Templars and appropriate their wealth. But he had to make his move by surprise because of the Templars' military strength. So at daybreak on Friday, October 13, 1307, Philip's soldiers seized every Templar they could lay their hands on, including the Grand Master Jacques de Molay and the Master of Normandy. The Templars were tortured, and many confessed to various crimes, including the worship of the "head," although they stated that only the highest officials ever saw the original. Some of the Templars died under torture rather than confess, and most of those who confessed later asked forgiveness for giving way. In 1314 DeMolay and the Master of Normandy renounced their confessions and asserted the innocence of the Templars. Philip ordered their immediate execution, and they were burned to death. The Master of Normandy was Geoffrey de Charney.

Apparently the Templars had come into possession of the Shroud after the fall of Constantinople, perhaps taking it as security for a loan or purchasing it outright. They then worshiped the Holy Shroud as the sacred burial cloth and image of the Lord, keeping their worship secret precisely to avoid charges of idolatry. When Philip's raiders came, somehow DeCharney managed to rescue the Shroud and spirit it out to his family.

He then died without revealing the secret.

DeCharney's son, also named Geoffrey, kept his possession of the Shroud secret as well. But after his death in battle in 1356, his wife, Jeanne, apparently needing money to support her young son, brought out the Shroud to exhibit it, the first time it had been seen publicly in over 150 years. Such shock and consternation were caused, including charges of forgery, that she put the Shroud away. Finally her son, another Geoffrey, received permission to exhibit the Shroud in the family's church in Lirey. At his death the Shroud passed to his only heir, his daughter, Margaret. Margaret had no close relatives and so searched for a worthy recipient for the Shroud at her death. She chose the family of Savoy, noted for its piety and ideals.

The House of Savoy exhibited the Shroud in Chambery, France until 1578, when it was moved to Turin, Italy, the new Savoy capital. The Shroud remains in Turin, exhibited only rarely. In 1983 the last Savoy heir willed the Shroud to the Vatican, and the holy relic is now the property of the Church.

The Shroud has thus survived a first century persecution of Christians, repeated Edessan floods, an Edessan earthquake, Moslem invasion, Crusader looting, destruction of the Knights Templars, a 1532 fire, and a serious arson attempt in 1972. Every building which housed the Shroud before the 15th century has long since been destroyed, but the Shroud remains, the most sacred relic in all the world.

Review Questions

1. Name Louis IX's mother and wife and tell how they were important to him as king. What kind of king was Louis IX?
2. What titles did Frederick II give himself? What was his attitude toward the Catholic Church? How did he attack the Pope? Who stopped him and how?
3. What happened on the seventh crusade?
4. What was the attitude of the Aquino family when Thomas wanted to join the Dominicans? Why? How did they try to stop him?
5. Thomas wanted to show that there is no contradiction between what two things? Name his two main books. What was the "two truths" controversy? What was Thomas' answer to this controversy?
6. What happened at Louis IX's banquet? What was Thomas' answer to the Manichees?

7. For what feast did Thomas write the liturgy? How did Thomas explain the Eucharist? What happened after he had written this explanation?

8. How did Thomas feel about his writings at the end of his life? Why did he feel this way?

9. What were the guilds? How did they help their members?

10. How did all parts of society contribute to the building of Chartres cathedral? What characterized the architecture of the cathedrals of the Middle Ages?

11. Describe the accomplishments of the Middle Ages in the following areas: chivalry, serfdom, education, science, art, literature.

12. What was the Babylonian Captivity? What effect did it have on the Church? How was it ended?

13. What was the Great Schism? What effect did it have on the Church? How was it ended?

14. What is nationalism? Why would nationalism be against the values of the High Middle Ages? What was the cause of the Hundred Years War? What was the role of Joan of Arc in this war? What were its results?

15. What was the Black Death? What was its effect on Europe? How did it help to bring the High Middle Ages to an end?

16. When were the last Crusaders withdrawn from the Holy Land? Who carried on the tradition of the Crusaders? What happened at the second siege of Constantinople? Give the date.

17. How did Pope Calixtus stop the Turks?

18. What happened at the Siege of Rhodes?

19. What is the evidence that the Knights Templars possessed the Shroud from 1204-1307?

20. List the owners and places where the Shroud has been since then.

Projects

1. Prepare an illustrated report on Notre Dame Cathedral in Paris and on Saint Chapelle in Paris.

2. Prepare a detailed report on knighthood and chivalry.

3. Imagine that you grew up in Chartres during the building of the Great Cathedral. Write an account of your memories.

4. Write a report on the guilds or on medieval universities.

5. Write a "biography" of the Holy Shroud from the time of Christ to the present day.

Chapter Sixteen
Spain Becomes a Great Power

AFTER THE MOSLEM WHIRLWIND had swept across North Africa, through Spain and up to the heart of France—to be stopped there by Charles Martel at the Battle of Tours—only one small strip of land in all the area remained in Christian hands: the mountains of the Asturias. Here Pelayo and his followers had sworn an oath to fight the Moslems until they died. These few men held off the mightiest power in the world at the Battle of Covadonga, thereby preserving a tiny bit of Spain to serve as a base for rewinning the rest of the country. This great effort, known as the *Reconquista*, took 770 years.

The Reconquista

In 794 the Moslems decided to wipe out the Asturias kingdom, now ruled by Alfonso II, known as the Chaste because he never married. A Moslem army too strong for Alfonso to meet in the open field marched on his new capital of Oviedo. The town was taken and sacked, but Alfonso escaped. In 795, 10,000 Moslem cavalry, with infantry support, attacked the beleaguered Catholic kingdom again. The Moslems won two victories, driving Alfonso into the mountains. So certain were the Moslems of ultimate victory that they went south to winter quarters, planning to complete the conquest in the spring.

But Alfonso was made of the same stuff as Pelayo, and he would not give up. Somehow he and his men survived the cruel winter. So little food was available that the men could not stay together. Alfonso allowed them to scatter, but when he recalled them in the spring they all came. They seemed scarcely stronger than the "thirty barbarians perched on a rock" of Pelayo's day, but they held on. The Moslems couldn't win the ultimate victory.

By 798 Alfonso was even able to launch an amazing counterattack, marching all the way to Lisbon. He regained Oviedo and rebuilt the Church of the Twelve Apostles, which the Moslems had sacked. A big morale boost came in 825 with the discovery of the bones of the Apostle St. James in Campostella (Field of the Star). Alfonso built the shrine of Santiago (St. James) de Campostella, and the Apostle became the patron saint of the Reconquista.

Alfonso was still successfully fighting off Moslems in his 70's. When he died around 843 he was described in these words: "Friend of God and of man, he sent his glorious soul to Heaven after bearing the burdens of rule through 52 years, chaste, sober, spotless, pious, and full of glory. He lived a life most chaste, never taking a wife, and from the kingdom of earth he passed to the kingdom of Heaven."

Little by little, with hard fought battles, territory was re-won from the Moslems and feudal rule set up. By 955 Navarra (in the north) and Leon and Castile (in the central plains) were free; by 1063 Aragon in the east was independent.

During the rule of the weak Alfonso VI of Castile, the Christian warriors were led by the great Spanish hero, Rodrigo Diaz, better known as El Cid Campeador (Lord or Master, Expert Warrior). Alfonso soon became jealous of his more able, moral and respected vassal. He exiled him from Castile.

Then on June 30, 1086, a huge Moslem host from Africa landed by the Rock of Gibraltar. The Spanish Moslems had grown weak, but there was nothing weak about these Africans or about their leader Yusuf ibn-Tashfin. They represented the greatest threat to Christian Spain in a hundred years. The two armies met in October near the village Sagrajas.

The Christians attacked first and broke the Moslem line. But Yusuf never panicked. He sent a picked force to attack the camp behind the Christian lines. Alfonso fell back to protect it. Then Yusuf ordered a thunderous drum roll—a sound the Christians had never heard in battle before—and sent his elite unit, 4,000 towering blacks from Nigeria armed with enormous swords, straight toward Alfonso. The Christian line disintegrated, and Alfonso was wounded, barely escaping with his life. Yusuf had the heads of the Christian dead cut off and put in a pile, from the top of which the Moslem call to prayer was cried the next day.

In desperation, Alfonso recalled El Cid, who immediately obeyed the summons, renewing his pledge of fealty to the man who had treated him unjustly. He occupied Valencia, a major Moslem kingdom, ruling it in the name of a Moslem ally, al-Qadir. Then in the spring of 1092, Yusuf inflicted another stinging defeat on Alfonso, and sent an army toward Valencia, conquering everything along the way. Al-Qadir tried to flee with his treasures; he was caught, killed, and his body buried among dead camels.

El Cid received word of the crisis. Later he said that all he had with him at that desperate moment were his horse, his sword, and four loaves of bread. But he rode on toward Valencia. He gathered an army, won a series of battles, and by the summer of 1093 had Valencia under siege. He personally led his army to do battle in the streets of the suburbs; in July the city surrendered to him.

In the summer of 1094 Yusuf, too elderly to lead the army himself, sent his nephew and 150,000 men to destroy El Cid. But El Cid did not wait to be destroyed. He led his men out of the city, taking the Moslems by surprise. They fought the Battle of Cuarte with lances and swords. Valencia was held.

El Cid became the great national hero of Spain, not only for his valor in battle, but for his honor and nobility, for he never broke faith with the lord who had broken faith with him.

The Reconquista went on. On July 16, 1212, the largest Spanish Christian army met the largest Moslem army ever assembled in Spain. The Moors lined up on the south bank of a stream running through small plains among hills, an area known as Las Navas de Tolosa. The Moors formed across the plains, with the heavily wooded rocky slopes at their backs. They are reported as having 100,000 mounted men, with a considerable number of infantry.

The Christians were divided into three groups—center, left and right. In the center was King Alfonso VIII and Archbishop Rodrigo, before whom was borne an enormous red cross with a shield at its base. The Christians attacked, with violent fighting all along the line. On the wings the Christians gradually forced the Moors back, and the farther they pushed them, the worse it became for the Moslems, who were being driven into trees and rocks.

In the center, the Moslems held, for they had their best troops there. At one point Alfonso cried, "Archbishop, it is here we ought to die!" The Archbishop replied: "No, sire, it is here we should live and conquer!" The Christian knights did not give way. The banner of the cross was carried forward, and the Spaniards attacked furiously. The Moslem leader fell back and the battle turned into a rout—a decisive victory for Spain.

The Christians had defeated the best troops the Moslems had, and thereafter the quality of the Moorish army declined. The Castillian kings took over the headwaters of all the great rivers and the control of the roads that paralleled them, so that all the parts of Spain could communicate with each other.

The next great hero of the Reconquista was King St. Ferdinand of Castile (1217-1252). A cousin of St. Louis IX of France, St. Ferdinand captured Cordoba, a major Moslem kingdom, in 1236 after a long siege. He brought back from Cordoba the bells of Santiago de Campostella, which had been stolen in a Moslem raid in 977. He took Seville in 1248, leaving only Granada in Moslem hands. Like his famous cousin, St. Ferdinand ruled as a Christian king. Throughout his kingdom, he established monasteries and convents, set up just courts to meet the grievances of the people, and encouraged education and culture. Everywhere in Spain, both in the lands newly rewon and in the lands long freed from Moslem control, Christian civilization flourished.

Isabel

After the death of St. Ferdinand, Christian Spain had fewer problems coming from the Moslems and more difficulties coming from itself. Spain was still far from being a united country, and civil war raged within the various kingdoms, as one faction after another sought control. The noblemen had far too much power, so that no strong central authority existed to keep order.

When Henry IV became king of Castile in 1454, the situation went out of control. He gave away his money and his power to any nobleman who threatened him, because he wanted nothing so much as to be left in peace. Criminals were unchecked, and the kingdom was close to anarchy. Henry's heir was his half-sister, Isabel—a green-eyed blonde whose striking beauty was matched by a brilliant mind and unshakable courage. Where Henry was weak, Isabel was strong. The nobles had no desire to see her on the throne of Castile, since she would surely curb their abuses. A powerful group of enemies challenged Isabel, stopping at almost nothing to keep her off the throne of Castile.

Much of the controversy revolved around whom the young princess would marry. If she could be married to some cooperative nobleman, her influence would be curbed. Normally Henry would have had the final say as to his half-sister's husband. But Isabel had ideas of her own. She determined that she would marry young Ferdinand, prince of Aragon and heir to its crown, and for many months secret messages in code passed back and forth between her supporters and his to arrange the marriage.

But Isabel's enemies knew at least partly what was going on and even attempted to kidnap her to prevent the marriage. Finally, in 1469, when Isabel was 18 and Ferdinand 17, Henry rode south with his army to put down a rebellion. Isabel made up her mind that the wedding must be delayed no longer and sent a message to Ferdinand. Her enemies heard of her plans and began to come after her. Friendly troops arrived to help Isabel, but at the same time came a message from Ferdinand saying that he was needed in Aragon to lead the army.

Isabel was near despair. If she and Ferdinand could not be married at this time, she would surely be forced into a marriage with King Alfonso the Fat of Portugal. She wrote a desperate letter to Ferdinand—"Come, come, for the love of God"—and sent it by her fastest rider.

When Ferdinand received her plea, he forgot all about the fighting in Aragon. His advisers warned that Henry's troops were blocking all the roads. Why not get past in disguise? he excitedly suggested. He would take three of his friends; he knew just whom. They could pretend to be traveling merchants, and he would be their mule driver. He would go; he must go.

In disguise, they crossed the border and rode toward Valladolid, where Isabel waited. The plan worked, and they crossed safely through enemy territory. He arrived on October 11. On October 18, they were married. Their marriage was a true love match and a genuine partnership.

On December 12, 1472, Henry died. Isabel went to Mass to pray for his soul. On her return, she heard her name shouted in the windy streets: "Long live Queen Isabel!" The next day the ancient crown of Castillian monarchs was placed on her head, and she began the reign which would lead Spain to peace, unity and greatness.

Ferdinand and Isabel Unite Spain

The first challenge facing Ferdinand and Isabel was a Portuguese attack as Alfonso the Fat brought his armies across the border. Henry had let the military deteriorate to such a degree that Ferdinand and Isabel had nothing with which to counter the threat. Isabel rode throughout the kingdom, raising money and recruiting soldiers. Ferdinand trained the army she had created for him. Alfonso was defeated, and the borders of Castile were safe.

Then the king and queen had to re-establish order within Castile. Isabel and Ferdinand were popular with the townspeople, the lower nobility (those who had not gained much power), the Church and the peasant farmers. The common people and the poor loved them and supported them during the civil wars. Before long, the opposition to their reign was defeated, and Isabel and Ferdinand were firmly in charge of the government.

But much remained to be done to make Spain fully prosperous and peaceful once again. Because of the anarchy of Henry's reign, crime was frequent and justice infrequent. Isabel and Ferdinand traveled from place to place throughout the kingdom, setting up their court and listening to the grievances of everyone. From the windy mountains in the north, through the barren central plain, to the fertile valleys and olive groves of the south, Ferdinand and Isabel judged controversies and handed down just and wise decisions. They established local police forces called the Santa Hermandad (Holy Brotherhood) to deal with the bandits, and appointed competent local government officials to preserve order. Ferdinand and Isabel reduced crime and violence, rid the government of corruption, and raised the country's moral standards, which had been abysmally low under Henry.

One incident which occurred during this time will illustrate the kind of ruler Isabel was. Isabel was resting in Tordesillas, when she received frightening news from Segovia: revolt had broken out and her baby daughter Isabel, with only a few loyal friends, was besieged in a tower of the Alcazar (royal palace). Isabel ordered horses saddled immediately, and with only three friends, rode all night to reach Segovia. When she arrived, the bishop came out of the city gate to welcome her. But he told her that she should leave her friends outside the wall because they were not popular with the leaders of the rebellion. Said Isabel: "Tell those citizens of Segovia that I am Queen of Castile, and this city is mine, for the king my father left it to me; and to enter what is mine I do not need any laws or conditions that they may lay down for me." Then, with her friends—but with no soldiers or any guard—she rode into the city. She rode to the Alcazar and asked that all the people of the town who had grievances should come to her. They told her that the rebellion had started because of dissatisfaction with the mayor of the city. She listened carefully, said that she would remove him from office while she investigated the matter, and guaranteed that she would be personally responsible to see that they were well-governed. They shouted "Viva La Reina"—"Long live the Queen!" The rebels surrendered, she entered the castle and embraced her daughter, then rode in triumph through the city.

With Spain firmly united behind them, Isabel and Ferdinand turned toward the enemy in the south: the Moslems in Granada, always threatening Christian Spain, making frequent raids to burn homes and carry off captives to be sold into slavery. Isabel had a vision of Spain as a leading power in Europe, advancing the cause of Christ, but her vision could not come true until all of Spain was once again in Christian hands. So in 1481, Isabel and Ferdinand launched the last phase of the Reconquista.

Because of the mountainous terrain in the south of Spain, the conquest had to proceed slowly, by besieging and capturing one stronghold after another. Cavalry troops were virtually useless and all depended on artillery and infantry. The people fought with the fervor of Crusaders—and the war, after all, was a Crusade, a defense of Christendom against the Moslems. At times the cause seemed hopeless—at one point Isabel pawned her jewels to raise money for the war.

At last on January 2, 1492, Boabdil—the last Moslem ruler in Spain—surrendered to Isabel and Ferdinand. At the highest point in the great Moorish city of Granada, the silver cross of the Crusade was erected, along with the flag of Saint James. The soldiers knelt in the dust to give thanks, and with them knelt the Ferdinand and Isabel, their son and daughters. Then the pennants of the King and Queen were raised, while the army shouted "Castile! for the invincible monarchs, Don Fernando and Dona Isabel!"

The Inquisition

One other task within Spain faced Isabel. During the years of turmoil, the Church had become weak and corrupt. Isabel was a fervent Catholic, putting the cause of Christ first in all she did. Furthermore, she knew that Spain's unity as a nation depended upon a strong Church—Spain might as well not exist if it were not Catholic through and through. She set about reforming the Church, raising the educational and moral standards of the clergy. Many abuses were halted, including the practice of selling indulgences, which would cause much grief in the rest of Europe.

One of the most serious problems the Church faced was the number of Jews and Moors who had been baptized Catholics and risen to high positions in the government and the Church without really believing in Christian doctrine. These false Conversos and Moriscos (converted Jews and Moors) were a threat to the Church and to Spain, and a way had to be found of determining who was a true Christian and loyal Spaniard and who was a traitor. Isabel knew that not all the Conversos and Moriscos were enemies-her own confessor was a Converso as was the husband of her best friend. But to protect the innocent, the guilty had to be found.

The method Isabel chose was the *Inquisition*: a court which would examine evidence and judge whether a person was a faithful Christian or an enemy of Church and country. At the beginning of the Inquisition, there were many abuses—some innocent people suffered and torture was used frequently. At this point the Pope stepped in and appointed new Inquisitors, with the Grand Inquisitor (head of the Inquisition) being a Dominican monk named Tomas de Torquemada. Torquemada reformed the procedure of the Inquisition to ensure that justice would be done. He made its procedures more lenient and improved conditions in the prisons. He personally examined appeals from the accused and gave money to help the families of those on trial.

The actions of the Inquisitors are often criticized, usually as a means of attacking Spain by those who resent the strong Catholic character of the country. One criticism is that the Inquisition used torture. It did, though less so under Torquemada than before him. Torture is wrong, and the Church has since condemned any use of torture. But at the time, all governments routinely used torture as a means of extracting confessions. Though the fact that a sin is routinely committed does not justify it, the Inquisitors were most probably acting in good faith, and they should not be singled out as unusually evil.

A second attack is that the Inquisition's judgments led to the execution of the guilty. People in modern times consider it wrong to execute people for not truly believing in the religion they professed, but that is not in fact why they were executed. Those found guilty were traitors to the state and to the Church, and treason has almost always been recognized as a crime justifying capital punishment. Furthermore, those found guilty were always given a chance to repent. Only if they refused to repent or if they relapsed into their crimes after promising repentance were they executed. Finally, only 2,000 were executed, a small percentage of the 100,000 put on trial.

A final charge is that the method of execution, burning at the stake, was unusually barbaric. But the 16th century was a brutal time. In England capital punishment consisted of being hanged, cut down while still alive, disembowelled, and then cut into four pieces (hanged, drawn and quartered); in France, it was to be boiled alive. Again, Spain should not be singled out for condemnation.

The Inquisition, in fact, though not perfect, was a more just court than most. Often, people charged with regular crimes would pretend to be heretics so that they could be transferred to the custody of the Inquisition, whose prisoners were better treated.

Looking at the Inquisition historically, we see that it avoided more deaths than it caused. Because Spain was united religiously as well as politically, it did not suffer the religious wars which came when Protestantism began in other countries. Furthermore, a few years later other parts of Europe went through a witchcraft hysteria, when many people were executed as witches on only the flimsiest of evidence, or no evidence at all (30,000 in England, 100,000 in Germany). In Spain, the Inquisition investigated charges of witchcraft and found them baseless, thus saving many innocent people from death.

All the efforts of Ferdinand and Isabel—ending civil war, restoring order and justice, completing the Reconquista, reforming the Church—brought peace and prosperity to Spain. The latter years of their reign and the years immediately following are known as Spain's Golden Age, when art, literature, culture and science reached a high point. During the 16th century, Spain was the intellectual capital of the world, with scholars coming from all over Europe to study there.

Out of Spain's optimism, joy and excitement came the explorations and discoveries which were to open up our own hemisphere and bring about the settlement of a whole new world.

The New World

In the early 1400's, Prince Henry of Portugal was intensely interested in explorations. He built a home at Sagres on the coast, and would climb to the highest hill with his telescope, looking out to sea for his ships to come in. Because of his encouragement of sea explorations, he is known as Prince Henry the Navigator.

Prince Henry's main interest was the discovery of a sea route to India and the islands of the Indian Ocean. Others were equally interested because these areas were the sources of the spices which were necessary to preserve food in those days. Without pepper and other spices from the Indies, food would spoil, since refrigeration had not been invented. Since the southern hemisphere was almost totally unknown, all the spices were brought by overland caravans, which were in constant danger from bandits, as well as being subject to taxes levied by all the small kingdoms through which they passed. In addition, Christendom hoped to gain a military advantage by finding a way to sail around Moslem lands. Prince Henry was also motivated by the desire to convert any pagan people who would be found in newly discovered lands.

Prince Henry sent his ship captains sailing south down the coast of Africa, looking for a way through. At first progress was very slow, because the sailors were afraid of the unknown. Finally, in the 1480's, Bartolomeo Diaz reached the Cape of Good Hope—the southern tip of Africa. In 1498, Vasco da Gama reached India by sailing all around Africa. Prince Henry did not live to see this great triumph, but without his encouragement and enthusiasm it would have been delayed many more years.

Portugal opened up the East Indies to Europe, but Spain was to open up the New World. The credit goes to Christopher Columbus, who had the vision, and to Queen Isabel, who supported him in his dream.

Columbus had a totally new idea for reaching the Indies—sailing west instead of east. His mathematics were wrong: he believed the earth to be much smaller than it really was. But nothing was wrong with his courage or his vision. He, unlike anyone else of the time, was willing to sail into totally unknown waters, in search of a totally new way to the East. He had a deep faith and a passionate conviction that he was the man chosen by God to reach Asia by a new route and to bring the Christian faith to the people there. It was this deep faith which convinced Isabel to support his venture, though many of her advisers knew that Columbus' calculations as to the size of the earth were incorrect. Isabel was not much impressed by numbers; she was impressed by Columbus' courage and his character, and she sent him off across the ocean in the name of Castile. On his ships flew a white flag bearing a green cross, on either side of which was a crown. Under one crown was the letter F for Ferdinand; under the other the letter I for Isabel.

The voyage west was rather easy, as Columbus' three ships caught the trade winds and made good time. But after reaching what he thought were the Indies, Columbus' troubles began. His largest ship, the *Santa Maria*, ran aground on Christmas Eve when the officer on watch went to sleep. The ship had to be abandoned, and some of the crew stayed behind in a hastily constructed fort. The captain of the *Pinta* disliked Columbus and frequently caused trouble, even disappearing with the ship for a time.

The voyage home was incredibly difficult. Columbus sailed the *Nina*—a very small ship—through the zone of the westerlies during the worst winter Europe had experienced in years. His ship was battered and broken, and for days on end he couldn't see the sun or the stars for navigation. At one point he even put a written account of his discoveries into a bottle and dropped it overboard, hoping that it would be found if his ship were wrecked.

But at last he landed safely and sent a message of triumph to Isabel. Columbus' voyage opened the door to the conquest and colonization of the New World.

Thus did the glories of the High Middle Ages continue to glow in Spain even after they had diminished in the rest of Europe. This accomplishment is the work of the great Queen Isabel, who richly deserves the title bestowed on her by the Pope: *La Reina Catolica*, the Catholic Queen.

Review Questions

1. How did each of the following contribute to the Reconquista: Alfonso the Chaste, El Cid, Las Navas de Tolosa, St. Ferdinand.
2. Why was Spain in the mid-fifteenth century in a state of near anarchy?
3. Summarize the character of Queen Isabel.
4. List each of the problems Isabel and Ferdinand faced and tell how they solved them.
5. How did Isabel and Ferdinand complete the Reconquista?
6. What was the Inquisition? Why did Isabel establish it? Who was Tomas de Torquemada?
7. List each of the charges made against Spain because of the Inquisition and answer each.
8. How did the Inquisition save more lives that it cost?
9. Who was Prince Henry the Navigator? What achievement resulted from his efforts?
10. Why was Columbus' plan unique? Why did Isabel support him?
11. What were the problems on his voyage? What was the main result of his efforts?
12. Why is it true to say that the High Middle Ages lasted longer in Spain than anywhere else?

Projects

1. Write an imaginary eyewitness account of one of the events in this chapter. (Some possibilities: the marriage of Ferdinand and Isabel, the Battle of Las Navas de Tolosa, an event on Columbus' voyage, the con-

quest of Granada, Prince Henry welcomes a ship back from explorations along the coast of Africa.) Or put on a play about the event.

2. Draw a map of Spain and locate all the places named in this chapter.

3. Prepare a bulletin board on Spain or a display of the ways Spain influenced the U.S.

4. Plan and prepare a lunch of Spanish dishes.

Chapter Seventeen
Revolt and Counterattack

IN THE LAST THREE CHAPTERS we discussed the glories and the goodness of the Middle Ages: the Gothic cathedrals soaring toward the sky, illuminated by their multi-colored stained glass windows; the knights of Christendom—led by Raymond, Richard, St. Louis—riding toward Jerusalem to free it from the Moslems; the ships sailing out of the Golden Age of Spain and into the New World. But we have also seen the effects of problems in the Church, nationalism, and the Black Death, all of which would help to bring the High Middle Ages to an end.

The Renaissance

Just as the Dark Ages had given way to the Middle Ages, so gradually did the Middle Ages give way to the *Renaissance*, which began in Italy around the middle of the 14th century. The word Renaissance means rebirth. The name was chosen because of rebirth of interest in the culture, art and ideas of classical civilization (ancient Greece and Rome). Some of this interest was good—it led to achievements in art and architecture, for example. Some of it was silly—people wore togas and celebrated the holidays which the Romans had celebrated. And some of it was harmful. Many of the Renaissance scholars regarded Christian culture as inferior to classical civilization. They thought Christianity put too many limits on the human mind and human behavior. They became skeptical of Christian teachings, not wanting to accept anything on faith. Led by a man named Machiavelli, they developed theories of government which said that the end—growth of power for the government and its leader—justified any means that might be used, no matter how dishonest or unjust. All of these ideas were part of the philosophy of *humanism*: a pride and confidence in the human mind and a stress on human accomplishments. The humanists could have had a good effect, by helping men use their abilities to become better men. Some humanists did this. But others began almost to worship man and human nature rather than God.

We have already seen the turmoil in the Church caused by the Babylonian Captivity and the Great Schism. The Church in the Renaissance was also weakened by nationalism, humanism, and the corrupting effects of wealth and power.

Church offices provided high incomes, which led to the evil of simony. Then, once a bishop or cardinal had gained his office through simony, he often tried to get as much wealth as he could. Bishops frequently lived outside their dioceses and totally neglected spiritual duties. A bishop of Strasbourg named Rupert von Simmern held his office for 38 years and never once said Mass. Churchmen in high positions would give favors, money and offices to members of their families without regard to their merits. This is called *nepotism*. Many bishops and priests led immoral lives.

Nevertheless, most of the people were loyal, faithful Catholics, serving God as best they could. The Church was free from heresy. If a strong, holy Pope had taken office after the Great Schism, he could have reformed the Church. But the papacy, as the most powerful and potentially most wealthy office in the Church, was the most desirable office in the Church. Cardinals and bishops would do everything they could to be elected Pope, including getting votes by bribery and blackmail. Once in office, they were not likely to reform the system that had put them there, especially since it was through the system that they could make themselves and their families wealthy.

Three Popes of the Renaissance show why the Church was suffering. A Spaniard named Rodrigo Borgia became Pope in 1492, taking the name Alexander VI. Though he and his family were not especially popular among the Cardinals who elected the Pope, Alexander promised wealth and high offices to his rivals, thereby buying his election. Once elected, Alexander's main goal was to make the Borgia family powerful in Italy and throughout Europe. Alexander used every kind of diplomatic and political weapon he had to give his illegitimate son Cesare a dominant position in the wild affairs of Italian politics. He lived in luxury, lavishly decorating his quarters in the Vatican. He brought his illegitimate children to the Vatican and didn't even pretend that they were anything other than what they actually were.

Alexander died in 1503, to be followed by an elderly Pope who reigned for only a few weeks. The next Pope was Julius II, whose primary goal was to unite Italy under the domination of the papacy. Early in his reign he set about destroying Cesare Borgia. Then he rode out at the head of his army, doing battle with the other city states in Italy in an attempt to bring them under his control. Julius was in fact a talented general and a skilled diplomat, but he had no interest in spiritual matters—except insofar as he could use them to achieve his political aims.

Leo X succeeded Julius in 1513. He was from the Medici family of Florence, who had been ardent patrons of the arts. Leo X showed himself a true Medici, taking far more interest in the Vatican's art collection than in spiritual matters. He was worldly and materialistic, doing nothing to provide the Church with the reforms it needed.

With Popes such as these, the people could easily forget that Christ had made a careful distinction between the powers He gave the head of His Church and the morality of the Pope himself. That is one of the reasons why Christ had chosen the Apostle who denied Him to be the first Pope: to show that Christ would protect the Church even when the Pope acted wrongly. But the immoralities of Alexander, Julius and Leo were so evident, even though none of them taught heresy, that many people came to believe that Christ had abandoned the Catholic Church. Christendom was like a pile of dry tinder, awaiting a spark to set it off into a roaring fire.

Martin Luther

The spark came from Germany, from a 34-year-old monk in the Augustinian order. He was a professor at the University of Wittenberg, admired for his brilliance. He lived from 1483-1546, and his name was Martin Luther.

Luther had a despairing belief in his own sinfulness. He meditated often on Hell, death, punishment and Christ as stern judge instead of loving Savior. Once he wrote that he "hated God and was angry at Him." He came to feel that his own sins were so great that not even God was powerful enough to forgive them, that he could do nothing to make himself holy. Finally Luther concluded that only faith could save him. Nothing he could *do* could possibly persuade God to forgive his sins, because they were so great. But if he believed in Christ as the Redeemer, then God would overlook his sins and pretend they weren't there.

This idea of Luther's was totally different from Christianity as it had been believed and taught since the time of Christ. Orthodox Christianity had taught that Christ's death on the cross earned grace for us. Grace then made the Christian into a *new man*. It wasn't that God overlooked the person's sins, but that the sins were gone. Any action performed in the state of grace and united to Christ was meritorious. Through these actions, the person earned more grace, growing holier and closer to God. Luther believed that man stayed the same, but that God would no longer punish him for his sins if he had faith. He also taught that nothing we did had any merit at all, that we couldn't earn more grace, that we couldn't become holier. We were evil men whom God would take into His presence anyway if we believed in Christ. Luther became so extreme in this view that he wrote, "Be a sinner and sin on bravely, but have stronger faith and rejoice in Christ, who is the victor of sin, death, and the world. Do not for a moment imagine that this life is the abiding place of justice: sin must be committed. To you it ought to be sufficient that you acknowledge the Lamb that takes away the sins of the world; the sin cannot tear you away from him, even though you commit adultery a hundred times a day and commit as many murders."

On October 31, 1517, Luther lit the spark which would send his new doctrines racing like wildfire throughout Christendom. On the church door in Wittenberg he nailed a document called the *95 Theses,* which called for a debate on the idea of indulgences. An indulgence is a removal of some or all of the punishment due to already forgiven sin because of the performance of a good deed or the saying of a prayer. The Pope had granted a special plenary indulgence to those who would donate money toward the building of St. Peter's Basilica in Rome. But inaccurate preaching, which misrepresented the Church's true teaching, plus the financial ramifications of the indulgence—the Pope was allowing the local bishop to keep half of the receipts to pay off a large debt to the Fuggers' banking house— combined to cause scandal. The Church was falsely accused of "selling" indulgences.

But Luther condemned the whole idea of indulgences. He said that we could never do anything that would remove the punishment we deserved. He also denied the authority of the Church to issue indulgences.

Various Catholic leaders prepared answers to Luther's document, and the two sides argued back and forth for some months. Then on August 7, 1518, Pope Leo summoned Luther to Rome within sixty days. Luther said he was not well enough to come. So the Pope sent a legate, St. Cajetan, to meet with Luther. Luther refused to meet with him. He felt confident in his position because he was gaining support in his attack on the Church.

Luther's support came from three groups. Many of the German peasants resented the power and wealth of the Church, which—because of their rapidly growing nationalism—they regarded as a foreign power. The middle classes (businessmen, merchants and manufacturers) were beginning to practice a form of capitalism. They regarded the Church as an enemy since it condemned some of their business practices. Most importantly, some of the noblemen thought that by rejecting the Church they could get more power and seize Church lands to increase their wealth.

In 1520 Pope Leo formally excommunicated Luther and condemned 41 separate doctrines that he taught. The Pope called upon Luther to recant within sixty days. But Luther had no intention of taking back one single word. He declared: "As for me, the die is cast: I despise alike the favor and fury of Rome; I do not wish to be reconciled with her, or ever to hold any communion with her. Let her condemn and burn my books; I, in turn, unless I can find no fire, will condemn and publicly burn the whole pontifical law, that swamp of heresies." The Protestant Revolt had begun.

John Calvin

Luther provided the emotional energy that started Protestantism. John Calvin (1509-1564) provided the intellectual energy. Calvin, a Frenchman, developed a whole new version of Christianity, which he published in 1536 in a book called *The Institutes of the Christian Religion*. This book spread rapidly through Europe and seemed to give the people a new faith to replace Catholicism.

Calvin taught the total depravity doctrine: that man is totally evil, "an ape, a wild and savage beast," with a load of sin so heavy and inescapable that man can only submit to it. He taught predestination, that man has no free will, but that everything he does, even his sins, are predetermined by God. He taught the doctrine of the Elect: that God chooses certain people, the Elect, whom He will save, the rest being the Reprobates, whom He will damn. The Elect can be recognized by several characteristics: they have faith; they lead sinless lives; they are materially prosperous, since God rewards His chosen people.

Calvin left France because the French king was strongly opposed to the new heresies. He went to Geneva, Switzerland, where he harshly condemned everyone in sight, so that the Genevans ordered him to leave. But he later became somewhat less critical, and since his books had made him famous, the Genevans invited him back. There he set up his "ideal" City-Church, with the Elect—those who had accepted his religion—running all affairs, both religious and political.

Calvinism was important in the history of the United States. The Puritans who settled New England were Calvinists, who wanted to set up a City-Church—or a City on a Hill, as they called it—in America.

A Revolt, Not a Reformation

The reasons for the early successes of Luther and Calvin are not hard to see. The widespread evils in the society of the time made it seem that everything men did was evil, as Luther and Calvin taught. Because of the behavior of the Popes, it was difficult to regard them as the spiritual leaders of Christendom. It was easy to believe that the Church had turned away from Christ at some point in its past history, as Luther claimed. And humanism and nationalism persuaded men that they would be better off without the Catholic Church.

Historians call the actions of Luther and Calvin a "Reformation." But it was really a Revolt. They didn't reform anything. If they had actually tried to reform the Church, much grief could have been avoided, since the Church was crying out to be reformed. It would, in fact, be reformed and led to new glories within just a few years. But instead they revolted against all existing authority, both spiritual and temporal. They were not just demanding "freedom of conscience." As we have seen, in those times religion was so interwoven throughout society that it could not be changed without tearing society apart. Luther and Calvin weren't attacking just ideas, but society itself.

In addition, Luther and Calvin opposed the Christian notion of community. To a Catholic, all other Catholics on earth, all the saints in Heaven and the Blessed Virgin Mary can help him to live a holier life. Luther and Calvin taught that no one could help a person spiritually. Each man and woman was alone.

Luther and Calvin eliminated all the special helps toward salvation which Catholics had: Mass, the Sacraments, special devotions such as the rosary, religious pictures and statues, customs which encouraged men to be good Christians, festivals and celebrations which showed men that Christianity was a joy as well as a challenge. Then Luther and Calvin had nothing to put in their place.

A final quote from Luther will clearly illustrate that he was leading a revolt, not a reformation: "If the madness of the Romanists [the Catholic Church] be continued, it seems to me that the only hope of salvation left is that Emperor, kings, and princes take up arms and attack this pest of the earth, and thus bring matters to a conclusion, no longer by words but by steel. . . . If a thief is punished by a halter, a murderer by the sword, and a heretic by fire, why should not we, with all our weapons, attack these teachers of corruption, these Popes, Cardinals, and all the rabble of the Roman Sodom, and wash our hands in their blood?"

One important point must be made here. The more extreme statements of Luther and Calvin are not necessarily the beliefs of Protestants today. The purpose of this discussion is to show how the Protestant Revolt began and its nature, not to judge any individual Protestant, living or dead.

Charles V

In view of the nature of this revolt, Catholics—especially Catholic kings who were responsible for the welfare of their people—could not say to the followers of Luther and Calvin: "You are entitled to your ideas and we are entitled to ours. Let's be friends." The Lutherans and Calvinists were attacking everything good in society and Church, as well as condemning the evils. Therefore they had to be fought. The first man to lead the counterattack was crowned Holy Roman Emperor just slightly less than three years after Luther nailed his *95 Theses* to the door in Wittenberg.

It was October 23, 1520. The crowds had been gathering for days, filling the great cathedral in Aachen, which had been Charlemagne's capital city and was now the official residence of the Holy Roman Emperor. A new emperor was to be crowned, a young man only twenty years old. The ceremony began early in the morning. The newly elected emperor swore to preserve Catholicism, protect the Church, govern justly, care for widows and orphans, and respect the Pope. Turning to the people in the cathedral, the Archbishop asked them: "Will you be obedient to this prince and lord?" Loud and joyful was their reply: "We will!"

The new emperor was Charles V. His father had been the irresponsible and immature Philip the Handsome, his mother Queen Juana of Castile, better known as Juana la Loca (Juana the Insane). At the age of 15, upon the death of his father, he had become Duke of Burgundy, the middle area of Charlemagne's old Empire, including what is now the Low Countries. At 16, he had become King of Spain and the Spanish possessions in the New World, when his grandfather King Ferdinand died. Now he had been elected Holy Roman Emperor, ruling Germany, Austria, central Europe and part of Italy, with the added responsibility of defending the Church.

With this great territory came great problems: the Protestant Revolt, threatening to tear Christendom apart; the Turks, menacing Europe anew by taking captives and raiding cities; the French, who were trying to take over Italy and gain control of the papacy as in the days of the Babylonian Captivity; the New World, where justice and order were needed.

To meet these challenges, Charles' parents had given him little, but others had given him much. He had been raised by his Aunt Margaret in Burgundy, where the ideals of the Middle Ages remained alive, so that Charles learned the responsibilities of a just monarch. His grandmother on his mother's side was Isabel of Castile, the great Spanish queen, whose example of devotion to the Church and to the welfare of her people could never fail to inspire Charles and give him courage. On his father's side, Charles was a Hapsburg, the family which had first emerged as a power in European politics with the election of Rudolf I as Holy Roman Emperor is 1273. This remarkable family understood the responsibilities of the Holy Roman Emperor as no one else ever did save Charlemagne and Otto I, and were to wear the crown continuously from 1483 to 1918. Charles' grandfather, Maximilian I, had brought the Hapsburgs to new heights of accomplishment in the ruling of central Europe, but his goal had not been personal or family glory but the good of Austria (the family homeland), the good of the Empire and the good of all Christendom. Even more than his talented grandfather, Charles was to fulfill these weighty responsibilities.

Charles came to the throne with a maturity far beyond his age. He was motivated by four basic ideals. First of all he regarded the Empire as a sacred trust given him by God, as serious as a religious vocation. He would care deeply for his people and always put them first. Secondly, he believed in the concept of monarchy of the Middle Ages, with checks and balances limiting a king's power. He would not use his vast Empire to gain wealth and power for himself. Thirdly, he acknowledged his responsibilities to the Church and to Catholicism. Fourthly, he held to the ideal of Christendom as opposed to nationalism. Though he ruled many different nationalities, he would try to keep them united, rather than allowing any one group to put its selfish interests ahead of the others. Motivated by these ideals, Charles would rule for 36 years. Almost single-handedly he would hold off the enemies of Christendom.

Charles Against the World

Charles would spend his life fighting three enemies: an internal enemy, (the Lutherans), an external enemy (the Turks), and a traitor (Francis I, king of France, who should have helped Charles but instead aided both of his other enemies).

The first major problem Charles had to face was Martin Luther, whose rebellion was spreading throughout the Empire. We have already seen that Luther was not merely changing religious beliefs but the way people lived, the whole structure of society. Luther rejected any authority above the individual person's conscience. Charles knew this could lead to anarchy, and wanted to spare his people these sufferings, just as he wanted to restore the unity of Christendom.

Charles called the political and religious leaders of the Empire to meet in Worms in 1521. He invited Luther to this meeting, called the *Diet of Worms*, asking him to present his beliefs so that some solution could be found to all the problems that had arisen.

Imagine how the people in Worms must have felt at the idea of a meeting between these two men: the rebel monk, 38 years old, who was trying to oppose a Church that was more than a millenium and a half old, and the 21-year-old Emperor, who had dedicated his life to defending that Church. Charles hoped that some areas of agreement could be found, that Luther could be persuaded to abandon his heresies.

But Luther intended no compromise. He stood before the Diet, proclaiming, "So long as I cannot be disproved by Holy Writ or clear reason, so long I neither can nor will withdraw anything, for it is both criminal and dangerous to act against conscience." The next day, Charles replied:

> You know that I am born of the most Christian emperors of the noble German nation, of the Catholic Kings of Spain, the Archdukes of Austria, the Dukes of Burgundy, who were all to the death true sons of the Roman Church ... Thus I am determined to hold fast ... For it is certain that a single monk must err if he stands against the opinion of all Christendom. Otherwise Christendom itself would have erred for more than a thousand years. Therefore I am determined to set my kingdoms and dominions, my friends, my body, my blood, my life, my soul upon it.

Thus we see the contrast between Luther's appeal to individual conscience and Charles' appeal to obedience to the Divine authority of the Church, a contrast which is one of the fundamental differences between Catholicism and Protestantism.

Luther was allowed to leave Worms in safety. Then Charles issued the *Edict of Worms*, declaring that no one in the Empire was to protect the heretic, that he must in no way be allowed to preach or spread his beliefs. But Charles was not a dictator who could enforce his decree with armed force. He still believed in checks and balances. Some German noblemen, who wanted to increase their own power, ignored the Edict and protected Luther.

Charles then began to urge that the Pope call a major council of all the bishops to reform the evils in the Church and to bring the Lutherans back into the Church. If Pope Clement VII had listened to Charles and called a council at that time, most of the territory lost to the Lutherans could have been regained. But this Pope was weak and kept finding excuses for delaying the council; and when his successor, Paul III, did call a council, the Protestants felt strong enough to defy it and the king of France refused to cooperate.

In 1522 Charles had to fight the Knights' War, a revolt of pro-Lutheran noblemen, and in 1524 the Peasants' Revolt, an ill-led uprising of peasants who had been influenced by Luther's rejection of Charles' authority. Charles put down both revolts successfully, but they showed that the Lutherans wanted more than just freedom of conscience: they wanted power.

Besides his love and loyalty to the Church, Charles had an additional reason for restoring the unity of Christendom. Christians would need all their strength in order to withstand the new advances of the Moslem Turks. In 1522 the Turkish sultan was Suleiman the Magnificant—destined to be the last great ruler of the Turks, whose sultans thereafter became corrupt and materialistic. He determined to defeat the Knights of St. John at Rhodes no matter what the cost. His fleets blocked all the ports of the island; his army had more than one hundred thousand men. On Rhodes were 600 knights and 5,000 foot soldiers.

Slowly the Turks wore down the defenses. Then on September 2, they launched an all-out assault. They stormed the walls guarded by the knights from Italy, then the walls defended by Spain. But the Grand Master—L'Isle Adam—rallied his men. Three hundred knights died to regain the walls of Italy, hundreds of women and children were killed by the Turks, several of the leading knights fell—but the attack was repulsed. The Turkish army was about to raise the siege and sail away. It was then that the unforeseeable occurred. A traitor had sent a message to the Turks: "The defenders cannot hold out any longer. There is not a man without wounds. There is no powder left. Persist but a little and the city is yours."

The knights could defeat foes in an honest battle. But they could not overcome treachery. L'Isle Adam was forced to sign a peace treaty, in order to spare the lives of the innocent people on Rhodes who would have been slaughtered when the Turks broke through the walls—as they would soon have done. On the evening of December 31, L'Isle Adam was the last knight to leave the island of Rhodes, which even his superhuman bravery could not save. He withdrew his knights to the island of Malta, which Charles gave him for the rent payment of one falcon per year. Suleiman was so impressed with the bravery of L'Isle Adam that he ordered the story of his heroic deeds to be read in the mosques throughout his empire.

The Turks also pressed into Europe on land and in 1526 annihilated the army of Hungary at the Battle of Mohacs, killing King Louis of Hungary. The Turks now controlled Hungary and stood at the borders of Austria, the very gates of western Europe. Because Charles' brother Ferdinand had married Anne of Bohemia, sister of Louis, Ferdinand assumed the crown of Hungary and Bohemia, though Hungary was at the moment in enemy hands.

At the very same moment that Charles was putting down Lutheran rebellions and hearing the news of the fall of Rhodes and Hungary, Charles had to fight the French, who had invaded the territory of the Holy Roman Empire in northern Italy (the First Italian War, 1521-1526). In 1524 Francis I entered Italy in person. This led to the Battle of Pavia on February 24, 1525, a great victory for Charles' troops. Francis was captured and put under house arrest in Spain. After long negotiations, Francis signed the Treaty of Madrid. He renounced his claims on Milan, Genoa, Naples, Flanders and Burgundy, on the condition that he be released from captivity. To seal the agreement, Francis was betrothed to Charles' sister Eleanor. Once he was released, however, Francis renounced the treaty. As well as refusing to call a council, Pope Clement VII allied himself with Francis in the struggles against Charles.

About the only good news Charles had in 1526 was his marriage to Isabel of Portugal, a true love match and a deeply happy marriage.

In 1527 the French war in Italy flared up again (Second Italian War). Because of his other responsibilities, the main troops Charles had available to fight the French were Germans, many with Lutheran tendencies. Also because of his many burdens, Charles was short of money and was unable to pay the troops in Italy on time. The soldiers became angry and finally broke out in violence, running wild in Rome and even imprisoning

Clement VII. Known as the *Sack of Rome,* this event was deeply regretted by Charles. Though he has been blamed for the Sack, it was in no way his fault, but he had to live with the consequences. (The Pope was released from imprisonment in December 1527.)

In 1528 Charles went personally to Rome to make his peace with Clement and to try to persuade him once again to call a council. In 1529 Charles' aunt Margaret and Francis' mother, Louise of Savoy, joined forces to arrange a peace between Francis and Charles, known as the Treaty of Cambrai or the *Ladies' Peace.* Francis kept Burgundy, but relinquished his Italian claims to Charles. The marriage of Francis and Eleanor finally took place.

1529 also brought good news on the Moslem front. Having taken Hungary, the Turks confidently marched on Vienna, the Hapsburg capital. Under the heroic leadership of the Austrian Count Nicholas, German and Spanish troops fought off a Turkish force that outnumbered them 350,000 to 24,000.

On the Lutheran front, a Diet was held in 1529 at Speier, at which Ferdinand pushed through a strongly Catholic decree. A group of Lutheran princes and towns issued the Protestation of April 19, 1529, and for the first time the Lutheran rebels were called Protestants. In 1530 the Diet of Augsburg was held, as Charles worked hard to reconcile the Lutherans. The Protestants again would not cooperate, even arming for war. Charles, beset with enemies, could not afford another war, so in 1532 he issued the *Peace of Nurnberg,* which allowed Protestants to practice their religion until a council could be called. Charles especially needed a time of peace so that he could launch an assault against the Turks. Francis I, who should have been helping Charles against Turks and Lutherans, instead was arranging treaties with both.

In 1535 Charles personally led a major victory against the Moslems in Tunis, North Africa, overcoming the heat and disease of that miserable climate to defeat the enemy. In 1536 Francis again declared war on Charles, the Third Italian War. He also attacked Spanish territory in the Netherlands, where Charles' sister Mary was untiring in organizing the defense of the country. She held off the invaders and they had to withdraw. In 1539 Charles suffered a great personal blow when his beloved wife Isabel died.

Besides all else, Charles also reformed the system of justice in the Holy Roman Empire, issuing a new and better law code. He financed Ferdinand Magellan's voyage, the first to circumnavigate the globe, and other explorations of the New World. He tried to bring justice to the natives of the New World, though tragically his wishes were not always followed since he was too far away.

The burdens he carried would have driven a lesser man to insanity or to greed for power or to weakness and failure. But not Charles. He simply accepted the burdens as part of the role in life God had given him, and gave everything he had within himself to meet his responsibilities wisely.

Catholics and Lutherans Fight to a Draw

The Lutherans' refusal to compromise led to increasing disorder and uncertainty in Germany. Fighting broke out, and Charles thought that a military victory against the Protestants might restore Catholic unity. The key battle was fought on April 24, 1547 at Muhlberg. The Protestant troops were on the opposite side of the River Elbe from the imperial forces. Charles personally led his men across the river. When they arrived, the Protestant leader tried to escape in the woods, but Charles and his men defeated him decisively. Charles reported: "I came, I saw, and God conquered."

After his victory, Charles issued a decree called the *Interim of Augsburg*. Still hoping to make friends of the Lutherans, the Interim permitted Protestants to keep all the land they had already seized. It also permitted the Protestants to continue some of their changes which were not heretical—such as allowing both Bread and Wine to be received at Communion. This settlement might have worked, but the man Charles appointed to enforce it—Maurice of Saxony—betrayed Charles. He revealed himself as a Lutheran and started a rebellion. The peace for which Charles had worked so hard collapsed.

At last Charles concluded that the Protestants were not going to return to the Church no matter what he did. In order to bring an end to fighting and bloodshed, he approved the *Peace of Augsburg* in 1555, decreeing that the official religion of any area within the Empire would be the religion of the nobleman ruling that area. If a Lutheran ruled an area, the people would be Lutheran; if a Catholic nobleman was in authority, the people would be Catholic.

Charles had come a long way since the triumphant day in Aachen, 1520. He had turned back the Turks, halted Francis I's power play, put a stop to Protestant advances. He had failed to win the Lutherans back to the true Faith. Now, with these successes and failures behind him, he was tired, old and ill. In 1556 he abdicated (resigned), the imperial crown going to his brother, Ferdinand, and the crowns of Spain and Burgundy to his son Philip. Among his parting words to Philip was this testament: "Seeing that human affairs are beset by doubt, I can give you no general rules save to trust in Almighty God. You will show this best by defending the faith." As he formally handed Philip his authority, he told his son that he had found Christendom torn in pieces and beset with foes against whom he had fought for the greater part of his life. He continued: "I have gone nine times to Germany, six to Spain, seven to Italy . . . four times to France, twice to England, and twice again to Africa . . . I have done what I could and I am sorry that I could not do better . . . My son, always honor religion; keep the Catholic Faith in all its purity; respect the laws of the country as sacred and inviolable, and never attempt to trespass on the rights and privileges of your subjects . . ."

Then the most powerful man in the world willingly—even gladly—surrendered every bit of that power and retired to a monastery near Yuste in Spain to prepare to meet the God he had served so long and so well.

Every other monarch in Europe at this time—Francis I, Henry VIII, even the Pope—had selfish goals. Charles alone fought for the ideal of a united Christendom. He was not totally successful, but without him the Protestants and the Turks would almost certainly have overwhelmed Europe. Charles died in 1558. His life is summed up in a painting by the great artist Titian. The Holy Trinity is enthroned in Heaven, with the angels, saints and the Blessed Virgin Mary. Before them kneel Charles and his beloved wife, adoring the Triune God. The imperial crown is cast aside, unnoticed. All Charles' attention is on God, where it belongs.

Review Questions

1. How did the Renaissance get its name? What is humanism?
2. What were some of the evils in the Church at this time?
3. How did Alexander VI, Julius II and Leo X help to bring about the Protestant Revolt?
4. What were Luther's main teachings? How did they differ from orthodox Christianity?
5. Who were Luther's followers? Why did they support him?
6. What was the importance of John Calvin to the spread of Protestantism? Summarize his main doctrines.
7. Show how Protestantism was a revolt and not a reformation.
8. What territories did Charles V rule? What was his background? What ideals motivated him? Who were his three main enemies?

9. When did Charles and Luther confront each other? What did Charles hope to do? What happened? What decree did Charles issue? Why didn't it work?
10. Summarize the events and outcome of the three Italian Wars. How else did Francis hinder Charles' efforts to restore Christian unity?
11. What happened at the Siege of Rhodes? At the Battle of Mohacs?
12. What were the two occasions when Charles' armies defeated the Turks?
13. What happened at the Diet of Speier? Diet of Augsburg?
14. Why did Charles go to war with the Lutherans? What was the outcome?
15. What was the Interim of Augsburg? Why wasn't it enforced? What was the Peace of Augsburg?
16. Why did Charles abdicate? What did he do after abdicating?
17. Summarize the successes and failures of Charles V.

Projects

1. Prepare a bulletin board or display of the artistic achievements of the Renaissance.
2. Prepare a chart of the main teachings of Luther and Calvin and show how they contradict Christianity as it had been taught and lived.
3. Read a description of one of the following: Battle of Muhlberg, Battle of Pavia, Siege of Vienna. Prepare a presentation of the battle including a map of the area where it was fought, a diagram of the key points in the battle, a summary of the results, and a list of the participants.
4. Prepare a large map showing the territories ruled by Charles V, marking the locations of the key events in this chapter.

Chapter Eighteen
England Against the Faith

AFTER BEING DRIVEN OUT of France at the end of the Hundred Years War, England soon plunged into civil war. King Henry VI was insane, and the resulting confusion caused rival forces to fight for the throne. These civil wars were the *Wars of the Roses*, so called because the symbols of the rival York and Lancaster families were red and white roses. By 1483 the throne was in the hands of Richard III of the Yorks. He was challenged by Henry Tudor, who had no real claim to the throne but who was supported by the Lancasters. At the Battle of Bosworth Field (1485), Richard was killed. Henry found the royal crown hanging on a bush and promptly placed it on his own head, beginning the Tudor dynasty. Thus Henry VII came to the throne by force and was not the rightful king. Henry began centralizing power, eroding the system of checks and balances which had stopped his predecessors Henry II and John from doing the same thing. He died in 1509, succeeded by his red-haired son, who was crowned King Henry VIII.

Henry VIII's Rebellion

Henry was a man of many talents who thoroughly enjoyed life. He wrote music, went hunting, had a huge appetite, loved to dance. Yet he was also interested in serious matters. When Lutheranism began to appear in England, he wrote a pamphlet attacking Luther's doctrines, called In *Defense of the Seven Sacraments*. In 1521 the Pope awarded him the title, "Defender of the Faith."

Henry was married to a dark-eyed princess of Spain, Catherine of

Aragon, daughter of Ferdinand and Isabel. Catherine had originally been married to Henry's older brother Arthur. But when he died only four months after the marriage, Catherine was betrothed to Henry for political reasons—Henry's father and King Ferdinand both wanted to preserve peace between England and Spain. Henry had been fond of Catherine when they married, but he had one great disappointment in their marriage: they had no sons. Henry desperately wanted a son to carry on the Tudor dynasty, but his only living child was a daughter Mary (born 1516). All Catherine's sons had died at birth or a few days after.

Then in 1527 Henry fell madly in love with Anne Boleyn, a young woman recently returned to England from France. Anne was strong-willed and ambitious, and she informed Henry that she wanted him to marry her. Ordinarily, young women—even attractive, intelligent ones—did not say such things to kings, but Anne was no ordinary woman. And Henry was so much in love with her that he wanted to give her what she wanted.

Henry decided that he must have his marriage to Catherine annulled. Then he could marry Anne and she could bear him sons. An annulment is a decree that two people had never really been married though they might have believed themselves to be. The idea of divorce did not exist in those days because of Catholic teaching on the permanence of marriage. Therefore Henry had to find some legal reason for having his marriage to Catherine declared invalid (never having been a real marriage).

In 1527 Henry's chancellor, Cardinal Wolsey, a corrupt, worldly churchman, sent an appeal to Rome asking for an annulment. He argued that the Church requires a dispensation (special permission) for a man to marry his brother's widow and that no dispensation had been received in the case of Henry and Catherine. Pope Clement VII sent a legate, Cardinal Campeggio, to England to hold a hearing on the issue. Henry tried to persuade Catherine not to contest the annulment. But Catherine was Isabel's daughter. Like her mother, she knew that the most important thing in the world was to love God—even more so since she was a queen, who must set an example for the people she ruled. She knew that her marriage to Henry was valid and refused to give in. Henry tried every pressure he could, even taking Mary away from her mother and forbidding them to see each other.

Cardinal Campeggio took testimony on the issue and finally ruled against Henry in 1529. Furious, Henry blamed Wolsey, removing him from office and sending him away in disgrace. As he lay dying in poverty and misery, Wolsey declared, "If I had served my God half so well as I had served my king, He would not leave me to die in this place."

Henry then turned to his close friend, Thomas More, asking him to be chancellor. Thomas was a devout Catholic and agreed to take the position only on the condition that Henry not involve him in the annulment controversy. Henry made the promise but he had no intention of letting the matter drop. He wanted Anne for his wife and he wanted sons, and he would let nothing stand in his way.

Finally, two clever and ambitious men came on the scene to advise Henry: Thomas Cromwell, a politician, and Thomas Cranmer, a bishop. They told Henry it didn't really matter if the Church would not annul his marriage. He was a king and didn't have to take orders from the Church. They urged Henry to declare himself head of the Church in England, and to require all the bishops to take an oath to him as their spiritual as well as temporal leader. Both men had selfish motives for what they were doing. Cromwell wanted to make himself wealthy by seizing Church lands. Cranmer wanted to change the Church in England from Catholic to Protestant and to make himself the most powerful Church official in the kingdom.

Henry went along with their plan. Thomas More would not and resigned as chancellor in 1532, Cromwell taking his place. In January 1533 Henry married Anne in a hasty and secret ceremony. In March Cranmer, whom Henry had appointed Archbishop of Canterbury, declared the marriage of Henry and Catherine annulled, and Catherine was sent off to a lonely and distant part of the kingdom, deprived of her income and most of her servants. Anne was crowned queen, but most of the ordinary people did not like her. They had been fond of Catherine and accused Anne of having bewitched Henry.

Meanwhile, his astrologers assured Henry and Henry assured everyone else that the child Anne was expecting was a boy. But when the baby was born in September, it was a girl, Elizabeth. Henry had broken with the Pope on the grounds that he needed a male heir. He did not even attend the christening of his new daughter.

But he would not recall the forces he had set in motion. In 1534 Parliament passed the *Act of Supremacy*, formally taking England into schism by declaring Henry the head of the Church in England and proclaiming Elizabeth and any other children he might have by Anne to be legitimate heirs to the throne. Bishops and important citizens were required to take the Oath of Supremacy, affirming their allegiance to Henry as head of the Church in England.

Thomas More refused to take the oath and was imprisoned in the Tower of London. He was joined by the only one of all England's bishops who also refused: John Fisher. Both men were convicted of treason and beheaded in 1536. That same year, Cromwell ordered the suppression of the monasteries and the confiscation of their lands. He distributed this land, which was a primary source of wealth in England, among his friends, creating a new class of wealthy men who would do anything to keep the Church from returning to power.

When the suppression of the monasteries was announced, loyal Catholics in the north of England rose up in opposition. This rising, known as the *Pilgrimage of Grace*, was led by Robert Aske, who carried a banner showing Christ's bleeding wounds. He mustered an army and could have taken London, but did not want to overthrow the king since his goal was the re-establishment of the true Church. Henry sent a promise to call a Parliament to consider their grievances and promised amnesty to the participants. Aske and his followers trusted Henry, but he promptly broke both promises. Peasants were hanged in villages; monks were hanged on timber from the steeple; Aske was executed. Altogether 150 people were killed, including one woman who was burned to death. The Pilgrimage of Grace was the only serious opposition to Henry's takeover of the English Church.

Meanwhile, Anne Boleyn proved herself no more capable than Catherine either of retaining Henry's love or of providing him with a male heir. After Elizabeth, Anne delivered only dead children. Anne became desperate. She had brought much suffering to England in order to be queen, but having failed to please Henry she knew her very life was in danger. She tried to persuade Henry to execute Catherine and Mary, thinking that if they were out of the way the people might come to love her as their queen. But Henry had other ideas. He had now fallen in love with another young girl at court, Jane Seymour. Cromwell, ever obliging, trumped up charges of treason against Anne. She was tried and convicted. Henry signed her death warrant and she was beheaded, less than three years after her coronation as Queen of England, and just a few months after her rival Catherine had died a holy death.

Within a month of Anne's execution, Henry married Jane Seymour, who produced Henry's only living son, Edward, in 1537. But she died within twelve days of the birth. In 1540 Henry married a German princess, Anne of Cleves, who unwittingly brought about Cromwell's downfall. Cromwell arranged the marriage to get a foreign ally for Henry, but poor Anne turned out to be ugly. This enraged Henry, who wanted revenge. He had his marriage to Anne annulled and sent her home, then set about investigating Cromwell's affairs. He found that Thomas had enriched himself at the expense of everyone, even Henry. He promptly had Cromwell executed. That same year he married 19-year-old Catherine Howard, whom he executed for adultery in 1542. His last wife was Catherine Paar, whom he married in 1543 and who outlived him.

Henry himself finally died in 1547, having separated England from the Catholic Church simply to satisfy his own desires.

The Church in England Becomes Heretical

As Henry's health had declined, there were struggles for control of the young, sickly Edward, his heir, because control of Edward meant control of the country. Thomas Cranmer won out and set to work making the Church thoroughly Protestant. Henry had been schismatic, refusing to accept the authority of the Pope, but not heretical. Cranmer was heretical as well.

His special target was the Mass. Official Church of England documents during Henry's reign downgraded its importance; as soon as Henry was dead, Cranmer replaced the Mass with a "communion service." He wrote the Book of Common Prayer in 1552 which denied the sacrificial character of the Mass and that the bread and wine were changed into Christ's Body and Blood at the "communion service." But because the "communion service" looked the same in many ways as the Mass, many of the ordinary people did not understand the fundamental change that had been made. It was years before they were fully aware that their religion was no longer Catholic.

When Edward died in 1553, Henry's oldest daughter Mary was the rightful queen. Some Protestants tried to keep her off the throne by proclaiming as queen a Protestant cousin, Lady Jane Grey. But the people wanted Mary and refused to accept Lady Jane. Thus England had a Catholic monarch again.

Queen Mary Tudor

Mary was 37 when she came to the throne of England, but all that she had suffered made her seem much older. She had seen her mother cast aside by the man she loved, deprived of her rightful title as Queen of England. She had seen Catherine die, suffering not so much because of what had happened to her personally, but because Christ's Church had been abandoned by England. She had seen her father become a cruel, wicked man, under the influence of Cromwell and Cranmer. She herself had been shunted about and kept under watch for fear she would escape to her cousin Charles V, who could have mounted an invasion to put her on the throne. She had been kept from her mother, snubbed and degraded, and had lived in fear for her life. She had been forced to endure every kind of pressure to persuade her to deny the authority of the Pope. She had seen England leave the Catholic Church primarily to satisfy the ambitions of evil men.

She wanted more than anything in the world to restore Catholicism to her country. First she abolished the Act of Supremacy and the Book of Common Prayer. Next she arranged a marriage between herself and Charles V's son, Philip of Spain, great-grandson of Ferdinand and Isabel and a loyal Catholic. Though she was much older than Philip, he admired and cared for her. Mary's most fervent prayer was that she and Philip would have a child who would be a Catholic heir to the throne, but the marriage remained childless.

Then she arrested Cranmer and the other Protestant leaders who had tried to keep her off the throne. She had them tried for treason and executed. These executions are the source of the "Bloody Mary" legend which has made Mary one of history's most maligned persons. The source of the propaganda is a book by a rabid anti-Catholic, Foxe's *Book of Martyrs*, written five years after Mary's death. In his book, Foxe purported to tell the tales of 273 people "martyred" by Mary for their religious beliefs. A careful study of the book, however, shows that 169 of the persons in it are listed only by name and were most probably criminals who would have been executed no matter who was ruling. That leaves 104 names of persons who were executed by Mary for a religion-related reason. However, it is important to realize that Protestant leaders tried to keep Mary off the throne and were plotting against her once she came to the throne. They were guilty of treason, a capital offense in any country. Furthermore, the 104 executions were fewer than the martyrdoms under her father or her sister, Elizabeth. Henry executed 150 people after the Pilgrimage of Grace alone, after having promised them amnesty; his total number of victims was 649. Elizabeth martyred 189 in England and was responsible for the deaths of many more in Ireland, as we shall see. Thus Mary Tudor has been unfairly named "Bloody Mary." "Bloody Henry" or "Bloody Elizabeth" would be much more accurate names.

Mary reigned only five years. On her deathbed she was faced with the crucial question of designating an heir. Since Anne Boleyn was not Henry's rightful wife, Elizabeth was illegitimate and had no right to the throne. The rightful heir should have been Mary Stuart, granddaughter of Henry's sister Margaret and James IV of Scotland. But Mary Stuart was at that time married to Francis, who was heir to the French throne. Philip was afraid that if Mary became queen of England, there would an English-Scottish-French alliance against Spain. Thus he urged Mary to accept Elizabeth as an heir. Mary did not trust Elizabeth, but Elizabeth swore an oath to the dying queen that she would continue Mary's efforts to restore the Catholic Church to England. Mary accepted the promises and named Elizabeth her heir. Philip's selfish political decision was to have disastrous consequences for England and ultimately for Spain as well. Philip was later a great Catholic leader, but this serious mistake weighed heavily on his conscience.

In 1558 Elizabeth became Queen of England. She was to reign until 1603, 45 years, sealing the doom of the Catholic Church in England.

Queen Elizabeth I

Elizabeth's reign displayed a strange combination of features. She seemed to have a talent for leadership; yet her major policies were devised by one of her ministers. Some real achievements occurred during her reign—much of the finest English literature was written during this time, for example; yet she launched a vicious and bloody persecution. She kept all Europe guessing as to whom she would marry; yet she died unmarried. At least part of the explanation can be found in the personality of the man who became her secretary of state.

During Mary's reign a minor official of the government named William Cecil had walked about court carrying a huge rosary, to convince Mary that he was on her side in the religious struggle. But when Elizabeth became queen, he threw away the rosary and revealed himself as a Protestant. He became Elizabeth's secretary of state and persuaded Elizabeth that she depended on the Protestants for her survival since only they would regard her as the legitimate heir to the throne.

Cecil, like Thomas Cromwell before him, cared for nothing except power. He was a deadly, life-long enemy of the Catholic Church. But he was cleverer even than Cromwell. He set up the first fully formed intelligence network in Europe, with spies everywhere. He also used hired assassins. Cecil remained chief minister of England until his death, and was then succeeded by his son, Robert, who served until 1613. This length of service was very unusual in the confused and dangerous politics of 16th and 17th century Europe.

Under Cecil's urging, Elizabeth did not take long to break her promise to Mary and Philip. At her coronation Mass, she forbade the elevation of the Host during the Consecration, and she struck the name of the Pope from the list of sovereigns to be notified of her accession to the throne. She restored the Act of Supremacy and the Book of Common Prayer. She removed from office all but one of England's bishops (all but two of whom died in prison), replacing them with new ones consecrated according to an invalid formula and rejecting the Catholic view of the Mass and priesthood. This meant that they were not truly bishops. Since they were not bishops, they could not truly ordain priests. Since the priests were not truly ordained, they couldn't change bread and wine into Christ's Body and Blood. Though some Anglicans (members of the Church of England) still believed in transubstantiation, the bread and wine on their altars remained simply bread and wine. Her invalidly consecrated bishops "ordained" "priests" in lots; they were mediocre but loyal to her. All was done skillfully, so that the people didn't fully realize what was happening. The majority of the ordinary people thought it safer simply to obey Elizabeth; Anglicanism came to be equated with patriotism.

The Elizabethan Persecution

Elizabeth is often referred to as "Good Queen Bess," but the English Catholics of her time would not have agreed with that nickname. In Elizabethan England, there were fines for non-attendance at Anglican services; Mass was illegal; anyone caught attending Mass could be fined and imprisoned and had to take the Oath of Supremacy; the penalty for the second refusal of the oath was death; bringing objects of devotion (rosaries, pictures of saints) into the country was penalized by confiscation of property; reconciling anyone to the Church or being reconciled to the Church was high treason; priests could be executed as traitors. Informers were paid to report on priests and Catholic activity.

Here are the stories of the martyrdoms of a Catholic laywoman and a priest, which illustrate the lot of Catholics under "Good Queen Bess."

Margaret Clitherow was married to a merchant in York and was the mother of several children. In a secret room in her home she hid priests who would say Mass for the Catholics in York. She was arrested several times and imprisoned in miserable circumstances because she would not attend Anglican services.

Finally the police broke into her home when the priest was there and threw them both into prison. At her trial, Margaret admitted that Mass had been said in her home, that she was proud of having had it there, and that she would have it again if she had the chance. She was martyred by being crushed under heavy stones, a particularly slow and painful death. Yet during her agony, she was cheerful, offering her sufferings to God and praying for those who persecuted her.

Edmund Campion was born in 1538 and was an Oxford professor by the time he was 17, brilliant and popular. Campion had probably taken the Oath of Supremacy and attended Protestant services. As he continued his studies he realized that all of his readings of the Fathers of the Church were against the Protestant position. But he convinced himself that heresy was really a small point and that he shouldn't cut himself off from worldly success for "mere" matters of doctrine.

By 1568, though, the lines were hardening with Catholics suffering serious repression. Campion had to take a stand. In 1569, he openly professed himself a Catholic. His term as proctor of the university had come to an end, and he hoped that he could still have an honorable life as a Catholic layman. He went to Ireland as a tutor.

But in 1570, Elizabeth began cracking down in Ireland. Campion went to Douai, Belgium, where a seminary for Englishmen had been set up. Campion realized how much of a compromiser he had been in the past; he heard an insistent call to martyrdom. In 1573 he left for Rome, on foot, alone, to become a Jesuit. He said his first Mass on September 8, 1578.

Campion taught for two years, then prepared to go to England with Robert Persons. They crossed the Channel on June 24, 1580, disguised as jewelers, with false names and false identities. In England, Masses were said in secret, with the sacred vessels kept behind sliding panels and priests smuggled through concealed passages.

Campion and Persons successfully entered England, then went to London, where Persons arranged lodging in the house of a young layman, George Gilbert. For the first three months, Campion traveled throughout the countryside, visiting about 50 houses, saying Mass and administering the Sacraments. The procedure was that when he would arrive at a house, word would go out to Catholics in the neighborhood. They would come at night for confession and counseling. Early next morning, he would celebrate Mass and distribute Communion. Campion even found time to write first a pamphlet and then a book attacking Protestant doctrine. These were secretly printed and distributed.

In July 1581 Campion was staying the weekend at Lydon House, a Catholic center. Eliot, a professional priest-hunter in Cecil's pay who had been in jail for manslaughter and then released because he promised to turn informer, came to the house. He attended Campion's Mass at which the sermon was on the theme, "Jerusalem, thou who killest prophets." Eliot brought troops to search the house, but Campion was hiding in a "priest hole" and the search was unsuccessful. A guard of 60 was left behind.

At daybreak the next day, the search began again, but by now even Eliot was losing heart. He knew that Campion had been there, but perhaps he had changed his plans. Suddenly a man named Jenkins noticed a chink of light in the well over the stairs, and seizing a crowbar, revealed the back of the hiding place. Then Jenkins called, "I have found the traitor."

Campion was taken to London. On the way there, he told Eliot that he forgave him and urged him to repent and go to confession, but Eliot refused. Campion was ridden into town on a horse with a sign on his hat reading "Campion the Seditious Jesuit." He was imprisoned in a miserable cell in the Tower of London, where it was impossible to stand up or lie down at full length.

Campion was brought before Elizabeth. He acknowledged her as queen but only in temporal matters. She told him that if he abandoned his faith and became a Protestant minister, there was no limit to the heights he might reach. He refused. He was returned to the Tower and put on the rack as Cecil tried to get him to reveal the names of other Catholics. He was so injured by his tortures that at his trial he could not even lift his hand to take the oath. Finally, on false evidence he was convicted of treason, being sentenced to hanging, drawing, and quartering. At his execution on December 1, he made his final statement: "I am a Catholic man and a priest; in that faith I have lived and in that faith I intend to die. If you esteem my religion treason, then I am guilty; as for other treason I have never committed any, God is my judge."

Because of the courage of people like Margaret and Father Campion, Catholicism was kept secretly alive. But the public practice of the Faith was ended, and those who chose to remain faithful to the true Church knew that they were risking their very lives in doing so.

Mary Stuart, Queen of Scots

Catholics in England and throughout Europe could not regard Elizabeth as the rightful ruler of England. (That was the excuse used by Elizabeth for executing Catholics for treason.) The rightful queen was the tall, red-haired beauty, Mary Stuart, known as Mary Queen of Scots.

Mary had gone to France, the home of her mother's family, the

Guises, in 1548 at the age of six, to be brought up to be the bride of the heir to the French throne. She was already the queen of Scotland, since her father's death when she was six days old, but her mother stayed behind to rule Scotland as regent.

In 1558, Mary and Francis were married, and the happy young couple assumed that they would have many years before the responsibility of ruling France was theirs. But in 1559, the 41-year-old king of France, Henry II, died after ten days of great agony. He had been jousting in a tournament to celebrate the betrothal of his daughter, Isabel Valois, to Philip of Spain, and had insisted on one more pass. As the two jousters came together, their lances shattered, the jagged end of his opponent's lance pushing through Henry's throat and eye, lodging a sliver of metal in his brain.

Only sixteen years old, Francis had wept: "What will I do if he dies? What will I do if he dies?" Totally lacking the strength to be king, his reign might nevertheless have been successful thanks to the influence of his wife, who was a much stronger person than he was, and her French relatives, the Guise family, the bravest, most noble and most dedicated of France's Catholic families. But within a year Francis was dead, his brain half rotted away. Mary was at odds with her mother-in-law, Catherine d'Medici, who now held power in France as regent for her younger son, Charles IX. Mary decided to return to Scotland.

Mary's mother had died the same year as Francis (1560), and the country was being ruled by her half-brother, James Moray, an illegitimate son of her father, and his Protestant friends. Scottish Calvinists under the leadership of John Knox dominated the country and made clear their opposition to Mary's rule. A mob attempted to disrupt her first Sunday Mass in Holyrood Chapel, Knox proclaiming that one Mass was a worse disaster than 10,000 armed troops invading the land. He wrote "First Blast of the Trumpet against the Monstrous Regiment of Women," in which he attacked the idea of women (primarily Mary Stuart) as rulers because they were "weak, frail, impatient, feeble, foolish . . ."

Mary decreed that Protestantism could be practiced and did not persecute anyone because of religion. She wanted to keep peace and order in Scotland in order to achieve her main goal, which was to persuade Elizabeth to name Mary to succeed to the throne of England when Elizabeth died. Mary believed that this would be the best way eventually to bring Catholicism back to England.

But Mary's first major mistake was to fall madly in love with a young English nobleman named Henry Darnley. Darnley was spoiled and immature, but also handsome and good company. Mary was lonely since the death of her husband and felt the need of a king to help her rule. They were married in 1565, but Mary soon lost her love for Darnley because of his arrogance and egotism.

The Protestant noblemen played on Darnley's ambition and won him to their side in a plot against Mary. They killed her trusted adviser, David Rizzio, before her eyes and imprisoned her. But Mary then persuaded the weak-willed Darnley that the noblemen were just using him for their own advantage. He helped her escape, and she rallied loyal noblemen to her side, especially James Bothwell, who was her main support.

She returned triumphantly to Edinburgh, where her son James was born on June 19, 1566. She now relied solely on Bothwell. Darnley became ill and lived isolated in a house at Kirk o'Field, outside Edinburgh. On February 9, 1567, in a plot arranged by Bothwell, gunpowder was exploded in Darnley's house and he was strangled while trying to escape.

Mary was not involved in the murder plot, but she made no attempt to find those responsible, leading many people at the time to believe her guilty. What turned the people against her even more was that she married Bothwell just three months later (May 15). The rebellion broke out again. When she was weak and sick from a miscarriage in July, the rebels forced her to abdicate in favor of her son, who was taken from her and crowned king at the age of 13 months. She never saw him again.

Bothwell abandoned Mary and escaped to Denmark where he was eventually captured and imprisoned, dying in captivity. Mary was imprisoned at Lochleven Castle, but her guards were impressed by her and helped her to escape. She joined with loyal Scottish noblemen, led by the Seton clan, who fought the Protestants at the Battle of Langside. After her army was defeated, she felt she had no choice but to flee to England. She hoped that Elizabeth, a fellow queen, would protect her. But Elizabeth, and more especially Cecil, had no intention of protecting a rival. Mary was arrested on charges of cooperation in the plot to kill Darnley.

At her trial, the chief evidence was the *Casket Letters*, which Moray had sent down to England and which were set forth as letters from Bothwell to Mary, implicating her in Darnley's murder. The letters are now known to be forgeries, but Mary was convicted on the basis of them, in a trial at which she was not even allowed to appear, in a court which had no authority to judge the Queen of Scotland for alleged crimes committed on Scottish soil.

Mary was placed in captivity (1568), while Cecil tried to persuade

Elizabeth to have her executed. But Elizabeth was not prepared to go that far, and allowed Mary to live. During her imprisonment, Mary repented her past sins and grew closer to God.

Thus the Protestant Elizabeth remained securely on the throne of Protestant England, while Cecil developed his plans to make all of Europe Protestant as well.

Review Questions

1. Who founded the Tudor Dynasty? How did he do it?
2. Why did Henry want to divorce Catherine? How was the divorce brought about?
3. What was his first attempt to have his marriage annulled? What happened?
4. Who persuaded Henry to make himself head of the Church? What were their motives?
5. What was the Act of Supremacy? Who refused to take the Oath of Supremacy and what happened to them?
6. What was the suppression of the monasteries? the Pilgrimage of Grace? What happened to it?
7. What happened to Anne Boleyn? Who was Henry's next wife? Who was his only son?
8. What happened to Cromwell and why?
9. What happened to the Church during the reign of Edward? Who was responsible?
10. What attempt was made to keep Mary Tudor from coming to the throne?
11. What steps did she take to restore the Catholic Church to England?
12. How did she get the name "Bloody Mary"? Why is it undeserved?
13. Why did Mary name Elizabeth as her heir?
14. How did Elizabeth and Cecil complete the abolition of Catholicism in England?
15. Summarize the story of the martyrdom of Margaret Clitherow. Of Edmund Campion.
16. Why was Mary Stuart the rightful queen of England? Why was she living in France? Why did she return to Scotland?
17. Who opposed her in Scotland? Why? How?
18. Why was her marriage to Darnley a mistake? How did Darnley die? Why was Mary blamed?

19. How did Mary lose her throne?
20. Why did Mary go to England? What happened to her there?

Projects

1. As far as anyone knows, Elizabeth and Mary Stuart never met. But imagine that they did. Write or act out an imaginary account of their conversation.
2. Make a chart of Henry's six wives, with the important facts about each.
3. Find out about an English martyr and give a report on him or her.
4. Write a letter that Catherine of Aragon might have written during her exile after Henry married Anne. Address it to her daughter, Mary.
5. Do a report on the controversial subject of whether Richard III was guilty of the murder of his two nephews in the Tower of London.

Chapter Nineteen
The Catholic Defense

THOUGH CHARLES' SON, Philip II, did not rule the Holy Roman Empire, he was still the most powerful king of his time, ruling Spain, Burgundy, and the New World. Like his father, he accepted the responsibility of defending Christendom against the attacks of the Protestants and the Turks.

Christ and Satan War for France

Philip was crowned king of Spain in 1556. In 1557 he returned to England, where he saw Mary Tudor for the last time and persuaded her to name Elizabeth as her heir. Philip soon learned that he had made a grievous mistake. He and Cecil became great adversaries and confronted each other in many countries in Europe, Philip defending the Church and Cecil seeking her overthrow.

In 1559 Philip achieved a victory which had escaped his father. At the *Battle of San Quentin*, Spanish troops decisively defeated the French, resulting in a peace treaty with King Henry II of France. In thanksgiving to God, Philip began the construction of a monastery-palace in honor of St. Lawrence, on whose feastday the victory was won, in the small town of *El Escorial* near Madrid. This building symbolizes Philip's character: strong, unostentatious, centered on Christ. It contains his "throne"—a simple canvas stool under a painting of the Crucifixion, and the magnificent basilica where he would slip in quietly to pray as he bore the great burdens of his office.

One of the provisions of the treaty arranged the marriage of Philip and Isabel of Valois, at the celebration of which Henry II was killed. Philip took his gentle, lovely wife home, leaving France under the rule of Francis II and Mary Stuart, assisted by the Guises.

Calvinism had made strong headway among French aristocrats (though the majority of the ordinary French people held to the Catholic Church), as nobles saw the new religion as a means of wresting political power from the crown and from the Catholic nobility. With Henry II dead and a weak, young king on the throne, the *Huguenots* (French Calvinists) under the leadership of Admiral Coligny saw an opportunity to seize power. In March 1560 came the shadowy plot known as the Conspiracy or *Tumult of Amboise*, in which certain Huguenots—probably with Cecil's connivance and with the support of Calvin himself, who had said that it was lawful to slay those who hindered the preaching of Calvinism—attempted to kidnap Francis and murder the Guises. They hoped to control Francis and influence him to be Calvinist. The plot was uncovered and the head of the Guise family, Duke Francis, moved against the ringleaders.

Furious at the failure of their plot, and encouraged by Cecil, who urged them to make good use of "their pen and weapons," the Huguenots began the Wars of Religion in France, sweeping the country with a wave of diabolical anti-Catholic atrocities during 1561. Churches were devastated; nuns and priests were scourged and killed; the tombs of saints were violated. At Montpellier the Huguenots sacked 60 churches and killed 150 priests and monks. The famous monastery of Cluny, from which had come the great reform of the Church in the tenth and eleventh centuries, was looted. All that remained of two of France's most famous saints, Irenaeus of Lyons and Martin of Tours, was thrown into the Loire River; the incorrupt body of St. Francis of Paola was taken from its tomb, dragged through the streets and burned.

By this time, Francis II had died; and Catherine d'Medici, Henry II's widow, was ruling in the name of the young Charles IX. Philip sent money and 7000 soldiers to help Catherine put down the Huguenot rebellion. Cecil sent money and arms to the Huguenots. On December 19, 1562, the Duke of Guise besieged the Huguenots at Orleans. The Huguenots attacked so furiously that the Catholic cavalry was routed. The Calvinists were singing victory songs, when suddenly the Spanish infantry counterattacked and won the day. The Duke of Guise continued the siege. He would surely have won and ended the war, but he was shot by a poisoned bullet from the gun of a Calvinist who had joined the Catholic army specifically for the purpose of assassinating the great Catholic leader. The Duke died, forgiving his murderer and praying God to forgive him. Catherine made a humiliating surrender to the Huguenots, giving them many concessions and ensuring that religious strife would continue to rack her country. Catherine would wield power for thirty years, manipulating her children as so many pawns on a chessboard, seeking power for herself and her family, putting personal gain ahead of the rights of the Church.

Catherine was already well-practiced in defying the Church. Forced into a political marriage at 14 (to further Francis I's ambitions in Italy), she had felt her position threatened because she had borne no children after ten years of marriage. Prayers and pilgrimages had not relieved her barrenness. So she turned from God to a power she felt could get things done more efficiently: witchcraft and devil worship. On January 19, 1544, Francis was born, and Catherine bore a child a year for the next decade.

But no one can defy the laws of God without eventually suffering the consequences. And the consequences for the children Catherine bore were frightening to behold: Francis, dead before he was 17, his brain half-rotted away; Isabel, a loving and loyal wife to Philip, but dead in her early 20's; Claude, crippled from birth and welcoming her death at 27; Louis, Jean, Victor, all dead within a year of their baptisms; Charles, insane and dead at 24; Hercule, stunted and misshapen, dead at 30; Marguerite, so beautiful that men traveled hundreds of miles simply to look at her, yet never able to bear children and pursuing a life of immorality with terrible energy until she grew old and sick and ugly and returned to the God her mother had forsaken; Henri, greedy, perverted, assassinated in his 38th year.

No one can sin except through his own free will choice, but sometimes the innocent suffer because of the sins of others. Catherine's children were responsible for their own souls, but each one of them suffered because of their mother's sins. And so, tragically, did France.

The Siege of Malta

While the monastery at El Escorial was being built, Philip would often come to the little town to watch the building progress. On a hill overlooking the town was a rock formation in the shape of a chair. Here Philip would sit, looking down on the workmen and looking forward to the day when the monastery-palace would be completed. But even in this peaceful little town, Philip could not escape the crises afflicting his realm.

One of the most worrisome was the Turks, on the march once again. Suleiman the Magnificent, the Turkish ruler, planned to conquer the island of Malta, where the Knights of St. John had taken refuge after their defeat at Rhodes. From there he would move to Sicily, Italy and southern Europe. He had sworn to feed his horses at the high altar of St. Peter's in Rome. Suleiman was pouring all the lavish wealth of his empire into this campaign. Philip meanwhile was trying to borrow money—he never had enough—and build a fleet of ships from scratch, to defend against the Turks.

The Grand Master of the Knights, La Valette, had, at age 47, survived a year as a Turkish galley slave. At the time of the siege, he was 71, the same age as Suleiman. The Turks had 31,000 men in 180 ships; the Knights had 641 with 8000 auxiliaries. As the Turkish fleet approached Malta, La Valette, ordered the Blessed Sacrament to be carried in procession, begging God for help in the coming battle.

On May 25, 1565, the Turks began to batter away with their artillery at the castle of St. Elmo. La Valette had instructed the Knights there to hold out as long as possible to allow more time to prepare other defenses and for Philip's fleet to arrive. The Turks assaulted no less than six times in one day, but each time the Knights drove them back, though hundreds of Knights were killed. After 18 days of attacks, the Knights there had been reduced to 60 men. The commander asked permission to fight their way out and join the main force. La Valette asked them to hold on longer. The Knights held out 13 more days. Then at last their strength was spent. The Turks broke through the walls, torturing and slaughtering everyone there.

Now the Turks attacked the main fortress and the rest of the Knights. La Valette sent urgent messages to Philip, pleading for help. Philip did everything he could, but would his ships get to Malta in time? The people of Malta helped by throwing stones and pouring boiling water on the Turks and by fighting a battle in the water with swimming Turks who tried to cut through defenses placed in the harbor.

By August 19 the Turks had opened three breaches in the walls. In the four-hour battle that followed, the white-haired Grand Master charged them, sword in hand. Even women fought on the walls, while children brought food and supplies and tended the wounded. The struggle went on, until only 600 defenders remained. The walls were reduced to crumbled stone. The Christians were so short of ammunition that they were firing back the cannon balls shot by the Turks.

As the sun rose on September 6, the Turks prepared to finish off the Christians. But during the night the Spanish army and fleet had arrived. The Spanish marched on the Turkish camp. The Turks were forced to flee to their ships and escape. Malta and Christian Europe were saved.

War in the Netherlands

Following close upon Calvinist gains in France, Cecil begin stirring up trouble in the Low Countries (also known as the Netherlands, or Holland and Belgium). William of Orange, who took favors from Philip and promised loyalty, plotted against him behind his back with Cecil and Coligny. The Protestant nobles were against Philip for religious reasons primarily, but they also wanted political freedom and complete control of the wealth of the Low Countries. In 1566 a group of the noblemen came before Margaret of Parma, Philip's governor in the Netherlands, with insolent demands. One of her companions said, "Don't be afraid of these beggars," so the next time they came dressed in rags. Their rebellion is therefore sometimes called the *Revolt of the Beggars.* Margaret was willing to consider such of their requests as were reasonable and Philip himself had made concessions, but they were not willing to compromise: they wanted Spain and the Catholic Church out of the Netherlands.

On August 16, 1566, the great cathedral of Antwerp was gutted by a Calvinist mob. They began by smashing the statue of the Blessed Virgin Mary that had been carried in solemn procession the preceding Sunday; they chopped off the heads of statues of Christ with axes and transfixed other images and pictures of Christ with swords; they assaulted a great old crucifix, which displayed the two thieves between whom Christ was crucified, leaving untouched the thieves, but hacking the form of Christ to pieces. They smashed stained glass windows and the great organ, and stole and defiled the vessels and plate. From Antwerp the destruction spread all over the Low Countries, until in the incredibly short time of six weeks the churches in more than 400 towns and villages had been sacked. In Antwerp alone more than 25 churches were devastated in the one terrible night of August 16-17. Not a finger was raised to stop the destruction in Antwerp or in most of the other towns. In Brussels, however, one of the great churches of the city was defended against the attackers by a lone Spanish soldier with a pike, who held the door until help came and the rioters were driven off. Small wonder that Philip believed that what was needed in the Netherlands at that point was a few more Spanish soldiers like that one.

When the full horror of this *Calvinist Fury* became clear to Philip, he called together his advisers of the Royal Council. One man dominated the deliberations: the Duke of Alba, tall, straight, harsh and outspoken, a deeply dedicated Catholic. The Calvinists, Alba argued, were indulging their greed for wealth by sacking the churches, but what was worse, they were committing blasphemy and sacrilege against God and His Church. Spain must take a firm, uncompromising stand, using whatever military force was necessary to put a stop to these outrages. Philip heeded this advice, putting Alba at the head of a Spanish army and sending it into the Low Countries to fight in the service of Christ the King.

But Protestant troops from all over Europe poured into Holland, and Calvinists introduced the bloody practice of slaughtering disarmed prisoners. Alba was furious, believing that such barbaric practices must be harshly countered. He ordered the arrest and trial of men guilty of destroying churches, desecrating the Host, or leading rebellion against the rightful king, Philip II. Two leaders of the rebels, Egmont and Hoorne, were executed in June 1568; other men prominent in the Calvinist Fury and later atrocities were also executed or received lesser punishments. Anyone who returned to the Catholic religion was pardoned. The Calvinists named these proceedings the *Council of Blood*, but the Calvinists had been the first to shed blood, and none was executed but those found guilty of the highest crimes. The Calvinists frequently published imaginary atrocities supposedly committed by the Spanish in order to make it appear as if Protestants were persecuted.

In November 1568 four Spanish ships sought refuge in Plymouth harbor from Huguenot pirates ranging the English Channel. They contained an enormous quantity of Spanish money, borrowed by Philip in Genoa to pay Alba's army in the Netherlands. The Spanish ambassador asked that the ships either be escorted to Antwerp or the money shipped overland to Dover and thence to Antwerp. Cecil blandly told the Spanish ambassador that he was investigating the question of who owned the money. In fact he was in touch with the bankers who had loaned Philip the money, persuading them to declare that the money would go to Elizabeth instead of to Philip. For years Alba and Philip tried to pry the money out of Cecil, naturally to no avail. Meanwhile the Spanish troops in the Netherlands went unpaid, and some of them began to plunder the countryside, increasing Spain's unpopularity in the Low Countries. Finally, to pay them, Philip was forced to increase taxes, which angered the rebels further.

Philip had still another heavy burden to bear at this time. For many years he had only one son, Carlos (the child of his first wife, Maria of Portugal), who was the successor to the throne. But Carlos was unbalanced. On one occasion when a bootmaker brought him a pair of ill-fitting shoes, Don

Carlos cut up the shoes, fried the pieces and made the man eat them. When the war in the Netherlands broke out, Carlos demanded command of the Spanish army. When he was refused, he attempted to murder the Spanish general, Alba. Later he let it be known that he hated his father and wished him dead. Finally, he devised a plot whereby he would flee to the Protestants in Germany. If they could have gained control of the heir to the Spanish throne (as they controlled the heir to the Scottish throne and attempted to control the young French king), their position would have been enormously strengthened. William Cecil may have been involved in this scheme.

Deeply grieved, Philip was forced to put his son under house arrest to prevent his joining the Protestants. When Carlos died in 1568, Protestant propagandists accused Philip of murdering his son, but there is no evidence whatsoever that he was responsible for Carlos' death (though as a traitor, Carlos could justly have been subject to the death penalty).

The same year his only son died, Philip also lost Queen Isabel, becoming a widower for the third time. In 1570 Philip married Anne of Austria; she bore him four sons in the next four years, but only the youngest (Philip) lived to adulthood.

Philip Against the World

Again Philip faced a threat from the Turks. Suleiman's son Selim the Grim prepared a new assault. In 1571 his army conquered Cyprus. The Turkish commander promised to spare the lives of the civilians there, but butchered every one of them. The Turkish fleet was once again poised to attack Europe.

Pope St. Pius V called for a new crusade. The only ruler in Europe who answered the call was Philip. He put his half-brother Don Juan of Austria in charge of a naval expedition against the Turks. Don Juan was sometimes foolish but always brave. When he was younger he had tried to run away to join the forces going to Malta. A little later he commanded an army which suppressed a Moslem revolt. Now was his moment of glory.

As Pope Pius asked all the people of Rome to join in praying the rosary for the success of the battle, Don Juan sailed his fleet to Lepanto, near Greece. To prepare himself spiritually for the battle he fasted for three days, and his soldiers went to Confession and Communion. On the day of the battle he held high a crucifix, calling to his men: "Do you now humble the pride of the enemy and win glory in this holy fight. Live or die, be conquerors; if you die, you go to Heaven."

As the Turkish ships advanced in a half-moon formation, Don Juan knelt and prayed. At that moment the wind, which had thus far favored the Turks, shifted to the west, and the Christian ships sped forward. First the ships fired cannon at one another. Then they came together, and the men fought in hand-to-hand combat. When the Christians captured the ship of the Turkish captain, shouts of victory burst from the Christians, as they hoisted the flag of Christ Crucified to the enemy masthead. The Turks took to flight, having lost 224 ships and 25,000 men. Ten thousand Christian galley slaves were freed. The Turks never again attacked Christian Europe by sea.

In Rome at that very moment—the afternoon of October 7—Pius V was walking in the Vatican with his treasurer. Suddenly he stepped aside, opened the window and stood watching the sky. Then turning to his companion he said, "Go with God. This is not the time for business, but to give thanks to Jesus Christ, for our fleet has just conquered." In gratitude to Our Lady, Pius declared that October 7, the day of the battle, would be celebrated as the Feast of the Most Holy Rosary, and it is still celebrated to this day.

Meanwhile in France, Catherine d'Medici, who of course had sent no aid in response to the Pope's call for a crusade against the Turks, was becoming fearful that the Huguenots were gaining too much power over Charles, as her son came to rely more on Coligny and less on his mother. On August 22, 1572, Catherine tried to have Coligny assassinated, but the assassin failed and only wounded him. Catherine now feared that her son would find out her involvement in the assassination attempt. So she deliberately provoked Charles—whose mind was unbalanced—into an insane rage, so that he ordered the murder of all the Huguenot leaders in Paris. Catherine and Henri of Guise, Duke Francis' son, drew up the list. On August 24, the feast of St. Bartholomew, soldiers of the French king systematically struck down the Huguenot leaders. But having unleashed the violence, Charles and Catherine were unable to stop it, and the soldiers ran wild, killing nearly 5,000 Huguenots, including women and children, in what is known as the *St. Bartholomew's Day Massacre*. This atrocity gave the Calvinists further anti-Catholic propaganda, though Catherine had ordered the killings not for the sake of the Church but to increase her own power.

Under the leadership of William of Orange, the Calvinists in the Netherlands carried on their rebellion. Philip recalled Alba, hoping that a change of tactics might bring the war to an end and restore peace to the ravaged country. Philip sent the hero of Lepanto, Don Juan of Austria, to take charge. But Don Juan delayed his departure for the Netherlands. During this leaderless time, the Spanish troops in Antwerp, unpaid for a year and more, ran wild in pillage, burning and massacre, a *Spanish Fury* grimly reminiscent of the Calvinist Fury in that same city that had begun the war, except that no sacrilege was involved.

When Don Juan finally arrived, he used a combination of heroism, charm and dedication to stave off the total disaster for the Catholic cause in the Netherlands that seemed sure to follow the Spanish Fury. He had a cross emblazoned with the words "In this sign we defeated the Turks; in this sign we will defeat the heretics," and on the last day of January 1578, he shattered the army of William of Orange in the Battle of Gembloux. In the excitement of victory, Don Juan even considered a daring mission to England to rescue Mary Stuart, marry her and seize the throne of England for its rightful queen.

The Calvinists were goaded to a second Calvinist Fury, sacking churches and monasteries and expelling priests from areas they controlled. On the feast of Corpus Christi in 1578—a day on which the Blessed Sacrament was carried in procession—Calvinists throughout the Low Countries attacked the processions and desecrated the Sacred Host.

Burned out by his battles in defense of Christendom, Don Juan died a sudden and premature death. He was succeeded as governor of the Netherlands by Alexander Farnese, Prince of Parma, called the greatest soldier of his age, who gradually rebuilt Philip's position in the Netherlands until by 1585 he had regained Antwerp and seemed on the verge of total victory. Then Cecil stepped in once more. Negotiations with Dutch commissioners were held all through the summer at Cecil's home, and on August 25 an offer to send 5000 English infantry and 1000 cavalry was sent to Holland in Cecil's own handwriting. The war went on, with Parma ensuring that the Spanish Netherlands (present-day Belgium) at least would remain Catholic but unable to win the smashing victory needed against the combined Dutch and English forces.

"In My End Is My Beginning"

Cecil never rested in his attempts to eliminate Catholic influence in Europe. In 1585 he and his chief of secret service, Walsingham, had Parliament enact the Act of Association, which provided for the death penalty for all plotters against Elizabeth and for the person on whose behalf the plot was arranged, even if he or she were ignorant of the plot. The only person likely to be put on the throne if Elizabeth were overthrown was Mary Stuart. Thus the Act was aimed directly at the Catholic Queen of Scots. That same year Mary was moved to Tutbury prison, in much more uncomfortable circumstances than her previous confinement. Her jailor was Amyas Paulet, a rabid Puritan, who made Mary's life miserable.

Once the Act of Association was passed, Cecil and Walsingham did not wait for a plot to develop. They stirred up some young Catholic noblemen, led by Anthony Babington, to plot to rescue Mary Stuart and put her on the throne. They did this through an *agent provocateur*, or double agent, one who persuades one group that he is on their side when he is in fact working for their enemy. Walsingham's *agent provocateur* convinced Babington and his friends that their plot would succeed and that Spain would help. This episode is known as the *Babington Plot*.

Babington wrote letters to Mary discussing the plot, which he thought were being secretly smuggled in to her. In fact, Walsingham read all the letters in transit, as he also read Mary's replies. Mary had been careful regarding escape attempts proposed to her in the past, but she was particularly upset at this time because she had just been informed that her son James had totally repudiated her. Thus her replies to Babington were more incautious than they might otherwise have been. She expressed interest in the escape plan, though she never at any point agreed to or approved of the overthrow and assassination of Elizabeth.

After several letters had passed back and forth, Babington was arrested. Though already in prison, Mary was formally re-arrested and charged with the crime of plotting Elizabeth's overthrow. She was taken to Fotheringay and all her belongings confiscated except, as she put it, "my royal blood and my Catholic faith."

At her trial she was completely self-possessed and dignified. She argued that the court had no jurisdiction over the queen of another country and that her only goal in communicating with Babington was to effect her own rescue. She took advantage of the forum to protest the Elizabethan persecution of Catholics. She was not allowed a lawyer, and the verdict was decided before the trial began. She was found guilty and sentenced to beheading.

Before the sentence could be carried out, Elizabeth had to sign the death warrant. But again Elizabeth held back from ordering the death of a fellow queen. She hinted to Paulet that he should murder Mary to save Elizabeth the trouble of signing the warrant, but Paulet indignantly refused. In January of 1587, Elizabeth signed the warrant under pressure from Cecil, but still held back from giving it to him. Finally Cecil took the warrant without Elizabeth's permission and delivered it to Fotheringay. The execution was set for February 8.

Mary's jailers refused to let her have a priest before she died and tried to persuade her to accept a Protestant minister. Mary absolutely refused. She spent the night before her execution in prayer, the sound of hammering on her scaffold in the background. The morning of her execution, they knocked on her door. She said that she was praying. They didn't believe her, suspecting her of some resistance. But when they broke into the room, they found her kneeling before a Crucifix. On the scaffold a Protestant minister again attempted to pray with her, but she refused him. She prayed by herself, especially offering her prayers for England, the country in which she had been imprisoned 19 years, nearly half her life. She died with dignity and courage, surrendering her soul to God, fulfilling her motto, "In my end is my beginning."

The Spanish Armada

When word came to Philip that Mary Stuart had been executed, Philip realized that the only chance of restoring Catholicism to England and reuniting Christendom would be to invade England. He had already been considering such an invasion because of Cecil's continued attacks on Catholic Europe and because of English pirate raids, led by Francis Drake, on Spanish ports both in Spain and in the New World, which caused destruction of cities and the deaths of civilians. Now, he knew that it was at least partly his fault that Elizabeth was on the throne and he felt a great responsibility to English Catholics. Furthermore, Mary Stuart had written to him before her death that she had disinherited her son and would name Philip as her rightful heir because he had English royal blood through his mother. So Philip ordered the assembling of a huge fleet, called the Armada. This fleet would hold off the English navy so that Parma's army in the Netherlands could come across the English Channel and land on the English coast, hoping thereafter to win victories and put Philip's daughter Isabel on the throne.

Philip felt so strongly his responsibility for Mary Stuart's death that he personally oversaw every detail of the Armada. Unfortunately Philip had no experience in naval warfare and would make mistakes which actually hurt the Armada. He intended Santa Cruz, Spain's best seaman, to be the commander, but he died before the fleet was ready. So Philip then chose the Duke of Medina Sidonia, a strong Catholic and skilled military commander. But Medina Sidonia had no experience at sea and relied too heavily on Philip's instructions.

The Armada would consist of 130 ships, many of them converted merchant ships since Spain did not have that many warships. These ships would slow down the rest of the fleet. In addition, the normal method of naval warfare in those days was for the ships to ram one another so that soldiers could board the enemy ship and capture it. Thus on both bow and stern were built up fighting castles, or large wooden structures, to carry the soldiers in preparation for boarding. These fighting castles further slowed down the Armada and made the ships less maneuverable. The ships would carry 30,000 men, 20,000 of whom were soldiers, and were hence overcrowded. The contractors Philip hired to provide food and water for the ships cheated him, selling him food which soon rotted and water casks which leaked. The sailing date was set for May 11, but the wind changed almost as soon as the ships left Lisbon harbor and it was two weeks before they could get on their way again. This caused further depletions of supplies, which in turn caused illness. Thus even before the voyage began, the Armada was beset with serious problems.

Finally, the Armada was underway. But on June 19 a terrible storm hit. The fleet scattered and it was not until July 20 that the Armada was able to reassemble with all damage repaired. Then the fleet sailed up the English side of the Channel, because Philip had ordered it, perhaps because he had an inadequate knowledge of the French side. This put Medina Sidonia's ships in sight of the enemy all the way and meant that he would have to fight before he ever got to where Parma was waiting.

Meanwhile Drake and Lord Howard prepared the English fleet. They had the idea of razing (tearing down) the fighting castles to make their ships more maneuverable and faster (hence they were called "race-built" ships). Without their castles, the English ships seemed smaller, though the total tonnage on the two sides was probably about equal. Drake and Howard decided to pursue a strategy of fighting by guns from long range instead of ramming and grappling.

On July 31 off Plymouth the two fleets skirmished for the first time. The Spanish learned how compact and fast the British ships were and that there would be little chance of boarding them. The British learned that the Spanish tightly packed formation would prevent their guns from doing much damage to the fleet as a whole.

The second battle was August 2 off Portland Bill. An immense amount of powder and shot blazed away but very little hurt was done to either fleet. But Howard did figure out from this battle a new tactic. Instead of sailing all his ships in abreast, firing all at once, he would sail them in a line which would move past the Spanish fleet, each ship firing in turn. He also divided his ships into four squadrons to stop the smaller ships from wasting shot. All of his new tactics would become a permanent part of naval warfare.

The English were now short of ammunition but could easily put to shore to get more supplies. The Spanish, also running short of all supplies, had no choice but to continue moving slowly up the Channel. By now Medina Sidonia was worried about Parma. He sent frantic letters to the Prince, asking him to get his men on boats and move them across the Channel. But Parma had never particularly liked the whole Armada strategy. He refused to budge, using as an excuse that he didn't have the right kind of boats. He at first did not answer Medina Sidonia at all; then finally he said that he could move in about two weeks—but Medina Sidonia could not survive in the Channel two more weeks.

Medina Sidonia anchored his fleet near Calais, while he sent more messages to Parma. Now the English had a new plan. On the night of August 7/8, they prepared eight fireships—old ships loaded with explosives to turn them into floating bombs. Medina Sidonia expected that the British might use fireships, so he had given his captains orders that if that happened, they were to cut their anchors and sail out of the way in as good order as possible. That is what they did. The Spanish ships got away so that the fireships didn't actually do any damage to the ships themselves, but the Spanish ships had lost their main anchors and had been driven out of formation. What was worse, the wind was blowing them onto the shore.

So the next day the British ordered an attack, the Battle of Gravelines. For the first time, the British came up close enough to do serious damage to the Spanish ships. The Spanish shot was inferior, often breaking up as soon as it left the gun or hit the enemy ship, so it did not do as much damage. Furthermore the Spanish ships were weakened because most of them were carrying guns that were too big for the ship; every time they'd fire, a great strain was put on the timbers and the ships were starting to break apart. The Armada might have been destroyed but a squall of wind and heavy rain came up and the British were forced to retire.

But the Spanish peril was not ended. A strong wind was blowing them to shallow water where their ships would run aground. Medina Sidonia ordered his men to pray since that seemed their only hope. Suddenly the wind shifted, and the Spanish escaped to deep water.

Medina Sidonia's ships had survived but there was no way he could continue the battle. Furthermore, the winds were blowing in such a way that his only hope was to sail north around Scotland and Ireland and then back to Spain. The voyage was a nightmare. The ships were in bad condition. The men were weak, wounded, and sick. Supplies were so low that the men were rationed to eight ounces of biscuit, one pint of water and one-half pint of wine per day, Medina Sidonia allowing himself the same ration as his sailors. The weather was cold and wet. Though Medina Sidonia navigated with great courage and skill, 26 ships were wrecked on the Irish coast. If the men made it safely to shore, they were often massacred by English or robbed by the poor Irish who regarded any shipwrecked person as a prize (though sometimes, after robbing them, they would help them escape from the British). Some 6,000 Spaniards met miserable deaths in Ireland or off its shores. On the rest of the voyage, many of the ships literally fell apart. Medina Sidonia finally brought home about half of his ships and a third of his men.

The Spanish and English had fought what was the first modern naval battle in history. It was fought with sailing ships and cannon rather than galleys, ramming and hand-to-hand combat. The defeat of the Armada assured Elizabeth's continuing on the throne, made England the greatest naval power in the world, and brought an end to Philip's hopes of restoring English Catholicism.

When the news came to Philip he accepted it as God's will. He ordered the monks at El Escorial to sing a *Te Deum*—a hymn of praise to God. Like his great-grandmother Isabel, he knew better than to question the crosses God asked him to bear.

The War of Three Henries

Just as Cecil never rested in his attacks on the Church, so Philip could never rest as leader of the Catholic defense. Events in France were rapidly coming to a climax that would pit the two great adversaries against each other yet again.

In 1574 Charles IX died, and Henri III became king of France. By 1584 it was clear that he would be the last of the Valois line. His closest male relative was King Henri Bourbon of Navarre, the husband of Henri III's sister Marguerite and an apostate Catholic who had become a Calvinist to secure his rule over Calvinist Navarre. The Catholic League under Henri Guise, who also had a claim to the throne as a descendant of Charlemagne, opposed the succession of a Calvinist to the throne of the

Eldest Daughter of the Church. Henri III at first reluctantly supported the League, then switched to the support of Henri of Navarre. This struggle for power in France was known as the *War of the Three Henries*.

Guise inflicted a smashing defeat on the Huguenots. He entered Paris in triumph as the king cowered in the Louvre Palace, afraid that Guise would seize his kingdom. The people cheered Guise wildly, but he sent his allegiance to the king, who invited Guise to a conference in his room. There, on a bitterly cold morning just before Christmas 1588, six hired assassins struck down the Catholic leader, who said, "This for my sins," as he died, perhaps recalling his part in the Bartholomew's Day Massacre. Henri proclaimed: "At last I am king of France." His mother struggled out of her sickbed to tell him, "Pray God that you do not prove to be king of nothing." Not long after Catherine herself died, according to one contemporary "with great repentance for her sins against God."

Henri III did not remain king of anything for very long. On August 2, 1589, an assassin struck him down with a dagger in his stomach. As he lay dying, he named Henri of Navarre as his successor, but the Catholic League controlled most of France and refused to accept him. Henri needed money for an army, and he knew exactly where to go for it. Cecil received Henri's ambassador at his own home in London, where he personally handed him 20,000 pounds. Henri said later that he had never seen so much money together in one place before, but within a year Cecil saw that Henri got three times that amount. He began winning battles, and by the summer of 1590 only Paris held out, two months under siege with 13,000 dead of starvation.

Philip saw his duty clearly. He ordered Parma to leave the Netherlands with his best men and march at once to the relief of Paris. He forced Henri to raise the siege and then defeated him in a second battle. Henri—who had switched religions three times already and was not known for religious fervor—decided that he could switch again. Some historians record that he announced "Paris is worth a Mass," but whether or not he actually said it, that statement summarized his views. He made a profession of faith in St. Denis in 1593 and entered Paris as its Catholic king. France had been saved for the Faith.

The Nine Years War

The epic struggle went on. In Ireland the Elizabethan persecution was perhaps even more vicious than in England. Ulster was the stronghold of anti-English resistance, and two clans especially held fast to the idea that

Ireland must be free of foreign rule: the O'Neills and the O'Donnells (also known as Clan Connell or Tirconnail). As the 16th century drew on, so worried did the English become about Clan Connell that they kidnapped the heir to the leadership of the clan—the fourteen-year-old Hugh (nicknamed Red Hugh). Red Hugh was imprisoned in a castle in Dublin, then an English stronghold. In 1591, after being imprisoned for four years, Red Hugh and a companion escaped on Christmas Eve, climbing through a window and down the wall using the sheets off their beds. They swam the icy waters of the moat and fled into the snowy hills around Dublin. They hid in the mountains for two days—without food or adequate clothing. Hugh's friend finally died of exposure, and Hugh himself was near death when his clansmen rescued him.

The O'Donnells and the O'Neills made an alliance and began the *Nine Years' War* against Elizabethan oppression. At first, under the leadership of Red Hugh and Hugh O'Neill, the Irish were everywhere victorious, restoring freedom and property to the Irish. The greatest Irish victory was the Battle of Blackwater, also known as the Battle of Yellow Ford (August 14, 1598). O'Neill and O'Donnell with about 5,000 men faced Elizabeth's general Bagenal, who had about 4,500 men. On the morning of the battle, O'Donnell inspired his men by reading a prophecy from St. Berchan of a great victory at the Yellow Ford. Bagenal, for his part, offered a 2000 pound reward for the head of O'Neill or O'Donnell. O'Neill had his men in entrenchments, in front of which he had prepared pits covered with grass. When Bagenal charged, his men and horses rolled into the pits and perished. He brought up new forces. The Irish charged with bagpipes wailing, shouting their war cry, "O'Donnell Aboo!" The English were forced back by the furious onslaught of the Irish. Then a cart of gunpowder exploded and the English were put to utter rout. Three thousand English were dead, the worst disaster Elizabeth suffered in her reign. With the exception of Dublin and a few walled towns, all Ireland was now in the hands of its own leaders.

William Cecil died in 1598, but his son Robert took his place. The Irish war went on. In 1599 Elizabeth tried again, sending over a force of 20,000 men under Robert Devereaux, the Earl of Essex, a royal favorite, handsome, reckless, courageous. She gave him great sums of money and withdrew troops from the Netherlands, where they had been fighting Philip's forces. O'Neill won a smashing victory over Essex, and then he came up against O'Donnell on August 15, the Feast of the Assumption. Before the battle, O'Donnell told his troops, "By the help of the Most Blessed

Virgin Mary, Mother of God, we will this day utterly destroy the heretical enemy whom we have always hereto worsted. We fasted yesterday in honor of the Virgin, and today we celebrate her feast. Therefore in her name let us fight stoutly and bravely the enemies of the Virgin and we shall gain the victory." The Irish won this battle at Ballaghboy, with the English suffering ten times as many casualties. Essex tried to negotiate a treaty with O'Neill, which made Elizabeth even more furious, as she wrote, "To trust this traitor upon oath is to trust the devil upon his religion." Essex panicked and sailed for London without permission. He entered Elizabeth's rooms unannounced and covered with mud, finding the queen without her makeup and without the orange wig which usually covered her bald head. Elizabeth was livid. Essex was imprisoned and in disgrace. He tried to lead a rebellion and died in February 1601.

Elizabeth and Cecil continued to pour resources into Ireland, and the Irish called on Spain for aid. Finally the combined Irish-Spanish force was defeated at the Battle of Kinsale, primarily because the Spaniards did not attack when they were supposed to. Red Hugh decided that he must seek help abroad and took ship for Spain. On his way to Valladolid, he suddenly died a mysterious death—poisoned by a spy, well known to George Carew, an English governor in Ireland very close to Robert Cecil.

Neither side could win the war, so finally, after Elizabeth's death, her successor James I made a treaty giving the Irish freedom of religion, restoring their lands to the rightful owners, and granting amnesty to O'Neill and the other leaders, in return for the Irish leaders' accepting English rule over Ireland. But James came under such vicious attacks from Protestant forces in England that he broke the treaty. The persecution of Catholics was resumed. The leaders were subject to arrest and had to flee to Europe (the *Flight of the Earls*). The English seized the estates of the O'Neills and the O'Donnells, which covered six of the nine counties of Ulster. Protestants from England settled in Ulster. This is known as the *Ulster Plantation*. These English Protestants were given the land only on the condition that they would never intermarry with the Irish, never resell the land to any Irishman, take part in no Irish customs, and support the English army on Irish soil. The Irishmen in Ulster were driven to the woods, the mountains and the moors, where many of them starved.

But the Nine Years War had good results as well. Because Elizabeth had to withdraw troops from the Netherlands, the Spanish were able to preserve Belgium as a Catholic country, though Holland became independent and Protestant. The Irish were united as never before in their belief in an Ireland free and independent. The Faith of the Irish was strengthened. So the heroic sacrifices of the Irish leaders were not in vain.

Two Deaths

Neither Philip nor Elizabeth lived to see the end of the Nine Years War. Word of the Irish victory at Blackwater had come to Philip as he lay dying in his small room which had a window overlooking the high altar of the great church of San Lorenzo. For 53 days of pain he could scarcely move. At one point the doctors had to lance a painful ulcer on his knee. The pain was so excruciating (since they had no anesthetics) that he asked a priest to read from the Bible the account of the sufferings of Christ so that he could think of that instead of his own sufferings. With his young son Philip at his side so that he could see how a Catholic king should meet death, Philip II died on September 14, 1598, and was buried in the monastery in a plain coffin, as he had wished.

Elizabeth lived until 1603. By the middle of March, everyone knew she was dying though no one could specify the disease. She was always thirsty and restless, refusing to eat or to go to bed. She sat on the floor, staring straight ahead, never closing her eyes. When urged to go to her bed, she screamed that she could not bear the nightmares she had. Anglican clergymen came to her but she sent them away, calling them "hedge priests" (invalid priests). She feared assassins hiding in the darkness. For two weeks she sat thus, until she finally fell unconscious and was carried to her bed, where she died without another word.

Philip II had continued the great work of his father. He sent missionaries to the New World and to the Philippines, which are named for him. He kept Spain united and at peace. Lutheranism made no further advances in Germany. He was unable to restore Catholicism to England or to rescue the Irish, but his troops helped France remain Catholic, and his ships helped stop the Turks. He was unable to save Holland for the Faith, but kept Belgium.

The monastery-palace of San Lorenzo dominates the little town of El Escorial. Within the basilica is a beautiful high altar. On one side are statues of Charles and his wife kneeling; on the other, of Philip and his last wife, Anne of Austria. The structure is a symbol of Spain, the Spain which Charles and Philip kept at peace—and of Catholicism, which they protected and advanced throughout the world.

Review Questions

1. When did Philip defeat the French? What monument did he build to commemorate the victory?
2. How did the Wars of Religion break out in France? What happened at the Battle of Orleans? How and why did Catherine d'Medici aid the Huguenots?
3. What had Catherine done to have children? What were the consequences?
4. How did the Catholics win the Siege of Malta?
5. How did war break out in the Netherlands? What were the goals of the rebels? What was the Calvinist Fury? the "Council of Blood"? How did Cecil aid the rebels?
6. Summarize the problems Philip had with his son. How were the Protestants involved?
7. What happened at the Battle of Lepanto? What were the consequences?
8. What was the St. Bartholomew's Day Massacre? Who was responsible? What was its effect on the Catholic cause?
9. What was the Spanish Fury? What was its cause? What did Don Juan do in the Netherlands?
10. How did Cecil bring about the death of Mary Stuart? Describe her death.
11. Why did Philip decide to send the Armada? What problems afflicted it before it sailed? During the voyage?
12. Summarize the battles fought between the British and the Spanish fleets. Why were the Spanish forced to retreat? What happened on the voyage home?
13. What were the consequences of the Armada expedition?
14. Summarize the events of the War of Three Henries, including the involvements of Cecil and Philip. What were the results of the war?
15. Why did the Nine Years' War break out? What happened at the Battle of Blackwater? Summarize the other important events in the war.
16. What were the terms of the treaty ending the war? How did the British break the treaty? What were the good results of the war?
17. Contrast the deaths of Philip and Elizabeth.

Projects

1. Make a model or draw an illustration of San Lorenzo del Escorial.
2. Imagine that you are one of the characters in this chapter. Pretend

that you are near the end of your life. Write a letter to one of your children or to a friend, summarizing what you have learned in your life and giving advice on the basis of what you know.

3. Read a description of one of the following: Battle of San Quentin, Siege of Paris, Siege of Malta, Battle of Lepanto, Battle of the Spanish Armada. Prepare a presentation of the battle including a map of the area where it was fought, a diagram of key points in the battle, a summary of the results, and a list of the participants.

4. Make a chart showing the conflict between Philip and Cecil in every area. List the main events in each area and tell who won in that area.

Chapter Twenty
The Catholic Offense

WHILE CHARLES V AND PHILIP II were defending Christendom against its enemies, the Church went on the offensive. It was not enough for Catholics simply to stop Protestant advances. The Church had to reform and renew itself, to win back lost territory, and to go into the newly discovered lands to win souls for Christ. The Church did all these things during the sixteenth century, a period in the Church's history known as the Counter-Reformation—or, better, the *Catholic Reformation.*

Ignatius and the Jesuits

It was the spring of 1521. The French were besieging Pamplona, the capital of Navarre, then an independent kingdom between France and Spain. One of the Spanish soldiers was thirty-year-old Inigo Lopez. Inigo's greatest love in life was soldiering—he would rather fight in battles than eat or sleep. Though he was only five feet tall, he made up in bravery what he lacked in size.

The French siege lasted six hours, by which time one wall of the fortress had crumbled and the gates had been breached. The attackers began to storm the palace. Inigo dashed to the gap in the wall with drawn sword. While he was fighting, a cannon ball smashed his legs, shattering one and wounding the other. As soon as he fell, the French captured the fortress. When they found Inigo bleeding and groaning on the ground, they took him prisoner. But they treated him well because of his great courage.

Two weeks later he was sent home to Loyola in the Basque country of Spain. The next months of Inigo's life were long and painful. The doc-

264

tors tried to repair his shattered leg, but with the primitive surgical skills of the time they caused more suffering than benefit. They had to re-break and re-set the leg, in an operation in which Inigo almost died. When he discovered a deformity below the kneecap, he insisted on a second excruciating operation. For the rest of his life he would walk with a limp and suffer pains in his legs.

Confined to bed, Inigo asked for books to read. He would have preferred stories of chivalry and knighthood, but all that were available were religious books. Inigo had never been especially religious, being more interested in fighting his fellow man than in loving him. But to pass the time, he read the books. By the time he was finally able to walk again, his life had utterly changed. His illness brought him face to face with Christ. Before, he had been able to ignore Christ. Now he could not. He had to choose, and he chose to reform his life. He would remain a soldier, but now he would be a soldier for Christ, dedicating his life solely to the service of the Son of God.

Realizing his great need for penance, he made a pilgrimage—on foot, limping all the way—to the monastery of Our Lady of Montserrat in March 1522. There he kept an all-night vigil, like the knights of the Middle Ages, and consecrated himself to the service of Christ. He gave away his fine clothes; he placed his sword on the altar, never to take it up again. Then he spent ten months in nearby Manresa, in prayer, penance, study, and hospital work.

He began to preach and teach, attracting admirers but also stirring up anger by his condemnations of evil, once being beaten almost to death. In 1523 he went to Rome as the first leg of a pilgrimage to the Holy Land, then walked to Venice to get a ship. In the Holy Land he was attacked several times by robbers and became ill from the bad water. On the way home, the ship sprang a leak. Back in Europe he was arrested by both the French and Imperial forces at different times, accused of being in the pay of the other. But to Inigo, all these sufferings were just so many more sacrifices that he could joyfully offer to God.

He then decided to go to school, to make up for the education he had never had, so that he could better proclaim the Gospel. He began by sitting with small children in their schools, ignoring the ridicule. He went to the University of Alcala in Spain and then in 1528 to the greatest university in the world, the University of Paris. Much older than other students, never having enough money, he spent his spare time trying to convert his fellow students and professors to more fervent Catholicism.

When he found someone who would listen, he would use a small book which he had written earlier. It was called the *Spiritual Exercises*, and was a means of bringing the individual to a deeper love of God. The Exercises took four weeks: the first on sin and repentance, the second on the life of Christ, the third on the Passion and death of Our Lord, the fourth on His Resurrection and Ascension. The Exercises had a great effect on those who made them under Inigo's direction. People who had led sinful lives or lives indifferent to God became fervent Catholics. The book became a classic of literature, and the Exercises are still performed today.

Inigo's roommates were two much younger men named Peter Favre and Francis Xavier. Peter was captivated by Inigo's personality and became a loyal follower. Francis was more difficult. He preferred being a fighter and a playboy to religion. But Inigo never gave up. Eventually his courtesy, good humor and patience wore down Francis' resistance, and he too repented his sins and became Inigo's devoted disciple.

Inigo gathered four other disciples around him in Paris. The seven took private vows to devote themselves to serving the Holy Name of Jesus. They called themselves the *Society of Jesus*, which became known to history as the *Jesuits*. Inigo changed his name to Ignatius, to honor an early saint. He is known to history as St. Ignatius of Loyola.

The Jesuits began with just seven men. But though they were often persecuted and criticized, even by fellow Catholics, their numbers grew. They were looked upon with suspicion because they did not follow the practices of earlier religious orders. For example, they took a special vow of obedience to the Pope, promising to do whatever he asked of them. Because of Ignatius' military background, the Jesuits were organized like an army, with firm discipline, strict obedience and careful training, based on the Spiritual Exercises. The Jesuits were approved by Pope Paul III in 1540, and Ignatius was elected the first General with only one dissenting vote, his own.

Jesuits went throughout Europe, establishing schools and universities to give Catholics the training they had lacked. They preached and gave retreats based on the Spiritual Exercises, to help Catholics improve their spiritual life. They sent missionaries all over the world. Many went into the newly Protestant countries, winning back large areas to the Church. Sometimes they suffered martyrdom, as in England, where many Jesuit priests were hanged during the Elizabethan persecution.

By 1556, Ignatius' seven followers had grown to a thousand. Their numbers would increase far beyond that, but Ignatius would see that success from Heaven. Since his injury in the war, Ignatius had suffered constantly from his leg wounds and other ailments. That he lived as long as he did seemed a miracle. Finally, in 1556, Ignatius died peacefully, almost alone, in his small room in the Jesuit college in Rome. His spiritual sons grieved that their founder and leader had been taken from them. But they rejoiced, because they knew that he was being richly rewarded in Heaven.

The Church Is Reformed

The Catholic Reformation was not simply a reaction against the Protestants. It was more like earlier times in the Church, such as that of the Cluny saints, where wise and holy men and women reformed the Church. The Jesuits were a vital element in the reform, but as in all other reforms, the papacy had to take the lead.

The first reforming Pope was Paul III, elected in 1534. He tightened discipline among priests and bishops, curbed abuses in indulgences, forbade the enslavement of the American Indians, and began preparations for a general council which would work out in greater detail the needed reforms.

Quarrels and disagreements delayed the council time and again. Its most important work was done in 1562 and 1563 in Trent in northern Italy. During these years the bishops managed to work in harmony and face up to the crises afflicting the Church. Work was done in two areas: discipline and doctrine.

The Council met head on the complaints which Protestants—and Catholics—had about the conditions in the Church. Among its reforms were the following: bishops were required to live in their dioceses; granting of indulgences in return for contributions of money was forbidden; seminaries were set up to train priests; bishops were required to be sure that a candidate for the priesthood was properly prepared before ordaining him; pastors of parishes were required to be qualified; priests were ordered to give an example of holy life; monks were required to live in their monasteries and to adhere to their vows; kings were forbidden to interfere in the affairs of the Church. The length of this list shows how desperately the Church needed to be reformed.

But more was needed. The Protestants had spread confusion because they claimed to be teaching the true doctrines of Christ. The ordinary Catholic, who had little education, couldn't be sure what the true doctrines really were. So the Council of Trent *defined* (stated the exact meaning of) the doctrines which the Catholic Church had always taught. Among the doctrines defined were these: baptism removes sins rather than just covering them up; man is truly transformed by grace; faith alone cannot save a man because he also needs hope and charity; by good works a man can merit an increase of grace; grace is offered to all, not just to the Elect; there are seven Sacraments; Purgatory exists; saints should be honored; indulgences may be granted.

The reforms of the Council of Trent were put into effect by Pope Pius V, who was elected in 1566. A greater contrast to the Popes of the Renaissance could hardly be found. He lived in a bare room, spent hours in prayer and meditation on the Passion of Christ, wore a plain white cassock instead of rich robes. The people of Rome were so impressed with his holiness that they wanted to put up a statue of him, but of course he refused to permit it. Pius V, who is now a saint, saw that the work of the Council was carried out, began to get rid of simony and nepotism, and called for the crusade against the Turks at Lepanto. He had great devotion to Mary and to the Rosary, crediting the praying of the Rosary with the victory of Lepanto.

Reforming Saints

The Pope and Council having done their part, the Catholic offense was carried on by the many saints who lived during this time, of whom we will consider the most historically significant.

Charles Borromeo: Charles first came to Rome when Paul III made him a Cardinal at the age of 22. Since Charles was Paul's nephew, most people considered this appointment just another example of nepotism. But Charles was no ordinary Pope's nephew. He was both talented and holy.

After the Council, he went to Milan, Italy, to take over his duties as bishop there. He is the best example of a bishop of the Catholic Reformation, carrying out the reforms of the Council of Trent. When he arrived, the people of Milan must have been rather curious, since he was the first bishop to live in the city in sixty years. He found that his priests didn't know Latin, that empty churches were being used as barns, and that monasteries were favorite gathering spots for dances and parties.

Charles began to travel throughout his diocese, finding out what reforms were needed. He set up a seminary to train priests. He instituted strict discipline, having priests do penance until they reformed their lives. Charles set up hospitals and schools of religious doctrine. Charles set an example for all his priests by living a simple life of prayer and penance, avoiding the wealth and display which had been characteristic of bishops during the Renaissance.

Not everyone was pleased with Charles. One disgruntled priest shot at him at point blank range—but the bullet miraculously did no harm, though powder burns were found on Charles' clothes.

Besides the reforms, Charles also showed his deep charity for his people during a serious outbreak of the plague. Ignoring the danger to his own life, Charles went from house to house, ministering to the sick and bringing the Sacraments to the dying.

By the time he died, the diocese of Milan had become disciplined and spiritual, a true example of what the Church should be.

Teresa of Avila and John of the Cross. The religious orders were also greatly in need of reform. Teresa of Avila had entered the Carmelite convent of the Incarnation in her home town, but found little spirituality there. The nuns kept their own property, could receive visitors at all hours, and neglected prayer and penance. Teresa herself saw little wrong with this life, until—like St. Ignatius—she underwent a conversion to deep spirituality.

After many obstacles, she received permission to start a small Carmelite convent of her own in Avila, which she named after St. Joseph. With 20 other nuns she returned the convent to the ideals of the early Carmelites, living in complete poverty, earning only enough money to buy a minimum of food by weaving cloth. They went barefoot and wore rough robes. Most of their day was devoted to mental prayer. Teresa wrote several books on mental prayer and frequently had visions of Christ.

Teresa set up many reformed Carmelite convents in Spain. Some of her nuns carried the reforms throughout Europe. Eventually one of the convents—that in Belgium—would send the first Carmelites to the United States.

John of the Cross was somewhat younger than Teresa and greatly influenced by her. He did for Carmelite priests what Teresa did for the nuns. Like Teresa, he faced many obstacles. Once he was even imprisoned by his fellow Carmelites who would try anything to stop his reforms. John bore all his sufferings patiently. Eventually he too won out, setting up a small monastery where he and a few followers could live in complete poverty and penance. His reform spread throughout Spain and the world.

Philip Neri: Philip had tried being a merchant, as the other members of his family were, but was totally unsuited for the job. So the tall, bushy-bearded young man came to Rome, where he instantly won friends by his humor and kindness. His reforms were directed at ordinary priests and laypeople. He would preach in the plazas of Rome, gathering large crowds by his jokes. He would shame people into repenting of their sins by showing them how ridiculous they were. Once they repented, they were loyal to Philip thereafter.

He did not believe in complicated organizations. Instead he set up what he called oratories—places where priests and laypeople could gather as friends to pray, discuss spiritual matters and enjoy each other's company. He was called the Apostle of Rome because of the good effects he had on that city. Rome had been the center of Renaissance corruption. Now it became the center of Catholic Reformation holiness.

Souls Regained

Charles, Teresa, John and Philip worked among already Catholic people. Some of them were not living very good lives, true, but they had remained Catholic. Two other saints took their apostolates to the Protestants to persuade them to return to the true Church.

Peter Canisius: Peter became a Jesuit in 1543. He went to Germany in 1549, where he worked most of the time until his death in 1597. Peter went from one end of the country to the other, founding schools, reforming universities (which were centers of Protestantism), debating the truths of Catholicism with Protestants. He wrote three catechisms of varying levels of difficulty for children of different ages. They were so popular and so effective that they were reprinted many times and translated into other languages. Within five years after Peter arrived, he was the most influential man in Germany.

Protestantism had made much headway in Germany because many intellectuals had adopted it, making Catholicism appear to be the religion of the ignorant. By his debates, his writings and his teachings, Peter showed that Catholicism was thoroughly rational, that the Protestant arguments were not convincing.

By his efforts, Peter won Bavaria (southern Germany) and the Rhineland (central Germany) back to the Catholic Church. He also won converts in Austria, Hungary, Bohemia and Poland. Poland had become largely Protestant, but thanks to the efforts of Peter and other Jesuits, it returned to the Church and is still Catholic today despite Communist persecution.

Francis de Sales: Francis was bishop of Annecy in France, but his main attention was directed toward Calvinist Switzerland. In 1594 he made up his mind to regain the province of Chablais from the Calvinists. At this time only about a hundred of Chablais' 25,000 inhabitants were Catholics. Francis went into Chablais, patiently going from town to town preaching and teaching, accepting ridicule and discouragement without ever giving up. When people refused to listen to his sermons, he passed out leaflets and put them up on town notice boards. By 1598 he had succeeded: Chablais was Catholic once again.

These six saints show the power of individual people—with God's help—to change history by having a great effect on the way people live. They spread the Catholic Reformation throughout Europe by their actions, their sacrifices and their prayers.

To the Ends of the Earth

In 1540 St. Ignatius said farewell to his former roommate and faithful friend, one of the original group of seven Jesuits, Francis Xavier. The king of Portugal had asked for missionaries to take the Gospel to the Portuguese colonies in India, and Francis eagerly accepted the assignment. The two men probably realized that they would never see each other again. For the next twelve years, Francis was to work in the Far East, taking Christianity to strange and often hostile lands, until he finally died while trying to get into one of the strangest of all.

Francis' missionary efforts began on board the ship *Santiago* sailing to India. The conditions on board were miserable, and the voyage, which normally took six months, in this case took thirteen. Francis ministered to emigrants, slaves and crew members, amazing everyone by his willingness to do the least desirable tasks and to care for anyone no matter what his condition.

Arriving in India, Francis had to suffer burning heat and monsoon rains. The local officials didn't like him because he befriended the natives, regarded as little more than animals by the Portuguese colonists. Francis' health deteriorated in the miserable climate, but he continued traveling, making hundreds of converts. Within 30 days, Francis converted more Indians than all the Portuguese had in 50 years.

Then he was sent to Malaysia, where he worked for a time. It was here that he met a Japanese, one of the few who traveled outside Japan. Francis converted him, baptizing him with the name Paul. Paul asked Francis to return with him to Japan and to bring Christ to his people. Francis couldn't have been happier and received permission to journey even farther from home.

In Japan the obstacles were overwhelming. Francis was mocked and ridiculed. He had to learn the complicated Japanese language. He was unprepared for the bitterly cold winter and sat shivering in his room by a small charcoal fire, laboring over the Japanese alphabet. Nevertheless he made many converts before Ignatius summoned him back to India to set up a college there.

But Francis had still wider horizons in mind: the mysterious land of China. The arrangements to get into the country were extremely difficult since the Chinese hated and mistrusted all foreigners. But Francis kept trying until a fever struck him down on a small island off the China coast, where he died. This man who had brought thousands to Christianity died with only two companions. He was buried in India, where his body remained incorrupt.

Francis was almost single-handedly responsible for establishing Christianity in Japan. He built such good foundations for the Church there that other Jesuits were able to carry on his work. Fifteen years after he left Japan, there were 150,000 Christians. By 1592 there were 300,000.

Tragically, a new shogun (ruler) came to the throne who was encouraged by the British and the Dutch to hate the Jesuits and all Catholics because, it was said, they were trying to take over Japan. In 1623 he began a vicious persecution, worse than anything the Church had seen since the days of Diocletian. He thought he had eliminated Catholicism, but a few brave people kept the faith alive, baptizing their children, saying the rosary, and passing on Christian doctrine though there were no priests to say Mass or hear confessions. When missionaries were finally allowed back into Japan in the 19th century, these Christian communities—numbering some 20,000-50,000 Catholics—came out of hiding and were the foundation for the rebuilding of Catholicism in Japan. Francis had done his work well.

In India Francis' work was carried on by another Jesuit, Roberto di Nobili, who adopted the dress and customs of the Brahmin caste in order to be more readily accepted by the Indians. Roberto faced the supreme difficulty of explaining Catholic truth to a society that did not believe that truth existed, that nothing either was or was not. But he did his work so well that his Indian converts bestowed on him the name *Teacher of Reality*.

Though Francis died trying to get into China, the Jesuits were far from ready to give up that country. The task of evangelizing the mysterious land was given to a young Italian, Matteo Ricci, the oldest of 13 children of an Italian nobleman. Because of Matteo's talents in science and mathematics, a Chinese official invited him to come to China.

But Matteo could not simply walk up and down the streets preaching

Christ. The Chinese thought they possessed all the world's wisdom. On their maps, China was as big as the rest of the world put together. Matteo had to adopt Chinese customs, Chinese dress, the Chinese language—he became as much a Chinese as the Chinese themselves, except for his religion.

Slowly Matteo won the respect of the wealthy, educated people in some of the important cities of China. The Chinese were not very religious, but Matteo showed them that the reason and morality they prized came from a Supreme Being, the Lord of Heaven. Gradually he gained converts, though his progress was painfully slow.

He had hoped to meet the emperor, to get permission from him to preach Christianity in all of China. It took him 16 years just to get into the Forbidden City in Peking, where the emperor lived, and then he did so only because the emperor was fascinated with a striking clock which Matteo had brought from Europe. But Matteo never did meet the emperor face to face, though he was once ceremoniously ushered into the emperor's throne room and required to bow to his empty throne.

Nevertheless the Catholic community grew. They built churches in several cities and even started a novitiate to train Chinese monks. Matteo had planted a seed which others after him would cultivate until it bore fruit. Matteo was buried in China, the land he had adopted as his own. By 1650, 40 years after his death, Chinese Catholics numbered 150,000. Through his patience and care, Matteo had opened up to Christianity and the West the most inaccessible country of his time.

In the newly discovered lands of the Western Hemisphere, missionaries followed close on the heels of the Conquistadors. First Hernando Cortez destroyed the evil Aztec Empire of Mexico and ended its thousands of human sacrifices; then Franciscan missionaries came to bring the Gospel to the people. After the Blessed Mother appeared at Guadalupe and left her miraculous image on the cloak of a poor Indian, nearly the whole population was converted in less than a century. In Brazil Jesuits converted cannibals and set up Christian villages for their Indian converts. Though French Calvinist pirates often attacked the missionaries' ships and killed all on board, the Jesuits kept sending more priests until by 1584 100,000 converts had been made. In the rest of Latin America Jesuits and Franciscans spread the Gospel and civilized the Indians, helping to create a Catholic society.

By its missionary efforts the Church showed how healthy it really was. It had lost one-third of its territory to the Protestant Revolt. It more than made up for this loss with the new lands won for Christ.

The Glory of the Baroque

The optimism and devotion to the Church produced by the Catholic Reformation led to new achievements in art and architecture. These were also an answer to the Protestants, who built plain churches because they thought artistic beauty had no place in worship. The new style in art and architecture was called *Baroque*. Churches were filled with statues and paintings, bright colors, gold and silver, elaborate decorations.

The rebuilding of St. Peter's was completed at this time with the interior in the Baroque style, primarily the work of the artist Bernini. Over the tomb of St. Peter stood the high altar with twisting, gilded columns. On the piers supporting the dome stood colossal statues of St. Andrew, St. Longinus, St. Helena and St. Veronica. In the chapel enshrining St. Peter's chair were gold stained glass windows and gilded, larger than life-size statues of Doctors of the Church.

The Church had halted the advance of its enemies, reformed itself, won new lands for Christ, proclaimed the glory of God in stone and paint. The Church had survived and triumphed in the crisis of the Protestant Revolt as it had survived and triumphed in all previous crises. Christ's promise to Peter had been kept.

Review Questions

1. What was the background of Ignatius of Loyola? What caused him to change his life?
2. Summarize his life from his conversion to the founding of the Jesuits. What were the Spiritual Exercises?
3. Describe the founding of the Jesuit order.
4. What were the accomplishments of Pope Paul III?
5. List the achievements of the Council of Trent in doctrine and discipline.
6. How did Pius V continue the reforms of the Church?
7. What part did each of the following play in the Catholic Reformation: Charles Borromeo, Teresa of Avila, John of the Cross, Philip Neri?
8. Where and how did Peter Canisius and Francis de Sales bring people back to the Church?
9. Summarize the achievements of Francis Xavier.
10. Briefly summarize the history of Catholicism in Japan.
11. Summarize the achievements of Roberto di Nobili and Matteo Ricci.

12. Summarize the missionary activity in the New World.
13. What was the Baroque? What did it symbolize?

Projects

1. On an outline map of the world, indicate the important missionary achievements of the Catholic Reformation.
2. Choose one of the characters in this chapter. Read part of a biography of his or her life to find an interesting incident. Retell the incident in your own words.
3. Prepare an illustrated report on one of the missionary countries mentioned in this chapter. Tell something about its history, its customs, its art and architecture and anything else you think important.
4. Prepare a play dramatizing important events in the life of St. Ignatius.

Chapter Twenty One
The Age of France

THE EPIC STRUGGLES FOR CHRISTENDOM begun in the sixteenth century continued in the seventeenth. Again the Holy Roman Empire defended Christendom while France sided with her enemies. And God continued to send saints and heroes to lead and inspire the Church and her people.

The Scientific Revolution

History in the seventeenth century was not made only on the battlefields and in the cloisters. During this century, there was a great explosion in scientific knowledge. New inventions such as the telescope led to new discoveries. Probably the greatest genius of the scientific revolution was Isaac Newton (1642-1727). This brilliant Englishman made many of his discoveries by the time he was 25. At the age of 24 he published his theory on the universal law of gravitation. He explained planetary motion and developed laws of motion. He wrote the *Principia Mathematica.* He made discoveries in optics and discovered the principles of calculus. Though many of his theories have been superseded by Einstein's work, his laws accurately explain the visible motions of the universe.

Another Englishman, William Harvey, played an important role in the area of medicine. In 1628 he discovered the circulation of blood. Harvey emphasized the use of experiment, observation and dissection in medicine, rather than relying on classical authorities.

In terms of its effect on science, the scientific revolution was all to the good. But it had harmful consequences philosophically and theologically. Philosophically, there came to be an exaggerated emphasis on the powers of the human mind and a kind of intellectual pride. Also, many men adopted *determinism*. Since the universe was seen to follow unalterable and pre-determined laws, it was thought by many that man could not alter his destiny either, thus denying free will.

This intellectual pride led to the theology of *Deism*: the belief that God had created the universe but exercised no providence over it nor cared about individual human beings. Since the universe seemed to operate according to rigid laws, God was thought to be unnecessary to its day-to-day operation. Although most men still acknowledged God as Creator, many intellectual leaders saw no further need of God after the creation, and certainly no need of Him in their daily lives.

Out of the scientific revolution came a controversy which has been used ever since to attack the Church, the Galileo case. There are two main areas of attack: that the Church persecuted and severely punished Galileo for his scientific beliefs, which now everyone knows to be true; and that the Church condemned his scientific beliefs as heretical, thus showing that the Church is not infallible. By studying the actual historical facts of the Galileo case, we can see that both of these charges are false.

The majority of people prior to the time of Galileo believed in *geocentrism*: that the earth was the center of the universe and that all heavenly bodies revolved around the earth. This theory seemed to accord with Scripture, which in one place, for example, speaks of Joshua making the sun stand still. Also, since the Son of God became incarnate on earth, it seemed fitting that the earth be the center of the universe. However, in 1543 Copernicus, a Polish monk, had published *Revolutions of the Celestial Orbs*, which had advanced the theory of *heliocentrism*: that the sun was the center of the solar system and that the earth revolved around the sun. The book was dedicated to Pope Paul III and received a respectful hearing in the Vatican. Martin Luther, on the other hand, violently condemned it. Protestants based their religion on a literal interpretation of the Scriptures. Therefore if a scientific theory contradicted the literal meaning of a passage in Scripture, they would either have to condemn the theory or abandon their belief in Scripture. Since they had nothing but Scripture, they were forced to condemn the theory.

Enter Galileo. He held the chair of mathematics at the University of Pisa and later at Padua, where he was nicknamed "the Wrangler" because he was always starting arguments. He acquired and improved a telescope, discovering the moons of Jupiter, the motions of which were an argument against geocentrism. He published a booklet called *Starry Messenger* and began to push for heliocentrism.

In 1611 Galileo went to Rome to advance his theories, where he had a cordial audience with Pope Paul V. Cardinal Robert Bellarmine, a Jesuit scholar, was intrigued with Galileo's theories but concerned with the disruption a too hasty publication of them could produce in the minds of ordinary Catholics. He was especially concerned because Galileo had a tendency to mock his opponents and overstate his case.

The Church officials were willing that heliocentrism be taught as a hypothesis (not a fact) and discussed in scientific circles, so long as the faith of the ordinary people was safeguarded. But Galileo began to teach his theory loudly and widely, insisting that it was proven fact. It was not yet proven; not enough data existed to prove it. Finally, on February 19, 1616 two propositions advanced by Galileo were submitted by the Court of the Inquisition to the Holy Office in the Vatican for advice regarding their orthodoxy: 1. "the sun is the center of the world and hence immovable of local motion." 2. "the Earth is not the center of the world, nor immovable but moves according to the whole of itself." On February 24 the theologians in the Holy Office stated that they found the first proposition "foolish and absurd philosophically and formally heretical . . ." and the second "to receive the same censure in philosophy and, as regards theological truth, to be at least erroneous in faith."

The next day Pope Paul V was notified of their opinion. He asked Cardinal Bellarmine to warn Galileo that if he did not abstain from discussing his theory as fact, he could be imprisoned. Galileo accepted this warning, and all was quiet for sixteen years.

But in 1632 Galileo published his *Dialogue on the Great World Systems,* which once again advanced heliocentrism. He was called before the Inquisition. The proceedings were not of the highest quality. Galileo's enemies produced a forged document stating that Galileo had been absolutely forbidden to teach heliocentrism, instead of being forbidden to teach it as fact; and Galileo lied about the circumstances of the publication of his book. The Inquisition, on June 22, 1633, decreed that Galileo had rendered himself "vehemently suspected of heresy." He was to renounce his errors before the Inquisition, which he did, and he was placed under comfortable house arrest. That his arrest was not painful is shown by the fact that while under arrest he wrote an important book on mechanics, including his theories on acceleration, motion and inertia.

With these facts, we can now refute the two charges. As for the first charge, Galileo was clearly not persecuted, nor did he seem to suffer much for his views. Such punishment as he received he brought upon himself by refusing to moderate his statements or to take account of the dangers to the faith of ordinary people by widespread teaching of his ideas.

As for the second charge, at no time did any *official* Church teaching condemn heliocentrism as heretical. The Pope did not, nor did any bishop, nor did the Inquisition itself. The only statement was a theological *opinion* issued by the theologians of the Holy Office. Theological opinion does not represent the Magisterium (official teaching) of the Church.

Other scientists then and later were perfectly willing to accept Church guidance in this area, and gradually heliocentrism came to be accepted.

Spain and the Holy Roman Empire

In Spain there was a painful contrast between the rulers of the sixteenth and seventeenth centuries. Philip II died at the end of the sixteenth century. He had been much loved by the Spanish people, much hated by his enemies, a man who would always do what he thought right no matter what it cost him. The Spanish kings who ruled in the seventeenth century were weak men, who could not always cope with Spain's many responsibilities: the government of the New World; continued aggression in Germany and the Netherlands; the hostility of France; the needs of the Church. The strength of the Hapsburgs had been reduced by too much inbreeding, and the weight of all these responsibilities on men who could not handle them well gradually weakened Spain so that it began to slip from its position as dominant nation in Europe.

Philip II's son, Philip III, ruled from 1598-1621. Philip III lacked his father's sense of responsibility and left government in the hands of the court favorite, the Duke of Lerma. Lerma was corrupt and greedy and used his position to manipulate Spain's finances so that his friends received huge estates and to create a wealthy court nobility, while the Spanish economy declined.

Philip III was succeeded by his son, Philip IV, who ruled from 1621-1665. Philip IV wavered back and forth. He knew his responsibilities and would at times put forth great efforts to meet them. He corresponded with the Spanish mystic, Venerable Mary of Agreda, and would try to follow her advice on how to be a wise and moral ruler. But the heavy burdens on his shoulders would at other times be too much for him, and he would seek escape in riding, hunting, and the theater. He also delegated much authority to his chief minister. But Philip IV's minister, Olivares, was an upright man, nothing like the corrupt Lerma. He recognized Spain's duties as a leading Catholic power in Europe and endeavored to meet them. But the wrecking of the economy that Lerma had accomplished left Spain heavily dependent on the gold and silver of the New World to finance its wars in defense of Christendom. This dependency would lead to many problems.

In the Holy Roman Empire, Charles V's brother Ferdinand I ruled wisely from 1556-1564. He was succeeded by Maximilian II (1564-1576), who was himself a Catholic but was not strong enough to do anything about the spread of Protestantism throughout the Empire. His nephew, Rudolph II (1576-1612), was next on the throne. Rudolph was feeble and ir-resolute. He became engrossed in alchemy and eventually went insane. He was succeeded by his brother Matthias (1612-1619).

This power vacuum in Europe, left by the decline in quality of the rulers of Spain and the Holy Roman Empire, would soon be filled by France.

A Cardinal against Christendom

As you will remember, Henry of Navarre had become king of France as Henry IV in 1594, after he agreed to become a Catholic. He founded the *Bourbon* dynasty. Henry issued the *Edict of Nantes* in 1598, which gave Protestants freedom of worship and equal political rights with Catholics, including the right to have their own fortified cities and their own army. Henry was assassinated in 1610 by an unbalanced Catholic, being succeeded by his son Louis XIII, who was only nine.

Louis was brought up by his mother, Marie d'Medici, who dominated the boy and kept him from developing a strong personality. But as Louis grew old enough to reign on his own, he desperately wanted to be a strong king. Since he didn't have the strength within himself, he came to depend on his chief minister, Armand de Richelieu. Richelieu was the man pri-marily responsible for France's emergence as the leading power in Europe.

Richelieu, born 1585, came from a noble family in France. But his fa-ther died when he was five, and his mother had to struggle to uphold the family's place in society. Richelieu never forgot this misery in his child-hood and all his life struggled to make the Richelieus one of the great families of France. As the third son of the family, he was intended for the army (the first son would inherit the estates, the second son was destined for the Church to hold the family's hereditary diocese). But the second son decided to become a monk, and Richelieu was advanced to take his place in the seminary. Clearly he did not have a religious vocation, as later events were to confirm. Nevertheless, he was made a bishop and then a cardinal.

Richelieu made friends with Queen Marie d'Medici. He was very good at flattering the Italian queen, who was not particularly popular in France. This flattery, plus Richelieu's administrative talents, helped him to rise quickly in the court. As Louis grew up, he too recognized Richelieu's talents and came to rely on the Cardinal as the main person who could give him what he wanted: absolute rule of France.

For his part, Richelieu had two goals: to make the king all powerful in France and to make France all powerful in Europe.

The first step toward achieving goal number one was to break the power of the Huguenots. Richelieu knew that the king could not be all powerful (which meant that Richelieu could not be all powerful) until the semi-independence of the Huguenots was destroyed. So in 1628 Richelieu personally commanded an army to besiege the chief Huguenot city, La Rochelle. The siege lasted a year. Louis XIII was there at the beginning but became bored and left. Richelieu did not leave. Eventually the population of La Rochelle had been reduced to one-fourth of its original 30,000, and the city was forced to capitulate. By September 1629, Huguenot resistance had ceased.

The establishment of a bureaucracy was the second step in the achievement of goal number one. Richelieu did not believe in the medieval idea of checks and balances. He wanted to centralize power in the hands of the king, a system known as *absolutism.* Therefore he set up a large and complicated organization of government officials (a *bureaucracy*) throughout the kingdom. This meant that even in areas which the king never visited, his presence would be felt through his bureaucrats who could act in the king's name and with the king's authority. These bureaucrats would make the decisions that the local communities had formerly made themselves.

The third step was the elimination of the influence of Marie d'Medici. On November 11, 1630, known as the *Day of the Dupes,* Richelieu persuaded Louis to reject his mother's advice and to send her away. Marie started a rebellion with several noblemen and Louis' younger brother, but Richelieu had it crushed easily and Marie went into exile. Henceforth there was no one to challenge the king's absolute authority, with unfortunate consequences for the French people.

The achievement of goal number two—to make France all powerful in Europe—came about through the Thirty Years War.

The Beginning of the Thirty Years War

A crisis developed in the Holy Roman Empire in the early years of the seventeenth century. The Holy Roman Emperor Matthias, old and sick and soon to die, had no children. The most likely candidate for Emperor was his cousin, Ferdinand, son of Maximilian II's younger brother Charles. According to custom, the Holy Roman Emperor was elected by seven electors. Ferdinand had one serious drawback in the minds of the three electors who were Lutheran: Ferdinand was a devout Catholic. He had been educated by the Jesuits and had made it clear that if he became Emperor he would revive efforts to re-establish Catholicism throughout Germany. Besides the three Lutheran electors, three Catholic bishops and the king of Bohemia were also electors. Ferdinand himself had become king of Bohemia when Matthias abdicated that office in his favor in early 1618. His vote along with the votes of the three bishops would give him a majority.

But on May 23, 1618 the Bohemian Protestants revolted. They seized the two Hapsburg governors in Prague (the capital city) and threw them out of a window. Fortunately for the governors, they landed on a pile of garbage and so were not killed. But though they still had their lives, they no longer had any power. This event is known as the *Defenestration of Prague* (*fenster* is the German word for window).

The Protestants deposed Ferdinand as king of Bohemia, electing the Protestant Frederick of the Palatinate in his place. But before messengers could get to Vienna with the news, the seven electors—Ferdinand representing Bohemia—had elected Ferdinand and solemnly sworn him as Holy Roman Emperor.

Protestant leaders throughout the Empire urged Frederick to lead a revolt against Ferdinand. Frederick was reluctant to do so, but eventually fighting broke out. This was the beginning of the *Thirty Years War*. If the Catholic Hapsburgs won, Christendom might be reunited. If they lost, the split in Christendom would be permanent.

The war can be divided into four phases. Phase I ran from the outbreak of the war until 1623, with the Catholic general Tilly against the Lutheran general Mansfeld, who followed a policy of plundering the countryside for food and supplies, leaving destruction everywhere his army went. The key battle was fought early in the war, November 8, 1620, the *Battle of the White Mountain*. Tilly devastated the Lutheran army in Bohemia. The war should have ended at this point but instead came:

Phase II—the Intervention of Denmark. Denmark, of course, had no reason to become involved in this war but the Danish Lutherans wanted to break the power of the Catholic Hapsburgs. To counter this intervention, the Austrian Hapsburgs called on the assistance of their Spanish cousins, assistance which Olivares willingly supplied, realizing what was at stake—the existence of the Holy Roman Empire as a Catholic power. Wallenstein became the Catholic commander. He was an able general, though not a particularly moral man, being primarily interested in power and wealth for himself. Nevertheless, the combined Austrian and Spanish armies crushed the Lutherans, so that Ferdinand was able to issue the *Edict of Restitution* in 1629. This declared that the Protestants must restore all Church property that they had seized since the Peace of Augsburg (1555). The Lutherans were to be allowed freedom of worship, but not Calvinists or other Protestants. In additon, Ferdinand dismissed Wallenstein, who he feared was becoming too powerful.

It appeared at last as if the Empire was to have peace.

War Breaks Out Anew

The Empire would have had peace, if it hadn't been for the scheming cardinal in Paris. Richelieu hated the Hapsburgs, and he couldn't stand to see them victorious in central Europe. Unless they could be defeated, Richelieu could not achieve his second goal.

Since the German and Bohemian Lutherans had shown themselves unable to accomplish anything in the battlefield, and since the king of Denmark had been defeated, Richelieu communicated with the king of Sweden—the young and handsome Gustavus Adolphus. Gustavus Adolphus was more than willing to fight Catholics at any opportunity—all he needed was money. And that Richelieu provided. At the head of an army of 30,000 foot soldiers and 6,000 cavalry, Gustavus marched into Germany from the north in 1631, beginning Phase III of the war.

In 1628 occurred an event which was to have serious consequences for the Catholic side in the Thirty Years War. The entire Spanish treasure fleet from the New World was captured by Dutch pirates. As we have already seen, Spain was dependent on the New World silver and gold for its economic survival. Olivares had to raise money somehow when the war was renewed, so he resorted for the first time to direct taxation. Angry revolts soon broke out in Portugal and Catalonia (a province of Spain), resulting in Olivares' downfall. The financial situation in Spain became so desperate that at one point royal officials even tore down the curtains in the palace to sell them to raise money to carry on the war.

Gustavus knew that he had to go up against the Spanish soldiers, heretofore unbeatable. The Spaniards fought in formations of pikemen with 16-30 rows, with guns planted carefully across the front and cavalry on the wings. The guns at this time were clumsy—they had to be mounted on supports to be shot. But Gustavus invented a means of lightening the musket and turned two-thirds of his infantrymen into musketeers. He took away their armor so that they could move rapidly. He trained his horsemen to ride at a gallop, shooting and using their swords—and to keep going, right through the formation of pikemen. He invented a light cannon, which could be easily moved on the battlefield.

Gustavus won a series of victories and brought his army into central Germany. At Breitenfeld, just north of Leipzig, he and Tilly met for the first time, on September 17, 1631. The Spanish cavalry attacked, but were shot down by the Swedish guns. The Spanish infantrymen advanced but were subjected to a rain of bullets. The Swedish cavalry charged and cut down Imperial troops at the side and rear. The Spaniards were brave but they could not stand up to the withering musket fire. By evening they retreated, leaving 7,000 dead and 6,000 prisoners. Gustavus received a nickname: Lion of the North.

Gustavus continued to win. Tilly was fatally wounded at the River Lech in April 1632. Reluctantly, Ferdinand recalled Wallenstein. After a series of minor battles, Gustavus and Wallenstein confronted each other at the little town of Lutzen, southwest of Leipzig.

Wallenstein had his Spanish troops in a solid defensive position, believing that even Gustavus' tactics could not dislodge them. As the battle wore on, Wallenstein's plan seemed to be working though his men suffered numerous casualties. A heavy mist came up, so that the Swedes couldn't fire their cannon. The Swedish cavalry wing went out too far and was about to be surrounded. A messenger came to Gustavus to tell him about the cavalry, and with four companions the king rode out to see what was happening. In the mist, he rode into a pocket of enemy troops and was killed. His death was the turning point of the battle.

Marshal Kniphausen rode back to the second in command, Duke Bernard, to tell him that Gustavus was dead, adding that he thought they could make a good retreat. "Retreat!" cried Bernard. "This is not the time to talk of retreat, but of revenge!" He snatched off his helmet and rode down the line of troops, shouting in a great, booming voice, "Swedes! They have killed the king!"

The Swedes were roused into a fury. They charged forward in such a rage that later Imperial troops were found who had been strangled. The Spaniards retreated and fled. Even though he was killed, Gustavus had won the day.

The death of Gustavus Adolphus, however, greatly reduced the power of the Protestant rebels. Ferdinand II's son, Prince Ferdinand, took command of the Catholic army and won a smashing victory at the *Battle of Nordlingen* in Bavaria in 1635, which broke the power of the Swedes. Thus Phase III ended, as had the earlier phases, with the Catholics victorious.

Now came Phase IV, the direct intervention of France. Richelieu could not allow the Hapsburgs to remain victorious if he were to achieve his second goal. So he declared war on Philip IV and sent French troops into Germany to keep the Empire in chaos. The French decisively defeated the Spanish at the Battle of Rocroi, 1643, and the German countryside was pillaged.

Wallenstein was assassinated in 1634; Ferdinand died in 1637. Richelieu died in 1642, followed by Louis in 1643. Finally both sides were too exhausted to continue the war, and the *Treaty of Westphalia* was signed in 1648.

The Thirty Years War had several important effects: 1) The most important is that the Treaty of Westphalia marked the acceptance of a permanently split Christendom. 2) Hence, nationalism became supreme, and the goal of each government was to gain as much power for itself as it could. 3) This in turn led to almost constant warfare. 4) War had become much more deadly and destructive. 5) Germany was devastated. 6) France emerged as the most powerful nation in Europe. Richelieu had achieved his second goal, though he did not live long enough to see it.

The Sun King

In France, Louis XIII was succeeded by his four year old son Louis XIV. A story is told that as his father lay dying, the little boy was brought in to see him. "Who are you?" the king asked. Replied his son: "I am Louis XIV." Whether the story is true or not, it is certainly something Louis might have said, even at that early age. He always regarded himself as a king, supreme over all.

While he was growing up, Louis XIV's chief minister was Cardinal Mazarin. Mazarin died when Louis was 22. When asked who his chief minister would be now, Louis replied that he himself would be. He took the government totally into his own hands and ruled as an absolute monarch until he died in 1715 at 76.

Louis began by perfecting and expanding the bureaucracy, increasing its size from 600 employees to 10,000, thereby tightening the king's control over every aspect of public life. Louis' political views are well-summarized in his motto: "L'etat c'est moi," which means "I am the state."

Louis also reorganized the French army, turning it into a complex military machine of more than 400,000 men. His army decisively defeated that of Philip IV in 1659, after which the *Treaty of the Pyrenees* was concluded, giving France the land which the two countries had both claimed. In 1667 he launched the War of Revolution against his brother-in-law, Charles II of Spain, in an attempt to seize the Spanish Netherlands. England, Holland, and Sweden joined in an alliance against him, thus involving almost all Europe in the war. The war dragged on until the Peace of Nijmegen in 1678 in which Louis got some though not all the land he wanted. In 1689 Louis touched off the War of the League of Augsburg by his attempts to gain more land in Germany.

To raise money for these seemingly never-ending wars, Louis appointed an able finance minister, Colbert, who organized and controlled the economy. He required accurate bookkeeping and regular audits and dismissed corrupt officials and dishonest tax collectors. But he did not reform the tax system itself, which put the heaviest burden of all on the poor while the nobility paid virtually nothing.

Louis also used the money raised by Colbert to build a luxurious, enormously expensive palace at Versailles outside Paris. Among the extravagances of Versailles were 1000 orange trees, chimneys gilded with copper, a zoo with leopards, lions, camels and elephants, enormous crystal chandeliers, 2400 fountains, exotic birds, two million flowerpots so that the flowers in the gardens could be changed every day, marble statues throughout the palace, and elaborate entertainments for his guests. Throughout Versailles could be seen images of the sun, because Louis gave himself the title *Sun King*, claiming that his power was as vast as the sun's.

In religious matters Louis regarded the Huguenots as both politically and religiously dangerous. First he harassed the Protestants in every way he could think of. He had a special body of soldiers called dragoons who made life miserable for the Calvinists. Finally, against the advice of the Pope, Louis revoked the Edict of Nantes in 1685, forbidding the practice of Protestantism and ordering that all Protestants become Catholic or leave France.

Louis also came into direct conflict with Pope Innocent XI (1676-

1689). Innocent was the best of the seventeenth century Popes, and has been beatified. He reorganized the Vatican finances, improved the morality of the clergy and supported the Hapsburgs against the Turks. He clashed with Louis on the subject of *Gallicanism*, a French schismatic movement similar to Anglicanism in England. Gallicanism held that the king of France was not subject to the Pope in temporal matters; that a council was superior in authority to the Pope; and that the Pope was inferior to the Gallican (French) Church. In essence, Louis wanted to be head of the Church in France as the king of England was head of the Church in England. The Pope refused to give in to Louis. When a French diocese became vacant, the Pope would not fill it with the candidate that Louis wanted. Innocent also appointed as Archbishop of Cologne the candidate favored by the Holy Roman Emperor, not the candidate favored by Louis. In retaliation, Louis seized the papal territory of Avignon, imprisoning the papal nuncio (representative). But the Pope remained firm, and Louis never quite dared to take France entirely into schism.

One beneficial policy of Louis XIV was his support of the great French explorations of North America and the settlement of Canada. In 1608 Samuel de Champlain had founded Quebec and by 1615 had reached the Great Lakes. In 1642 Montreal became a mission center. But it was under Louis' reign that colonists came to Canada (or New France as it was called) and troops subdued the fierce Iroquois Indians. Jesuit missionaries preached the Gospel to the Indians. Many of the Jesuits died heroic martyrs' deaths after horrible tortures: St. Isaac Jogues and St. John de Brebeuf are the best known. By 1672 Quebec had 6,000 people, with a flourishing fish and fur trade. Father Marquette and Louis Joliet went down the Mississippi River as far as what is now Arkansas. Shortly thereafter Robert de La Salle went to the mouth of the Mississippi. By 1700 France had an inland empire stretching from Quebec to the Gulf of Mexico, throughout all of which missionaries were winning souls for Christ.

The Catholic Revival

Though the Thirty Years War had ended in a defeat for the Catholic cause, the Church and the Catholic countries of Europe soon showed their continued strength and vigor. In France, the corruption, immorality and extravagance of the French court at Versailles was balanced by a sunburst of holiness in the Church in France. St. Vincent de Paul persuaded many of Paris' richest ladies to devote time and money to the care of orphans, prisoners, the destitute and others who before his time had been left to suffer untended. St. Vincent founded the Daughters of Charity as an order of nuns who would consecrate their lives to the service of the poor. He preached against the persecution of the Huguenots, warning that genuine conversion could come only through love and good example, not through force.

Also at this time, an unknown nun, Margaret Mary Alacoque, received the apparitions of the Sacred Heart of Jesus with His message of infinite love and mercy for sinful men. These apparitions were a direct heavenly answer to the heresy of *Jansenism*, which was a kind of Catholic Calvinism, seeing God as stern and angry and man as almost always unworthy to approach the Sacraments. The Sacred Heart told Margaret Mary, "Behold this heart which has so loved men," and encouraged the frequent reception of Holy Communion, particularly on the First Friday of each month. Though Margaret Mary was ridiculed and disbelieved by the nuns in her order, eventually devotion to the Sacred Heart spread throughout the world, as Our Lord bestowed rich blessings on those who responded to His burning love.

If in France the seventeenth century saw a manifestation of the power of God's love, in Sweden there was a manifestation of the power of God's truth. Gustavus Adolphus had no sons. When he was killed at Lutzen, his young daughter Christina became Queen of Sweden. A brilliant girl, she was not satisfied with Lutheran doctrines, which lacked intellectual rigor. She brought the French scientist, Descartes, to Stockholm to serve as her tutor. Her studies with him convinced her that only in the Catholic Church could she find intellectual and spiritual satisfaction. Yet she was queen of a country where it was illegal to become a Catholic. She took instructions secretly. Then she abdicated and fled the country in disguise. She took refuge first in the Spanish Netherlands, then went on to Innsbruck, where she was formally received into the Catholic Church. She spent most of the rest of her life in Rome and is buried in St. Peter's Basilica, having sacrificed the wealth, power and prestige of the throne of Sweden to follow her conscience into the Catholic Church.

Christina was succeeded on the throne of Sweden by her cousin Charles X Gustavus, who immediately provided the Catholic cause a chance to win on the battlefield.

In 1654, the year of Christina's abdication, the Swedes invaded Catholic Poland. The Swedish army still possessed the skill and the weapons which Gustavus Adolphus had given them. The Lutherans took Warsaw in September 1655, then Krakow. King John Casimir, abandoned and discouraged, fled the capital and took refuge in Silesia. Most of the noblemen likewise had fled or gone over to the enemy. The few remaining faithful noblemen looked for a place to make a last stand and chose the monastery-fortress of Czestochowa.

In Czestochowa was the greatest treasure of Poland—the Black Madonna, an ancient painting of the Blessed Mother. Enshrined in the monastery chapel, the painting was a pilgrimage destination of the Polish people, whose devotion to the Blessed Mother has always characterized their piety. The noblemen were welcomed by Abbot Kordecki, who promised the prayers and support of the monks.

The Lutheran general Muller brought his army up to Czestochowa, the last obstacle in the way of total conquest of Poland. He sent in a message to Abbot Kordecki: Be reasonable; surrender now and avoid bloodshed. Abbot Kordecki absolutely refused. Then began the Siege of Czestochowa. Somehow everything seemed to go wrong for the Lutherans. At one point they launched a mighty cannon ball over the monastery walls, only to have it come flying back and land in the middle of their dinner table. They offered bribes to Kordecki if he would surrender, argued with him that it was unseemly for monks to be engaged in military action, all to no avail.

The Catholic resistance was firm, but life in the monastery was not easy as supplies dwindled and the number of wounded increased. Came Christmas Day. The monastery had few supplies left. Nevertheless, Kordecki ordered a great feast and celebration in honor of the birthday of Our Lord. The Lutherans heard the singing and rejoicing. Surely the Catholics must be well-supplied if they could celebrate so joyfully. It is also said that the Lutherans saw in the sky a vision of the Blessed Mother, defending the monastery. Despairing of victory, they raised the siege.

Hearing of this defeat, John Casimir returned to Poland. Suddenly proud of their country, the people rallied around their king. When John Casimir reached Lvov, he made a double vow: Mary henceforth was to be venerated as Queen of the Crown of Poland; when Poland was freed from the Lutherans, the peasants would be liberated from serfdom. On June 30, 1656, the Lutherans were driven from Warsaw. In 1660, the Lutherans signed a treaty and Poland was saved. John Casimir kept his vows, and Our Lady of Czestochowa has ever after been honored as Queen of Poland.

Defeat of the Turks

The second Catholic battlefield triumph in the seventeenth century came against the Turks. The victories over the Turks can best be chronicled by following the career of Prince Eugene of Savoy.

Born in 1663, Eugene was brought up in the corrupt French court. At first he was attracted by the luxurious life-style, but he eventually rejected it totally. When Louis XIV refused him a post in the French army, he left France forever and went to Austria. He was accepted by Emperor Leopold I, who had just fled Vienna to escape the oncoming Turks (1683).

The Turks were mounting their strongest attack against Europe since the first siege of Vienna in 1529. One hundred carriages were required to transport the harem alone. A total of 200,000 were encamped outside Vienna, under command of the Grand Vizier Kara Mustapha, nicknamed "scourge of humanity." Mustapha could easily have taken Vienna since there were only 10,000 troops inside, but he wanted to be sure that he could get all the loot for himself, so he decided to starve out the city. Eugene joined the army of the Duke of Lorraine, which was coming to the city's rescue.

Also on the way to the city was a Polish army, under command of the Polish king, John Sobieski. He had decided to risk his country's safety upon the personal request of Innocent XI that he help defend Vienna—for if Vienna fell, all Christian Europe would be open to the rampaging Turks.

Mustapha was confident, enjoying the siege in his luxuriously equipped tent. Inside the city, the Viennese tightened their belts and reinforced the walls and prayed to the Blessed Mother for protection. Behind the city was a forested hill, the Weinerwald (Viennese Forest). Mustapha had not fortified the hill, believing that no one could possibly bring an army over the hill and through the thick forest. So that is exactly what Sobieski did. On September 12, 1683, 24,000 Poles under Sobieski and 21,000 Imperial troops under the Duke of Lorraine came over the hill to fall upon the surprised Turks. Though they greatly outnumbered the Catholic forces, the undisciplined, unprepared Turks were no match for their determined opponents. By the end of the day, the Turks had fled, leaving behind much of their treasure, including Kara Mustapha's tent. That evening Sobieski sent a message to the Pope which echoed Charles V's victory cry after Muhlberg: "I came; I saw; God conquered." Vienna, and Christian Europe, had been saved, and Pope Innocent declared September 12 the Feast of the Holy Name of Mary in thanksgiving for Our Lady's intercession.

Eugene acquitted himself so well in the battle that he was soon given a regimental command. During the summer of 1684 he fought at Buda, the

Turkish military headquarters, his regiment shattering a Turkish relief force. In 1685 Eugene covered himself with glory in the Turkish defeats at Neuhausel and Gran and was made a major general. In 1686 the Catholic forces took Buda, Eugene being twice wounded in the battle. In 1687 the relentless counterattack continued as Eugene's cavalry brigade played a large role in the defeat of the Turks at Mohacs. He was promoted to lieutenant general and rejoiced as Archduke Josef received the Crown of St. Stephen at Buda on December 9.

The Turks lost Athens to Venice in 1687 (though the Parthenon, in use as a powder magazine, was severely damaged by a Venetian bomb). In September 1688, the Hapsburg army took Belgrade, the key Turkish position on the lower Danube. Eugene received a sabre cut which penetrated his helmet. For the next ten years, Eugene had to turn his attention from the Turks to fight in the War of the League of Augsburg against the French, who as usual were refusing to make common cause against the enemies of Christendom. (Louis XIV, in fact, had supported the Turks.) The war had little significance except insofar as it kept the Hapsburgs from defeating the Turks. Eugene became a Field Marshal in 1692, the highest rank in the Hapsburg army, and the war finally ended in 1697.

In the meantime, the Turks had recaptured Belgrade, but now Eugene was free to launch a new campaign against them. As he was organizing his army, he learned that the Turks had put a bridge of boats across the Theiss River at Zenta and that the Turkish army was crossing into Transylvania. Though his men had already marched ten hours that day, he marched them on to the attack. He threw his men against the Turkish camp, forcing the foe up against the river. He pressed forward with assault after assault. The *Battle of Zenta* (September 11, 1697) finally ended with 20,000 Turks killed, another 10,000 drowned and only 300 dead among Eugene's forces (and he even captured 60,000 camels!).

The Battle of Zenta broke the back of the Turkish army. On January 26, 1699 the Turks signed the Treaty of Carlowitz, the first time ever that they had negotiated with the Catholic forces. Transylvania and most of Hungary were restored to the Holy Roman Empire. The Turks had made their last attack on Christian Europe.

Review Questions

1. What was the scientific revolution? Name two Englishmen who were leaders in the scientific revolution and describe their contributions.

2. What was the good result of the scientific revolution? What were its harmful results?

3. What is geocentrism? What is heliocentrism? What did Copernicus say about these two theories? What in general was the Church's position?

4. What charges are made against the Church in the Galileo case? Refute the two charges.

5. How did Philip III and Philip IV weaken Spain?

6. Summarize the background of Richelieu. What were his two goals for France?

7. Summarize the three steps in the achievement of his first goal.

8. Why did the Thirty Years War break out?

9. Who were the leaders and what were the events and results of Phase I?

10. Who were the leaders and what were the events and results of Phase II?

11. What happened to Spain between Phase II and Phase III? Why was this important?

12. Why did Sweden come into the war? Summarize the victories won by Gustavus Adolphus. How did the Catholics counterattack?

13. Who were the leaders and what were the events and results of Phase IV?

14. What were the results of the Thirty Years War?

15. Summarize the character of Louis XIV. How did he increase absolutism in France? What was the harmful aspect of his financial policies?

16. Summarize the wars in which he was involved.

17. Besides warfare, how did Louis XIV further waste money in France?

18. What was Louis' policy toward Protestants? Summarize his conflict with Innocent XI.

19. What beneficial policy did Louis XIV pursue?

20. Summarize the achievements of the great French saints of the 17th century.

21. Tell the story of the conversion of Queen Christina of Sweden.

22. Summarize the Catholic success at Czestochowa.

23. Summarize the Catholic success at the Siege of Vienna.

24. Summarize the victories of Eugene of Savoy over the Turks.

25. What was the significance of the Treaty of Carlowitz?

Projects

1. Report on French explorations and settlements in the New World.
2. Give an illustrated report on Versailles, or build a model of it.
3. Imagine that you are Cardinal Richelieu or Louis XIV near the end of your life. Write a justification of the things you have done during your life.
4. Make a poster of the promises of the Sacred Heart to St. Margaret Mary.

Chapter Twenty Two
The Rise and Fall of the Stuarts

ALTHOUGH ENGLAND WAS INVOLVED in affairs on the continent of Europe during the seventeenth century, Englishmen were mainly occupied with struggles of their own. Two conflicts were waged on English soil during this century: Would England retain a limited government with king and parliament checking each other, or would wealthy noblemen and the newly rich capitalists and bankers control the government? Would England remain anti-Catholic or would it permit a Catholic monarch to reign? Both these conflicts were fought out by members of one dynasty: the Stuarts, descendants of Mary Stuart, Queen of Scots.

James I

Queen Elizabeth died with no children. The next in line for the throne was Mary Stuart's only child, James, who had been taken from her when a baby and raised as a Protestant. He had been King James VI of Scotland, and upon Elizabeth's death was proclaimed James I of England. The dominant church in Scotland was the Presbyterian, but upon receiving the English crown—which he had long coveted—James willingly became an Anglican.

James was an absolute monarch who believed in the *Divine Right of Kings*: that anything a king did was sanctioned by God. This belief was quite different from that of Charles V or Philip II, who believed that the king was responsible to God and must rule in harmony with God's laws. Because of his attitude James came into conflict with Parliament but for the wrong reasons. The members of Parliament were not interested in defending the rights of the people but in getting power for themselves. Parliament did not represent the ordinary people. Only owners of a substantial amount of property could vote. This put Parliament in the hands of the noblemen and the newly wealthy bankers and capitalists, who had gained their wealth from the seizure of Catholic property and in no way were defenders of the rights of the ordinary people.

In England, Parliament could come into session only if summoned by the king and could be dissolved by the king when he didn't need it any longer. James would have preferred not to summon it at all. But only Parliament had the power to vote taxes and revenues for the monarchy. The king had some sources of income himself, but because James' life style was so extravagant, they were never enough for him. So he had to call Parliament into session, even though he never got along with it.

When James first became king, he did not enforce the anti-Catholic laws. But Robert Cecil could not allow this toleration to continue. James was frightened into renewing the anti-Catholic persecution by the *Gunpowder Plot*. The full truth about the Gunpowder Plot may never be known, but here are the facts.

On Saturday, October 26, 1605, a mysterious letter was delivered to the Catholic Lord Monteagle, warning him to stay away from Parliament when it convened on November 5. The letter was badly written, with no punctuation and no capital letters. Lord Monteagle immediately took the letter to Robert Cecil, who stated that he feared some kind of Catholic violence against Parliament, since a Catholic nobleman had been warned not to attend its meeting. So Cecil ordered a search of the cellars of Parliament, and on November 4 found a Yorkshire soldier-of-fortune named Guy Fawkes standing guard over barrels of gunpowder. Fawkes was arrested. James I was terrified of gunpowder because of the way his father had died. (Darnley's house had been blown up and he was killed while attempting to escape.) He ordered the torturing of Guy Fawkes. On November 8 Fawkes finally confessed under torture and named others involved. Cecil announced that Catholics had been plotting to blow up Parliament when the king and his two sons were there, put his daughter Elizabeth on the throne, and bring her up as a Catholic. Fawkes and others were executed, and for centuries afterwards, the English people celebrated "Guy Fawkes Day" on November 5 with bonfires.

Many historians believe, however, that Robert Cecil organized the whole plot precisely to turn James solidly against Catholics. Here is the evidence: How could the plotters get gunpowder when it was a government monopoly? Why did Cecil refuse to allow an investigation into missing stores of powder in the Tower of London? How did the plotters get access to the house next to Parliament (from which they had tunneled into the cellars of Parliament), since it belonged to a government official (who conveniently died on November 5)? Why were two leading conspirators immediately shot instead of being taken alive? The government claimed that it did not know the identity of the conspirators until Fawkes confessed under torture on November 8, yet why were a number of conspirators arrested on November 5? Why was the assembly of Parliament postponed from February (when the plotters weren't yet ready) until November (when they were)? Even at the time, some observers thought the whole plot was a government frame-up.

The result was exactly what Cecil wanted. James I turned unalterably against Catholics and increased the laws against them.

Specifically, James broke the treaty with Ireland and enforced the Act of Uniformity, which required everyone to attend Anglican services. Besides harassing Catholics, the Act of Uniformity also affected small Protestant groups which wanted a simpler church with few ceremonies and no bishops. One of these groups, the Separatists, left England and came to America in 1620, where they were later known as Pilgrims. James also opposed the Puritans, English Calvinists who wanted to make the Church of England more like the Calvinist churches and less like the Catholic Church. His dislike of them stemmed from his unpleasant memories of the stern Calvinists who had raised him in Scotland.

Charles I

Charles I came to the throne when James I died in 1625. The new king differed from his father in many ways. He was much more orderly and dignified. He was a religious man, with a strong belief that a king was responsible to God for his rule. He therefore took his authority and his responsibilities seriously. Religiously, Charles antagonized many Englishmen by his sympathies for Catholicism. Charles had married a French Catholic princess, Henrietta Maria, the daughter of Henry IV and the sister of Louis XIII. He did not enforce the laws against the Catholics and permitted the Irish to practice their religion in private. He was a "High Church" Anglican; that is, he insisted on the full rituals of the Anglican Church—including candles, incense and other things which the Puritans thought encouraged "popery." On the other hand, he had some leading Puritan speakers and writers arrested and severely punished by flogging, the pillory and occasionally mutilation (having an ear cut off, for example). Charles was friendly toward Spain (a Catholic country) but an enemy of Holland (a Protestant country). Many people feared that Charles would become a Catholic and try to make England Catholic once again. As a result, many Puritans left England and settled in America.

Like his father, Charles had trouble with Parliament. The differences between Charles and the members of Parliament were so great that Charles dissolved it in 1629, reigning without it for eleven years. To raise the money he needed, he collected taxes which had been levied in the past but had been ignored for some time. He took over the power to set customs duties (taxes paid when goods are shipped into or out of a country). And he started to collect a tax called Ship Money throughout the country instead of just in seacoast towns as previously. These measures caused much unrest. In parts of England, the sheriffs had trouble collecting the taxes because the people refused to pay.

But a problem was coming to a head which would force Charles to summon Parliament. In July 1637 a mandatory new high church prayer book was to be introduced throughout England and Scotland. In Scotland the Calvinists encouraged the rejection of the new prayer book and there was widespread disobedience throughout the country. On February 28, 1638 leaders of the Scots met at Greyfriars Church in Edinburgh, where they signed a document known as the *Covenant*, which rejected the Church of England and declared allegiance to Calvinism. Then the doors of the church were opened and the people allowed in to sign. They kept coming for three days. Copies of the Covenant were carried over all Scotland for signature. The Covenanters, as they were known, prepared for armed resistance to the king.

At first Charles seemed to hope that the rebellion would just go away—he didn't even make a formal announcement of it to his council until July 1. By the time he finally marched his troops to the north of England near the Scottish border on March 30, 1639, the Covenanters had seized Edinburgh Castle, carrying away arms, powder and the crown jewels. After two dismal defeats by the Covenanters, Charles signed the Pacification of Berwick, ending the First Scots War.

But he did not intend the Scots to defy his authority for ever. He called a Parliament to raise money to wage all-out war. In this Parliament, which assembled April 13, 1640, the Puritans won the elections to most of the seats in the House of Commons and proceeded to stir up hostility to the king. So Charles dissolved it on May 5, and it is therefore known as the

Short Parliament.

Charles could send Parliament away, but the Scots wouldn't go away. The Second Scots War broke out in August when the Scots crossed into England, forcing the king's troops to flee. In October Charles had to agree to an armistice, leaving the Scots in control of six counties in England. Once again he felt he had no choice but to call Parliament. This Parliament, which began meeting on November 3, 1640, came to be known as the *Long Parliament*, because it met for thirteen years.

Again the Puritans dominated and this time their goal was nothing less than control of the government. On November 23, Parliament passed the Grand Remonstrance, totally condemning the king's policies. In December, they introduced a bill for the impeachment of the queen. Disgusted, Charles sent troops to arrest the Puritan leaders, but they were forewarned and escaped. The Puritans controlled London, and Charles and the royal family had to leave the capital city for their own safety. John Pym, the Puritan leader, said that if the king returned, Parliament would put him on trial for his life for the crime of breach of Parliament (attempting to deny Parliament its authority). In response to this hatred of the king and all he stood for, there was an outbreak of anti-Catholicism, with Catholic houses ransacked and religious objects destroyed. Charles began to organize an army, and Parliament responded with an army of its own under the leadership of Oliver Cromwell. Thus began the *First Civil War*.

The first battle between the Royalists (Charles' supporters, nicknamed Cavaliers) and the Puritans (nicknamed Roundheads) was fought at Edgehill on October 23. The Roundheads had more enthusiasm than training, and the Royalists easily won.

But Cromwell was not easily defeated. He set about training his army, turning his undisciplined men who thought they could win on faith alone into a superb army, later known as the New Model Army (nicknamed Ironsides). In July 1644 the Ironsides won a decisive victory at Marston Moor, and in June of 1645, the first Civil War came to an end with the Battle of Naseby, when the rebels won a resounding victory and captured 5,000 Royalist prisoners. King Charles himself was placed under house arrest under control of the Scots.

But Charles wasn't ready to give up either. He secretly negotiated with the Scots, promising them a Calvinist church in return for their support. Since they would rather be ruled by a Scottish Stuart than English Puritans, they supported him. The *Second Civil War* broke out in 1648. But though Charles had found some friends among the Scots, he had not found a better army. Despite being outnumbered three to one, Cromwell defeated the combined Royalist-Covenanter force at Preston.

The Puritans had no intention of letting Charles fight them again. Originally they had wanted England to be ruled by Parliament with a figurehead king. Now their leaders did not want a king at all; they wanted Charles tried and executed.

There was, of course, no legal or constitutional authority for Parliament to kill the king of England. Whatever faults he had, Charles was still the rightful king. But the Puritans had become drunk with power. Charles was illegally tried and sentenced to die as "tyrant, traitor, murderer, public enemy." At his trial, Charles warned the people of the consequences of defying lawful authority: "How can any free-born citizen of England call life or anything he possesses his own, if power without right daily destroy the old fundamental laws of the land? I speak not for my own right alone but also for the true liberty of all my subjects, which consists not in the power of government, but in living under such laws and such a government as may give the people the best assurance of their lives and their property."

The execution date was January 30, 1649. As Charles prepared to walk to the scaffold where he would be beheaded, he was calm and courageous. He asked one of his servants to get him an extra shirt since it was chilly—he didn't want to shiver and have his enemies think he was frightened. Saying, "I fear not death; I bless my God I am prepared," he died nobly and unafraid.

The Puritan Interregnum

Parliament was now supreme and unchallenged. But the Long Parliament had become the *Rump* (remnant) *Parliament* when the Puritans had quarreled among themselves, splitting into two factions called the Presbyterians and the Independents, with the Independents chasing the Presbyterians out, leaving just sixty members left. Cromwell assumed control and began governing England with the title *Lord Protector*. Cromwell's rule is known as the *Puritan* or *Cromwellian Interregnum* (between kings).

Parliament had complained that Charles was an absolute monarch. But Cromwell was a dictator. He divided the country into eleven military districts, each ruled by a major-general, a combination tax collector and policeman. Taxes went up far higher than under Charles (because of Cromwell's wars, discussed below), beggars roamed the streets, and highwaymen infested the roads. Throughout England Cromwell enforced Puritan standards—even the celebration of Christmas was outlawed. However much the people may have believed that Charles I had too much power, at least he had never spied on their personal lives as Cromwell's Puritan government now did.

In February 1649 the Irish rose in favor of Charles I's oldest son, the rightful king, Charles II. Cromwell personally led an invasion of Ireland, bringing death and destruction. He and his army sacked the city of Drogheda for three days. At the end of this terror, only 30 men were left alive out of 3,000, and no one could count the number of women and children killed. In Wexford, 2,000 were killed, including 300 women gathered around the Celtic high cross in the market place. After eight months, Ireland was subdued.

The whole of Ireland was landlordised. This meant that no Irishman could own land—it was in the hands of English landlords. Under penalty of death, no Irishman was allowed east of the Shannon River after May 1, 1654. The Irish were forced into Connaught, the least fertile, least productive province. Irishmen of an age to be soldiers were given a choice: death or exile. 34,000 of them fled to Europe (the "Flight of the Wild Geese"). Thousands of orphaned Irish children were sold into slavery in the West Indies. It is estimated that half the native population of Ireland perished.

On June 24, 1649, Charles II landed in Scotland. Against his better judgment he signed the Covenant in order to get the support of the Scots against Cromwell. At the Battle of Dunbar, September 3, Cromwell easily defeated the Scots. Charles then joined the army in person, and they occupied the city of Worcester. But Cromwell's Ironsides were still the best soldiers around, and the Scots were crushed. Charles barely escaped capture and hid in the estates of two Catholic families in the neighborhood, once spending an entire day in an oak tree (the "Royal Oak of Boscobel") while Cromwellian soldiers prowled around beneath. Finally, assisted by the Catholic priest Father John Huddleston, Charles escaped the area in disguise and sailed back to France, still the rightful king of England but also an almost penniless suppliant at the French court.

Cromwell had subdued the Scots and the Irish, but now he had trouble with Parliament. Just as Parliament had not given Charles everything he wanted, so they did not now give Cromwell everything he wanted. And just as Charles had concluded that he must dissolve Parliament, so Cromwell came to the same conclusion. He marched into the House of Commons, stationing soldiers at the entrances. He stalked into the middle of the chamber. On a table lay the mace—the symbol since the Middle

Ages of Parliament's power to legislate. He walked up and down, shouting at the members of Parliament and insulting them. Finally he said: "You are no Parliament. I will put an end to your sitting." He called in his troops and threw the mace to the floor, shouting, "Take away these baubles." The legislators fled in fear.

Charles I was convicted as tyrant, traitor, murderer, public enemy. But surely those words applied much more truly to Oliver Cromwell.

Cromwell died in 1658. His son Richard succeeded him as Lord Protector, but by this time the people were tired of Puritanism. They were more than ready to welcome back the rightful king: Charles II.

Charles II

The return of a Stuart king to the throne of England is known as the *Restoration*. When Charles arrived back in England he stated that he did not want "to go on my travels again." That is, he set as his primary goal remaining on the throne and would not do anything that would jeopardize his position. Thus he would make whatever compromises were necessary to keep support of the Protestant leadership. But he had a second goal as well: to insure the Stuart succession. As we shall see, this was a harder goal to achieve.

Charles arrived back in England in 1660. He was crowned in April 1661 and soon after arranged a marriage for himself with a Portuguese princess, Catherine of Braganza. Catherine was a devout Catholic and Charles made no attempt to interfere with her private practice of her faith, nor would he allow anyone else to do so. Catherine was charming and good-natured and soon earned the affection of Charles and of the English people.

In the first year of his reign, he made the first of his many compromises to retain Protestant support. He permitted Parliament to pass the *Clarendon Code*, which penalized non-Anglicans. The code, of course, was primarily directed against Catholics.

In 1672 Charles' goal number two came up against a huge obstacle. By this time it seemed obvious that Catherine would be unable to bear children. Thus Charles' heir was his brother James. But early in that year, James entered the Catholic Church, largely through the influence of his wife Anne Hyde, herself a Catholic convert and recently dead of cancer. Shortly after James' conversion became public knowledge, Parliament passed the *Test Act*, which required every office holder to take public communion in the Anglican Church. Charles tried to persuade James to take communion but continue his practice of Catholicism in private, but James had too much integrity. He was a Catholic and would be a Catholic both privately and publicly. So he was forced to resign his office as Lord High Admiral. He further angered the Protestants by his choice of a second wife: an Italian Catholic princess, Mary of Modena, whom he married in 1673.

In order to keep goal number two on track, Charles made another compromise. He took charge of James' two daughters by Anne Hyde, Mary and Anne, had them raised Protestants, and arranged marriages for them with Protestant princes. Mary was wed to William of Orange, heir to the Dutch throne, in 1677, and later Anne married Prince George of Denmark. Charles believed that the Protestants would accept James as his heir, even though he was a Catholic, if they knew that James would be succeeded by a Protestant daughter.

In 1678, the *Titus Oates Plot*—also known as the *Popish Plot*—revealed the depth of anti-Catholic feeling in England and the extent of Charles' willingness to go along with it. Oates had been an Anglican, then a Catholic, then an apostate. He claimed to know of a fantastic French plot to assassinate Charles and even James and then take over England. Supposedly involved were Catherine's doctor and Mary of Modena's secretary. Anti-Catholic hysteria spread throughout London, and fashionable ladies concealed pistols in their muffs as protection against Jesuit revolutionaries. Five Catholic noblemen had been accused by Oates. There was no other evidence against them, but the House of Commons ordered their arrest. One of them, Lord Stafford, was condemned to execution; and Charles signed the death warrant, though he knew it was unjust. "I sign with tears in my eyes." In Ireland Bishop Oliver Plunkett was arrested for high treason. His trial had to be held in England because no Irish jury would have convicted him. He was found guilty and executed (and has since been canonized). Charles also permitted this execution.

Feeling its power, Parliament now attempted two further moves. They began pressuring Charles to divorce Catherine and marry a Protestant princess to produce Protestant heirs, and they introduced an *Act of Exclusion*, which would have barred any Catholic from sitting on the throne of England. At last, the Protestants had found two compromises which Charles would not make. Charles remained loyal to his wife and would not hear of divorce. And he remained loyal to his brother. When Parliament insisted on the Act of Exclusion, Charles dissolved them in 1681 and ruled without them for the rest of his reign, obtaining the money he needed from a secret treaty with France.

Charles ruled for 25 years. Finally, in February of 1685, he knew he was dying. Anglican Bishop Ken came to Charles, but the king declined to receive communion. Catherine, Mary of Modena and James wanted to get a priest to Charles, so on Thursday, February 5, James whispered in Charles' ear, asking him if he wanted to see a priest. Charles replied, "Yes, with all my heart." None other than Father Huddleston was in Catherine's rooms; he had once formed part of her household, since part of the marriage agreement had stated that she could have priests to attend her. Father was disguised in wig and cassock and hidden in a small room just off the king's with a private communicating door. James cleared the room except for two loyal Protestant nobles who would be witnesses and then brought in the priest. Charles said, "You that saved my body are now come to save my soul." Charles answered Father's questions clearly, confessed, made an Act of Contrition, was anointed, received Holy Communion, and held the crucifix while Father Huddleston recited the prayers for the dying. Charles died the next day at noon, a member of the Catholic Church.

The Glorious Revolution

Now James took the throne as James II. Not only was James a Catholic, but he was a strong Catholic, who would do nothing to hide his beliefs. He allowed Mass to be celebrated in public, annulled all the anti-Catholic laws including the Test Act, and published a Declaration of Indulgence, declaring that all men were equal under the law no matter what religion they professed.

But James was in his fifties—the age at which his brother died. Next in line was the Protestant Mary. So the Protestants decided they could afford to wait until James died. Then rumors began to go around the court that Queen Mary was pregnant, and before long the rumors were known to be true. On June 10, 1688, a son—James Francis Edward Stuart—was born. He was next in line for the throne of England (sons having precedence over daughters). And he was baptized a Catholic.

Secret messages went back and forth across the English Channel to Mary's husband William in Holland. With one hand William wrote a letter to his father-in-law congratulating him on the birth of the prince. With the other hand he organized an invading army to seize the throne. James himself always said exactly what he meant and assumed others did as well. Right up until the last minute he did not believe that William would betray him.

On November 5, William landed with his troops in England. He was not well received by the people, who may not have liked Catholics but liked Dutchmen no better. In addition, James had the larger army. But for a second time James was betrayed by one he trusted. The leading general in James' army, John Churchill (later the Duke of Marlborough), told the king that he would send his troops to battle William's. Instead he sent them to William and then went himself, becoming William's leading general. Even James' younger daughter Anne and her husband joined the enemy.

James sent his wife and baby across the Channel to France and then followed himself across a stormy sea. William marched triumphantly to London. Englishmen call this the *Glorious Revolution*. The victorious Whigs (the dominant party in Parliament, mostly wealthy Protestants) decreed: "King James having endeavored to subvert the constitution of this kingdom by breaking his original contract between king and people, and by advice of Jesuits and other wicked persons having violated the fundamental laws ... has abdicated the government." They awarded the crown jointly to Mary (1689-94) and William III (1689-1702).

The Glorious Revolution had two important and lasting results. First, Parliament was now dominant in England. William owed his crown to Parliament and did not dare defy them. Parliamentary supremacy was assured by the passage of the Bill of Rights which greatly reduced king's powers in favor of Parliament.

The second result was the victory of Protestantism. The Act of Toleration of 1689, despite its name, denied the rights of Catholics, providing toleration only for all Protestant sects. The Test Act was restored. All non-Anglicans had to contribute to the Anglican Church. Catholics were forbidden to inherit land, own arms or a horse, or send their children to be educated abroad. Priests might be imprisoned for life if discovered saying Mass. Then the Act of Succession of 1701 excluded Catholics or spouses of Catholics from the throne of England.

But James was not quite ready to give up the throne that belonged to him. On March 19, 1689, he landed in Ireland, inaugurating the *War of English Succession*. The Irish parliament declared the country independent of England, and Irishmen rallied around James.

William's troops were better equipped than the Irish, and James hurt his own cause by his indecisiveness and his refusal to use the talents of the great Irish general, Patrick Sarsfield. On July 12, 1690, the armies met at the Battle of the Boyne, a river near Dublin. The Williamites were able to cross the river, but a greatly outnumbered group of Irishmen fought them to a draw, while the main body of the Irish army made an orderly retreat into Dublin. The Irish army had not really been defeated, but James had been. He had fought a long time for the things he believed in, and he just couldn't face fighting anymore. He left Ireland for France.

After James left, Sarsfield refused to surrender. The war went on, as the undrilled, poorly armed Irish fought their wealthier, better-equipped foes. Eventually the Irish army found itself besieged in the city of Limerick. A trumpeter rode forward: "Open your gates! Let the King of England in!" The reply came: "Limerick will not open her gates, will not surrender!" Meanwhile Sarsfield and a few men slipped out of the city and on an all-night ride captured William's supply train, blowing up English ammunition and powder.

Ten thousand Dutch and English soldiers marched on Limerick. For three hours Irish infantry fought them off. Slowly the Irish line was pushed back; the enemy entered the city. A fierce hand-to-hand fight went on in the streets, women as well as men defending the city. The Irish cavalry rode behind the English army and attacked. The English were forced to retreat—Limerick was saved.

William went back to England, leaving Churchill in command. Despite the heroic defense of Limerick, the English won other battles. Finally, in October 1691, the Irish were exhausted. To continue to fight would only waste lives. William offered Sarsfield honorable terms. A solemn treaty was signed giving Irish Catholics the right to exercise their religion, to have the rights of citizens, and to be preserved from all disturbances.

This treaty was the *Treaty of Limerick*. It was signed on a stone known as the Treaty Stone, which sits today in the city square of Limerick where all can see it. It symbolizes the deceit and tyranny of the English.

For when the ink on the treaty was scarcely dry, Parliament passed the *Penal Laws*, whose goal was to obliterate Irish Catholics from the face of the earth. Irish Catholics were forbidden to practice their religion, to receive an education, to hold public office, to engage in business, to purchase land, to inherit land, to rent any land worth more than 30 shillings a year, to earn profit from land.

The Irish fiercely held to their religion and their culture. They attended secret Masses celebrated in hiding places called Mass rocks. Teachers in disguise taught in hidden schools called hedge schools. The Irish refused to let the poverty into which they were forced destroy them. They accepted every hardship and suffering, never surrendering, holding fast to their Irish heritage and praying for the day when they could be free of English tyranny.

The Last Attempts to Restore the Rightful King

William and Mary had no children. They were succeeded by Mary's sister Anne, who also had no heirs, since her 17 children all died before she did.

The rightful king was young James, the son of James II, who lived in France where his parents brought him up to realize his responsibilities as a Catholic and as a king. As his father lay dying in 1701, he wrote a long manuscript on kingship for his son. Article one stated: "Serve God as a perfect Christian and like a worthy child of the Roman Church, let no human consideration of what ever nature so ever be ever capable to draw you from it." Throughout his life, there would be pressures on James to become a Protestant so that he could go back to England and resume the throne, but he was not even tempted.

When Anne died in 1714, the throne passed to the German George of Hanover, the grandson of Charles I's sister Elizabeth. Though he was not the rightful king, and couldn't even speak English, he was the closest relative who was a Protestant. And he was totally controlled by Parliament.

In September 1715, Jacobite (pro-James) forces raised James' blue and gold standard in the north of Scotland, in a rising known as "The '15." They won victories but failed to take the key fortress of Edinburgh Castle. Young Catholic Lord Derwentwater in the north of England raised an army of about 1600 and made some gains. But the Jacobite forces had no really good general, and the Scots and English quarreled about where they should attack first. Then at the battle of Sheriffmuir, the right wing of each side broke and gave chase to the other's left, with each side claiming victory. The Jacobites' only hope lay in beating Lord Argyll, but the Jacobites did not press the attack, and the English government had time to summon troops from the continent.

This was the end of James' hopes in England and Scotland, but he did not know it. James was still in France, frustrated because he did not know what was going on in his homeland. He decided he must return to the British Isles, though he had to go in disguise because British spies were after him. James was ill but finally crossed the Channel, setting foot on English soil for the first time in 27 years on January 1, 1716. He was welcomed by the nobles, but his army was in a pitiful state. The men wanted to fight, but the generals persuaded James not to. Then James wanted to retreat to the north and raise his standard near Aberdeen at an excellent defensive position. But the generals said he would be risking his life to no purpose. Thwarted at every turn, James withdrew to Flanders on February 4, never to see Scotland again.

James spent the rest of his life off and on trying to raise troops and money for another invasion but never receiving the help he needed. He married Clementina Sobieski (granddaughter of John Sobieski) and had two sons, Charles and Henry (who became a Cardinal).

James' son Charles was known as Bonnie Prince Charlie because of his good looks. In 1745 he landed in Scotland in secret, with only seven companions, determined, he said, to win the throne or die ("The '45"). Word of Charlie's daring landing spread through the Highlands of the north of Scotland, still Catholic. The Highland clans were founded on family loyalty and were therefore loyal to the family which should rightly wear the crowns of England and Scotland. They rallied to Charlie's side, their symbol a white rose. Filled with enthusiasm, they won major victories at Edinburgh and Prestonpans.

The army marched into England, toward London. But then Charles' troubles began. He had hoped for French aid. It didn't come. He had hoped for support from discontented Englishmen. It didn't come. Still Charles wanted to risk everything in an attack on London. But the Highland chiefs refused to move.

Having come so far, the Highlanders had to turn around and march back into Scotland. Charles was heartbroken. He stopped marching with his men, riding silently in a carriage. They won another battle, but were running short of supplies. And the army was being pursued by an English army under the command of King George's son, William, Duke of Cumberland.

In the middle of April 1746, the two armies were near Culloden. This was not a favorable location for the famous Highland tactic of charging the enemy, guns firing and swords waving—but for some reason Charles did not move the army.

Finally with food running low the generals planned a secret night march to surprise Cumberland's army about 2:00 A.M. But everything went wrong, the men straggled behind, and by 2:00 A.M. they were still several miles from Cumberland's camp. Charles wanted to go on—Charles always wanted to go on. The generals said no. They turned the men around and marched them all the way back.

Now the Highlanders were not only without food but without sleep as well. Cumberland attacked by firing his cannon into the Highlanders. Man after man fell. For some reason Charles didn't order an attack right away. When he finally did, it was too late. His men were destroyed. The battle lasted only 25 minutes.

The Duke of Cumberland ordered the slaughter of any Highlander who was found. For this he was known to the Scots as Butcher Boy Cumberland. Later the English named a flower in his honor: Sweet William. The Scots, for their part, named a weed Stinking Billy.

Charles escaped and hid in the Highlands for five months. Though a reward of $100,000 was offered for him, none of the Scots betrayed him. He finally escaped back to France. The Scots had a song, asking Bonnie Prince Charlie: "Will be no come back again?" But he never came back. He wandered around Europe, wasting his life and ruining his health by drinking too much.

The great Stuart adventure had ended. Charles I, James II, James, the son of James II, Bonnie Prince Charlie—brave men all. But in England, Protestantism and Parliament triumphed. Catholicism would never be restored, and the king would be a figurehead, with power in the hands of the men who had money.

Review Questions

1. What were the political views of James I? Why did he come into conflict with Parliament? Who dominated Parliament?
2. What was the Gunpowder Plot? Summarize the evidence that Robert Cecil was responsible. What were the consequences of this plot?
3. How did Charles I differ from James I?
4. Why did the First Scots War break out? What happened during this war?
5. What was the Short Parliament? What happened during the Second Scots War? Why did Charles summon Parliament after this war?
6. Summarize the conflict between Charles and Parliament up to the outbreak of war.
7. What happened during the First Civil War? During the Second Civil War?
8. Why did the Puritans execute the king? Why did they have no right to do so? Describe Charles' death.
9. What was England like during Cromwell's rule?
10. What happened in Ireland during Cromwell's rule?

11. Describe Charles II's attempt to gain the throne and what happened to him.
12. What did Cromwell do to Parliament? How does Cromwell's indictment of Charles actually apply to Cromwell?
13. What was the Restoration? What were Charles II's two goals?
14. List and explain the compromises Charles made to achieve his goals.
15. What were the two compromises he would not make?
16. Describe the conversion of Charles II.
17. How did James restore religious toleration to England?
18. What was the cause of the Glorious Revolution? Why did it succeed?
19. What were the two chief results of the Glorious Revolution? Summarize the laws which brought them about.
20. Summarize the events of the War of the English Succession.
21. What were the results of this war?
22. Who succeeded William and Mary? Who succeeded this person? Who was the rightful king? Why did the rightful king not come to the throne?
23. Describe the events of The '15.
24. Describe the events of The '45. Why did it fail?
25. What were the results of The '45?

Projects

1. Conduct a trial of Charles I.
2. Do research in current sources and write an essay showing how present troubles in Ireland are related to the events in this chapter.
3. Write an account of events in this chapter from the point of view of one of the characters.
4. Make a chart of the English succession from Elizabeth to George I.

Chapter Twenty Three
Liberals and Despots

THE SIXTEENTH CENTURY saw the major rebellion against the authority of the Church by men who said that the individual conscience was supreme in matters of religion. As a result they also rejected the society which the Church had created. Nevertheless, in spite of these rejections, men still had very strong beliefs and feelings about spiritual matters. They were willing to fight and die for what they believed.

During the seventeenth century much of this spirit still existed; the Thirty Years War, for example, began as a religious war. Then under the influence of Richelieu in France and Parliament in England the conflicts of the seventeenth century changed from religious to power struggles. Richelieu wanted France to be powerful even if he had to support Protestants to defeat the Hapsburgs. Parliament in England wanted to be supreme, whether the king was Catholic or Protestant.

The Rise of Liberalism

In the eighteenth century, the decline in morality and the rejection of authority reached bottom among the intellectual and political leaders of European society. Because France dominated Europe politically, it also dominated Europe culturally and intellectually. To get an idea what sort of culture and ideas were coming out of France, we will pay a visit to a meeting house in Paris. The men there are *Freemasons*—a partially secret organization which aimed at substituting itself for the Church. A group of Freemasons was called a lodge, and the most important lodge in Paris was that named the Nine Sisters, most of whose members were artists, scientists and scholars.

Eavesdropping on a conversation which could have occurred there, we would find that a member named Voltaire is the man to whom everyone else attends. As the others listen, he would probably say something like this:

"The Church is evil because it requires obedience and insists that men believe what it calls 'truths.' Nonsense! As my good friend Jean Jacques Rousseau says, every man's mind is pure and should be protected from the corrupting influences of any authority—Church, king, parents."

Georges Jacques Danton, a lawyer, pounds the table to emphasize his words: "Yes, yes! The Church must be smashed! And the king along with it! Men must be free to guide their own lives without the hateful meddling of any higher power. If only men were left alone they would build a perfect society on earth and we would need no talk of Heaven."

Voltaire continues in a calmer tone: "Men must be free to speak and to print any ideas they wish. They must be free to live by any moral standards they choose—even if they choose to have none. The law must not restrain them. The priests must be stopped from teaching and spreading their wicked notions of morality and truth."

A new member asks: "But we must have some government. If not a king what then?"

The others laugh and then look to Voltaire for an answer: "First, we must eliminate all authority which tries to tell men what to do. Then the people themselves can set up their government and make their laws. They will automatically do what is right for them so long as they are kept free from the evil influences of Church and king and family. Read Rousseau's *Social Contract*; he explains it all. A government set up by the people would, of course, have all the power it needed to keep evil influences such as religion from creeping back into society."

Another member, Count de Gebeline, interrupts: "I agree completely that the whole idea of a church helping men to be good is pure superstition—a ridiculous notion in our wise and intelligent times. Men contain within their own bodies all the strength they need to overcome every evil, physical or spiritual. You must all come over to Montmarte Street to meet the great Anton Frederick Mesmer. With the exception of the illustrious people here tonight, he is the greatest man now alive. In the center of his drawing room, he has an oaken tub with a solution of sulphuric acid. From the lid project movable iron rods. A person who is ill—in mind or body—has only to sit by the tub and take a rod in his hand. The evil will pass out of his body and strength will flow in when Mesmer walks by and touches the diseased parts of his body with his iron rod."

Voltaire sums it all up: "We must destroy the superstitions of the Church so that true scientists like Mesmer can remake the world. We must destroy the monarchy and the old ways of government so that the people can make their own laws. We must destroy authority so that men can be free to be good and happy. We must crush the evil things!"

When the meeting finally ended, the members would return to their homes determined to spread far and wide the ideas discussed at the lodge. These ideas are known as *liberalism*, which may be summarized as follows: Liberalism is a philosophy which rejects moral absolutes and authority, especially religious authority. It is usually opposed to hereditary monarchy. It emphasizes that men should be free to do whatever they want in moral matters. It usually approves the elimination of opposition, by violence if necessary.

Not all persons who call themselves liberals today would agree with all parts of this definition, but it describes the philosophy which profoundly affected history in the eighteenth century and after.

The eighteenth century is known as the *Age of Reason* or the *Enlightenment*, on the theory that men had finally outgrown everything that hindered them from knowing truth and leading perfect lives (specifically religious faith). They thought they would cure society of all that ailed it. But perhaps the following story will illustrate what their cure was really like:

A talented actress named Sophie Arnold took her pet dog, which was quite ill, to Mesmer. Mesmer, wearing his lilac silk coat, performed his rites and cast his spells. He returned the dog to Sophie, pronouncing him cured. A few days later, the dog died. Whereupon Sophie commented: "What a consolation I took him to Mesmer! At least the poor animal died cured!"

Bourbon Kings in France and Spain

Charles II, who ruled Spain from 1665-1700, was the last Spanish Hapsburg. Because of all the Hapsburg intermarriage (both Philip II and Philip IV had married their own nieces), Charles was afflicted with every sort of illness. He had no heirs, and at his death a struggle broke out between rival claimants to the throne. Louis XIV's wife was Philip IV's daughter; therefore his grandson had a claim to the throne of Spain. The Holy Roman Emperor Leopold I had married Philip IV's other daughter; therefore his son had a claim to the Spanish throne. Most of Europe did not want to see France and Spain come under one ruler, so united with the

Holy Roman Empire to prevent this in the *War of the Spanish Succession.*

Two great generals commanded for the Imperial side: Eugene of Savoy (who had won his fame defeating the Turks) and the Duke of Marlborough (John Churchill, the general who had betrayed James II; though his moral values were questionable, he was an able military strategist). At the beginning of 1704, the Allied army under Marlborough was on the Dutch frontier and the lower Rhine. Austrian armies were in Italy and Germany. The Allies agreed that the two armies should link up on the Danube to attempt a knock-out blow of the French forces. Eugene left Vienna to take command of the Imperial army in Germany. He surprised the French by moving his men quickly to join Marlborough, which he did on August 12. The two generals decided to attack the unsuspecting French the next day. At the battle, known as the Battle of Blenheim for a nearby village, the Allies had 52,000, the French 56,000. Eugene would attack the left after a long march through difficult country; he would be outnumbered. Marlborough would attack with superior force near the center. In the early afternoon, a French counterattack threatened to divide the Allied army in two. Though Eugene's men were under attack, he sent an Imperial brigade to help Marlborough hold the line. At 5:00 P.M. a final charge routed the French.

Though the war dragged on with Eugene winning further victories, Blenheim was the most important. Peace negotiations were finally held in 1713. Louis XIV's grandson became Philip V of Spain, but the French guaranteed that the two governments would never be united. So Louis XIV's power grab was largely thwarted.

But the French and Spanish people had nothing to cheer about. Under Charles III (Philip V's son) Spain was under the same absolutist rule that Richelieu had set up in France. Gone were the days of Hapsburg limited government and local rights. Taxes were raised. The Spanish colonies in the New World, which had local self government under the Hapsburgs, were brought under absolutist rule, and their wealth was exploited to benefit Spain alone.

In France, the corrupt and selfish Louis XV (1715-1775) succeeded his great-grandfather on the throne. At least Louis XIV had been an able king, but Louis XV had no ruling talents and didn't care. When reproached for his spendthrift and oppressive policies, which could cause the people to rebel, he replied: "Apres moi, le deluge"; "After me, the flood." By this he meant that he didn't care what happened after he died, even if it were a "deluge." The members of the French and Spanish courts spent money as if it were water, lived in gorgeous palaces, and spent their days and nights in a ceaseless round of parties, balls, gambling, frivolity. During the Middle Ages and later, kings and noblemen had understood the real world. Charles V, leading his soldiers, knew pain and death and ugliness. But the eighteenth century noblemen pretended that none of these things existed. Government officials were motivated by selfishness and a desire for power. They fought constant wars, broke their promises and betrayed their friends.

The Church in the eighteenth century was slipping back into some of the evils which had afflicted it earlier. Especially in France, many of the bishops were little different from wealthy noblemen, and some had been infected by liberalism. At one point a man was proposed as archbishop of Paris who did not even believe in God. The faith of the ordinary people and the parish priests was still strong, but the leadership, where it was not corrupt, was too often weak.

The Bourbons hated the Jesuits because St. Ignatius' order represented an independent and spiritually powerful force which commanded the loyalty and love of Catholics throughout Europe and the New World. To eliminate their influence, Charles III first expelled the Jesuits from Spain and all Spanish possessions. Then he told Pope Clement XIV that if he did not suppress the Jesuits (order them disbanded), he would take Spain into schism. Clement was too weak to resist this threat, though he knew that what he was doing was wrong, declaring on his deathbed: "I have cut off my right hand." The Society of Jesus went out of existence, not to be re-established until 1814.

Hanover Kings and Parliament in England

In England the situation might have seemed different on the surface, since Parliament, rather than an absolute monarch, held power. And England did not have the lavish and extravagant court life which drained the wealth of France. Yet evils there still were. Parliament was dominated by wealthy noblemen, many of whom held their seats through nepotism or bribery. There was scarcely another country in Europe where so many crimes were punishable by death, and the number of capital offenses was being increased; 33 new capital crimes were created in the reign of George II alone. The enclosure movement took away the lands which peasant farmers had worked for years, forcing these formerly independent men to become tenants (dependent on the landlord) or unemployed. The Hanover kings took little interest in the problems of the poor, while the wealthy aristocrats who controlled the government were slowly being infected with liberalism.

One beneficial result from the spread of liberalism was that as the English leaders became less devoted to Protestantism, they became less hostile to Catholicism. In 1778 a Catholic Relief Bill did away with rewards for informers and abolished life imprisonment for priests. A second Relief Bill in 1791 eliminated most legal penalties for Catholics.

England was just as eager for power as their rivals on the continent, and England and France engaged in a series of wars with battles fought both in Europe and the New World. The most significant was the *Seven Years War* (1756-1763), which grew out of rivalries for trade in the New World between France and England. A key battle was the Battle of Quebec, Canada (where the war was known as the French and Indian War), where the British general led a secret night march up the cliffs upon which Quebec was built. Both commanding generals were killed, but the English were victorious. As a result, England replaced France as the dominant power overseas and challenged her position in Europe.

After the French and Indian War, the English government attempted to raise money to pay its war debts through taxing the American colonies. Since the earliest days of the English settlements in America, Parliament had never before attempted to control their affairs nor levy internal taxes. So the new taxes and English blundering in attempts to enforce them created an ever-growing hostility among the leaders of the colonists, and the idea of rebellion became popular, especially in New England and Virginia.

When the American War for Independence broke out, the Americans proved to be much better fighters than the English expected. And George Washington was an outstanding leader who held the colonial army together through the difficult early months of the war, refusing to admit defeat. Then the French came to the Americans' aid, tipping the balance in favor of the colonists, who won the final victory at the Battle of Yorktown. Thus was a new nation born which would eventually have a great influence on the future history of the world.

The Romanovs in Russia

It would be some time, however, before this influence was exercised, as the new nation needed time to grow, and most of Europe was able to ignore the United States for the time being. They could not so easily ignore another nation just beginning to have an influence on European politics. This was not a new nation. In fact it was very old, and larger than the rest of Europe put together. But it had never before the eighteenth century had any significant effect on the history of the world. That nation was Russia.

Through the seventeenth century most of Russia was still close to barbarism. Few people could read or write, even among the noblemen. Many of the poor people were still serfs, bound to the land as during the Dark Ages. The ruler was more absolutist than any king in Europe, and life in the court of the Tsar (sometimes spelled Czar; it is the Russian word for emperor) was cruel and often horrifying. Various factions fought for power, and murder was the most popular weapon. The religion of most of the people was Russian Orthodox, which had most of the same beliefs as the Catholic Church but tended to be much more emotional and mystical.

The Romanov dynasty ruled Russia. On April 27, 1682 Tsar Theodore died. His ten-year-old son Peter was proclaimed Tsar. But another faction supported Peter's elder half-brother Ivan. A conspiracy to put Ivan on the throne led to the revolt of the military men called the Streltsy, who massacred a group of boyars (noblemen). On July 5, Peter, standing by his mother's side on the steps of the main entrance to the Kremlin (the royal palace), watched while the Streltsy stabbed to death the opposing leaders. The Streltsy proceeded to run wild, looting houses and rioting. This introduction to life in the Russian court left a permanent mark on Peter; ever after he hated the Kremlin.

When Peter finally became Tsar in his own right, he made up his mind that Russia must be backward no longer. In 1695 he sent a Grand Embassy from Moscow to Germany, Holland and England to learn European ways of shipbuilding, warfare and armaments manufacture in order to make Russia a power in European politics. Disguised as a soldier, Peter went along, though his disguise fooled no one since he was almost seven feet tall and unmistakable in any crowd. During the trip, Peter personally worked in shipyards and studied navigation. He and his noblemen also appalled Europe with their bad manners, as the time Peter picked up a ten-year-old princess by the ears to kiss her.

But the trip was a success. Russia modernized its army and navy and in 1709 defeated Sweden in the Great Northern War to give Russia new territory and a more open road to Europe. He moved his capital from Moscow to the newly conquered land, building a city named St. Petersburg. He grabbed a pair of scissors and went around cutting off the floor-length beards of the boyars, insisting that they look like Europeans, even if they didn't act like them.

Though the evils of the court had not much changed—Peter condemned his own son to death, for example—and though the ordinary people were no better off, Russia was now a power in Europe. In 1721 the Russian Senate gave Peter the title of "the Great," and that is how he is known to history.

Peter the Great died in 1725, and from 1725-1762 Russia was ruled by a series of undistinguished sovereigns, with intrigues, plots and corruption commonplace. Empress Elizabeth (1741-1762) had no children, so she chose her German nephew Peter to succeed her, and arranged his marriage with the German princess Catherine. Catherine and Peter couldn't stand each other, and Peter was himself no fit Tsar. For example, he was so childish that he spent most of his time playing with toy soldiers made of wax. When a mouse ate one of the soldiers, he caught it, court martialed it, and had it hanged in punishment. Finally Catherine deposed her husband and murdered him, assuming the throne herself.

Catherine had not the slightest rightful claim to the throne and was interested only in amassing power. She was primarily responsible for the partition of Poland (see below) and seized the Crimea and the Caucasus from weakened Turkey. She was one of a number of European rulers of the eighteenth century known as *Enlightened Despots*, because they adopted many liberal ideas, especially a contempt for religion, while at the same time keeping most of their absolutist powers. She pretended concern for the people but increased the power of the nobility over the serfs. Her punishments for those she disliked were cruel and arbitrary. Yet she is known as "the Great" because she increased Russia by 200,000 square miles and 17 million population. She was succeeded by her illegitimate son Paul, who despised his mother so much that he passed a law decreeing that no woman could rule Russia. Paul was assassinated, to be followed by his son Alexander I.

Hohenzollerns in Prussia

Still another nation emerged onto the stage of history in the eighteenth century. Though the Thirty Years War left Germany in a weakened condition, a few of the states began to emerge as more powerful than the others. One of these was Prussia, a Protestant state in northeast Germany, which became a virtually independent kingdom in 1701 under the Hohenzollern dynasty. Its leaders had one goal: making the Prussian army the best in the world. Boys were drafted into the army at an early age. Discipline was harsh; the slightest mistake was severely punished. The generals learned the newest techniques of warfare and made sure their troops knew them well. Soon Prussia had the finest army in Europe.

In 1740 Frederick II—later known as Frederick the Great—became king of Prussia. Frederick was motivated by two things: liberalism and militarism. Like Catherine the Great, he was an Enlightened Despot. Frederick was a close friend of Voltaire and founded the Academy of Science and Literature to spread liberal ideas. At the same time he wrote to Voltaire boasting that he had increased "the forces of the state by sixteen battalions, five squadrons of hussars and a squadron of lifeguards." Frederick cared nothing for moral values and everything for power, and he had the well-trained, tightly disciplined army needed to seize that power.

Maria Teresa in Austria

Louis XV, Charles III, George III, Catherine the Great, Frederick the Great—all were typical of the eighteenth century rejection of Church and morality. But one eighteenth century ruler towers above the rest. This ruler believed in justice, in peace, in God and the Church, in the rights of the people.

In Austria the Hapsburg Holy Roman Emperor Charles VI was nearing the end of his life. He was obsessed with the idea of making the Hapsburg succession absolutely secure so that no one could challenge his heirs. His task was made more difficult by the fact that he had no sons, only a daughter, Maria Teresa. Charles feared for Maria Teresa with all the greedy governments around her. So he bribed all the major powers in Europe to sign the *Pragmatic Sanction*, a document which decreed that they would recognize Maria Teresa as rightful ruler of the Hapsburg possessions and make no attempts to seize Austrian territory. Charles nearly bankrupted his treasury to get the Pragmatic Sanction signed, but he would have been better advised to spend the money building up his army. No one took promises seriously in the eighteenth century. When Charles died in 1740 and his blonde, 23-year-old daughter ascended the throne, she was threatened on all sides.

Because Maria Teresa's father had always hoped to have a son, he never properly trained his daughter to rule. Most of the other nations in Europe believed that she could be easily conquered and proceeded to ignore their solemn promises in the Pragmatic Sanction. The leader of Maria Teresa's enemies was Frederick the Great. Only two months after her father's death, Frederick marched 30,000 troops into Silesia, Austrian territory, and the English ambassador tried to persuade her to let Frederick have it. Count Charles Albert of Bavaria claimed the throne because Charles VI had left no male heirs, and his claim was backed by France, which was soon involved in the war.

Maria Teresa stood alone—even her advisers recommended giving in to Frederick. She knew that if she gave in, her enemies would not be satisfied with Silesia but would continue to attack Austria. She went to Hungary, under Hapsburg rule but with a large measure of self-government, where she stood before their Diet and asked them to come to her defense. The Hungarians had fallen in love with their beautiful young queen. They responded with infantry and cavalry. Maria Teresa sent a message to the English ambassador: "Not only for political reasons, but from conscience and honor, I will not consent to part with much in Silesia. No sooner is one enemy satisfied than another starts up; another, and then another must be appeased, and all at my expense." Europe learned that Maria Teresa was no helpless woman who could be pushed around. She was intelligent, brave and stubborn—the equal of any man ruling at that time, and better than most.

The *War of the Austrian Succession* went on for seven years before peace was concluded in 1748. At the end of the war, Austria was recognized throughout Europe as a major power. Maria Teresa's husband Francis Stephen was elected Holy Roman Emperor, though Maria Teresa actually did the ruling and made the decisions for her good-natured but rather ineffectual husband. The Holy Roman Empire, which Maria Teresa's father had brought to the verge of collapse, was now strong.

Throughout the rest of her reign she had three main concerns: strengthening Austria, improving the lives of her subjects, and raising her children (she had 16, nine of whom lived to adulthood). Maria Teresa was deeply religious and believed in the holy character of her responsibilities as ruler. That she was not a typical eighteenth century ruler can be seen in one of the first things she did upon becoming queen. She disguised herself and went among the people to find the things that troubled them.

After the war had established Maria Teresa's position throughout Europe, she turned her attention to Austria itself. Charles' extravagances and the war had nearly wrecked Austria's economy. Against strong opposition, Maria Teresa put through a tax reform program which reduced taxes on the poor and for the first time taxed noblemen. With this money, Maria paid for a well-trained, well-equipped army. She set up a new system of courts, faster and fairer. She reformed education so that even the poor could go to school. She helped the peasants gain freedom from their landlords so that they could own their own property and be self-supporting. Unlike the other monarchs in Europe at this time, Maria Teresa really cared for her people. She saw herself as their servant, rather than the other way around.

The Partitions of Poland

Maria Teresa has one serious blot on her record: the part she played in the partition of Poland. After the heroic defense of Vienna led by John Sobieski and the Polish army, Poland went into a decline. The almost constant fighting of the seventeenth century against the Swedes and Turks had ruined Poland economically. Russia, growing in power, looked covetously at Poland and manipulated the election of King Augustus II. Peter the Great then dragged Poland into his war against Sweden. Before long it was clear that Russia was the real master of Poland. After Augustus II died, Russia put his son Augustus III on the throne. He spent his entire reign in Germany while Russia used Poland as a roadside inn to move her armies into Europe. Catherine the Great selected the next king of Poland, Stanislaus Augustus, and helped him to crush a patriotic rebellion which broke out in 1768, led by Bishop Krasinki and Casimir Pulaski (who eventually died in America).

By this time Catherine had made up her mind that instead of going to the trouble of ruling Poland through Polish kings, she would simply annex Poland to Russia. Frederick the Great found out about her ambitions and decided to prevent their fulfillment. His motive was not concern for Poland; rather he wanted a share of Poland for himself. Frederick and Catherine then put pressure on Maria Teresa to join them so that she wouldn't help the Poles rebel against them. Against her better judgment, Maria Teresa went along with it.

In 1772 the first partition of Poland took place, Catherine taking an eastern section, Frederick taking West Prussia and a northern section, and Austria taking Galicia. In 1793 after Maria Teresa's death, Russia and Prussia took more pieces of Poland. Then in 1795, one year before Catherine's death, and with Maria Teresa's grandson Francis on the Austrian throne, all three countries completed the dismemberment of Poland, removing it from the map. Both Russia and Prussia persecuted the Poles in their sections, but Austria granted the Poles limited self-government.

Except for this one mistake, Maria Teresa was clearly an exception to the eighteenth century rule: rivalry and warfare, absolutism and oppression, liberalism and irreligion. This mixture would soon erupt into horror and bloodshed, in the destruction of the Christian social order and the birth of the modern world.

Review Questions

1. What were the Freemasons? Who was the chief liberal leader and what did he believe?
2. What did Mesmer and Rousseau believe?
3. Define liberalism.
4. Why was the 18th century called the Age of Reason or the Enlightenment? Why were these terms inaccurate?
5. How did the Bourbons come to the throne of Spain?
6. Describe the rule of Charles III in Spain.
7. Describe the rule of Louis XV in France.
8. Why did the Bourbons hate the Jesuits? Why did the Pope suppress the Jesuits?
9. How did England share in the evils of the 18th century?
10. What was the Seven Years War? What were its results?
11. Why did the American colonies rebel? Why was the rebellion successful?
12. How did Russia differ from the rest of Europe? How did Peter the Great change Russia?
13. Describe the rule of Catherine the Great.
14. Describe the rule of Frederick the Great in Prussia.
15. How did Maria Teresa differ from other 18th century rulers?
16. What was the War of the Austrian Succession? What were its results?
17. What were Maria Teresa's accomplishments in Austria?
18. What were the Partitions of Poland? Who participated in each?

Projects

1. Report on the American Revolution or the French and Indian War.
2. List the ideas of liberalism and explain what is wrong with each.
3. Report on the Kremlin or build a model of it.

4. Act out or write a conversation among the main rulers of this time.

Chapter Twenty Four
The French Revolution

THE FRENCH REVOLUTION is a pivotal event in the history of Western civilization. We need a detailed understanding of this event to understand the enemies the Church has fought ever since and to understand the evils of our own times (such as Communism) which are consequences of the French Revolution.

The common view of the French Revolution is that it was a justified rebellion of oppressed lower classes against a tyrannical king, corrupt nobility and insensitive Church. The French Revolution is also sometimes seen as similar to the American Revolution—a blow for freedom and self-government, struck against tyranny. As we shall see, some parts of this view are correct, but others are false, and a great deal of the truth about the French Revolution has been left out.

We have already seen how the totally Catholic kingdom of Louis IX and the High Middle Ages was destroyed: by the Protestant Revolt and the Wars of Religion; by the absolutism created by Richelieu; by the extravagance of Louis XIV; by the corruption of Louis XV. The results for France were the creation of a parasitical nobility which contributed little to society and lived on the taxes levied on the middle and lower classes, the wasteful extravagance symbolized by Versailles, and an unjust tax system. The worst consequences were felt in the cities, especially Paris, where there was massive unemployment and poverty. The peasants were better off because they worked the land and could be self-sufficient, but France was still far from the healthy conditions of Louis IX's reign. So when Louis XV died in 1774, there is no question that conditions in France were very bad and that the upper classes lived luxuriously at the expense of the middle and lower classes.

Louis XV was succeeded by Louis XVI, who was married to Maria Teresa's youngest daughter, Marie Antoinette. In the minds of most people who know anything about them, Antoinette is pictured as extravagant, foolish, immoral and irresponsible. Louis is pictured as stupid, dull, dictatorial and totally unconcerned about his people. The most often repeated condemnation is the legend that Marie Antoinette said, "Let them eat cake," when confronted with the hunger of the poor, who had no bread. The statement was actually made by the wife of Louis XV. Antoinette's enemies later attributed the statement to her. Although Louis did have a somewhat weak character, and though Antoinette, especially in her youth, did tend toward frivolity and thoughtless actions, both genuinely cared for the welfare of the people of France.

Louis and Antoinette had the tragic misfortune to rule France during the worst period in its history. They have therefore been blamed for all of the evils of this time. But if we study the facts of the second half of the eighteenth century in France, we will see that Louis and Antoinette were not the causes of the evil but its victims.

Louis and Antoinette Serve France

Louis was not a brilliant man, but he knew right from wrong and cared deeply for his people. At his first cabinet meeting, he told his ministers: "Above all, gentlemen, do not forget St. Louis' maxim: 'Everything unjust is impossible.' " He stated that his economic policy must include "no bankruptcy, no increase in taxes, no borrowing." Since his government had inherited huge debts he could not reduce taxes right away, but he ordered that no taxes be increased. To save money he greatly reduced expenditures at Versailles and stopped paying noblemen who did nothing. He ended government control of the grain trade, thereby reducing the prices paid by the ordinary people for bread. He made the courts more just, improved conditions in the prisons, and abolished the torture of accused prisoners. He ended the custom of *corvee*, which had required all the peasants to work two weeks a year without pay on public roads. He replaced corvee with a tax on property owners and insisted on paying his own share. He provided free medical care to the poor. He re-established parlements—local judicial bodies—thereby reducing the absolute power of the king and returning some governmental authority to the localities. He granted civil rights to Protestants, and set an example of loyal Catholicism in his own life.

For her part, Antoinette was determined to love and understand her new country. She paid for and guided the education of destitute children and served poor people in her own kitchens. She encouraged the opera and the ballet. She changed fashions in dress from overly elaborate and expensive styles to simplicity and naturalness and reduced luxury and lavishness in court balls. Her main weakness was gambling for high stakes, but Louis paid all her gambling debts out of his own pocket and she eventually stopped the practice. She was devoted to Louis and to her children.

The king and queen were so popular with the ordinary people that in the winter of 1784, the Parisians built first a statue of the king, then one of Antoinette in snow and ice, with this sign beside it: "Take your place near our kindly King, Queen whose beauty surpasses your charms; this frail monument is of snow and ice, but our wishes for you are warmer."

By the tenth year of Louis' reign, 1785, all seemed to be going well. His third child, a son, had just been born. The harvest was abundant. Business was good. Visitors crowded to Paris to buy the luxury goods the king and queen denied themselves. With time, France could be fully reformed and a new age of peace and prosperity begun.

But Louis and Antoinette were to be denied the time they and their country needed.

The King's Enemies

Two very powerful forces were working against Louis and Antoinette. The first was the wealthy noblemen of France. Under Louis XIV and Louis XV, they had grown accustomed to living in luxury while rarely being called to account for it. They craved a life of frivolity, wit and immorality. Louis and Antoinette denied them these things. Louis reduced expenditures and insisted that noblemen pay their debts. He and Antoinette were faithful to each other and were loyal to the Church. Therefore the wealthy and powerful in the land began to hate the king and queen. They wrote vicious pamphlets about them, accusing them of all the evils of which the writers themselves were guilty.

The other force was the liberals. They hated the king and queen because they hated all authority. Though they also despised the noblemen, the liberals were more than happy to join forces with them in condemning Louis and Antoinette and spreading lies about them. Some of their writings were so immoral that even today they cannot be seen without special permission. Gradually this propaganda began to be read by the ordinary people who assumed that at least some of it must be true. They began to turn against the king and queen who had done so much for them.

Problems began to come to a head when Louis proposed a new tax reform to help pay for, among other things, the expenses Louis had incurred when he came to the aid of the United States during its War for Independence. Previously the income tax had been 10%, but the richest paid nothing. Louis' tax would be 2 1/2%-5%, to be paid by all who had the ability to pay. The new system would increase the total amount raised but would reduce the amount paid by the poor. But Louis' enemies emphasized in the newspapers only that the government was going to make more money, without saying a word about the reduced taxes for the poor. Louis' enemies stirred up rebellions around the country and began a loud outcry demanding that Louis call into session the Estates General.

The *Estates General* was France's equivalent to Parliament and hadn't met since 1614. Louis was not eager to call it because the last time it had met it had accomplished nothing. But since it seemed that the people really wanted the Estates General, he issued a call for representatives of the three Estates—noblemen, clergy and ordinary citizens—to meet in Paris. Often during the days of crisis to come, Louis would go against his better judgment to do what the people seemed to want. A stronger king might have stood his ground and refused to be persuaded into doing something he thought unwise, but Louis was not especially strong and was convinced in his mind that if the majority of the people wanted something, it was probably the best thing to do. Unfortunately, what the liberals said the people wanted was not always what they really wanted; and even when it was, it was not always what was best for them or the country.

Before the Estates General actually met, Louis called for the people to send him Lists of Grievances—special letters stating what they wanted the Estates General to consider. Most of these letters showed that the people above all wanted a fair tax—which is what Louis wanted—and that they wanted to retain the essentials of the Catholic monarchy as they had known it. Unfortunately, the Third Estate (representatives of the ordinary people) was dominated by lawyers—360 out of 621 delegates—who had been infected by liberalism and wanted above all an end to authority. They were more concerned with imposing their ideas on France than with solving France's problems.

The Estates General opened on May 4, 1789—one of the most crucial years in all the history of Europe. From the beginning the Third Estate demanded a change in voting procedures. The traditional method of voting in the Estates General was that each estate would vote separately, and then cast its vote as a group. Thus the First and Second Estates could outvote the Third Estate, even though the Third Estate had more actual members. In 1789 the Third Estate insisted that all the estates meet as a mass, with each person's vote counting individually. Such a procedure would enable the liberals to dominate.

Louis should have done one of two things. He could have invited the Third Estate leaders to meet with him privately to work out an agreement to benefit France. Or he could have ordered them to work within the traditions of the country, forcibly removing them from Paris if they did not cooperate. But Louis was not strong enough to do either. Further, one of his sons died on June 4 and he went into mourning and seclusion at a crucial time.

The Third Estate, believing that nothing in France could stop them, broke away from the other estates and set themselves up as the official legislating body of France. They called themselves the *National Assembly*. The king and his advisers locked them out of the meeting hall, whereupon they met on a nearby tennis court on June 20 and swore the *Tennis Court Oath*: that they would not disband until they had given France a written constitution and a totally new government.

After the Tennis Court Oath, Louis called the leaders together and announced major reforms in the court and tax system. Liberal leader Mirabeau (who earlier had said, "I am a mad dog from whose bites despotism and privilege will die") told the king that the National Assembly intended to do all the reforming that was to be done. The liberals were able to persuade the majority of the First and Second Estates to join them. On June 27, Louis gave in and asked the three estates to merge. The liberals went wild in celebration and Louis had to call in troops to keep order. Mirabeau accused Louis of using force against the National Assembly.

From this point on, events in France moved with breakneck speed. From a condition where the people were somewhat discontented but willing to obey the laws, France plunged into chaos and horror.

Revolution: 1789

July 12-14: Paris at this time was crowded with high unemployment. Many people were hungry because hail had ruined the wheat harvest in 1788. Though the government had spent huge sums to import wheat, it was not enough. The unsettled conditions in Paris, plus Louis' calling in the troops, gave the liberals the chance to agitate the people of Paris. Mobs ran wild in the Paris streets and burned the police headquarters.

July 14: Men armed with hatchets broke down the chains of the draw-bridge of the old prison known as the Bastille, and the mob rushed in, massacring the 120 guards. The mob found only seven prisoners: four forgers, a young man who'd been put under guard by his family because of his evil life, and two insane men. But the *storming of the Bastille* became a symbol of freedom, and to this day July 14 is celebrated as France's independence day. Louis tried to reason with the Assembly, but they refused to listen.

August: There was violence throughout the countryside, known as the *Great Fear*. The anarchy in Paris caused a breakdown of food distribution, with consequent famine and plunder. There were wild rumors about "brigands": the cry would go up "the brigands are coming." No one knew exactly who the brigands were or when they were coming but people were in a state of terror. Armed men would gather to repel the supposed brigands, but would soon be stirred up by liberal leaders to attack the local chateaux. Many chateaux were burned and innocent people murdered.

August 26: The Assembly issued the *Declaration of the Rights of Man*. Many of the rights listed in this document resemble those in our own Bill of Rights. Thus the Declaration is often looked upon as a great blow for human freedom. But it was philosophically unsound. Catholic political tradition stated that rights came from God and therefore could be taken away by no one. In French Revolutionary liberalism the rights were seen as coming from the state or from the majority; hence in practical fact they could be taken away by the state or by the majority.

A major debate in the Assembly was on whether the king should have the right to veto acts of the Assembly. The Assembly split into two parts on this issue: the "right" or more conservative part which wanted to leave some powers to the king, and the "left" or more radical part which did not. Our own political terminology of left and right comes from the French Revolution, where the conservatives sat on the right side of the Assembly and the liberals on the left. As the months went on, the left would become increasingly more radical and the right would move into the position occupied by the former left so that soon no true conservatives remained.

October 5-6: The Flanders Regiment had demonstrated for the king, calling for their old uniforms and his colors (white and gold, as opposed to the red, white and blue tricolor of the Assembly), and rejecting the Assembly. The Paris liberals heard of this action and organized a mob of women (and some men dressed as women) to march on Versailles in protest. The mob marched to Versailles, demanding the queen's head and dismemberment. In an incredibly foolish action, Louis dismissed the loyal Flanders Regiment and called upon the disloyal National Guard for protection. The Marquis de Lafayette (who had fought in the American Revolution), arrived at Versailles with the National Guard of Paris about 10:00 P.M., but proceeded to go to sleep, leaving the gates inadequately guarded. The mob invaded the courtyard, driving back the guard. Their chief officer's head was cut off and put on a pike; other defenders were killed. The mob screamed for the king and for Antoinette, threatening to "cut her pretty throat." Antoinette fled to Louis' apartment just in time. The mob broke into her room and slashed her bed. Lafayette finally woke up and urged the king to move to Paris. He and Antoinette behaved with dignity and bravery. They took a carriage to Paris, followed by the howling mob, carrying heads of the officers of Louis' guard on pikes. The Assembly also came to Paris to meet, where they would be increasingly under the influence of the mob. Louis and Antoinette took up residence in the Tuileries palace. The palace at Versailles was never inhabited again.

October: A group called the *Jacobins* grew in power. The Jacobins taught that everyone should have complete freedom to do whatever he wanted.

November: Church lands were seized by the National Assembly to enrich its members.

Revolution: 1790-1791

February 1790: Monastic vows were prohibited and religious orders suppressed.

July 1790: The Assembly passed the *Civil Constitution of the Clergy*. Pastors and bishops were to be elected, with even non-Catholics voting. Priests and bishops who didn't take an oath to the Constitution could no longer serve. A liberal bishop named Talleyrand was one of the chief authors of the Civil Constitution. To their credit, only seven bishops and less than half the priests took the oath; the others served the people in secret. Pope Pius VI condemned the Civil Constitution, but in agony Louis signed it because he was afraid of more bloodshed. He became ill from the strain and guilt.

Autumn 1790: France was in chaos. Laws were not enforced and the people had no protection. Louis and Antoinette were virtual prisoners in the Tuileries, surrounded by armed guards.

June 20-25, 1791—*The Flight to Varennes*: The royal family, fearing for their lives, decided to escape from Paris. The attempted escape was primarily planned by Axel Fersen, a Swedish nobleman who greatly admired Antoinette. His basic plan was sensible. Louis and Antoinette would secretly leave the Tuileries and then be taken out of Paris by carriage, at night. Loyal troops would await them in three different towns which were safely away from the influence of Paris. Gradually their escort of loyal troops would increase until they reached the border, where they would rendezvous with a loyal army.

But though the plan was a good one, a number of mistakes were made in arranging its details. The royal party (which consisted of Louis, Antoinette, their two children, and Louis' sister Elisabeth) decided to travel in a huge, cumbersome, slow carriage called a berline, instead of in two light, fast carriages. There was room for a sixth person in the berline, but instead of taking an armed man, they took the Dauphin's governess. Fersen first presented the plan to the king and queen in early 1791, but instead of immediately acting on it, Louis procrastinated all through the winter and spring of 1791. Antoinette used her hairdresser to carry messages; he later panicked at a crucial time. The three chosen to be driver and footmen were not very strong or reliable.

On the night of June 20, Louis left the Tuileries in disguise. A man who bore a slight resemblance to the king had been coming into the Tuileries every day for two weeks and leaving about the time Louis planned to make his escape. On the chosen night, he exchanged clothes with the king, and the king easily walked out of the palace grounds. Antoinette, meanwhile, left separately with the children. On her way out, she almost ran into a guard. She ducked into a corner in the shadows and was so frightened that when it was safe to leave she took a wrong turn and got lost, thus losing a valuable half hour. Once she rejoined the king, they couldn't find the berline where it had been hidden outside Paris, so that they didn't finally leave the city until 2:00 A.M., at a time of year when it becomes light very early.

Once the party was finally underway, they did not travel at maximum speed and were then further delayed by a broken wheel. The first rendezvous with troops was to be at Pont-Sommevelle at 2:30 P.M. But the berline was running three hours late. The troops were frightened; a hostile mob had gathered because they thought the troops were there to collect rents. About 4:30 the troops couldn't take much more of the tension. Leonard, the hairdresser, panicked and rushed on to the next town, Ste. Menehould, and told the troops to disperse because the king had been captured and wasn't coming. The troops in this town had also encountered hostility. A man named Drouet, who owned an inn, was furious because the troops had stayed the previous night at the inn of his rival. Some of the troops were drunk. So at 5:30 they dispersed.

Louis meanwhile had come to Pont Sommevelle and found no troops, so he ordered the berline to go on. He arrived at Ste. Menehould at 6:00, again finding no troops. Again he had no choice but to go on. The next rendezvous point was Varennes, which was just 30 miles from their final destination.

Meanwhile Drouet had recognized Louis and Antoinette and realized that they were escaping. He decided to rush on to Varennes to rouse out the National Guard there to halt the escape. Varennes was divided into an upper and lower town, with a key bridge across the river between. The loyal troops were waiting in the lower town, but Louis entered the upper town. He had arrived in Varennes 20 minutes ahead of Drouet, but he was in the wrong part of town. He could find neither the troops nor the fresh horses he expected. Drouet arrived and immediately drove his cart across the bridge to block the way between Louis and his troops. Soon 6000 national guardsmen had arrived. Louis had to agree to return to Paris. The flight to freedom became the flight to Varennes and a failure. The royal family had lost its last chance to save itself, as Louis recognized when he said, "There is no king in France."

The trip back to Paris was a Via Dolorosa for the royal family, as liberal mobs spat on them and jeered at them at every stop. On the return trip, Antoinette's hair turned completely white. In the coach rode the liberal Barnave, appointed by the Assembly to guard the royal family. He was enormously impressed by Antoinette's dignity and courage and decided to try to help her later. He did so and was eventually guillotined.

July: Parish churches stood empty as the people flocked in secret to the *non-juring* priests, those who had not sworn the oath to the Civil Constitution of the Clergy.

September 14: The new constitution was finally adopted. The king had only one real power left to him: to veto laws. Everything else depended on voting and the will of the new *Legislative Assembly*.

October: The Legislative Assembly was divided into the small, weak remnants of the right; the Plain, who more or less felt that the Revolution had gone far enough; the Girondists, who wanted no king at all; and the Mountain (so-called because their seats were high up on the left side of the hall), who were the most radical Jacobins. Business was conducted in a state of chaos. Legislators threw things at each other; people in the audience screamed insults at legislators. The paper money printed by the Assembly rapidly declined in value and prices rose. A poor harvest resulted in a famine. The revolutionary government was extremely unpopular.

December 19: Louis vetoed a decree ordering the arrest of non-juring priests because he realized that hatred of God and the Church was at the heart of the Revolution. The propaganda against him became more vicious.

Revolution: 1792

April 20: In order to unite the country and take the people's minds off their troubles, the Legislative Assembly declared war on Austria, the beginning of 23 years of war for France and Europe. At first the army was weak and mutinous, infected by the liberal notion that all decisions should be made by voting (and how many soldiers are going to vote to go into battle?). Since Antoinette was Austrian, she was regarded as an enemy alien and hated more than ever. The Allied armies (Prussia and Austria) were under the command of the Prussian Duke of Brunswick, who brought his army to the French border with little or no resistance.

June 20: A mob came to the Tuileries demanding that Louis retract his veto of the law against priests. Louis put on a red "liberty cap" and calmed the mob down.

July: The Jacobins under the leadership of Robespierre, leader of the Paris Commune (revolutionary city government of Paris), wanted to get rid of the king altogether. The Jacobins called upon the Jacobin Mayor Mouraille of Marseilles for "600 men who know how to die." The call was answered, and a mob marched from Marseilles to Paris singing the revolutionary song, the "Marseillaise" (which is now France's national anthem).

August 10: At sunrise, Danton and the Commune seized the Paris City Hall and took over the rule of Paris. The Marseilles men then attacked the Tuileries. Louis decided to seek refuge in the Assembly. Louis, Antoinette and the children went to the Assembly and were placed in the stenographer's box.

Meanwhile the Marseillaise-led mob called on the Tuileries to surrender. The king's Swiss Guard refused with the words, "We would think ourselves dishonored!" The Guard had not been issued enough cartridges, the excuse being given that all ammunition was needed for the war. When the sound of battle reached Louis, the Assembly pressured him to order the Swiss to cease firing on French citizens.

Louis issued the fatal order. The heroic Swiss ceased firing and were massacred to the last man, along with everyone in the palace, including the cooks and the Dauphin's tutor—800 killed in all. In the evening, little boys rolled human heads along the streets.

The mob then came to the Assembly where they demanded Louis' suspension. The Assembly agreed, and Louis and his family spent the next two days in the stenographer's box and the nights in a nearby convent with hardly anything to eat. On August 12 the king was thrown into prison. Danton was dictator of France, and the Assembly struck a medal: "In memory of the glorious combat of the French people against tyranny at the Tuileries."

September: The arrest of the king apparently galvanized the Allied armies, and the Prussians crossed the frontier on August 19 under the Duke of Brunswick. The Allied successes frightened Jacobin leaders, who declared that the only reason the French army had lost was because of traitors in Paris. The Assembly decreed the imprisonment of all fathers, mothers, wives and children of the emigres (those who had fled France because of the Revolution) and all non-juring priests. Then under the leadership of Danton and Marat (a half-mad, militant atheist, so diseased that he had to spend part of each day in a special bath), 150 murderers were hired and sent into the prisons where they massacred 1400 prisoners—including many priests and girls down to ten years of age. In many cases the bodies were torn to pieces. The Church accounts the priests and bishops martyrs because some were offered the opportunity to save their lives by swearing the oath to accept the Civil Constitution of the Clergy. These are the *September Massacres*, which lasted from September 2-7.

September 20: Meanwhile the Allied army under Brunswick stood at Valmy. The Allies had every advantage, but Brunswick finally persuaded the king of Prussia, who was present at the battle, to call off the attack. The Prussians retreated, and the Revolutionary army proclaimed a great victory and marched to occupy Belgium, where there was looting, bloodshed, and the destruction of many art treasures. This was the last good chance the Allies had to overthrow the Revolution and save the royal family.

Why did Brunswick retreat? The full story has only recently been revealed. In the treasury in Paris was an enormous diamond (*part* of it later became the Hope Diamond) known as the Blue Diamond of the Golden Fleece. Thieves broke into the treasury and stole this diamond along with some other treasures. Suspected of the theft was Carra, a fervent Jacobin. A few days later he appeared at the camp of the Prussian army. Much later—long after Valmy—the Blue Diamond appeared in the Duke of

Brunswick's private collection. The Duke had thrown the Battle of Valmy in exchange for the Blue Diamond of the Golden Fleece; and the royal family, France, and all Europe would pay in blood for his greed.

September 5-21: The Legislative Assembly, under pressure from the Paris Commune and the Jacobins, had dissolved itself and called for elections for a new body to be called the *National Convention*. In the Convention, the Girondists were now the right and the Mountain the left. This makeup is not surprising because during the election, the Jacobins used threats and intimidation to keep conservatives from the polls. Rightist newspapers were suppressed, thugs stood at the voting booths, and there was no secret ballot. Out of seven million eligible voters, only 700,000 actually voted. Danton, Robespierre, and Marat were the leaders of the Convention.

On the first day of the Convention, September 21, the French monarchy was abolished. The Jacobins wanted the king's life as well as his throne, and the Girondins were too fearful to stop the regicide (murder of a king).

December: An illegal trial by the Assembly found Louis guilty of "conspiring against the general security of the state" and sentenced him to death. Some members of the National Convention wanted to submit the question of the king's execution to a vote of the people. Robespierre refused; he said that France no longer operated under the principle of majority rule. Saint-Just, a friend of Robespierre and one of the worst of the Jacobins, admitted that an appeal to the people would save the king. He added: "Caesar was put to death in the middle of the Senate, with no formalities beyond 22 dagger thrusts," implying that the king was lucky to have had any trial at all.

The Reign of Terror

January 21, 1793: As he mounted the scaffold to be executed, Louis proclaimed: "I die innocent of all the crimes laid to my charge; I pardon those who have occasioned my death; and I pray to God that the blood you are now going to shed may never be visited on France. And you, unfortunate people . . ." No one could hear his last words because the officer in charge ordered a drum roll, drowning out Louis' voice. The guillotine fell and France's king was dead.

The execution of the king was the beginning of the *Reign of Terror*, as the *Committee of Public Safety*, dominated by Robespierre, assumed absolute dictatorship of France. Antoinette, Elisabeth and the children (Marie Therese and Louis, now rightfully Louis XVII of France) were imprisoned in the Temple Tower. Francois Adrian Toulon was assigned as guard. He was an ardent revolutionary, but like Barnave was won over by Antoinette's dignity and courage. He devised a plan whereby the royal family would escape disguised in men's clothes. But the man who was to get them their passports so they could escape Paris backed out at the last minute. Furthermore the Tison couple, which was guarding the royal family, became suspicious. The plan had to be cancelled. Like Barnave, Toulon eventually paid with his life for his change of heart.

March: The killing of the king led to the *Rising in the Vendee*, a strongly Catholic farming region in the west of France. The two main leaders were a nobleman, the Marquis de Rochejacquelein, and a commoner, the coachman Cathelineau. Priests, nobles, and peasants were united in their opposition to the evils of the Revolution. With the battle cry of "Church and Crown," they won a series of victories, until worn down by the full strength of the French army.

July 3: Antoinette was separated from her seven-year-old son, in an attempt to break the wills of both of them. She was moved to the Concierge, a damp, gloomy, filthy prison. Louis was forced to sign documents accusing his mother of immoral acts.

Summer: The Girondins also attempted several risings against the Jacobins, but they were strong only where the people were motivated by traditional values. The Jacobin leaders began purging the Girondins from the Convention, and the revolts were savagely put down. In Toulon, for example, a thousand people were executed, including a 94-year-old man who had to be carried to the guillotine in a chair.

July: In Caen in Normandy a young woman named Charlotte Corday decided to take matters into her own hands. She had been a Girondin and in favor of the Revolution in its early days because she believed in liberal values. But she had become increasingly disillusioned as the Revolution became more and more bloodthirsty and began devouring those who had spearheaded it. She had somehow convinced herself that Marat was primarily responsible for the attacks on her fellow Girondins, and she made up her mind that if she could assassinate Marat, she could bring the bloodshed to an end. So on July 5, 1793 she bought a one-way ticket to Paris.

After she arrived, she bought a sharp knife and tried to obtain an appointment to see Marat. She was refused, so she finally forced her way into his apartment. She walked into his room, where he was soaking his diseased skin in his bath. Charlotte told Marat that she had a list of Girondins in Caen. Marat was delighted and told her that they would soon be dead.

As soon as he pronounced their death sentence, Charlotte pulled out her knife and stabbed Marat to death. She then calmly surrendered herself and went to her own execution convinced that she had saved France.

But France was not saved. In the Vendee Cathelineau was killed, and the British refused aid for the Vendeeans until they could capture a major port. Another attempt to help Antoinette escape (the "Plot of the Carnations"), which had the complicity of the police administrator, Michonis, another of her "conquests," failed. The Convention called for total mobilization and universal conscription, which produced a fresh army of 200,000. The Allies argued with each other and were unable to mount a concerted attack against the Revolutionary army. The mobs demanded more executions, and one of the delegates in the Convention, referring to the guillotine, announced: "Let us go to the foot of the great altar and attend the celebration of the Red Mass."

September: A communist economy was set up. Wages and prices were set by the government, but they had no relationship to what things were really worth; men were told what work to do. No one would cooperate so more executions were ordered. Many necessary items became extremely scarce and famine gripped the land.

October: Antoinette was interrogated by the Assembly. Though she was ill and exhausted, she did not fall into any of the traps which the questioners had prepared for her and answered with dignity and bravery. Her accusers could provide no evidence of the commission of any crime. Nevertheless she was found guilty and guillotined.

After Antoinette's execution, her court-appointed lawyer, who had defended her too spiritedly, was also arrested. The number of enemies she won over to her side clearly shows that she could not have been the monster she has been too often portrayed. Her saintly sister-in-law Elisabeth was also executed; Louis XVII later died of mistreatment; and Marie Therese was sent to Austria where she was used as a pawn in Austrian politics.

November: The worship of God was forbidden, to be replaced by the "goddess of reason." A new calendar was ordered, with the Year 1 of Liberty beginning September 22, 1792 (the first day after the abolition of the monarchy). The months were given new names, and the week was made ten days long. When one of the leaders was asked the purpose of the new calendar, he replied: "To abolish Sunday." Honorary and courtesy titles such as monsieur and madame were outlawed; all men had to be addressed as "citizen," all women as "citizeness."

December: The army of the Vendee, fighting for Church and Crown, was finally crushed. In reprisal, more than 1500 prisoners were killed by loading them aboard barges and sinking them in the river when the Revolutionary authorities decided they couldn't work their guillotines fast enough.

The Terror steadily worsened in Paris and throughout France. But Danton began to have glimmerings of conscience. His first wife died and he planned to marry again. But his wife-to-be would not marry him until he had been to confession. (Imagine the confession he could make!) Then in December he stood up in the Convention and called for an end to the Terror. His words were ignored. The bodies of former kings (including the body of James II of England, who had died in France) were disinterred, put in a common grave, and destroyed with lime. Everyone was terrified of Robespierre, who held absolute power of life and death.

February, 1794: Danton visited Robespierre in his rooms and they argued about the Terror. Robespierre insisted that not a single innocent person had been executed, and Danton walked out in disgust.

March: On March 19 Danton again urged an end to the Terror. On March 22, he pleaded with Robespierre for the release of imprisoned Convention delegates, but Robespierre said that they all must be guillotined. When Danton tried to embrace Robespierre, he found him "cold as ice." On March 31 Danton was arrested. He told his fellow prisoners: "Gentlemen, I had hoped to get you all out of this place. Unfortunately, I'm now shut up in it with you."

April: Danton said: "A year ago I established the Revolutionary Tribunal. I ask pardon of God and men." When Danton was brought to trial, Robespierre forced the Convention to pass a decree forbidding Danton from defending himself. Danton responded with, "You are murderers! Murderers! Look at them! Vile Robespierre! You too will go to the scaffold. You will follow me, Robespierre!" The jury, which was made up of seven of Danton's personal enemies, actually was ready to acquit him, when Fouquier-Tinville (the public prosecutor and one of the most bloodthirsty of the Jacobins) entered the room with letters from the Committee of Public Safety and coerced a verdict of death. On his way to the guillotine in the tumbril, Danton apparently made his confession and received absolution from a priest by the roadside.

Robespierre then decreed: "The Tribunal must be as active as crime itself and conclude every case within 24 hours." It did. The victims were not just the aristocrats, who had been the original target of the Revolution.

Anyone of even modest income or talent was regarded as an enemy of the Revolution and could be taken to the guillotine. Broz, who was 19 at the time of the Terror, wrote: "I saw Paris in those days of crime and mourning. From the stupefied expression on people's faces you would have said that it was a city desolated by plague. The laughter of a few cannibals alone interrupted the deadly silence which surrounded you."

June 10: Robespierre forced the passage of the *Law of 22 Prairial* (one of the new months in the Revolutionary calendar), ending all defense for persons on trial for their lives before the Revolutionary Tribunal. The guilty could include anyone who so much as said he was discontented with conditions. During the next seven weeks, 1,376 were guillotined. The best in France had been executed or were in hiding or were at the front. The country was governed by its worst and was on the verge of mass starvation.

July: Joseph Fouche, who had been co-governor of Lyon during the Terror there, returned to Paris. He quickly realized that Robespierre held absolute power and that no one's life was safe, even the lives of those who had participated actively in the Revolution. Even the deputies in the Convention were terrified of the dictator. (Remarked one deputy, after Robespierre simply looked at him: "He'll be supposing I was thinking about something!") But Fouche was not easily frightened and made up his mind to get Robespierre before Robespierre could get him.

After Robespierre had him expelled from the Jacobin Club in Paris, Fouche went into hiding, never sleeping in the same place for two nights in succession. He went to the members of the Convention and said: "Robespierre has a list and you're on it." He persuaded the deputies that he could save their lives if they would join him in a plot to overthrow Robespierre.

July 26: The Carmelite nuns of Compiegne were sent to the guillotine, the last martyrs of the Reign of Terror.

July 27: Fouche was finally ready. The Convention met and under Fouche's leadership voted the execution of Robespierre. Fleuriot, the Mayor of Paris and an ardent follower of Robespierre, attempted to rally the Commune and its army to Robespierre's defense. But Robespierre was not a man of action and did not know quite what to do. Hanriot, the commander of the National Guard, was drunk all day, riding through the streets yelling "Kill! Kill!" instead of organizing his troops. Robespierre was finally prevailed on about midnight to sign an appeal to the army to come to his rescue, but adherents of the Convention broke into his room and shot him in the jaw while he was signing. (We still have the half-signed, blood-stained paper.) Robespierre then lay on a table for six hours in the offices of the Committee of Public Safety. A passing workman, looking at his shattered jaw, said: "Yes, Robespierre, there is a God." Eight thousand people were in prison awaiting the guillotine in Paris when Robespierre was executed. The date in the Revolutionary calendar was 9 Thermidor so the overthrow of Robespierre is known as the *Thermidorian Reaction.*

The Rise of Napoleon

The Convention members had overthrown Robespierre to save their own lives. They had not intended a real change in the way France was governed. But the people demanded a change, and the Convention had to undo the communistic laws that had been passed, re-open the churches, suppress the Jacobins, and make peace with foreign enemies.

Nevertheless France still faced an acute crisis: famine, bankruptcy, popular uprisings, chaos. The Convention set up its own army to keep order in Paris. To command it, they hired a former protege of Robespierre's who had attracted notice at the siege of Toulon against the British. His name was Napoleon Bonaparte. The Convention passed a new constitution on August 22, 1795 and set up the Directory. Talleyrand, one of the original liberals who had managed to survive the Reign of Terror, soon emerged as a leader of the Directory.

The whole precarious system of government was in danger from popular uprisings, but Napoleon had the answer. All that was needed, he said, was "a whiff of grapeshot." The "whiff" (actually a cannonade) was fired into the mob on October 5, and order was restored in Paris.

Napoleon could keep order for the Directory but they couldn't do much for themselves. When they had their first meeting in the Luxembourg Palace, they had only one rotten table to work on and only one of them had thought of bringing some paper. Paper money was worthless, and the army was supported by pillage. They finally decided, as the Assembly had decided long before, that France's only hope of salvation was a war. Three armies were organized, two to march through the Danube Valley, one over the Alps into Austrian territory in Italy. Napoleon was given command of the Army of the Alps.

He was a wise choice. He immediately established authority over his soldiers, restoring the discipline that had been lost in the revolutionary hysteria. In the spring of 1796 he captured Turin, Lombardy and Milan. The dukes of Parma and Modena, the king of Naples and Pope Pius VI purchased truces at the price of large payments in money and art treasures.

Napoleon set up his own government in the conquered territory. The Directory didn't complain because he was winning and because money was pouring into the treasury. He called his new government the Cisalpine Republic, which was formally proclaimed on July 9, 1797.

On September 4, 1797, the radicals, supported by Napoleon, engineered a coup to seize control of the Directory. They reinstituted laws against priests and royalists. Prison ships replaced the guillotines. They were just as deadly, though not as fast. The Pope was referred to as "Citizen Pope," or, more ominously, "Pius the Last of Rome."

Then in February 1798 the French army occupied Rome, proclaiming the Roman Republic, breaking the earlier agreement with the Pope. Churches and other buildings were looted, and opposition was disposed of by firing squads. Pope Pius VI was past 80, partially paralyzed and enfeebled by age. He had earlier refused to flee and seek refuge in Naples and now had nowhere to turn. On February 20, the French officer Haller confronted the Pope, bullied him, demanded his abdication and tore the Fisherman's Ring from his finger. The Pope begged to be allowed to die in Rome. Haller replied: "I assure you one dies the same way everywhere." The Pope was forced into a carriage and escorted by a troop of boorish soldiers first to Siena and then to Val'Ema. Both of these cities were considered as too near Rome so then he was dragged in a Via Dolorosa to Florence, Turin, across the Alps to Briancon (too near Austria—move the Pope again), and then to Valence, France, where he arrived on July 14. Now completely paralyzed, he was imprisoned in a church there. Though he had been cheered all along the way to Valence, he was at the mercy of the French. They expected that he would die soon, and Napoleon had already said that when the Pope died, the army should prevent the election of another.

By May 1798, France controlled Holland, Switzerland and Italy. Napoleon knew that England was likely to be his major enemy so decided on an expedition to Egypt to cut the lines between Britain and India, thus isolating England and depriving it of its outposts. He set sail on May 19, 1798 with 300 ships, 16,000 sailors, and 38,000 soldiers. England was outwitted. Their fleet was waiting in the Channel, expecting an invasion of Ireland, when Napoleon seized Malta without a shot and then landed in Egypt. On July 21 at the foot of the Pyramids, the Egyptian army shattered itself against the French infantry squares in the *Battle of the Pyramids.*

Admiral Horatio Nelson pursued Napoleon. The French fleet was anchored at the mouth of the Nile, downwind, no sails up, in more or less a straight line, expecting no trouble. The men were unloading stores when the British attacked at 6:00 A.M. on August 1. The British ships sailed down either side of the anchored French ships, risking grounding on the shoals, a daring feat of seamanship. The British methodically finished off the French ships. The French admiral was badly wounded. He declared: "A French admiral ought to die on his deck," and did so. His second in command was also killed. The British set fire to the French magazines, which blew up. Only two French ships got away. Napoleon fled Egypt on August 24 to return to France, leaving most of his army behind.

The New Absolute Monarch

In May 1799, encouraged by the Battle of the Nile, Austro-Russian forces erased the Cisalpine Republic and threatened to cut the rest of the French in Italy off from France. A popular uprising against the French began in Tuscany, the Papal States and Naples. The people were motivated primarily by their loyalty to the Church and their opposition to revolutionary atheism. One of the first things the people did in the uprising was to uproot and burn the Trees of Liberty which the French had erected, replacing them with crosses. They then repaired the damage in the churches and reopened the monasteries and convents.

Under the leadership of Cardinal Fabrizio Ruffo, a congregation was formed called the Congregation of the Holy Faith (or, as they were usually known, *Sanfedisti*) with a military arm called the Army of the Holy Faith. The Sanfedisti were similar to the Vendeeans in France. They were armed with little more than scythes and shotguns, but they soon numbered in the tens of thousands. They captured Altamura and rescued alive three out of 48 priests and other persons who had been chained together and dropped into a ditch. They advanced on Naples, which they occupied in the middle of June. They gave generous terms to the French garrisons to secure peace and to avoid bloodshed.

On June 24 the British Admiral Nelson arrived and took over the direction of the anti-French forces. But in their short history, the Sanfedisti overthrew revolutionary regimes in Naples, Rome and Florence. They ended for the time being the Jacobin system in Italy and disproved the myth that the Revolution was supported by the ordinary people. The Sanfedisti were ordinary people, and they most emphatically did not support the Revolution.

The Sanfedisti at one time had hoped to be able to rescue Pope Pius

VI, but they were too late. On August 29, 1799 the Holy Father died at
Valence, begging forgiveness for his enemies. Just before he died, he offered a three-fold prayer: that peace be restored to Europe, that the Pope
be restored to Rome, and that the Church be restored to France. All three
of those prayers would be answered within the lifetime of the next Pontiff, but as Pius VI offered those prayers, all the evidence seemed to be
that no one living then would ever see the answer to his plea. The official
in charge certified the decease "of the said Giovanni Angelo Braschi, exer-
cising the profession of pontiff," and sent a report to Paris that the dead
Pope would certainly be the last. In earthly terms, his report seemed to be
exactly right.

Napoleon certainly behaved as if he had nothing to fear from the
Pope or from anyone else. He returned to Paris and was welcomed as the
conquering hero. He met with radical leaders and worked out a scheme
whereby the Directors would be bribed and intimidated to get out of the
way, thus permitting Napoleon to come before the Council of Five Hundred (France's newest legislative body) to get them to bestow power on
him and two other radicals.

The first part of the plan was easily accomplished. But when
Napoleon came before the Council (which tried to imitate the old Roman
Senate by dressing in togas), his speech was so inept that he was soundly
booed. But he pulled himself together and called in his troops, which had
been standing by, just in case. There followed a stampede of togas, and the
Coup d'Etat of Brumaire had succeeded (so called because it took place on
November 9, which was 18 Brumaire in the Revolutionary calendar).
Napoleon became First Consul (using the old Roman title) with two other
consuls who had no real power. The people ratified the Constitution of the
Year VIII (in the Revolutionary calendar) on December 24, 1799 by a vote
of 3,011,107 to 1,567 because they were grateful for someone who could at
last keep order. The effect of the constitution was to establish Napoleon as
dictator of France. The Revolutionary violence was over, order was restored, and France was ruled by an absolute monarch once more.

On November 30 the conclave, long delayed by the revolutionary upheavals, met in Venice to elect a new Pope. Only 35 out of 46 cardinals
were able to come. The cardinals were sharply divided between those who
wanted to elect a compromiser and those who wanted Pope who would
defy Napoleon. For three and a half months they argued. Finally on March
14, 1800, the cardinals elected Cardinal Chiaramonti, who had spent his
time at the conclave praying instead of seeking votes. He took the name of

Pius VII. At the time he was widely believed to be a compromiser, one who could get along with Napoleon. For fifteen years Europe would witness the struggle between these two men—the former monk and the all-conquering general.

Ten years of bloodshed, terror, famine and violence had brought France from absolute monarch to absolute monarch. The French Revolution had promised a stable government, sound finance, wise laws, peace and domestic order. The people had received anarchy, bankruptcy, communism, war and terror.

Many evils existed in France and eighteenth century Europe. They accumulated until they were like a pile of dynamite. The torch igniting the dynamite was liberalism: the beliefs that no authority, no responsibility exists; that men owe nothing to God; that man's mind is supreme. These ideas were born in the Renaissance and the Protestant Revolt, grew up in the seventeenth century, and reached a full, terrible adulthood in the eighteenth century, when they spread suffering and death throughout Europe.

Though Napoleon had restored order in France, he shared the revolutionary ideology and would proceed to spread revolutionary liberalism throughout Europe. The evils unleashed by the French Revolution would plague the world to this day. Both Nazism and Communism are children of the French Revolution because both these systems are based on the principle that the government owes nothing to God and that moral principles are chains to be crushed into dust. Wherever today men and governments reject God's authority and deny the necessity for applying morality to the social and political order, they are continuing the work of the French Revolution.

Review Questions

1. How had Louis XIII, Louis XIV and Louis XV helped create conditions that would lead to the French Revolution?
2. What is the common view of Louis XVI and Marie Antoinette? Give specific examples from the early years of their reign which refute this view.
3. Why did the noblemen oppose Louis and Antoinette? Why did the liberals oppose them?
4. What was the Estates General? Why did Louis call it?
5. Why did the liberals walk out of the Estates General? What was the Tennis Court Oath?

CHRIST THE KING—LORD OF HISTORY

6. What happened at the storming of the Bastille?
7. What was the Great Fear?
8. What was the Declaration of the Rights of Man? Why was it not really a guarantee of individual rights?
9. What is the origin of the political terms "left" and "right" and what does each mean?
10. What happened at the March on Versailles?
11. What actions did the National Assembly take against the Church before the Civil Constitution of the Clergy? What did this Constitution say?
12. What was the Flight to Varennes? Why did it fail? What was its chief significance?
13. Why did the Assembly declare war?
14. Who were the men from Marseilles? What did they do? What happened to Louis and Antoinette?
15. What were the September Massacres?
16. Why did the Allies lose the Battle of Valmy? What was its significance?
17. What was the National Convention? What was their first action?
18. Describe the trial and execution of King Louis.
19. What was the Reign of Terror? The Committee of Public Safety?
20. What was the Rising in the Vendee? What happened to it?
21. Describe the assassination of Marat.
22. Give examples showing Antoinette's ability to win liberals to her side. What is the significance of this fact?
23. List the laws enacted in the Reign of Terror.
24. Describe the conversion of Danton and its consequences.
25. Explain how Fouche brought about the end of the Reign of Terror.
26. What was the "whiff of grapeshot"?
27. Why did the Directory go to war? Summarize Napoleon's victories in this war.
28. Describe the arrest of the Pope and what happened afterwards, including his death and the prayer he offered at that time.
29. How did Napoleon win and lose in Egypt?
30. Who were the Sanfedisti and what did they do?
31. What happened at the Coup d'Etat of Brumaire?
32. Who was the new Pope? What was the general view of him?
33. How had the French Revolution broken its promises to the people?

Projects

1. Imagine that you lived in Paris during 1789-1799. Write a diary of the main events.
2. Conduct a trial of Louis or Antoinette.
3. Dramatize a scene from this chapter, such as Danton's meeting with Robespierre, the death of the Pope, or the overthrow of Robespierre.
4. Hold a "press conference" with students representing one or more of the characters in this chapter.

Chapter Twenty Five
The Age of Napoleon

THE CONTEMPT FOR RELIGION and lawful authority unleashed by the French Revolution had produced a man who wanted to conquer all of Europe and even dreamed of conquering Asia and America, the first man with such a desire since Christianity had come to the continent to teach men the dangers of pride and aggression. Added to his monstrous ambition were Napoleon's genius as a military commander and his skill as a political leader. The combination was for a time unstoppable.

Napoleon as First Consul

As Napoleon consolidated his position as First Consul, his foreign status appeared to be more shaky. Thanks to the Sanfedisti, Napoleon had lost his foothold in Italy, but he did not intend to allow this situation to last. In May he marched his army through all five Alpine passes into Italy. The early days were tough going. At one point Massena's army had to make bread out of sawdust; another time the army had to cut a road through a mountain around a fort after all attempts to reduce it had failed.

The key battle was the *Battle of Marengo* (in the Po River Valley), June 14, 1800. The Austrian army under Melas was cut off so Melas decided to attack France at dawn and fight his way through. He used artillery to break up the French infantry squares, then charged with cavalry. The French were retreating by noon. Melas turned the pursuit over to General Zach and sat down to write a dispatch to Austrian headquarters announcing the first ever Austrian victory over Napoleon Bonaparte.

It wasn't quite that simple, however. Napoleon had been at the rear and not arrived at the battle until 11:00. He asked his subordinate Desaix what he thought of the situation. Desaix replied: "The battle is wholly lost, but we have time to win another." Desaix hid reinforcements, then attacked Zach's rear guard, which was moving slowly because Zach insisted on keeping parade order, so confident was he that the battle was over and won. The French regrouped and then attacked from the other side, forcing the surrender of 2000 Austrians. Melas evacuated northern Italy, which was now in Napoleon's hands once again.

Meanwhile back in Paris, two familiar faces appeared in Napoleon's government. The Minister of Police was Joseph Fouche, who had once said, "The Republic must march to liberty over corpses." He now made sure that no opposition would arise against Napoleon.

At the same time, Napoleon appointed Talleyrand, who always landed on his feet, as Foreign Minister, and sent him off to Rome to negotiate with the Pope. Napoleon desired at least the appearances of reconciliation with the Church so he could count on the full support of the French people, who were still loyally Catholic.

On July 15, 1801, the *Concordat* (an agreement between a government and the Vatican) was concluded. Pope Pius VII recognized the French Republic as the official government of France. The dioceses would conform to the departments (new administrative divisions set up during the Revolution) rather than to their traditional boundaries. Bishops would be nominated by Napoleon and approved by the Pope. Priests would be appointed by bishops from an approved government list. Church property in France was not restored. In return, most of the papal lands were returned, the government would pay salaries of priests, freedom of worship was guaranteed, and the Catholic Church was recognized as the religion of the majority (but not as the official religion of France). Napoleon's liberal friends were angry that he had made any concessions to the Church, but his reply was, "I know what I'm doing. I'm working for the future." (A few of the liberals were so unhappy that they tried to jump out of the carriage on the way to the Mass in Notre Dame celebrating the adoption of the Concordat. Napoleon ordered them to stay. They revenged themselves by talking loudly all through the ceremony.) Loyal Catholics were angry at the Pope for making concessions to Napoleon, but the churches were reopened and a Gallican schism was avoided.

In February 1802 Napoleon issued the Organic Articles, a code of ecclesiastical law, which put restrictions on the Church. Bishops were forbidden to leave their dioceses, the state would control the seminaries, and no religious marriage would be valid without a civil certificate. Pius VII was not happy with this code, but there was nothing he could do. Nevertheless, the Church was far better off than it had been at any time during the Revolution.

On March 27, 1802, Napoleon concluded the *Treaty of Amiens* with England, the only major power he had not defeated. England recognized Napoleon's authority in Europe, while Napoleon agreed not to extend his conquests any further. Now all Europe was at peace with France, regarding the French Revolution as an accomplished fact.

In the summer of 1802, Napoleon maneuvered a plebiscite by which he became first consul for life, with the right of appointing his successor. The question of succession was uppermost on many minds. Napoleon and his wife, Josephine Beauharnais, had no children. So he arranged a marriage between Josephine's daughter by her first marriage, Hortense, and his younger brother Louis. Neither Louis nor Hortense was very happy about the marriage, but Josephine was delighted because she believed that by it she had forestalled an attempt by Napoleon to divorce her and marry a younger woman. Within a year Hortense gave birth to a son, Louis Napoleon, whom Napoleon accepted as his heir.

Napoleon Becomes Emperor

Now that Napoleon had peace in Europe he could turn his attention elsewhere. He wanted to build a colonial empire with the Louisiana territory as a base and the Caribbean island of Sant Domingue (now Haiti) as the stepping stone for shipping. But first he had to regain control over the island which had gained independence during the French Revolution under the leadership of a former black slave of genius, Toussaint L'Ouverture, a strong Catholic. Napoleon sent some of his finest troops to the New World, but his men fell victim to yellow fever and to ambushes which decimated them. In disgust, Napoleon granted the island its independence. Then he decided to wash his hands of the New World altogether and sold the Louisiana Territory to the upstart United States at a bargain price.

In 1803 Napoleon made hostile moves in Switzerland, so on May 18, 1803, England declared war. The early stages of the war were almost all sea battles. In 1804, French royalists devised a plot to assassinate Napoleon. Fouche knew all about it and encouraged the plot through double agents until he could arrest and execute the conspirators. Fouche then convinced the liberals who had not liked Napoleon that a Napoleonic dynasty was the only way to prevent the return of the Bourbons (two of Louis XVI's brothers were still alive and eager to return to power). Thus the liberals, who had destroyed the monarchy, now found themselves supporting an empire, as Napoleon held another plebiscite by which the people (with a vote of 3,000,000 to 3,000) approved the establishment of an empire. Napoleon at once set up a luxurious court which rivaled that of the Bourbon kings.

After five months of negotiation, Pope Pius VII agreed to a coronation of Napoleon in Paris. The Pope probably believed that he could gain concessions for the Church if he cooperated with the Emperor. The Pope journeyed to France, where Napoleon had prepared a lavish coronation ceremony. The night before the coronation, the Pope had an unusual visitor. Josephine, still afraid that Napoleon might divorce her, visited the Pope to tell him that she and Napoleon had never had a Church marriage, only a civil one. Josephine hoped that if the Pope insisted that Napoleon marry her in the Church, the Emperor would be less likely to divorce her. The Pope agreed that a Church ceremony must immediately be held, and Napoleon went along, his uncle, Cardinal Fesch, performing the hurried and private ceremony. At the actual coronation ceremony in Notre Dame, Napoleon seized the crown and placed it on his own head, then crowned Josephine. The Pope stayed in France for four months, though he was able to gain little for the Church. But the hierarchy and priests in France were so happy to be functioning again (Napoleon even changed the calendar back in 1806) that they were willing to flatter Napoleon as the price of being able to minister to the people.

Through it all, Napoleon made plans to invade England, saying, "Masters of the Channel for six hours and we are masters of the world." Six hours was a rather optimistic estimate; he would need more like six days to get everything loaded on flat bottomed boats, across the Channel, and unloaded in England for a successful invasion. But he couldn't even get six hours because he had no competent admirals in the French navy. The English fleet under Nelson was so strong that Villeneuve, admiral of the Combined Fleet (France and its ally Spain), did not dare attack it. With the English fleet in the way, the barges with the invading army could not leave port. Napoleon became impatient. He kept urging Villeneuve to sail. Once he even had a medal minted which proclaimed the invasion of England and the conquest of London. But the British fleet refused to cooperate.

At almost the same time as Villeneuve was working up his courage to tackle Admiral Nelson, Napoleon won the *Battle of Ulm* (October 14, 1805) against the Austrians. He had organized an elite corps of 22,000 cavalry to serve as a screen. The Austrians underestimated the size of the French force and were so thoroughly defeated that 70,000 out of the 84,000-man army were taken prisoners.

Napoleon finally abandoned his plans to invade England and ordered Villeneuve to evade the British blockade and sail to the Mediterranean, or be replaced. Villeneuve managed to get his ships out into the Atlantic but Nelson came in pursuit.

On October 21, 1805, 27 British ships commanded by Nelson sighted the 33 French and Spanish ships of the Combined Fleet off Cape Trafalgar, Spain. Nelson hoisted signal flags which read "Engage the enemy more closely" and never took them down. The British sailed in two columns toward the enemy, with Nelson's ship *Victory* taking on the 130-gun *Santissima Trinidad* and Villeneuve's *Bucentaure*. The British ships broke through the line and throughout the afternoon kept up a devastating fire. With one broadside, *Victory* dismounted 20 of *Bucentaure's* guns and wrecked the ship. At the same time gunfire from the next ship brought down Nelson himself, who lay painfully dying in the steaming hot hospital quarters, while his fleet destroyed 18 ships, captured four more, and damaged all but three of the rest so as to make them useless. This battle was the end of France's sea power, and played a crucial part in Napoleon's ultimate defeat, as the Emperor's dreams of conquering England sank beneath the waves of the ocean along with half his fleet.

The Sword and the Spirit

Napoleon's fleet had sunk off the coast of Spain, but his army marched on. Forbidding anyone to so much as mention Trafalgar in his presence, he marched the Grand Army down the Danube and occupied Vienna with almost no resistance on November 13. Russia and Austria combined forces against Napoleon. The two armies came together on December 3 at *Austerlitz*. Russian Tsar Alexander I and Holy Roman Emperor Francis II were present, along with Napoleon, so that the battle is sometimes called the Battle of Three Emperors. The Allied commanders believed Napoleon's troops to be spread along a thin line near Austerlitz and planned an attack at which they would break through that line at several points.

That was exactly what Napoleon wanted them to believe. The thin line was only a screen. Napoleon had a heavy concentration of troops at the key point. The battle began at dawn. By 10:00 A.M. the French had wiped out the Allied center, leaving the left and right wings isolated. By 11:00 A.M. the Allied right had broken and scattered. By twilight, Austrians and Russians had lost 30,000 men, as well as all their baggage, guns, food, ammunition and transport. The captured flags of the defeated units were carried back to Paris. This particular war was over.

After Austerlitz France received still more Austrian territory and set up the Confederation of the Rhine, to govern under French domination most of the German territory of the Holy Roman Empire. Francis II was forced to lay down the crown of Holy Roman Emperor, becoming Francis I of Austria.

Disturbed by Napoleon's encroachments into Germany, Prussia declared war against France. The forces came together at *Jena* on October 14, 1806. The French were outnumbered, so Napoleon decided to concentrate on the left wing of the Prussians, to overpower and roll it up, so as to gain time for his reserves. Napoleon demolished the Prussian left, his reserves came up, and he won an easy victory. At the same time, twenty miles away, a cavalry battle was fought at *Auerstadt*, where the French commander Davout was outnumbered (64,000 to 26,000) by Blucher's Prussians. Nevertheless the French refused to retreat, the Prussians broke, and the French pursued to annihilate the Prussians. Napoleon occupied Berlin and Prussia was incorporated into the French Empire. A great victory for France—but old General Blucher swore revenge, and Napoleon would eventually pay dearly for Jena and Auerstadt.

Back in France, Napoleon founded the University of France to control education throughout France, the first time such centralized control of education had been attempted in any country. He had two goals: to weaken tradition and the Church's influence; and to indoctrinate children so that they would accept the Revolution and Napoleon's influence.

At Berlin on November 21, 1806, Napoleon decreed the *Continental Blockade*, forbidding the countries under his domination to trade with England (mostly ineffective). England hit back with a total blockade of France and her colonies (mostly effective). Pope Pius VII refused to go along with the Continental Blockade. Napoleon's troops overran all of the Papal States except Rome itself. The Pope still stood his ground. On February 2, 1808, while the Pope was celebrating the Feast of the Purification, French troops occupied Rome, surrounded the Papal palace and arrested Papal officers. Through it all the Pope stayed calm.

Then Napoleon announced his intention to annex the Papal States to the Empire and to make the Pope his vassal. He sent representatives to Rome to demand that the Pope approve the proposal. But Pius VII, elected because he could get along with Napoleon, had made his last compromise. *"You may tell them in Paris,"* he roared, *"that they may hack me in pieces, they may skin me alive, but I shall never agree!"* Furious, Napoleon annexed the Papal States anyway (May 17, 1809). The tricolor was hoisted on Castle San Angelo in place of the Papal banner. The Pope excommunicated Napoleon, having the Papal bull posted on the walls of Rome by night. Contemptuous, Napoleon scoffed, "Does he imagine that the weapons will fall from the hands of my soldiers" because of this excommunication, and ordered his general to bring "this crazy fool" of a Pope to reason.

On the night of July 5, 1809, 400 French soldiers led by General Radet attacked the Pope's residence, the Quirinal Palace. First they tried scaling ladders over the walls, but the ladders broke. Then Radet attacked the gate with a hatchet, after which soldiers broke through the windows. The Pope sat calmly at a table, holding a crucifix. The soldiers burst in but were awed by the dignity of the Pope. They removed their hats, read their orders, genuflected, and kissed the Pope's ring. He was put into a carriage and taken out of Rome. But the soldiers did not know where to put the Pope because no town wanted the responsibility of being the Pope's jail. He was taken into France, then back to Italy, and finally imprisoned near Genoa. All along the way, Pius VII, like Pius VI before him, was cheered by the people. It was probably about this time that Napoleon said, in a flash of insight, "There are only two powers on earth, the sword and the spirit... In the long run the sword is always beaten by the spirit."

Napoleon had said of the Pope's arrest, "I don't want him to look like a prisoner." Nevertheless, he was isolated, confined, subject to searches, deprived of ink or paper. But Pius had been a Benedictine monk, so remained undisturbed in the midst of privation and refused to agree to any surrender of his temporal sovereignty. The cardinals were forced to leave Rome; Vatican Congregations were deprived of their superiors, staffs and archives. Pope Pius refused to appoint new bishops, leaving 27 dioceses empty. To all outward appearances, the sword had triumphed over the spirit.

War to the Death

In 1808 Napoleon and His Grand Army towered above Europe, having annihilated the armies of Russia, Austria and Prussia; forced Francis II to abandon the imperial title which the Hapsburgs had proudly carried since the fifteenth century; occupied Portugal; bullied the Pope; and brought all of Europe east of the Iberian Peninsula into submission. William Pitt, Prime Minister of England, had said after Austerlitz: "Roll up the map of Europe. We won't need it for the next ten years."

Spain, the western neighbor of Napoleon's empire, was at its weakest since Isabel had created the nation. To the rest of Europe, Spain was a joke: ignorant, dirty, old-fashioned, poor. Napoleon had coerced King Charles IV into signing a treaty of friendship with France, then tricked and threatened Charles and his son Ferdinand into abdicating in favor of Napoleon's brother Joseph in the spring of 1808. Arrogant French troops marched into the country, showing utter contempt for Spain, its customs and its religion. The rest of Europe bowed to Napoleon. The Spaniards rebelled. In Madrid on May 2, the people poured into the streets in opposition to the hated tyrant. French soldiers brutally and bloodily crushed the uprising, killing hundreds of people in cold blood. The Spaniards adopted a new motto: "If there be a Spaniard who weakens in the great struggle, let him remember at once May 2." The "great struggle" is known to history as the *Peninsular War*.

Aragon lies north and east of Madrid. Once an independent kingdom, it had united with Castile through the marriage of Isabel and Ferdinand, thus forming the foundation of modern Spain. The soil is red and rocky, and it is said that if you give a nail to an Aragonese, he will use his head instead of a hammer. The capital of Aragon is Zaragoza, a city of many churches, a miraculous statue—Our Lady of the Pillar—and dark, irregular, narrow streets. Of all the Spanish cities, Zaragoza was regarded as the worst.

But in Zaragoza still lived the spirit of Pelayo and the men who had sworn not to surrender to the Moslem conquerors but to restore Spain to Christianity. The Zaragozans would not submit to the French tyrant, who represented hatred of the Church and the evils of the French Revolution. When they received orders from Madrid to acknowledge Joseph Bonaparte as king of Spain, the people revolted, overthrew the city government and set up their own *junta* or governing body. They chose Jose Palafox as their leader. His first act was to visit the chapel of the Pillar Virgin to ask her intercession. His second was to organize the city as a military state, so that every able-bodied man became a soldier.

The French laughed at Palafox and his peasant army. On June 13 they easily defeated the poorly trained Zaragozans and forced them to flee in confusion and fear. The French general sent a message: Surrender now and save yourselves. The response of the Zaragozans was to stay up all night reinforcing the walls. The French general vowed to reduce the city to rubble "in spite of the 30,000 idiots who wish to oppose my war-experienced troops."

On June 15 General Lefebvre sent three columns against the crumbling Zaragozan walls. The Spanish rallied to the attack points, shooting and praying. They drove off the first attack in hand-to-hand combat. The few soldiers that broke into the city were bombarded with rocks by the people in the houses. When the Spaniards began to run out of shot, they filled their cannons with glass, nails and pieces of scrap metal. The French lost 700 men to the Spaniards' 300. That night, while they huddled around their campfires nursing their wounds, the French could hear the Spanish singing victory songs.

On June 30 the French began a cannon bombardment against the aged walls. On July 2 they attempted a pre-dawn surprise attack, but the Spaniards heard them coming and opened fire. At a key point of attack stood a 24-pound cannon. As the French surged forward, the gunner fell dead and the gun was there for the taking, giving the French an open corridor into the city. But out of nowhere came 24-year-old Augustina Zaragoza, her black eyes flashing. She seized the burning linstock and lit the fuse. The gun fired, decimating the French column. The attack was repulsed. Not one French soldier entered the city.

The French settled down to siege warfare, hoping to starve or bombard the Zaragozans into surrender. The Spaniards ran low on food and powder; huge holes were knocked in the walls. Then at 1:00 P.M. on August 4, the French cried, "Long live the Emperor!" and rushed into the city. They established a post just inside the walls, and their general sent a message to Spanish headquarters: "Peace and capitulation." Back came the Spanish reply: *"War, even to the knife!"*

The French tried to break through to the Corso, Zaragoza's main street. But the Spaniards forced them to fight for every street, every building. It took the French six days and nights to capture one house. Finally the French general decided that his losses were too heavy. By the morning of August 13, the city was free of French troops.

Joseph wrote to his brother, telling him that Spain couldn't be subdued without a hundred thousand gallows and hundreds of thousands of troops. Napoleon refused to listen. He marched into Spain with several corps of his Grand Army, the best soldiers in the world. He won battle after battle. By the end of November, Zaragoza was the only important city between Madrid and the Pyrenees not in French hands. By Christmas, a French force was camped outside Zaragoza with one of the most formidable trains of artillery and siege equipment ever assembled. They asked Palafox to surrender. He replied: "I do not know how to surrender."

At 6:30 A.M. on January 10, eight batteries opened fire. The walls began to crumble. The bombardment continued. Inside the city, the people were low on food and an epidemic of typhus added to the death toll. On January 27 the French attacked, breaking through the walls. But every church and monastery was a fortress, every house a small fort, every room a battleground. Every man, woman and child had a weapon, if only a knife or a pile of stones. The Spaniards fought and died before yielding a single yard.

No place was free from fighting. The French broke into a church to find the body of a young monk shot dead amid a pile of dying men while giving them the last rites; he was still holding the ciborium and consecrated Hosts. The French finally captured one house after four days of fighting only to be driven out when Spaniards climbed to the roof and dropped grenades down the chimney. General Lannes ordered that a tunnel be dug under every block of houses in turn and explosives set off, even if it meant that the city be turned to rubble with the whole population buried beneath it. The Spanish dug their own tunnels and fierce underground fighting raged. On February 10, 3,000 pounds of gunpowder exploded under the San Francisco monastery, but not until February 12 were the last defenders driven to the monastery tower, their only weapons being tiles from the floor which they hurled at the attackers. The French fought their way up the winding steps, stormed the tower at bayonet point and sent the Spaniards crashing to the ground below.

On February 19, with the streets filled with bodies because not enough people were left alive to bury the dead, the Junta was forced to surrender. On February 21, at midday, the surviving defenders marched out the Portillo Gate. One French observer wrote: "Most of them had such an unmilitary appearance that our men were saying quite loudly that we should never have had such trouble in overcoming such a rabble." They were sick, thin and filthy. But they marched proudly. When the French entered the city, they felt that they had conquered a vast graveyard.

The Zaragozans lost the battle, but the French were utterly devastated. The fact that untrained men, women and children had withstood the best troops in the world was a terrible blow to French morale. And it was a great boost to Spanish morale. The Spaniards kept up the rebellion with guerrilla warfare, named from the Spanish word for war, *guerra.* The guerrillas attacked French foraging parties and convoys; made secret, lightning fast raids against French troops; practiced a scorched earth policy—destroying the crops the French army lived on. For nearly four years, Napoleon lost 100 men, on the average, *every day* in Spain. The Spanish fought war to the death—the gradual death of the French army.

For God, Emperor and Homeland

The peasant rebellion against Napoleon in Spain was the most famous but not the only time that the common people rose up against the revolutionary tyrant. The strongly Catholic Tyrol region of Austria also rejected Napoleon, under the leadership of the peasant innkeeper, Andreas Hofer.

Hofer was born November 22, 1767. His father was an innkeeper; Andreas had limited education. After marrying Anna Ladwiner, he took over his father's business. Though he was not especially successful, his life was satisfying. He had many friends and was devoted to the Hapsburgs. He had gained some military experience by fighting in the militia from 1796-1805 as the revolutionary tide had rolled over Europe.

After Austerlitz, Austria was forced to cede the Tyrol to Bavaria, which had been allied with France. Hofer's loyalty to the Hapsburgs would not permit him to accept this change of rule. He joined with others to plan an uprising. He became commander of a detachment which defeated the Bavarians on April 11, 1806. When the French occupied Innsbruck, capital of the Tyrol, Hofer issued a general summons to the people. The French underestimated his strength and left only a small garrison, but many patriots rallied to Hofer's standard.

After a few skirmishes, Hofer and his peasant army, many armed only with pitchforks, broke into Innsbruck on May 30, 1809. The main battle was fought and won on the Berg Isel, the mountain which overlooks the city. For two months the Tyrolese were free from the French. Elsewhere, however, the Austrians were defeated and the Emperor announced that he was returning the Tyrol to the Bavarians. A French force marched in under General Lefebvre, only recently returned from Zaragoza where he had learned all too well what a peasant army could do. Hofer again rallied his people and on August 13-14 the second Battle of Berg Isel was fought. Hofer stood in the heat of battle and induced the weakening ranks to renew their efforts. Hofer won the day and took over the government of the Tyrol, preserving his simple peasant habits and piety. But the Austrians had been exhausted at the Battle of Wagram and signed the Treaty of Schonbrunn on October 14, which, among other things, gave the Tyrol back to Bavaria.

The Tyrolese, left to themselves, continued the war against the Bavarians and French with heroic courage. In the museum on the Berg Isel today hangs a painting entitled (in translation) "The Last Maximum Effort," showing determined farmers marching down a mountain road armed with their pitchforks and primitive weapons. On November 1 the third Battle of Berg Isel was fought against a much superior force, the Tyrolese losing. Hofer escaped and hid in the mountains, but a traitor gave him away. The heroic commander was dragged to Mantua amid insults and outrages. He was haled before a court, but without awaiting its sentence, Napoleon ordered him shot. He was taken out and placed before a French firing squad. Their guns blazed, but somehow Hofer was not killed. With a twinkle in his eye, he said, "You are very bad shots." They then fired again and Hofer was dead (February 20, 1810).

Shortly before his execution, Hofer said, "The Tyrol will be Austrian again." His prophecy came true three years later. On the Berg Isel now stands a larger than lifesize statue. The inscription reads: "Fur Gott, Kaiser, und Vaterland": "For God, Emperor, and Homeland." In the military museum in Vienna are statues of princes, archdukes and Emperors who led Austria in battle. In the midst of the royalty stands Andreas Hofer, innkeeper, patriot and hero.

Trying to ignore the bad reports coming in from Spain and the Tyrol, Napoleon at long last took the step Josephine had been dreading. Declaring that he had not really consented to the religious marriage with Josephine, Napoleon demanded of the hierarchy of France that they grant him an annulment. A commission of Paris bishops granted his demand. He then married the young Archduchess Marie-Louise, daughter of the Austrian Emperor, in April 1810, hoping at last to attain a direct heir. Fifteen cardinals refused to come to the wedding. They were deprived of their property, exiled and stripped of all ecclesiastical dignities. On March 20, 1811, Marie-Louise presented Napoleon with a son, Napoleon Jr., promptly crowned King of Rome. Napoleon announced: "Now begins the most glorious epoch of my reign."

Wellington in Iberia

Meanwhile back in the Iberian Peninsula, Sir Arthur Wellesley was granted command of the British army there. Before he left England, he said: "The French may overwhelm me, but I don't think they will outmaneuver me because I am not afraid of them as everyone else seems to be."

The French under General Soult occupied Oporto on the Portuguese coast, expecting the British attack to come from the sea. But Wellesley brought his men in from the other side, crossing the Dovro River in barges in broad daylight. Soult was so taken by surprise that he had to abandon his dinner. Wellesley entered the city and finished the meal. Soult and his army escaped into Spain, where they easily defeated the Spanish army.

Wellesley brought his army into Talavera in northwest Spain. He set up good defensive positions on the hills and waited for the French to attack. He knew he couldn't defeat the French in a head-on fight so he chose to use defensive strategy. The French launched four attacks on the British position on July 27 and 28 but the British held and the battle was won. After this battle Wellesley was raised to the peerage and became Viscount Wellington of Talavera, and it is as Wellington that he will henceforth be known.

The French, never stopped for long, regrouped and came after the British. Wellington's army, poorly provisioned, retreated to Portugal. Wellington didn't dare risk a large open-field battle, so he conceived the ingenious strategy which came to be known as the Lines of Torres Vedres. He secretly ordered the construction of impregnable defensive lines marking off a hilly quadrilateral surrounding Lisbon, with the coast as one leg of the quadrilateral. He fortified existing buildings and added others to make a total of about 150 hill forts commanding all the highways and passes to Lisbon. He dug ditches and scooped up earthen ramparts. He destroyed all crops and other supplies in the immediate vicinity of the lines and then withdrew his men inside. By October 10, 1810 his whole army was safely behind the lines, and the French had no idea what had happened. The first the French knew the lines even existed was when a captured cavalry patrol told the French that they were on their way back to "the lines."

The French camped outside the lines but were unable to break through them. Finally on March 5, 1811 the French, hungry and diseased, retreated, having lost 25,000 men in the five months they had watched the lines. Wellington's losses during the same time were only 4,000.

The Torres Vedres strategy had greatly weakened the French but Wellington still feared to make a direct attack. Finally Napoleon himself came indirectly to Wellington's aid by withdrawing a large number of troops from Spain in preparation for his attack on Russia.

Wellington marched toward Salamanca, arriving on June 17, 1812. The two armies marched and counter-marched, each waiting for the other to make the first mistake. Finally on July 22 the French were overextended and a gap opened up. Wellington smashed through the line, throwing the French into confusion. In 40 minutes Wellington defeated 40,000 men.

Wellington made a triumphal entry into Madrid on August 12. Brother Joseph fled. With the help of the guerrillas, Wellington harassed the French for the rest of the year. When good weather came again in 1813, Wellington was off in pursuit of Joseph. Joseph elected to fight near Vitoria. He also decided to make a grandstand so that his followers could watch him beat the English. The script didn't work out quite the way Joseph had planned, however. At the Battle of Vitoria, June 21, 1813, the French expected a frontal attack. Instead, Wellington sent a flanking attack on both left and right. Joseph ordered a retreat, and all was chaos. Joseph fled to France, and the French abandoned most of the country. Wellington himself crossed the French frontier in November. Spain belonged to the Spanish once again.

Napoleon vs. Russia

On June 23, 1812, 600,000 French and allied troops began crossing the Russian border. The largest army in the history of the world prepared to conquer the largest country in the world.

Napoleon's troops marched toward Moscow, but Napoleon didn't really expect they'd have to go that far. He assumed that his huge army could win a few decisive victories against the scattered Russian armies, and thereby bring Tsar Alexander to terms. But the Russian armies practiced a scorched earth policy so that the French couldn't get enough to eat and escaped Napoleon, finally uniting at Smolensk. Napoleon marched his men through the dust and heat of the Russian roads to Smolensk, but the Russian armies again slipped away and continued to retreat toward Moscow. Napoleon had already lost many men and was running ahead of his supplies. The next major city was 280 miles away: Moscow itself. Napoleon ordered his men onward.

Finally the Russian general, Mikhail Kutusov, who had devised the strategy of scorched earth and retreat, prepared for battle at Borodino. The battle came on September 7. Napoleon was not well. Instead of planning his usual brilliant strategy, he simply ordered a frontal assault, a direct attack on the Russian position. The battle went on all day. At one point the Russian center appeared to have broken, but Napoleon refused to order into battle the Imperial Guard (also known as the Old Guard), his best troops, because he wanted to keep one reserve force intact. At last his infantry captured a key Russian position, and Kutusov ordered a retreat. The French could be said to have won the battle, but their losses were extremely heavy. The Russians withdrew toward Moscow.

Napoleon said to his officers: "March on! We are going to break open the gates of Moscow!" But when they arrived, they found the city virtually deserted. Alexander I had decided to evacuate and burn the city to prevent the French from getting the supplies they desperately needed. Napoleon waited in the ruined city until October 19, then decided to march south to set up winter quarters in the fertile lands. But Kutusov was in the way. Napoleon was forced to turn his men back and march them west, along the same weary road they had followed to Moscow.

On November 5 they marched through the first snow of the season. Kutusov harassed them all along the way. At the Berezina River, Napoleon's troops had great difficulty getting across the cold, half-frozen river and suffered huge losses when the Russians attacked. The men had no winter clothing because Napoleon had expected to defeat the Russians earlier. His men made shoes out of their hats and wrapped themselves in pieces of sacking. They trudged through the snow, many falling by the wayside. (As the men's weapons fell from their frozen fingers, did Napoleon perhaps remember his contemptuous remarks at the time the Pope excommunicated him?)

Finally on December 5 Napoleon abandoned his army, returning to Poland by fast sled. By the time Marshal Ney got the last of the troops into Poland on December 14, there were only 1000 effective troops and a few thousand stragglers left—out of the more than half million men of the Grand Army who had marched into Russia six months before.

The Grand Army had been destroyed. Though Napoleon tried to build it up again, he could not succeed. At the *Battle of Nations* at Leipzig in October 1813, Austrian, Russian and Prussian armies combined to defeat the untrained French troops. At the same time, Wellington marched into southern France, and on March 31, 1814 the Allies captured Paris. Napoleon abdicated on April 11. The Allies gave him the island of Elba near Corsica: the Emperor of Europe had been reduced to one small island. On May 24, 1814 Pope Pius VII returned to Rome.

The Hundred Days

The victorious Allies—Russia, Austria, England, Prussia—appointed a five-man provisional government to rule France until the rightful king, Louis XVIII, could be re-installed. The government was headed by the eternal survivor, Talleyrand, who had been one of Napoleon's ministers and simultaneously a spy in the pay of Tsar Alexander. The Allied leaders met at the *Congress of Vienna* in September 1814 to determine what should be done with the remains of Napoleon's empire. But before any treaties could be signed, they received startling news. On February 26, 1815, supported by 1,500 soldiers, seven small ships, and his sister's jewels, Napoleon had set sail for France.

His initial force was so small that he could easily have been stopped, but no French soldier would raise his gun against him. Marshal Ney had ridden out with an army, promising to "bring Napoleon back in an iron cage." But when Napoleon and the troops came face to face, they abandoned Ney and came over to Bonaparte with a shout: "Long live the Emperor!"

The only blow known to have been struck against him occurred as his army triumphantly entered Paris. An old woman in the crowd, determined to express her loyalty to Louis XVIII, shouted "Vive le roi"—"Long live the king." A man next to her roared back, "Vive l'Empereur!" The woman promptly hit the man on the head with her ladle. And that was the only violence to mar Napoleon's entry into the capital city. He was carried shoulder high into the Tuileries, and all the Bourbon white and gold flags came down to be replaced once again by the red, white and blue revolutionary tricolor. Thus did Napoleon begin the rule known as the *Hundred Days*.

The Congress of Vienna was now transformed from a peace conference to a council of war. Wellington arrived in Brussels on April 4 to assume overall command.

Napoleon did not have as many men at his disposal as he had hoped. Shortly after he had re-entered Paris, the Vendee rose up again "for Church and Crown." Napoleon had to dispatch some 10,000 troops to put down the rebellion. These were troops Napoleon would sorely miss come June 18.

Wellington and Blucher outnumbered Napoleon, but were separated. Napoleon hoped to drive a wedge between English and Prussian armies so they couldn't unite to crush him. At Ligny on June 16, the Prussians were badly mauled. Blucher was thrown from his horse in the middle of a troop of retreating cavalry. The 73-year-old general was trampled, his life being saved only by the devotion of an aide. Wellington was unable to send any help to Blucher, and finally decided to pull his men back to make his stand near the village of Waterloo. Blucher had to spend the whole day of the 17th recovering from his injuries, and it seemed as if the elderly field marshal had been removed from the picture. Napoleon ordered General Grouchy to hold off Blucher's men, who were fourteen miles away from the British, while the Emperor faced the British forces. Throughout the night of the 17th, rain poured down on Belgium, and the stage was set for the Battle of Waterloo.

Waterloo

On the morning of June 18, Napoleon had originally intended to attack at dawn, then postponed the attack until 9:00, then finally ordered the attack at 11:00. He said that his purpose in the delay was to let the ground dry, but his main reason was contempt for Wellington and disbelief in the Prussian powers of recuperation. He said: "This affair is nothing more than eating breakfast." And that was the first of Napoleon's mistakes on Waterloo day.

The actual battle is divided into five phases.

Phase I: 11:30 A.M. The Hougoumont Chateau. The chateau was to the left of Napoleon's headquarters and was occupied by a force of British soldiers. Napoleon ordered his brother Jerome to lead an attack against the chateau to open the battle, hoping to feint the British forces out of position toward the chateau. The fighting at the chateau was tough and heroic, but the British were not fooled and kept their main lines intact. Nevertheless Jerome kept attacking, and Napoleon didn't tell him to stop, thus tying up two divisions later when Napoleon needed them. And that was Napoleon's second mistake on Waterloo day.

Phase II: 1:30-3:00 P.M. The Infantry Defeated. Marshal Ney sent d'Erlon's infantry toward the right of Napoleon's headquarters, where Wellington had positioned Dutch and Belgian troops. Both sides fought valiantly, but the French broke through the line and then were up against a line of Scots infantry. The French were about to overrun that line too, so Wellington ordered in a crack cavalry troop called the Royal Scots Greys. The cavalry rode forward and after fearsome fighting (4,500 infantry troops and 2,500 cavalry troops were lost), the infantry was repulsed. Never before had cavalry routed so great a body of infantry in formation. Meanwhile, valiant Blucher had risen from his bed of pain to bring his Prussians to Waterloo. Grouchy, whose orders from Napoleon were vague, did not really understand that his function was to intercept the Prussians and at all costs prevent them from reaching Waterloo. The Prussians began advancing, but from Wellington's vantage point they seemed hardly to be moving.

Phase III: 3:45-5:30 P.M. The Cavalry Repulsed. Having failed on the left and on the right, Napoleon now ordered Ney and the cavalry to take the farmhouse in the center of the British lines, the charge to be preceded by a ferocious barrage from the artillery. As the barrage began, Wellington ordered his men back 100 yards to take a safer position. Ney misinterpreted the movement, thinking that Wellington had ordered a retreat. Believing that Wellington's men were in disarray, he sent in the light cavalry. Wellington formed his men into infantry squares to receive the attack. The British began mowing down the horses. Whenever a soldier fell, the square simply pulled together to re-form without backing up, presenting a still-unbroken front to the charging horses. Napoleon then ordered 5,000 heavy cavalry forward, the last of Ney's reserve. The horsemen attacked the squares seven, eight times—one square was attacked no fewer than 23 times. Ney himself had four horses killed from under him. At 5:30 Ney tried an attack with a mixed force of 6,000 cavalry and infantry but was once again turned back.

Phase IV: 6:00-6:30 P.M. The Farmhouse. Napoleon's infantry had been repulsed, his cavalry wasted; the British army was on his front, the Prussians approaching on his flank. The Emperor ordered Ney to take the farmhouse—no matter what. In the farmhouse were 376 soldiers, who had beaten off all earlier attacks. They were now down to four or five rounds each. Ney sent the infantry, the cavalry, the guns. Now the British in the farmhouse numbered only 41. They had no cartridges left, only bayonets. At last the farmhouse and its gallant defenders were captured, leaving the center of Wellington's line at Ney's mercy. He began to batter with his artillery; one gun was only 300 yards from the British line. Wellington had few men available for relief and no time to bring them up. He ordered his men to stand to the last man, saying, "Night or the Prussians must come."

The Dreadful Pause: 6:30-7:00 P.M. Ney asked Napoleon for reinforcements. Napoleon did not send any. Instead of attacking immediately, Napoleon did nothing for half an hour, giving Wellington time to pull his men together and close up the gaps in his lines. This was the third and most crucial mistake Napoleon made on Waterloo day.

Phase V: 7:00-9:00 P.M. The Crisis. At last Napoleon brought up his finest reserves, the Imperial Guard. He personally led them to Ney at the farmhouse, 15,000 strong. They had a formidable and frightening reputation, regarded throughout Europe as almost invincible. Meanwhile, Wellington had hidden a regiment behind a ridge. The Imperial Guard advanced. Directly in front of them were Wellington's second line troops, young and raw. They faced the unbeatable Imperial Guard of Napoleon's Grand Army. Somehow the young soldiers stood. Then the hidden forces attacked. The Guard was repulsed. But they were not wiped out. Suddenly Wellington could see through his telescope that the enemy's right flank was turned: the Prussians had arrived. Wellington waved his hat three times toward the French and ordered a massive charge. The Scots Highlanders rushed down and liberated the farmhouse. The Prussian and British troops met. The Imperial Guard made one last stand and then surrendered. The French were defeated, though in the confusion Napoleon made his escape. Every single one of Wellington's aides was dead or wounded. Wellington's own assessment of the British victory was the "nearest run thing you ever saw in your life."

Napoleon made it back to Paris but could find no support. He surrendered to a British warship to avoid capture by his enemies in France. Thanks to Wellington's strategy, the heroism of the individual units in the British lines, the indomitable Blucher, the Vendee rising, and the Emperor's own mistakes, Napoleon had met his greatest and final defeat.

The Counter-Revolution

For the second time Napoleon was sent from France, but this time he was imprisoned on the dismal island of St. Helena in the South Atlantic Ocean, guarded day and night by British warships to be sure that he would not escape again. Although it was once assumed that he died of cancer, evidence later came to light that he was slowly poisoned by arsenic in his wine and food. The most likely culprit was a man in the pay of French Bourbons.

The Congress of Vienna completed its work, signing the final documents about the same time as news of Waterloo reached the Austrian capital. The Congress restored Louis XVIII to the throne of France (with, of course, Talleyrand as one of his ministers), fixed the boundaries of the Netherlands and Switzerland, settled disputes in Italy, and formed the various German states into a loose federation under the control of Austria.

Though Napoleon was gone, his legacy remained. He had spread revolutionary ideas throughout Europe, and Europe would never be the same again. The political leaders in Europe could be divided into roughly three groups. There were the revolutionaries, who wanted to continue the French Revolution and its philosophy in less bloody forms. They had accepted the notions of moral relativism and the denial of hereditary or hierarchical authority. They would call for representative government and democratic elections, but would often end up imposing their will through violence. Once in power they would persecute the Church and those who opposed them.

A second group was the *liberal absolutists*. They were similar to the Enlightened Despots of the preceding century. They shared many liberal values, especially opposition to the Church, but wanted to rule absolutely, without parliaments or elections.

The third group was the *traditionalists* or counter-revolutionaries. The traditionalists were thoroughly Catholic and respected the traditions of the people. They were in favor of a strong monarch on the throne but also believed in local self-government and in protecting the rights of the people, as the kings had done in the High Middle Ages.

The leading figure at the Congress of Vienna was also the leading traditionalist political leader in Europe for the next 40 years. He was Prince Clemens Metternich, the prime minister of the Hapsburg Empire. Although the Holy Roman Empire no longer existed, and Christendom was divided, Metternich had some of the vision which had motivated Charles V and others: that nationalism must take second place to peace and order throughout Europe.

And if his political ideas went back to the Middle Ages, so did his philosophy. Metternich was infected by none of the revolutionary ideas which had done so much damage in France and throughout Europe. He believed that right and wrong should be determined by natural reason and Divine law, not by majority rule. He believed that the Church must be honored and the kings' authority respected. The French Revolutionaries earlier and others in Europe now were talking about freedom above all else. But Metternich knew that freedom was not itself a goal, but a result of a society built on order and authority. The French Revolution showed what happened when freedom was made into a god; the Middle Ages showed how free men could be when authority maintained order.

Metternich summed up his views; "Without order as a foundation, the cry for freedom is nothing more than the attempt of some group or other to achieve its own ends. When actually carried out in practice, that cry for freedom will inevitably express itself in tyranny."

In the years after the Congress of Vienna, Metternich devoted all his energies to maintaining peace and order throughout Europe and to seeing that the revolutionary ideas which had torn France apart did not infect other nations. He developed a new kind of diplomacy called *Congress Diplomacy*, whereby heads of government or their representatives would meet to discuss controversies, rather than trying to settle them on the battlefield. He worked to maintain a *balance of power*, which means that no one nation could become stronger than others and thereby be tempted to go to war against its neighbors. He was instrumental in the adoption of the *Carlsbad Decrees*, by which the Austrian government kept watch over what was taught in the universities and printed in newspapers and books so that it was more difficult for revolutionary ideas to spread.

Metternich was not perfect, but for over 30 years he kept peace in Europe. He once referred to himself as a "rock of order," and that he was. His order was based on a respect for lawful authority—family, Church, king—and on a view of men which saw them as children of God rather than tools in the hands of absolutists or revolutionaries.

The Carlists

In Spain, the revolutionaries and the absolutists banded together to defeat the cause of the traditionalists, in the struggles known as the *Carlist Wars*.

After Napoleon's downfall, Ferdinand VII, the Bourbon king, was restored to the throne of Spain. Unfortunately Ferdinand had not learned much from France's recent experiences, ruling as a liberal absolutist. When the Bourbons had come to Spain, they had caused to be lawfully passed a law forbidding women to rule (the *Salic Law*). But Ferdinand had only a daughter, Isabel. He could have asked the Cortes (Spain's traditional law-making body) to bestow the succession lawfully on Isabel. Instead, under the influence of his liberal wife Maria Cristina, he simply decreed that Isabel would be queen. Since she was still a child when Ferdinand died, Maria Cristina dominated the government, ignoring Spain's traditions and despising its moral and religious principles by her immoral life.

Throughout Spain there were uprisings in favor of Ferdinand's brother Carlos, the rightful heir under Spanish law. Carlos, a traditionalist, had refused to rebel while his brother was still alive, but when Isabel was unlawfully placed on the throne, he crossed the frontier in disguise to assume command as King Carlos V. His supporters were the Carlists; the liberal opposition was known as the Cristinos. Unfortunately Carlos was not a very good leader, and the uprising appeared to be going nowhere. Then out of the mountains came Tomas Zumalacarregui, a great general who had gained military experience fighting at the Siege of Zaragoza, taking command of the Carlists. Maria Cristina sent out her general with 10,000 men, assuming that it would be easy to crush the upstart Carlists. But Zumalacarregui's ragged and ill-equipped men won battle after battle, usually against heavy odds.

France, England and Portugal supported the Cristinos. Maria Cristina's government raised money by seizing Church property and auctioning it off, thereby creating a wealthy class in Spain which oppressed the poor. Zumalacarregui began marching his army toward Madrid. Carlos ordered him to stop and besiege the city of Bilbao because they needed money. Zumalacarregui knew this was unwise but the king insisted. The Carlists lost the battle, but what was worse, their general was killed. Without his leadership the Carlists could not hold out against the superior government force. Carlos finally signed a treaty and withdrew into France. Thus ended the First Carlist War (1834-1839).

In 1840 discontent with Cristina's high-handed ways, even among her liberal friends, forced her to flee the country. Two liberal generals, Espartero and Narvaez, ruled practically as dictators for Isabel, who showed little interest in ruling and mainly imitated her mother's immorality. The traditionalists rose again in 1848 in the name of Carlos VI, son of Carlos V. But the younger Carlos had no leadership abilities and the Second Carlist War failed to accomplish anything.

In 1868 Isabel's scandalous misconduct became too much for her government to stand and she was declared deposed. The Cortes wanted to continue a monarchy and went searching for a king, finally offering the crown to the Duke of Aosta (Italy), who became King Amadeo I in 1871. Amadeo received no respect from the Spanish people, who contemptuously referred to the Italian upstart as "King Macaroni." He discovered that being a king was not what he really wanted after all and abdicated in 1873.

A small group of liberals then set up the First Spanish Republic, and Spain was in chaos. Thus the Third Carlist War broke out, led by Carlos VII, a grandson of the first Carlos. Carlos VII ruled the north of Spain, protecting traditional rights of local self-government and defending the Church. He won a stirring victory at Montejurra, but the Carlists still lacked money, supplies and a good general. When the Republic collapsed, Isabel's son Alfonso took the throne, gaining the support of the people by offering concessions to the Church. The Carlist movement collapsed, and Carlos VII left Spain in 1876, leaving the liberals in control.

Thus was Spain committed to liberalism, which led to many sufferings in the twentieth century. These sufferings could have been avoided if the rightful kings, the Carlists, had succeeded.

Review Questions

1. What happened at the Battle of Marengo? What were its results?
2. What role did Fouche and Talleyrand play in Napoleon's government?
3. Summarize the terms of the Concordat. Of the Organic Articles.
4. What were the terms of the Treaty of Amiens?
5. What happened to Napoleon's goal of establishing an empire in America?
6. How did Napoleon become Emperor? Describe his coronation.
7. Why did Napoleon's plans to invade England fail?
8. What happened at the Battle of Trafalgar? What was its significance?
9. What happened at the Battle of Austerlitz? What was its significance?
10. What happened at the Battles of Jena and Auerstadt? What was their significance?
11. Summarize the conflict between Napoleon and Pius VII.
12. Summarize the events of the Siege of Zaragoza. What was its significance? How did the Spanish people carry on the struggle against Napoleon?
13. What happened in the Tyrol? What does this show about the attitude of the ordinary people toward the Revolution?
14. List and briefly explain the victories of Wellington in the Peninsular War.
15. Summarize the events of Napoleon's Russian campaign. What was the result?
16. What happened at the Battle of Nations? What was done to Napoleon afterward?
17. What were the Hundred Days?
18. Summarize the events of the Battle of Waterloo.
19. List the reasons why Napoleon lost at Waterloo.
20. What was done to Napoleon after Waterloo? How did he probably die?
21. What was the Congress of Vienna? What did it do?
22. What were the three groups in European politics after Napoleon and

what did each believe?
23. Who was Metternich? What was his philosophy? What did he achieve?
24. What was the cause of the Carlist Wars?
25. Why did the traditionalists lose the Carlist Wars? What was the main result of this defeat?

Projects

1. Imagine that you are a member of Napoleon's Imperial Guard. Write a diary of your experiences from the Treaty of Amiens to the exile on St. Helena.
2. Prepare a diagram and an account of one of the battles in this chapter.
3. Draw a map of Europe. Show Napoleon's empire and the key events of this chapter.
4. Write or enact a conversation that Napoleon might have had with a visitor to St. Helena's.

Chapter Twenty Six
The Nineteenth Century

THE NINETEENTH CENTURY saw the revolutionary ideas which Napoleon had spread throughout Europe begin to bear fruit in one country after another. Only the Hapsburgs in Austria consistently held the line for traditionalism, but even there liberals could not be entirely suppressed. In addition, the Industrial Revolution brought in its wake the rise of Communism, a revolutionary ideology which would spread suffering and destruction throughout the world.

The Industrial Revolution

If we compare the eighteenth century to our own, probably the first difference we would notice is that of science, technology, industry and inventions. Before 1750, products were made in homes or small shops. Now, most products are manufactured in factories. Before 1750, transportation was no faster than a horse could run or a ship could pick up wind in its sails. Now we have cars, trains, steamships, airplanes, rockets. Communication was slow then; letters were carried on horseback from one place to another. Now we can communicate in seconds with any part of the world. Because products were made by hand in the past, the quantities that could be produced were small. Now products are made in the millions and are available to everyone. Most men lived on farms or in small towns. Now men live in large cities. Most men used to own their own land or property so that they could be economically independent. Now many people depend on a job in a business or factory. All of these changes from a simple, slow-moving way of life to a materialistic, complicated one are called the *Industrial Revolution.*

The beginning of the Industrial Revolution is usually dated at 1769, when James Watt, an Englishman, invented the modern steam engine, making possible much more rapid transportation and the manufacturing of large quantities of goods in a short amount of time. England took the lead in the Industrial Revolution, not only because the steam engine had been invented there but because the concentration of wealth in the hands of a few men as a result of the Protestant Revolt meant that they had the excess wealth or *capital* needed to build a factory and buy the machines to use in it.

The Industrial Revolution brought about great changes in the way people lived. Lured by the promise of a steady wage, as opposed to the uncertainties of farming, many people left their farms and moved near the factories. These settlements grew into towns, then cities, becoming more crowded all the time. Expenses were higher in the cities, since men could no longer grow or make most of what they needed. Thus the wages paid the head of the family were not always enough to support it, so women and children would have to go to work too. Since the whole family was dependent on factory income, the factory owner could often take advantage of them, paying low wages and requiring long hours in poor conditions, because the family would starve if they quit.

Thus *capitalism* came to dominate English society. Capitalism is an economic system whereby wealth and power and the means of production are concentrated in the hands of a few. Capitalism stands in contrast to the system of the Middle Ages, *distributism*, where wealth was more evenly divided because the individual would own his own tools, equipment and land and could therefore be independent and self-supporting.

These changes in the way people lived also had an effect on political ideas. Capitalists became dominant in the government and their main concern was more wealth. A new theory was developed called *laissez faire* (a French phrase meaning "leave alone"). Laissez faire means that the government was not to interfere in anything the capitalists did, even if they mistreated their employees. Laissez faire became widely accepted in England and America, probably because of the influence of the old Calvinist idea that the Elect were those who were materially successful.

Eventually conditions became so bad that Parliament was forced to pass the *Factory Act* in 1833. This act forbade the employment of children under nine. Children from 9-13 could not work more than 48 hours a week, and teenagers could not work more than 69 hours a week. The fact that it had to be enacted at all shows how bad conditions must have been and how much more still needed to be done.

The poor in England benefited somewhat by the Industrial Revolution. More goods were available and they had a little more money. But industrialization also brought evils in its wake. If a person was sick or injured or old and couldn't work, that was generally thought to be his bad luck and not the concern of the government or his employers; his equally poor neighbors in the factory towns couldn't help either. The Church, which had formerly provided charitable assistance, no longer had any power in England, being allowed barely to exist.

The Rise of Communism

Laissez faire capitalism also helped to lead to an even greater evil. Low wages and bad working conditions caused much discontent among workingmen. Liberals decided to take advantage of this discontent, motivated in part by a desire to help the poor but also by a desire to get more power and overturn authority. The economic theory of *socialism* appeared in France and England in the 1820's, demanding that government control the means of production, owning and operating factories and businesses. There were three types of socialism. The *utopian socialists* believed that society would be perfect if all men shared everything and no one owned property of his own. Some of the utopian socialists set up communal farms where people tried to live in accordance with these ideas. Most of them soon collapsed. *Fabian socialists* believed in bringing socialism into power through democratic and peaceful means, by electing socialists to office. The Fabians were strong in England.

But the *revolutionary socialists* were not content with peaceful communes and elections. They believed that property should be redistributed by force. These revolutionary socialists were the *Communists*.

The center of Communist activity was in Paris because of the strong influence of the French Revolution, and the Communists were sometimes nicknamed "Reds" because they adopted the color of the French Revolution. In 1843 Karl Marx, a German liberal with a wild shock of black hair and a bushy beard, came to Paris and soon adopted Communism wholeheartedly. He formed a working partnership with Friedrich Engels, the two of them believing that Communism should be explained scientifically and that workers themselves (the *proletariat*) should unite to overthrow the social order and set up a Communist society. Marxist Communism had three elements: socialism, atheism, and the *dialectic*. The dialectic was a philosophy taught by a German named Hegel, which declared that truth and moral absolutes do not exist but that all reality can be explained by violent struggle. Marx used the dialectic to justify the use of violence to overthrow capitalism and establish Communism.

In 1847 Marx and Engels were instrumental in the formation of the International Communist Federation, the first organized Communist group. Then in 1848 they published one of the most revolutionary, destructive documents in history: the *Communist Manifesto.* In the Manifesto Marx and Engels claimed that "the history of all human societies up to the present time has been the history of the class struggle." In other words, they said that society was divided between those who had wealth and those who didn't, and that all history was the story of the struggle between these two groups. The time had come, Marx and Engels wrote, for the proletariat to overthrow those in power and seize all power for themselves. Law, morality and religion were to be totally rejected, since they had been invented by those in power to oppress the weak. The Manifesto ended with these words: "The Communists openly proclaim that the only way they can achieve their aims is by the violent destruction of the old order of society. The ruling classes may well tremble at the thought of a Communist revolution! The proletarians have nothing to lose in the struggle apart from their chains. They have a whole world to conquer—workers of the world unite!"

The evil ideas of French Revolutionary liberalism lived again in the Communist Manifesto, but now they were being spread throughout the world. Because of the abuses of capitalism, Communism was accepted by significant numbers of dedicated, active men and women. These people would be tools in the hands of those who wanted to overthrow all authority in society and concentrate all power in their own hands. Christianity now faced a new and deadly enemy and would need all its resources to combat it.

Revolution in France

Despite the efforts of Metternich and other traditionalists, the revolutionary ideas spawned in Paris and spread by Napoleon took root throughout Europe. The first post-Napoleon revolution broke out, not surprisingly, in France itself.

After Waterloo, Louis XVIII, Louis XVI's brother, returned to the throne. Louis had fled from France during the Revolution and had not done as much to aid his brother as he perhaps could have, but when he came to the throne he ruled reasonably well. He was followed by his younger brother, Charles X, who began to rule in 1824. Charles was an absolutist, announcing, "I would rather saw wood than rule like an English king." Revolutionary liberals began stirring up hostility to Charles and his absolutism.

On July 18, 1830, a young Sister of Charity in Paris had the first in an extraordinary series of apparitions. Catherine Labouré was favored from heaven with the message of the Miraculous Medal in a series of visions of the Blessed Mother in her convent chapel. But Our Lady's message was not spiritual alone. She also predicted the coming upheavals in France, although Mary promised that the Sisters of Charity and their brother order the Vincentians would not be attacked.

On July 17 the Revolution of 1830 broke out. Churches were desecrated, priests and religious imprisoned, beaten and killed. Sister Rosalie of the Sisters of Charity had cared for a derelict who told her, "We sack the Archbishop's palace tomorrow." The sister warned the Archbishop and he went into hiding, protected by the Sisters of Charity. As Mary had promised, the Vincentians and the Sisters of Charity were spared.

But the violence continued in the streets of Paris. The revolution gained a great impetus when the Marquis de Lafayette announced his support of the radicals. The liberal absolutists in France had enough sense not to want a return to the days of the Terror. To forestall a liberal republic's coming to power, they turned to Louis Philippe, Duke of Orleans, and a great-great-great grandson of Louis XIII. Louis Philippe was liberal (his father had voted for Louis XVI's execution, although he too had later been guillotined), but also ambitious. Lafayette agreed to accept Louis Philippe as a replacement for Charles X, and he came to the throne. Not wanting to appear too royalist yet still wanting to have some royalist prerogatives, Louis Philippe chose to be known as "Citizen King," a combination of his royal title with the egalitarian designation by which all men were required to be known during the days of the Terror.

One of Citizen King's chief foreign ministers was, needless to say, Talleyrand. Talleyrand served Louis Philippe for four years, then retired to write his memoirs, in which he declared he "never had betrayed a government which had not betrayed itself first." He died in 1838 at the age of 84. Just before he died, he signed a declaration in which he rejected "the great errors which ... had troubled and afflicted the Catholic, Apostolic and Roman Church, and in which he himself had had the misfortune to fall."

For a time all was peaceful, although Catherine Labouré's continuing visions hinted at a return to violence and at the death of the next archbishop. Then in 1848, the year of the Communist Manifesto, the French liberal revolutionaries became fed up with Louis Philippe's feeble attempts to assert royal authority and erupted in violence again. The Citizen King abdicated, and the revolutionary mob proclaimed a republic in February. Chaos and fear reigned again. In June Paris witnessed some of the bloodiest street-fighting Europe had ever seen. Archbishop Affre came to the barricades to plead for an end to the bloodshed. He was shot. Finally an election was held in December, won by Prince Louis Napoleon, Napoleon's nephew whom he had originally proclaimed as his heir. In the midst of chaos, the people turned to the descendant of the man who had restored order in the midst of chaos once before.

Louis Napoleon's office was president, but he gradually began increasing his powers and acting like a king. In December 1851 a liberal rebellion broke out, but Louis Napoleon quickly suppressed it. He then deemed the time was ripe to rally the people to his side for the same step as his uncle had earlier taken. On November 2, 1852 he declared the empire re-established, with himself as Emperor Napoleon III (Napoleon's son would have been Napoleon II). His government was liberal absolutist, but from time to time he took steps which aided the Church, for example, the re-opening of the grotto at Lourdes after local anti-Catholic authorities had closed it. Most of these pro-Catholic actions were taken as the result of the influence of his wife, the Spanish countess Eugenie Montijo.

Revolution in Austria

For centuries the many nationality groups in the Hapsburg Empire had been largely resistant to nationalism, as the Empire was built on loyalty to the Hapsburgs and the emperor, whoever he might be, not to a nation. But French Revolutionary liberalism with its accompanying nationalism was infecting many intellectuals and political leaders in the Empire, and this infection would produce a serious illness.

The Metternich years were years of vigor for the Austrian Empire. They saw swift economic expansion, prosperity and a flourishing culture. Metternich was emperor in everything but name after the feeble-minded Ferdinand came to the throne in 1835. But his censorship policies did not really succeed, and liberal ideas spread among the upper class intellectuals. Nationalism was also at work, especially among the Hungarians and the Italians under Austrian rule.

In 1848 revolutions broke out in four areas of the Austrian Empire: Vienna itself, Budapest, Prague, and Lombardy-Venetia in Italy. Kossuth, a wildly radical leader, and the other liberals in Budapest wanted virtual independence for Hungary. They demanded national liberation, but during the short time they were in control, they proceeded to oppress violently the other nationality groups within their lands, especially in Croatia and Transylvania. In Italy the revolutionaries threw the Austrians out of Milan. In Prague General Windischgratz's wife was killed in one of the wild demonstrations. In Austria, Metternich was forced to resign.

Behind the scenes was a remarkable woman, Sophie of Bavaria, wife of Franz Karl, who was Emperor Ferdinand's brother. Sophie had always resented the fact that her husband could not be on the throne simply because he was younger, while a feeble-minded emperor played at ruling. Since Ferdinand had no children, Sophie's oldest son Franz Josef was next in line for the throne. So she energetically prepared him for the day when he would rule, even calling upon Metternich—whom she couldn't stand—to act as his tutor in political matters. With the revolution, Sophie saw her chance to hasten the day when Franz Josef could rule. She persuaded Ferdinand that he should abdicate as soon as Franz Josef turned 18 and therefore became eligible to rule—but that would not be until December 1848. So in the meantime, Sophie held things together, persuading Ferdinand to make all sorts of liberal promises to quiet the liberals, while calling upon generals Windischgratz and Radetzky to restore order throughout the Empire. Windischgratz successfully subdued the rebels in Vienna and Prague, though he was less successful in Hungary.

On December 2 Franz Josef at last assumed the throne. He would rule for 68 years. An intelligent, hard-working man, Franz Josef was totally dedicated to his people, regarding his high office as a God-given trust. He knew that the forces of liberalism and nationalism would be deadly for his people and therefore he opposed these forces with all of his strength. He insisted on the ceremonials of his office and is therefore often accused of being distant and autocratic. But these ceremonials were to him the symbol of his God-given authority; he wanted the people to realize how important to them the office of emperor was. For 68 years he held the Empire together. He made mistakes, as any man would over such a long span of time. But he was not motivated by selfishness or a hunger for power or the desire to conquer other nations. He longed only to preserve his Hapsburg heritage as Maximilian and Charles V and Ferdinand II and Maria Teresa before him had preserved it. It was not his fault, though it was his undoing, that the nations around him, almost without exception, were power-hungry and contemptuous of moral principle.

Once established on the throne, Franz Josef had the remaining revolutions put down. He removed Windischgratz from command in Hungary and asked the Russians for help. They proceeded to send 200,000 troops, and Hungary was forced into submission. Radetzky played his part by subduing the Italians with a crushing victory at Novara (March 26, 1849). The 83-year-old general was greatly aided by the Tyrolese, true to the memory of Andreas Hofer and as always loyal to the Emperor.

To be in charge of domestic policy, Franz Josef chose Bach, who proceeded to put through important reforms with the Emperor's approval. Among the reforms, which made Austria probably the most just nation in Europe, were the following: the judiciary reformed and separated from the executive to provide checks and balances; trial by jury established; internal passports abolished; taxation made more fair; local government strengthened; the "robot" (a requirement that peasants had to do a certain amount of work for the landlords) abolished; education reformed. Furthermore, the highest careers in the Imperial service, whether civil or military, were open to men of every class. The only requirement was talent. This situation was far different from England, for example, where the wealthy land-owning classes controlled society. The Austrian Empire also had industrialization without the evils of laissez-faire capitalism. In addition, the Austrian government officials were by and large efficient, humane and incorruptible. Franz Josef would never allow the strong to oppress the weak. When he made mistakes, they were the mistakes made by a father who is looking out for the best interests of his children but doesn't always see all aspects of a problem.

The military did not fare as well as other aspects of society. The head of the Imperial Military Chancellery was Karl Grunne, who persuaded Franz Josef to be Supreme Commander in fact as well as in name. This was not a wise decision, since Franz Josef did not have the talents needed for this job, although he was vitally interested in the military (and, in fact, almost always dressed in a military uniform and for most of his life slept on a camp cot). The Austrian military was backward and inefficient. Radetzky had made reforms in training and organization, but Grunne undid them. The Austrian army looked fine on the parade ground in their dress uniforms, but as experience would show did not do so well on the battlefield.

Franz Josef against the World

At this time the Moslem Empire of Turkey was weakening rapidly, leaving a power vacuum in the Balkans (southeastern Europe). Tsar

Nicholas I of Russia wanted to gobble up Turkish territory, all the way to Constantinople, but England and France were unalterably opposed to this expansion. Thus the stage was set for conflict. Since Austria bordered on these lands, Franz Josef would almost inevitably be drawn into any conflict, though his goal was not territory but peace and order.

Nicholas declared war on Turkey on October 1, 1853, using as his excuse the freeing of Christians living under Turkish rule. England and France entered this *Crimean War* on Turkey's side in March 1854. Franz Josef was bombarded from all sides. Nicholas wanted him in the war on Russia's side or at least to declare a firm neutrality; France and England wanted Austria on their side. Franz Josef could do none of these things. Neither side in this war was morally justified; even an open declaration of neutrality would be too much to Nicholas' advantage. So Franz Josef called for a peace conference and issued stern warnings to Nicholas not to cross the Danube. He successfully demanded that Nicholas evacuate the Danubian Principalities, a diplomatic triumph, but was not firm enough with England and France so that they maintained illusions that he was coming into the war on their side. When he didn't, they accused him of weakness and changeableness.

Probably one of the reasons for Franz Josef's failure in this area—which was a diplomatic failure only, not a failure of policy or of moral principle—was a problem in his personal life which would continue to afflict him for many years. Franz Josef the ruler was also Franz Josef the husband, and it is important to understand his wife and his marriage.

In 1853 Franz Josef's mother Sophie had arranged a marriage between her son and the Bavarian princess Helena. But when Franz Josef went to Bavaria to meet Helena, he fell madly in love with her sixteen-year-old sister Elizabeth, known as Sisi. Though beautiful, Sisi was immature, but Franz Josef put his foot down to his mother and said he would have no one but Sisi for his wife. So in April 1854 the two were married. Almost immediately problems began. Sisi and Sophie couldn't stand each other. Sophie constantly criticized Sisi as lacking in the proper behavior of an empress and Sisi reacted by behaving even more irresponsibly. She refused to participate in the court ceremonies demanded of her and became increasingly more vain and obsessed with her beauty. The constant bickering between Sophie and Sisi couldn't help but affect Franz Josef, who would come home to it from his draining duties each day. When the children were born, Sophie tried to dominate them. Franz Josef intervened on Sisi's side, but the tension remained. Sisi made constant demands on Franz Josef and showed little concern for the burdens he carried.

Meanwhile revolutionary forces were stirring again in Italy. In 1852 Count Camillo Cavour had become prime minister of Piedmont-Sardinia; his goal was to drive Austria out of Lombardy and Venetia and then to unite all of Italy under the rule of Piedmont-Sardinia. Though Lombardy and Venetia had lower taxes and more just administration than the rest of Italy, though the peasants and artisans there were happy under Austrian rule because they were prosperous and well-treated, the middle and upper classes and intellectuals were infected by revolutionary ideas and hated Austria.

As a first step in achieving his goal, Cavour had entered the Crimean War on the side of England and France. Piedmont had no logical or moral reason for being involved in the war, and the Italian troops made no real contribution to the outcome, but Cavour gained what he wanted: support from England and France for his moves against Austria. Napoleon III of France was especially eager to get involved because Cavour promised him the territories of Nice and Savoy should Austria be defeated in Italy. In addition, when he wasn't listening to Eugenie, Napoleon III was a friend of revolutionary nationalism.

Cavour maneuvered Austria into war first by calling up his military reserves and volunteers, the volunteers being chiefly fugitives eluding conscription in Lombardy, thus a direct provocation to Austria. Franz Josef then issued an ultimatum to Piedmont, directing her to demobilize in three days. This was a blunder on Franz Josef's part because it supplied Cavour with the excuse he needed to make it appear to the rest of Europe that Austria was picking on Piedmont. Franz Josef had nothing to gain and everything to lose from a war with Piedmont, but he nevertheless ordered General Gyulai to invade the Italian kingdom.

Once in the war, Franz Josef should have insisted that it be fought vigorously and ended quickly, but that policy was not followed either. General Gyulai moved so slowly that the French had time to bring in their troops to reinforce the Piedmontese.

The key battle was at *Solferino*, June 24, 1859. Franz Josef and Napoleon III were each in personal command of their armies, but neither man was really in command of the situation. The armies were enormous: 138,000 French and Piedmontese, 129,000 Austrians, fighting on a fifteen-mile front. Neither side was winning, but the carnage was appalling: 40,000 killed and wounded by the end of the day. Both emperors were shocked and shaken by the bloodshed. Fighting for Austria, the Hungarian Benedek was the best general on the field; he could have held his position for re-grouping the following day. But Franz Josef's heart was broken by the suf-fering he had seen, and he ordered a retreat. France could have cut the re-treat to pieces, but the Frenchmen were too tired to move. Both Napoleon and Franz Josef were eager to strike a quick bargain and put the agonies of the battlefield out of their minds. Franz Josef gave up Lombardy only, not Venetia, which made Cavour furious, but there was nothing he could do. But in the long run Piedmont benefited more than France, as Italy was eventually united under Piedmont's leadership. Napoleon III, on the other hand, began to think he was invincible, but he would soon find out that he wasn't. And Austria had lost a major territory, with the woeful state of its military revealed for all the world to see.

Bismarck and Prussia

As a result of the defeat at Solferino, Franz Josef felt that he must make concessions to the liberals at home to avoid their rebelling at this time of national crisis. The Emperor set up a parliament with limited pow-ers, but with the right to interfere in the budget. About the only thing the parliament did was to cut down military expenditures, a serious mistake. Franz Josef also had renewed personal problems as Sisi suffered the first of a series of breakdowns and began the compulsive traveling which would characterize the rest of her life. Franz Josef wrote her constantly, his love for her never flagging despite its immense drain on his emotional re-sources.

Now a new enemy was emerging. In 1861 Otto von Bismarck became chancellor of Prussia. Bismarck was an expert diplomat but it seemed as if his only moral principle was that anything was justified so long as it ad-vanced the cause of Prussia. Immediately upon coming to power he began strengthening the army. He purchased the new breech-loading rifle which made possible more rapid fire. The Austrian army could not purchase the new rifle because of budget cuts by parliament. Bismarck ignored Prussia's parliament and set up what was in fact absolute rule. Franz Josef, on the contrary, tried to encourage local governments, but in Hungary at least, the liberal leaders—who pretended to be concerned for the rights of the peo-ple—frustrated his efforts.

Bismarck's long term goal was the unification of the German states under Prussia. To achieve this goal, he had to defeat Austria, since many of these states were in the Empire. He enlisted Piedmont on his side with the promise of Venetia and then proceeded to maneuver Franz Josef into war.

He began moving troops in the direction of the province of Schleswig-Holstein, which was in the Empire. Then Piedmont made threatening troop movements. Austria mobilized against Piedmont, but Bismarck accused Franz Josef of mobilizing against Prussia and mobilized against Austria. Austria declared war (June 1866), the *Seven Weeks War.*

The Prussians were better prepared and able to move instantly the war was declared. Within five days all three Prussian armies were in Bohemia, some 221,000 men. Austria's only chance was to defeat the three armies individually. But they moved too fast and came together. In addition, their breech loaders enabled them to shoot three to five times as fast as the Austrians.

General Benedek decided that if the Austrian army was going down it would go down fighting. He pulled his army together to fight the Battle of Koniggratz (July 3). First Benedek used his artillery, but the Prussians moved slowly forward. Then he sent in his infantry. The Austrians fought heroically, but the Prussians advanced. Next there was a battle in the woods. In one part, the 27th Prussian Regiment went into battle with 3,000 men and 90 officers. They came out of the woods, having cleared out the Austrians, with fewer than 400 men and only two officers. The Austrians finally held, but at 3:30, the Prussian crown prince arrived with his army and threw in the fresh troops. The Austrians fought bravely but couldn't hold. Many units fought to the last man. One Austrian corps lost 10,000 men in twenty minutes. The battle and the war were over.

Then Bismarck made a generous peace so that he could have Austria on his side in the war against France that he knew was coming. Piedmont received Venetia (though the Italians had lost both a land and a sea battle to the Austrians), and the German territories were transferred from Austrian sovereignty to Prussian.

Now liberal pressure from the Hungarians was becoming almost irresistible. Franz Josef felt that to save the Empire, having lost the Italian and German territories, he must make far-reaching concessions to the Hungarians. The solution was the *Dual Monarchy.* Both the Austrian and Hungarian halves of the Empire would be granted parliaments. Each half would be independent of the other except for the army, the Ministry of Foreign Affairs, and certain finances connected with these. Franz Josef would be Emperor of Austria and king of Hungary—two crowns, one head.

In the same year, tragedy struck the royal family. Franz Josef's only brother had gone to Mexico at the request of Mexican traditionalists and with the military backing of Napoleon III to become Emperor of Mexico.

But liberal revolutionaries, supported in part by the United States, tried to overthrow his regime. Napoleon III withdrew his troops, leaving Maximilian virtually defenseless. After a heroic defense of the city of Queretaro, Maximilian was defeated and shot by a firing squad. A liberal revolutionary government took over in Mexico and for many years would not even permit Franz Josef to bring Maximilian's body back to Austria.

The Franco-Prussian War

Bismarck's next move was to maneuver Napoleon III into war, so that he could persuade Bavaria to unite with Prussia out of fear of France and so that he could humble France's pretensions. Napoleon III was more than willing to fight, believing himself invincible. When it looked as if the Prussian king was going to back down from fighting France, Bismarck published a doctored version of King Wilhelm's private account to him of his meeting with the French ambassador at Ems to make it look as if the Prussian king had broken off diplomatic relations. This document (known as the Ems telegram) caused such a public outcry in France that war was declared July 19, 1870, the *Franco-Prussian War*. Prussia had even less difficulty with the French armies than with the Austrians, and on September 3, Napoleon surrendered in person at Sedan, discovering that he was not quite the military equal of his famous uncle. Bavaria had united with Prussia, France had to surrender Alsace and Lorraine (two provinces from the old middle kingdom of Charlemagne's empire), and King Wilhelm was proclaimed Kaiser (Emperor) Wilhelm I of Germany, the ceremony taking place at Versailles to further humiliate the French. The French were bitter toward the Germans and harbored thoughts of revenge.

In the new German Empire, Bismarck put into effect an anti-Catholic policy, called the *kulturkampf* (culture war). The May Laws of 1873 required all priests to study at state universities and pass government examinations. All appointments of priests and bishops were subject to state approval. In 1872 all nuns except a few who worked as nurses were exiled. By 1879 over 11,000 priests were in prison.

Napoleon III was overthrown and the radical Paris Commune took over Paris on March 18, 1871. On March 30, the royalists began an attack from Versailles to try to regain the city. The Commune's National Guard counterattacked on April 3. It was little more than a mob, but very enthusiastic, routing the royalists. Paris was now under siege again, and many people fled the city.

On April 28 a five-member, all-powerful Committee of Public Safety was formed, under the leadership of police chief Raoul Rigault, atheistic, amoral, vicious. The Commune confiscated Church property, turning churches into Red Clubs. On April 4 Rigault arrested the Archbishop of Paris and organized a mass roundup of priests. In May the Commune went back to the revolutionary calendar, announcing that it was the 15th Floreal, year 79. Arrests multiplied.

On May 21 government troops entered through a bombarded, unguarded gate. They encountered bloody fighting at the barricades set up all through Paris, but the Versailles army was irresistible. The Commune burned large parts of Paris, partly for strategic reasons, partly for revenge. On the night of May 24, Rigault had hostages shot, including the Archbishop and four other priests. After about a week of fighting, the Commune had to surrender, and the Versailles army took revenge in many killings. The week was known as *Semaine Sanglante*, Bloody Week. The total dead on both sides was between twenty and twenty-five thousand.

A provisional government was set up. Two-thirds of the representatives in the government were in favor of restoring the monarchy, but they were divided between the liberal Orleanists, who favored the line of Louis Philippe, and the Legitimists, who favored the Count de Chambord, who was the rightful king and the grandson of Charles X. The two factions worked out an agreement. The Count de Chambord would be offered the crown to rule for the rest of his life; when he died, since he had no children, the Orleanist line would come in. On October 27, 1871 the crown was offered to the Count, who would have been King Henry V of France.

The Count de Chambord was not a power-hungry man. If he were to become king, it would be to benefit the people by turning France from liberalism to traditionalism. As a guarantee that he would be allowed to turn the country around and as a symbol of dedication to the Catholic France of old, the Count announced that he would not agree to be king unless the tricolor flag were abandoned and the white and gold fleur-de-lis of traditional France restored. The issue therefore came before the Assembly: the tricolor flag and a liberal republic or the fleur-de-lis and a traditional monarchy. By one vote the liberals won, 353-352. The Third Republic was proclaimed, which proceeded to enact anti-Catholic laws, and France never again returned to monarchy.

Franz Josef Carries On

In 1877 Russia again attacked Turkey, this time defeating them. An independent Bulgaria was created, but it was under the influence of Russia.

Serbia, Rumania and Montenegro became independent. Because Franz Josef had remained neutral during the conflict, Austria was permitted to occupy Bosnia and Herzegovina, two small principalities bordering on Serbia. Austria governed these territories wisely and the people in them were well off under Austrian administration, but the stage was set for two problems: conflict with Serbia, which felt she should rule the territories, and conflict with Russia, which wanted to be the dominant power in the Balkans. In October 1879 Bismarck concluded an alliance with Austria. With the addition of Italy in 1882, the alliance was known as the Triple Alliance. Franz Josef intended the alliance to be primarily defensive to counter the growing Russian power in the Balkans. Italy was added so that if Russia should attack Germany or Austria, they wouldn't have to worry about Italy's coming in on Russia's side.

In March 1888 Kaiser Wilhelm died after a long reign. He was succeeded by his son Frederick who was already dying of cancer and ruled only 99 days. On June 15 his 29-year-old son became Kaiser Wilhelm II. Wilhelm was an egotistical man who wanted to be the sole power in the realm, so in 1890 he dismissed Bismarck. He maintained the alliance with Austria, but felt that Germany should be the dominant partner. Nevertheless, in spite of some rough moments, Franz Josef kept Austria at peace for 48 years (from Koniggratz to the outbreak of World War I), an amazing achievement.

The Emperor was not to know peace in his personal life, however. Elizabeth was off on her incessant travels and channeled all her emotional energy into an obsessive love for her youngest daughter Valerie. But an even greater problem was the Crown Prince, Archduke Rudolf, Franz Josef's only son. Rudolf was enamored of liberal ideas and opposed to his father's policies. He drank compulsively, took drugs, sank into apathy and dissolution, looked much older than his thirty years. He totally lacked his father's self-discipline and sense of duty and honor; he inherited his mother's emotional instability. Finally, in January 1889 he committed suicide at Mayerling, the royal hunting lodge. Franz Josef had no choice but to bury his grief and carry on.

Yet another tragedy awaited the Emperor. After Rudolf's death, Elizabeth dressed always in black and wandered incessantly. In September 1898 she was in Geneva, preparing to take a steamer across the beautiful lake. As she walked on deck, a 26-year-old anarchist named Luigi Lucheni rushed up and pushed against her. At first the Empress simply continued walking, then collapsed on the deck. Lucheni had stabbed her with a long, thin knife, so thin that at first she didn't realize she had been stabbed. Within hours she was dead. When word came to Franz Josef, he cried, "Nothing has been spared me in this world. Nobody knows how much we loved each other."

After the death of Rudolf, the heir to the throne was Franz Josef's brother Karl Ludwig. But he died of typhoid in 1896 after drinking contaminated water from the Jordan River while on a pilgrimage. The new heir was his son, Franz Ferdinand. In 1894 in Prague, Franz Ferdinand met Countess Sophie Chotek. The two fell in love but kept their affection secret. Finally in 1899 Franz Ferdinand requested permission from the Emperor to marry Sophie. But Sophie was not of a high enough status to be eligible to marry the heir to the Imperial throne. Franz Josef forbade the marriage. Franz Ferdinand insisted on it. The Emperor and his heir were both stubborn men and neither would relent. At last Franz Josef agreed to a compromise: what was known as a morganatic marriage. This meant that Sophie would always be considered of inferior status and their children could never inherit the Imperial throne. Franz Ferdinand and Sophie believed that their love could survive any such handicaps and agreed to the conditions. They were married on June 28, 1900. Since Franz Ferdinand's sons could not inherit the throne, the next in line would be his nephew and godson Charles.

Thus as the century came to an end, Austria was at peace (though the growing closeness of England, France and Russia should have sounded warning signals in Vienna) and domestically stable (though the Hungarians and other liberals were still restless). Franz Josef had weathered public and personal storms such as few men had been required to endure. Yet he had sixteen more years to reign and the worst storm of all on the horizon.

Italy and the Pope

In June 1846 Pope Pius IX ascended the papal throne. Many of the liberals in Italy thought that he would be on their side or at least not oppose them, and some of his early actions, such as granting amnesty to political prisoners, permitting freedom of the press, and introducing laymen into the government of the Papal States, convinced them that Pius was indeed a liberal Pope. But when the 1848 revolution against Austria broke out in Italy, Pius issued a statement condemning the revolutionaries and urging all Italians to remain loyal to their rulers. So now the liberals were ready to turn against the Pope.

They did so in November 1848. A revolutionary mob invaded Rome and surrounded the Quirinal Palace, residence of the Pope. A Committee of Public Safety began ruling Rome, as the Pope was a prisoner in his own palace. But the Bavarian ambassador worked out an escape plan. Dressed as a simple priest, Pius went out of the Quirinal through a secret passageway. He was met by a small carriage which took him out of Rome, where he transferred to a large coach and was taken to safety.

The radicals tried to have elections for an assembly but only a few people bothered to vote. Some of those who did vote cast their ballots for Pope Pius or St. Peter. When the assembly finally met, it voted an end to the temporal power of the Pope and the establishment of a pure democracy to be called the Republic of Rome.

The Republic of Rome was short-lived. In June 1849 Louis Napoleon, no doubt urged by his wife, sent French troops to Italy and chased the revolutionaries out of Rome so that the Pope was able to return.

As we know, however, Cavour emerged as a leader of Italian unification under liberal rule. He gained Lombardy in 1859 and Naples and Sicily in 1860. In 1861 the Kingdom of Italy was proclaimed with Victor Emmanuel of Piedmont as the first king. Venetia was added to the kingdom after the Seven Weeks War, but the Papal States remained independent.

And so did Pope Pius IX, who refused to make any concessions to the liberals and in fact made it clear that he intended to exercise the full authority of his office. On December 8, 1854 he solemnly proclaimed the doctrine of the Immaculate Conception, that Mary had been full of grace from the first moment of her existence. Then in 1864 Pius issued the *Syllabus of Errors*, formally condemning the errors of liberalism. Finally, in 1869 he called the First Vatican Council, which proclaimed *papal infallibility*: the doctrine that the Pope cannot make a mistake when officially teaching the Church on matters of faith and morals.

The revolutionaries couldn't touch the Pope's spiritual authority but they waited their chance to usurp his temporal authority. The chance came in 1870. Napoleon III withdrew his troops from Rome to fight in the Franco-Prussian War. On October 2 the liberal leader Garibaldi and his troops annexed Rome, making it the capital of the Kingdom of Italy. Pope Pius IX now had no territory of his own. For many years (until 1929) the Pope was known as the *Prisoner of the Vatican.*

Since the Pope had lost his political power, many people believed that the papacy would soon collapse. But of course it didn't. Pius remained strong until the end. He was succeeded in 1878 by an equally strong Pope, Leo XIII. Leo refused to make any compromise with revolutionaries and anti-Church governments. In fact his firmness resulted in Bismarck's gradually lessening his persecution of the Church in Germany.

But Leo did not simply condemn errors. He was a great teacher, pointing out the positive actions that would counteract error. He is best known for his teachings in economics. Leo wrote a series of *social encyclicals*, the most important being *Rerum Novarum* in 1891, pointing out the evils of both capitalism and Communism. Leo taught that employers had a moral obligation to respect their workers, to pay them a fair wage sufficient to support their families in reasonable comfort, and to give them reasonable working hours and sufficient time off. Leo endorsed labor unions—associations of working men who band together to improve their wages and working conditions. At that time, most people condemned unions because the rights of capitalists were thought to take precedence over the rights of workers. But Leo showed that everyone's rights must be respected. Leo also encouraged workers to help each other and to pool their resources so that they could own their own businesses. He encouraged bishops to go among the workers and the poor to help them solve their problems.

Leo XIII is recognized as one of the greatest men of the nineteenth century even by non-Catholics, because his teachings recognized the good things in the Industrial Revolution while showing how the evils could be eliminated.

Imperialism

The nationalism of the nineteenth century, combined with the desire for cheap raw materials to supply the Industrial Revolution, produced another important development: *imperialism*, or the drive by European nations for political and economic control over non-Western areas of the world, such as Asia, Africa and the Middle East.

Great Britain was the first imperialist power. By the late eighteenth century, it had taken over India, which it would control until 1947. England's control of India is probably an example of imperialism at its best. Before England arrived on the scene, India was riddled with lawlessness and immoral customs. Some examples were Thuggee, suttee and the caste system (see Chapter Two). The British officials in India tracked down and eliminated the Thugs, outlawed suttee, and abolished the caste system, thereby making Indian society more just.

England also supplied an example of imperialism at its worst, in China. In the early 1800's England gained a foothold in the country. Englishmen built up a very profitable opium trade throughout China, bribing the Chinese government so that it wouldn't interfere. When a group of Chinese Protestant Christians known as the Taipings rebelled against the government and especially denounced the opium trade, the British authorities called upon one of their best generals, Charles Gordon, to command the Chinese army. Gordon, supposedly representing a Christian country, smashed the Taiping Rebellion. The British opium trade was safe.

Imperialist nations were also very greedy for Africa, which began to be explored in the second half of the 1800's. By World War I all of Africa except Liberia and Ethiopia was controlled by Europeans. This control lasted until the 1950's, when African nations began to get their independence. These independence movements often led to bloodshed because the nations the Europeans had carved out of the continent had no relationship to the realities of the African tribes, and because liberalism and Communism became strong forces in Africa.

But the opening up of Africa also brought Christianity, which made its appearance as Christian missionaries, especially the White Fathers of France, followed close behind the explorers. Almost daily these priests risked their lives, braving the climate, the unfriendly natives, tropical diseases, deadly snakes and poisonous insects to bring Christ to men and women who had never known him.

Ireland's Agony

With the rest of Europe occupied by the French Revolution, the Irish thought that perhaps they could gain their freedom at last. Some of the worst of the Penal Laws had been relaxed—Catholics could now at least go to Mass—but they still had no political or economic rights. Wolfe Tone—a Protestant but a believer in Irish independence—founded the United Irish Movement and communicated with the French, hoping for aid in overthrowing the British. The Irish began holding secret meetings and training for war. They hid weapons—mainly pikes, though they had a few guns. A rising was set for May 23, 1798, at which time the French were supposed to arrive with aid.

The *Rising of '98*, as it is known, is a story of great heroism on the part of the poorly armed, poorly led Irish. Though the French aid did not arrive on time, and though the British found out about the plot and arrested many of the leaders, small groups of rebels did rise up. They won a few great victories. In County Wexford, Father John Murphy, a Catholic priest, organized a small army. Father Murphy had worked for a peaceful settlement, but when the homes of the people and their church were burned, he told them: "It is better to die bravely in the field than be butchered in your homes." Father Murphy's men defeated the English garrison in Wexford on May 26. Then he marched his men to Enniscorthy, a key city. His men charged the city gate again and again. The British troops couldn't believe that these poorly armed men could fight so bravely. The Irish broke through the gate and took the city.

The British were furious at the Irish for daring to rebel against them. They proceeded to crush the rising with cruel severity. Many of the leaders were tortured and publicly hanged. Houses were torn apart to find hidden weapons. By July 23 the last of the Irish armies had to surrender.

Then in August, the French arrived. Their leader, General Humbert, was representing only himself, not the French government, and he had only a small force. He won some victories in Connaught and forced 3500 British troops to flee in a battle known as the Races of Castlebar. But his men were eventually surrounded and forced to return to France.

The rising had been crushed, but the Irish desire for freedom could never be crushed. In 1829 every Catholic parish in the country petitioned for *emancipation* (granting the rights of citizenship to Irish) on the same day at the same hour. This so impressed the British Parliament that they did relax some of their oppressive laws by passing the Catholic Emancipation Act.

In the 1840's the potato crop in Ireland failed several years in a row. Because English landlords owned most of the land, most of Ireland's crops were shipped to England and the people had only potatoes to eat. So when the crop failed, the Irish had no food. The English government, of course, could have prohibited the landlords from shipping grain to England so that it could feed the people in Ireland. But because of laissez faire, the government did not interfere. As the Irish died of hunger, shiploads of food left Ireland and went to England. With hunger came epidemics, and more Irish died. Many Irish came to the United States, selling everything they had to get space on board a ship. The ships came to be known as coffin ships because conditions on them were so bad that almost as many people arrived in America dead as alive. it is estimated that by the time the famine ended, Ireland's population had been cut in half.

But the agitation for freedom went on. During Easter Week in 1916, a group of Irish patriots led by the great hero Padraic Pearse seized the post office in Dulin and proclaimed Ireland's independence. But the *Easter Rebellion* lasted only a week. Pearse had to order his men to lay down their arms in order to avoid terrible slaughter. All of the leaders were executed except one—Eamon DeValera, who, having been born in America, was an American citizen, so the British were afraid to kill him.

The British began a reign of terror. Anyone suspected of having rebel sympathies or found possessing a weapon could be shot on sight. Irish homes were raided at night to find rebels. The British developed a Special Branch of the police force, which the Irish nicknamed Black and Tans, for the color of their uniform. The Black and Tans were not really policemen but terrorists, who were extremely cruel to Irish men, women and children. But the Irish refusal to give up, along with criticisms of the British tactics from other nations, persuaded the British leaders to arrange a truce and hold a conference with Irish leaders. They gave the Irish a choice—independence for the southern 26 counties with six counties of Ulster remaining part of Great Britain (this was known as *partition*) or "immediate and terrible war" within three days. The Irish agonized over their decision. The idea of allowing even six counties of their country to remain part of Great Britain was almost more than they could bear. But so was the idea of a terrible war which would cause further suffering for innocent people. By a majority of one vote, the Irish leaders approved partition. Ireland—or the Irish Free State as it is known—received its independence, with the six counties becoming part of the United Kingdom of Great Britain and Northern Ireland.

But Ireland's suffering wasn't over yet. Those who thought partition was wrong went to war against the Free State. For two years civil war raged. Peace finally came to Ireland on April 30, 1923, with a victory for the Free State. Partition has been a fact of Irish life to this day.

Review Questions

1. What was the Industrial Revolution?
2. What social changes did the Industrial Revolution produce? What was capitalism? What was laissez faire?
3. How did capitalism lead to the rise of socialism? What were the three types of socialism?
4. Who were the founders of Communism? What are the principles of Communism?
5. Summarize the events and results of the Revolution of 1830 in France.
6. Summarize the last years of Talleyrand's life.
7. Summarize the events and results of the Revolution of 1848 in France.
8. How did Louis Napoleon become Napoleon III? What were the

characteristics of his rule?

9. Where did revolutions break out in the Austrian Empire in 1848? What were the results of these revolutions?
10. What was Franz Josef's philosophy of ruling?
11. What domestic reforms did Franz Josef put through?
12. What was the Crimean War? What did Franz Josef do during this war? What were its results for him?
13. What personal problems did Franz Josef face because of his wife and mother?
14. How did Piedmont gain control of Lombardy?
15. How did Bismarck gain control of Austria's German territories?
16. What was the Dual Monarchy?
17. Why did the Franco-Prussian War break out? How did it lead to the establishment of the German Empire? What was the kulturkampf?
18. Summarize the events in France after the overthrow of Napoleon III?
19. What led to conflicts between Austria and Serbia and Austria and Russia?
20. What additional personal problems did Franz Josef have to bear?
21. Who became Franz Josef's heir? Why could this heir's children not inherit the throne? Who was next in line?
22. Why did the liberals think Pius IX was a liberal? When did they find out he was not?
23. What happened during the Revolution of 1848 in Rome?
24. What three actions did Pius IX take to assert his spiritual authority?
25. What happened in Rome in 1870?
26. What were the main achievements of Leo XIII?
27. What was imperialism? Give examples of the good and the harm done by imperialism.
28. What happened in Ireland in the Rising of '98? In the Irish potato famine?
29. What happened during the Easter Rebellion and immediately afterwards?
30. How did the Free State gain independence? What were the results of the Irish Civil War?

Projects

1. Choose one of the inventions of the Industrial Revolution and report on it. Include a diagram or picture and explain what effect it had.
2. Write a story about the Irish potato famine.

3. Report on conditions in factories during the Industrial Revolution.
4. Report on imperialism in a non-Western country.

Chapter Twenty Seven
World War I and
the Russian Revolution

WHEN THE TWENTIETH CENTURY BEGAN, Europe hadn't had a major war since the Franco-Prussian War in 1870. But prospects for continuing peace didn't look especially bright. We will examine the situation in each European country in the years just prior to World War I to see how this bloody and fateful conflict came about.

Western Europe

England was still dominated by the wealthy land-owning class, which was prosperous and optimistic with a sense of indestructibility. On June 22, 1897 Queen Victoria celebrated the Diamond Jubilee (60th anniversary) of her coronation; she was a symbol of the British Empire, which stretched all around the world. But change was coming, though no one suspected it at the time.

On January 24, 1901, Victoria died, to be succeeded by her son, Edward VII. Then in 1906 the Liberal Party came into power, under David Lloyd George, a Welshman. At last there was a reaction against laissez faire as workmen's compensation, old-age pensions, and eight-hour days for miners were enacted into law. The House of Lords lost its veto power and a new tax bill was passed. In 1910 Edward died, to be succeeded by George V. Royalty from all over Europe attended the funeral. An onlooker could reasonably conclude that the system of monarchy throughout Europe was permanent and unchangeable. He could not imagine that within ten years three emperors would be overthrown forever.

The domination of England by the wealthy, self-satisfied classes, even when the Liberal Party was in power, would mean that strategies and tactics in the coming war would be totally lacking in imagination and innovation, with deadly consequences. It would also mean that the English government would have such confidence in its own righteousness that it would not be interested in any peace initiatives that involved less than total surrender by the enemy.

France was under the government of Emile Combs, who closed all Catholic schools, seized Church property, suppressed religious orders, and put harsh restrictions on the Church. Because of his policies a strong counter-revolutionary movement grew up and was gaining in strength. The traditionalists might have been able to take power, if it had not been for the *Dreyfus Case* of 1894. Because of the Franco-Prussian War, hatred for Germany was at a peak in France. Thus when it was discovered that someone in the army was sending confidential information to Germany, there was a concerted effort to find the culprit. The officer corps in the army tended to be traditionalist, and they accused a Jewish officer named Alfred Dreyfus of being the spy. He was tried, convicted and sent to Devil's Island prison camp. During the whole case, France was split between the liberals, who defended Dreyfus, and the traditionalists, who believed him guilty. Eventually it was discovered that not only was Dreyfus innocent but the army officers had falsified evidence to bring about his conviction. Dreyfus was exonerated and brought back to France, though he still suffered from the physical effects of his imprisonment. The most important long-term effect of the Dreyfus Case was that the traditionalist movement in France was badly damaged, so that the liberal, anti-Catholic government was more firmly entrenched in power.

Germany was still ruled by Kaiser Wilhelm II. When he came to the throne, his first proclamation read: "We belong to each other, I and the army; we were born for each other." *Militarism* dominated society. The German army and hence the government was dominated by the Prussian Protestant aristocracy and therefore would not listen to any moral teachings that came from the Church. Like the English, the Germans were self-confident and believed themselves the best at everything. Thus there was a military rivalry between the two countries. Whenever one country would add to its military power, especially its navy, the other would do the same, only more so. The Krupp Arms Works at Essen, Germany, was the largest single business in Europe. The increase of population made possible by the Industrial Revolution's raising of the standard of living, along with the legacy of Napoleon I's mass armies, meant that European nations would have large armies. Thus there was a demand for more weapons, and Krupp gladly met the demand. The machine gun had been invented as had the small bore rifle, which provided distance and accuracy. At Waterloo soldiers had been able to fire three rounds per minute. Now they could fire sixteen.

Germany also felt it had a philosophical justification for militarism. The Germans believed in Darwin's teaching of survival of the fittest. It was a national dogma in Germany that war was justified as a conflict in which the stronger or superior race survived. Though many people now believe that the "master race" idea came to Germany with Hitler, it was actually there much earlier. Nietzsche had taught that "God is dead," and therefore men need not worry about moral commands, and that the Germans were a super-race. As the influence of religion faded in Germany, the worship of the nation took its place.

Italy, now a united nation, was anti-Catholic and chaotic. The Italian government had pretensions of being a great power and still coveted Austrian territory, especially the South Tyrol.

Austria-Hungary was discussed in detail in the last chapter. Franz Josef was ruling well but the tragedies in his life were taking their emotional toll. Liberal nationalists were active within the Empire, and the Serbians as well as the Italians wanted Austrian land.

In the *Vatican* Pius X (1903-1914) succeeded Leo XIII. Since canonized a saint, he led a holy, simple life, but he vigorously fought the evils of the times. He issued a condemnation of *Modernism*, the heresy which brought liberal doctrines into the Church, primarily by denying absolute truth and the reliability of the Scriptures. His last letter before he died was an appeal for peace. He was succeeded by Benedict XV (1914-1922).

Throughout Europe the *anarchist movement* was growing. The anarchists opposed all existing governments but especially monarchies, hated property and the ruling classes, preached the necessity of violence, and recognized no moral absolutes. From 1894-1914 six heads of state were assassinated by the anarchists: a president of France, two prime ministers of Spain, Empress Elizabeth of Austria, the king of Italy, and President McKinley of the United States.

In summary, on the surface the wealthy classes could believe that all was well and that their position was indestructible. But underneath, dark currents flowed, and the upper classes lacked the moral strength to deal with them. The examples that follow will illustrate the fundamental instability in Europe in the first decade of the twentieth century: 1905, Greeks in Crete revolt against Turkey; 1907, revolt in Rumania, French fleet bombards Casablanca; 1908, King Carlos I of Portugal and Crown Prince murdered, revolt in Macedonia, riots in Bohemia; 1910, revolt in Portugal; 1911, Italy declares war on Turkey; 1912, Turkey declares war on Bulgaria and Serbia; 1913, King George I of Greece murdered, Russia declares war on Bulgaria, Serbs invade Albania. Immense suffering was in store for Europe, but no one would have believed it possible.

Russia

Russia remained the most absolutist country in Europe. The Tsar was seen as the unifier of all Russia, but Russia was so large that he had to set up a bureaucracy to rule throughout the country. These local bureaucrats could be good or bad and there was a wide variation among them. When they were bad, they received the hatred of the people, who retained their love and loyalty to the Tsar, whoever he might be, whom they called their "Little Father." In most Russian homes, no matter how poor, a picture of the Tsar would hang near the icon of the Blessed Mother or the glorified Christ. The people were still in serfdom, but the condition of the serfs varied. Household serfs could rise to positions of authority or be skilled craftsmen, and their lot was good. The agricultural serfs labored on their master's estate and then on their own land; their lot depended largely on their master. The serfs in the worst condition were the factory serfs, who belonged to the owner of the factory and received barely enough to survive.

Nicholas I, the Tsar of the Crimean War, died in 1855, his death probably hastened by Russia's humiliation in that war. He was succeeded by his oldest son, Alexander II (1855-1881), who presided over the end of the war in January 1856.

Alexander II had made himself personally familiar with the conditions of the serfs. In 1861 he issued the *Emancipation Act*. All serfs were given personal freedom and a grant of land which was taken from the landlords. The landowners were paid by the state, and the peasants in turn were to refund the treasury by installment payments spread over a period of 49 years. Forty eight million serfs received their freedom; with their families, they made up eighty per cent of the population of Russia. Though the basic idea of freedom for the serfs was good and long overdue, the actual fact of emancipation led to many problems. Too many peasants had too little land; the payments to the treasury were too large for them to meet so they went into debt; the landlords received inadequate compensation and lacked the capital to develop what remained of their estates; many peasants experienced a strong sense of disorientation because of this abrupt change in the only way of life they knew. Perhaps Alexander should have gone more slowly, encouraging voluntary freeing or allowing liberal terms for buying freedom. Be that as it may, his attempt to improve the life of his people led to instability in Russian society.

Alexander put through other reforms as well. He reduced punishments in the army, applied conscription to the poor and rich alike, reduced terms in the army to six years (from 25), established universities, and instituted jury trials. His reign also saw the founding of the city of Vladivostok on the Pacific Coast so that Russia became a rival to Japan as a Pacific power. He also encouraged *Panslavism*, the idea that Russia was the guardian of all Slavic peoples. This meant in effect that Russia would rival Austria for control of the Slavic peoples in the Austrian Empire and that Serbia would receive Russia's support against Austria.

In spite of the reforms that Alexander had put through, liberal revolutionaries hated him because they hated all authority. On March 1, 1881, they assassinated the Tsar while he was riding in his carriage. That very day, Alexander had signed a limited reform program permitting a representative assembly, first in Russia's history, to work on draft legislation for Alexander's consideration.

Alexander II's son, Alexander III (1881-1894) now came to the throne. His father had tried to make reforms and had been murdered. His son ended all reforms and strengthened the police. Alexander III was also nationalistic and prejudiced against Catholics and Jews. He encouraged industrialization; the Trans-Siberian Railroad was completed at this time. But industrialization did not much benefit the lower classes.

In 1887 an amateurish plot to assassinate Alexander III was easily uncovered, and all the conspirators were hanged. One of them had a brother named Vladimir Iliych Ulyanov, who later adopted the pseudonym of Nicolai Lenin. Lenin was from a comfortable, middle class family; his father was a bureaucrat. But after his brother's execution, Lenin was not allowed to continue at the university because of his relationship to a convicted revolutionary. So Lenin read Marx and became a committed Communist. In 1895 he stirred up strikes in St. Petersburg and was sentenced to three years exile in Siberia, during which time he and nine Marxists founded the Russian Social Democrat Labor Party. This was the beginning of the career of a man who would change the world.

Nicholas and Alexandra

Alexander III died in 1894 to be succeeded by his oldest son Nicholas II. Nicholas believed that absolutism was the will of God and sincerely tried to put himself in God's hands. But like Louis XVI, who was also a good man who tried to do God's will, he was weak in a crisis. Nicholas was married to Alexandra, a German princess. Alexandra dominated the marriage and constantly involved herself in government affairs though she had little talent in this area. She had converted to the Russian Orthodox Church when she married Nicholas, and was totally wrapped up in the mysticism which tended to overshadow the rational, logical elements of Christianity in the Russian Church.

Nicholas and Alexandra had four daughters. Then in July 1904 a son, Alexis, was born, the heir to the throne. The rejoicing at his birth soon ended when it was discovered that the baby boy had hemophilia, a disorder which prevents the blood from clotting normally. The main danger from this disease is not from a cut, because pressure on the wound can usually halt the bleeding, but from a bruise, which produces internal bleeding. A strong sailor was appointed as Alexis' bodyguard when he became old enough to walk to try to protect him from falls or bumps that could cause bruises. But Alexis, like many hemophiliacs, seemed to thrive on taking chances. Not even the closest watch could prevent the bruises which would produce excruciating pain. Nicholas had to live with the shadow of his son's illness constantly hovering over him.

In 1904 Russia went to war with Japan, the *Russo-Japanese War.* Kaiser Wilhelm of Germany had more or less pushed Nicholas into this war because he wanted to keep Russia occupied. Japan had wanted Port Arthur and part of Manchuria from Korea. Russia said no, then seized it herself. Japan launched a surprise attack on Port Arthur. Russia had impossibly long supply lines and suffered defeat after defeat, including the sinking of almost the entire fleet at Tsushima, May 27. The hardships that the people suffered because of the war left them open to revolutionary agitation. The result was *Bloody Sunday*, January 9, 1905.

A Russian Orthodox priest, Father George Gapon, had organized a massive march to the Winter Palace where the workers would present a petition to the Tsar. To this day historians disagree on whether Gapon was sincerely interested in helping the workers or deliberately trying to stir up violence. Most of the people marching thought that the petition was a plea for the Tsar's protection from the factory owners; actually the document was revolutionary. The march itself was illegal, but the authorities made no attempt to stop it. Nicholas was not at the Winter Palace, but at Tsarskoe Selo, his country residence. He had no idea of the magnitude of the demonstration and had paid almost no attention to it. When the marchers converged on the Winter Palace, the troops fired into them, killing many, including women and children. When Nicholas found out what had happened, he met with a delegation of marchers but gave them only platitudes. He set up a commission to investigate the event, but it accomplished nothing. Nicholas' apparent indifference to the welfare of the workers led to strikes and further revolutionary violence, including the assassination of Nicholas' uncle.

Finally on October 30, 1905 Nicholas issued the *October Manifesto*, which provided for the establishment of a legislative body, the Duma, which would have power to make laws, not merely recommend them. The moderate liberals were satisfied, but the radicals were not: Lenin instigated a flare-up in Moscow which left a thousand dead. But the majority of the people were willing to accept Nicholas' will in this matter. The Duma was regarded as a step in the right direction, though the First Fundamental Law of Russia was maintained: "To the Emperor of all the Russias belongs the Supreme autocratic power . . ." Nicholas appointed a new prime minister, Stolypin, who put forth an excellent land reform program, creating a class of farmers known as the kulaks, who received land purchased from the incompetent and unproductive farmers. Stolypin was working hard for the good of Russia, but his reforms needed time and peace. He received neither. During 1906 and 1907 there were nearly 4,000 terrorist murders. Then in 1911, Stolypin himself was assassinated by a socialist revolutionary.

About this time appeared one of the strangest characters in history: Rasputin. Rasputin claimed to be a monk, but his religion consisted of the belief that anything he wanted he should have. He was tall and heavy, had a bushy beard and piercing eyes, and rarely washed. But he had a dominating personality, and Alexandra became convinced that he had been sent to her and Nicholas by God. This belief became firmly entrenched after the Spala incident.

The royal family was vacationing in Spala when Alexis fell and bruised himself. He began to suffer severe internal hemorrhaging, and the pressure from the blood inside his hip socket caused him unbearable pain. Alexandra nursed him day and night, becoming gray with fatigue and anguish. The doctors tried everything they could think of but nothing worked. Finally Alexandra telegraphed Rasputin. He sent a return telegram: "Tell the doctors not to bother the little one too much. He will be all right." Immediately Alexandra relaxed and became cheerful. She sent the doctors away. In a few hours the bleeding stopped and Alexis began a slow but steady recovery. Whether the child would have become well anyway or whether Alexandra's relaxation and ease after the telegram had a psychological effect on her son or whether Rasputin actually used some preternatural power, we do not know. But Alexandra attributed her son's recovery to a miracle worked by Rasputin, and his position in the palace became immovable. Even when clear evidence of his immoral life was brought to Alexandra, she refused to believe it. Nicholas allowed her to have her way, against his better judgment, and the people's respect for the royal family greatly declined.

The War Begins

We have seen the instability in Europe and the lack of moral principle on the part of most of Europe's leaders. Ironically, it was the country with the most moral government—Austria-Hungary—which was the first to declare war and open the conflict which was known at the time as the Great War and now is known as World War I.

The Austrian occupation of Bosnia-Herzegovina had been good for the inhabitants. They now had what they had not had before: roads, schools and order. Both Catholic and Moslem residents were happy. But the Serbs were not happy and were constantly agitating, trying to start trouble. A secret group known as the Black Hand was formed, with rituals that seemed almost diabolical. The members were mostly young Bosnians who wanted to break away from Austria. They were given asylum in Serbia. When word came out that the heir to the Austrian throne, Franz Ferdinand, would be visiting Sarajevo, the capital of Bosnia, the Black Hand planned his assassination. There is documentary evidence that Serbian government officials encouraged these plans and gave assistance to the plotters. The plan was successful, and Franz Ferdinand and Sophie were shot by Gavrilo Princip while riding in an open car in a motorcade through Sarajevo on June 28, 1914.

Franz Josef had now seen his brother, wife and heir murdered by revolutionaries. He saw no other recourse than stern punishment of those responsible, which included the Serbian government. Yet he did not behave rashly. He considered all alternatives before finally issuing an ultimatum to Serbia, almost a month after the murder. The main provisions included the eradication of anti-Austrian societies in Serbia and Austrian presence in Serbia until the terms were carried out.

Serbia was eager to provoke war with Austria because they believed that Russia would support them (Serbia) because of pan-Slavism. They therefore drafted a conciliatory response to the ultimatum to put themselves in a good light, agreeing to some of the less important provisions of the ultimatum, but at the same time ordering a mobilization of their army. After agonizing over his decision, Franz Josef ordered a mobilization, but only a partial one, directed solely against Serbia. He had no intention of fighting anyone else nor did he want anyone else to be drawn into the war.

Meanwhile, just after the Austrian ultimatum had been delivered, Nicholas, under pressure from his council, ordered a partial mobilization, believing that this might deter Austria from war or if war came Russia would be ready, since it took Russia so much longer to mobilize than it did anyone else. If Russia had limited itself to partial mobilization, it might still have been able to stay out of the war, but on July 30 the Russian general staff persuaded Nicholas, against his better judgment, to order a complete mobilization. The Russian general staff hoped that Russia would make great territorial gains as a result of the war. It was only after Russia had ordered its general mobilization that Austria gave in and ordered its own general mobilization.

Meanwhile, Germany was in a difficult situation of its own making. General Schlieffen, now dead, had developed the *Schlieffen Plan*. Germany believed that in any major war, it would have to fight on two fronts—Russia and France—because of the alliance between these two countries. The Schlieffen Plan was designed to meet this difficulty. The Plan was based on the premise that Russia would take at least six weeks to mobilize. Therefore as soon as war broke out, Germany would send a rapid invasion into France the shortest and easiest way possible—through Belgium. France would be quickly defeated by the time Russia mobilized. Then Germany at its leisure could defeat Russia. After the Russian general mobilization was announced, Germany sent an ultimatum to Russia: suspend "every war measure" within twelve hours. Of course, Russia would do no such thing, so Wilhelm issued the orders necessary to put the Schlieffen Plan into effect. Once the orders were issued, it was almost impossible to recall them. On August 1, the French ordered a general mobilization at 4:00 P.M., and the Germans declared war on Russia at 6:00 P.M. The Schlieffen Plan at first worked perfectly and the Germans invaded Belgium. England had promised to protect Belgium's neutrality, so on August 5 England declared war on Germany.

Only Austria and England had the semblance of a moral reason for becoming involved in the conflict. Russia's general mobilization and Germany's launching of the Schlieffen Plan were both unjustified actions which guaranteed that all of Europe would be involved in the war. As for the French, though they pretended to be an innocent party, they were eager for the war because they believed that they would at last be able to regain Alsace and Lorraine. The French even deliberately pulled back frontier troops ten kilometers to make the Germans appear more clearly the aggressors.

Though both sides enthusiastically proclaimed that theirs was the moral position, no side had the right to make that claim. World War I had no moral basis or justification for its beginning.

The Schlieffen Plan Fails

The Germans sent an ultimatum to Belgian King Albert II asking him to permit passage of German troops through Belgium without resistance. Albert said absolutely not, and the Belgians resisted heroically. Though they were no match for the German army, they fought much harder than the Germans had expected. The Germans were slowed down and the Schlieffen Plan timetable was thrown off. But the Germans were determined to crush Belgian resistance. Priests and other hostages were shot; a Zeppelin bombed Liege, killing nine civilians; a 98-ton siege gun with shells a yard long was brought up to subdue a Belgian fort. When they couldn't fight the army any more, the Belgians engaged in guerrilla warfare, especially cutting telephone and telegraph lines. Finally on August 20 Brussels was occupied.

Meanwhile the French had not come to the aid of the Belgians. Instead, they had their own plan: Plan 17, which involved taking Alsace and Lorraine and breaking through to the Rhine. The French plan was totally unrealistic, and from August 20-24 they fought four battles at the same time (Lorraine, Ardennes, Charleroi, Mons) and were wiped out in all of them.

On the eastern front, Germany was able to intercept all Russian messages, which were sent either with a very simple code or no code at all because some of the headquarters didn't have the key. The Russians also suffered from constant shortages of food and ammunition. Nevertheless the Russians were somehow able to mobilize in two weeks instead of the six expected by the Schlieffen Plan. Therefore Von Moltke, the German commander-in-chief, pulled out two corps from the western front and sent them east.

They were a little late for the *Battle of Tannenberg* (August 26-30), a German victory. General Samsonov's Second Army ceased to exist, and the Russian general, in desperation, shot himself on the field. The German army was clearly superior to the Russian, but the absence of two German corps from the western front was to have crucial results, as we shall see.

Britain moved quickly to dominate the seas and by the end of August controlled the Atlantic. Germany had built a huge fleet, but Kaiser Wilhelm wouldn't risk it on the high seas to keep commerce open. He didn't want anything to happen to it, being convinced that the very existence of the fleet would serve his purpose. Though Admiral von Tirpitz tried to bring about a more active policy, Wilhelm passively allowed the British to set up their blockade of Germany. This British superiority led to the development of the U-boats or submarines by the Germans, as a means of preventing ships from reaching Britain and of establishing a counter-blockade.

On the western front, German troops entered French territory on August 24, following the Schlieffen Plan strategy of an enveloping action to encircle the French army and annihilate it. But the Schlieffen Plan wasn't working out so well: Belgian resistance had slowed the Germans, the British Expeditionary Force had landed and was providing strong resistance, and the Germans desperately needed the two corps that had been sent to the eastern front when the Russians mobilized more quickly than expected. The French First and Second Armies had escaped from the German "envelope" and the Germans had an exposed flank. The French General Joffre announced a counterattack on the Marne River to stop the German advance. Too late Von Moltke realized the danger and ordered a regrouping. But his men were exhausted from 24-mile per day marches; they were disorganized and confused. Joffre's reinforcements, 6000 men, detrained in Paris but had no transportation to the front. So Joffre drafted 600 taxis into service. The men were rushed to the front and held the ground. After fierce fighting, the Germans retreated and established new lines. The British and French were unable to break these lines, but the Schlieffen Plan had been decisively defeated.

By the end of 1914, both sides had dug into trenches, in lines that would not vary more than ten miles in either direction in the next four years. The Germans held all but a strip of Belgium and about a tenth of France. To hold these lines thousands of lives would be lost, as the machine guns in the trenches mowed down the attacking soldiers. The horrors of life in the trenches were most apparent to the young men who had to live in the mud and blood day in and day out. The dispatches sent back to their home countries spoke only of glorious victories being won and of the importance of fighting until the wicked enemy would surrender unconditionally. The only moral course of action at this point would have been for the nations involved to have opened peace negotiations and put an end to the slaughter. But both sides were convinced that they were totally in the right and that they would soon win a decisive victory. No negotiations were held and the slaughter went on.

The War in 1915

During 1915 there was almost no movement on the western front, though both sides began using poison gas and despite enormous casualties, such as the 400,000 men lost when the French gained only three miles at the second battle of Artois. Several important events did happen during 1915, however.

The first was the German announcement on February 4 of a submarine blockade of Great Britain. On May 7, the Germans sank the *Lusitania* off the coast of Ireland, with a loss of 1198 lives, including 139 Americans. Despite being a passenger liner, the ship was loaded with munitions, including guncotton which exploded when the U-boat's torpedo struck it, causing the ship to sink much faster than it would otherwise have done with a consequently increased loss of life. The U.S. nearly came into the war at this time, but finally the Germans gave promises that no liners would be sunk in the future without warning and without some provision for the safety of non-combatants. These assurances were reasonably well observed for the next year.

In May and June the Austrians and Germans launched a great offensive in Galicia. The Russian army by this time was suffering from chaos in its supply lines and lacked rifles, artillery, ammunition and clothing. The offensive continued through the summer. Russia lost Poland and Lithuania and almost a million men. Strong opposition to the war and to the government for continuing the war was beginning to develop in Russia.

On May 23 Italy, which had originally been allied with Germany and Austria-Hungary, declared war on the Dual Monarchy. England and France had made secret agreements with Italy that it would receive the South Tyrol from Austria. The two Allies also agreed to support Italy in preventing the Pope from taking diplomatic steps for the conclusion of hostilities. The Italian intervention was not a great military success—the

Italians fought eleven successive battles in two years on the 60-mile front of the Isonzo River, with almost no gains—but they tied down a good portion of the Austrian army. More importantly, their secret agreements with England and France would stand in the way of peace negotiations.

Turkey had come into the war on the side of Germany, hoping to get back some of its territory from Russia. Winston Churchill of England suggested that the Allies open a second front in Turkey to force Turkey out of the war, open supply lines to Russia, and break the stalemate. So on May 24, the Allies invaded Turkey at *Gallipoli*. The idea was a good one. But the Turks knew of the plan well ahead of time so that the British bombardment was harmless. Then when the British forces landed, they were met by the same murderous machine gun fire as had decimated the ranks of their comrades on the western front. There were 120,000 Allied casualties and nothing was accomplished. The greatest tragedy was that the Allies were thus able to do nothing to help Russia and conditions there deteriorated.

Finally in September Nicholas II decided that the only way to save Russia from total defeat was to take over supreme command at the front. He could scarcely have made a worse decision. Russia needed to get out of the war, not prolong it. Nicholas was not qualified as a military commander. And worst of all, he left the government in Russia in the hands of Alexandra as regent—which meant that the government was actually in the hands of Rasputin. Rasputin removed every able man left in high position in the government and brought in weak, immoral men whom he controlled. The situation within Russia rapidly deteriorated.

1916

In February 1916 the Germans launched an attack against the French at Verdun. The French held, but casualties mounted. The Allies decided to launch a counterattack on the Somme, a strategically worthless area, to relieve the pressure on the French. General Douglas Haig was placed in command for the British, but he intended to use the same tactics that had gone nowhere in 1915.

The *Battle of the Somme* illustrates the murderous ineptness that characterized the Allied high command during the war. The Germans were aware from aerial reconnaissance that a major offensive was coming. So they improved their defensive positions, putting up new barbed wire with barbs as thick as a man's thumb, in some places at a depth of thirty yards. The British nevertheless went ahead with their plans.

They began with a terrific bombardment of two million shells. But the shells were of poor quality, sometimes bursting prematurely to kill gun crews and Allied infantry. The bombardment started on June 24 preparatory to an attack scheduled June 29, but at the request of the French the attack was postponed to July 1. Therefore the gun crews ran short of shells, and the Germans were able to recover from the bombardment.

The next mistake made by the high command was to postpone "zero hour" to 7:30 A.M. (at a time of the year when dawn came before 4:00 A.M.) instead of attacking when it was just barely light to have more of the element of surprise. This decision was made at the insistence of General Foch, who wanted the gunners to be able to observe the effect of the last stage of their bombardment. Then the high command was so sure the bombardment would be effective that the men were told to march toward the Germans at walking pace, carrying loads of 70 pounds.

The night before the attack, one of the generals sent out a "good luck" message to the men over field telephone, so that the Germans picked up the message and knew that the attack was imminent. Also the night before, the men had been brought up from trenches behind the lines, some coming a distance of ten miles. They were exhausted and crowded into water-logged trenches.

Finally at 7:30 A.M., the men were ordered out. The Germans were waiting for them. The first day, there were 60,000 British casualties, 8,000 German casualties. After the first day, Haig narrowed the lines from the original 25 miles down to six, the first sensible decision he had made. But the battle dragged on until November. Altogether there were 600,000 Allied casualties. They gained very little ground, though they inflicted many casualties (650,000) on the Germans. The pressure on Verdun was relieved, but that battle was dying off anyway.

The final scorecard on the Somme showed a gain of eight miles, at a total cost to both sides of 1,250,000 dead and wounded—or two and one half men per *inch*.

Also in 1916, Franz Josef died, to be succeeded by his 29-year-old great-nephew Charles. The new Emperor was a deeply spiritual Catholic, motivated by concern for the welfare of his people in the best Hapsburg tradition. He was determined to grant greater autonomy to the local nationality groups within the Empire. But before he could institute these reforms, the deadly war must be brought to an end. He first tried to persuade Kaiser Wilhelm to consider withdrawing from the war, allowing France to keep Alsace and Lorraine, in exchange for which Charles would surrender some of his own territory. Thus Charles was the only leader of the time who was willing to make territorial concessions. But the Kaiser flatly refused.

The situation in the Russian government went from bad to worse so that not even Nicholas could evade the truth. He finally decided to fire Protopopov, Rasputin's Minister of the Interior. When she heard of this decision, Alexandra, almost certainly under the urging of Rasputin, wrote emotional letters to Nicholas, putting every possible pressure on him to retain Protopopov. On November 27 she visited Nicholas at army headquarters. Nicholas capitulated. Later, he wrote to Alexandra; "Tender thanks for the severe written scolding. I read it with a smile, because you speak to me as though I was a child . . . Your poor little weak-willed hubby." And this was from a man who held the fate of one hundred and fifty million people in his hands.

Finally, a group of Russian aristocrats, led by Felix Yusupov and Vladimir Purishkevich, plotted the murder of Rasputin, hoping that by assassinating this man of evil they could save Russia. They planned to lure him to Yusupov's house and poison him with cyanide. They put enough to kill into each of three cakes and two glasses of wine.

Rasputin came, expecting to meet Yusupov's beautiful wife, Irina. He ate two of the cakes, drank the two glasses of wine—enough poison to kill four men. Nothing happened.

Then Yusupov brought out a revolver and fired at point blank range. Rasputin crashed to the floor, falling onto a white polar bear rug. There was no blood on the rug, only a small spot of blood on Rasputin's shirt, in spite of a bullet in the region of his heart. They could hear the rattling of his breath, but surely he was dying.

Moved by a sudden impulse, Yusupov went over and shook the body. the eyes opened; Rasputin grabbed Yusupov by the shoulder; he repeated his name over and over: "Felix, Felix, Felix, Felix . . ." Yusupov tore himself away and screamed. He rushed up the stairs. Rasputin followed, staggering up the stairs and out the door into the snowy courtyard. Purishkevich, a crack shot, pulled out his revolver. The first two bullets missed. The third bullet struck Rasputin in the shoulder, the fourth in the neck. Rasputin collapsed into the snow, and they dragged the body back into the house.

Again Rasputin wouldn't die. Again his eyes opened. Yusupov grabbed a leaded walking stick and beat him frantically until the body was still. They tied it with ropes and drove to the Neva River. They hurriedly threw it into a hole in the ice. On the way down the body struck either the bridge abutment or the ice, breaking its head open. They drove away.

Rasputin had been poisoned, enough to kill four men; shot, two fatal wounds; beaten and thrown against a bridge. But it was still alive under the water, where it should have frozen to death almost immediately in the ice-choked Neva River on the last day of the year. But the body breathed, for there was water in its lungs; it moved, for the ropes binding its hands were partially untied.

How at last did it die? No one knows. Perhaps an angel from Heaven finally intervened to conquer the devil which was apparently possessing the body. The next day, the body was recovered, entirely encased in ice, its lungs full of water, its right hand free of the rope and reaching out.

But the devil didn't really need the body anymore. Its work had been done. The royal family's prestige had been ruined; there was a power vacuum in Imperial Russia. And waiting in the wings to fill the vacuum were Nikolai Lenin and the Communist Party.

1917

At the beginning of 1917 the troops in the trenches on the western front could see so little purpose in their war that a popular song, sung to the tune of "Auld Lang Syne," was "We're here because we're here because we're here . . ." Several million men lived like moles along a 350-mile line. The ground had been so devastated by the constant fighting and the heavy rains that a wounded man could literally drown in the mud before he could be rescued. In Russia, the death(s) of Rasputin had not solved anything. On March 8 bread riots broke out in St. Petersburg as starving people tried to get food. Instead of suppressing the riots, the soldiers joined them. Nicholas had surrendered his authority to Alexandra and Rasputin; now he could not regain it. He signed the document of abdication, and Alexander Kerensky, a leader in the Duma, formed a government. The best thing Kerensky could have done for Russia was to get out of the war, but the Allies pressured him to stay in, and the slaughter of Russian soldiers continued. Many of the soldiers could take no more, and from March-August 1917, seven million men deserted the army.

Charles of Austria continued his efforts to make peace, embarking on a dangerous diplomatic venture. Charles' wife Zita came from the Bourbon-Parma family of Italy. Meeting secretly with two of her brothers, Sixtus and Xavier, Charles gave them the mission of carrying personal messages to Paris, offering to make concessions of Austrian territory if peace negotiations would begin. But neither Paris nor London was interested in negotiations; the Allied powers had made too many secret deals among themselves to be able to abandon the war and work for peace. A disloyal official in Charles' government revealed the secret peace mission—known as the "Sixtus Affair"—and all Charles' careful and arduous efforts collapsed. Except for the anguished appeals for sanity of Pope Benedict XV, Charles' efforts were the only serious attempt to end the war and prevent further slaughter.

In February Germany resumed unrestricted submarine warfare, gambling that they could starve out Britain before the United States could gear up for war. This German decision, along with the uncovering of a German plan to persuade Mexico to declare war on the United States, brought America into the war. The American declaration was a great morale boost for the Allies, but it would not be until 1918 that American troops would arrive in France in large numbers.

Back on the western front, the best any of the Allied generals could think of was more of the same. General Nivelle, commander-in-chief of the French forces, planned an offensive in which the British and French would attack one flank to draw German attention. Then the French would attack the other and break through to the coast. Once again there were delays in implementing the plan, because of the miserable weather and shortages of supplies. The plan of the Nivelle offensive appeared in some newspapers, and the Germans immediately fell back to new, stronger defensive positions. Incredibly, Nivelle insisted on going ahead with his plan.

On April 16, in a cold rain, the Nivelle offensive began. By April 17, the Allies had suffered 120,000 casualties to gain two miles. But Nivelle ordered the attack to continue. At last, on May 3, the men in the trenches had had enough. The 21st Division of the French army refused duty. Then the 120th Infantry did the same. The mutiny spread. The men announced that they would defend their positions against German attack but they themselves would not attack; they had fed the machine guns long enough. An entire regiment left for Paris to demand a negotiated peace. One regiment went to the front baa-ing, to show that they regarded themselves as lambs sent to slaughter. Desertions during the mutiny numbered 21,174. In desperation, the French government replaced Nivelle with Petain. He took stern measures. Two hundred fifty leaders were shot, 100 banished. Petain went personally to the units to promise help; generous leaves were given. But the French army was effectively finished. Now the British had to take over. But the British had only General Haig, and he had nothing original to offer. He planned the *Passchendaele* or *Flanders Campaign,* destined to be the bloodiest of a bloody war. The goal was to break through to Ostend on the coast, "only" 30 miles away.

Meanwhile in Switzerland, Lenin was watching events with interest. Lenin had great ambition and a desire for power. He saw an opportunity now to get what he wanted. He communicated with the German government, telling them that if they could get him safely back to Russia he would take over the government and immediately withdraw Russia from the war. The German government made arrangements to transport Lenin and some of his friends secretly back to St. Petersburg in a sealed railway car. Charles of Austria tried to persuade the Kaiser to abandon this dangerous plan, but Wilhelm wouldn't listen. Charles then prohibited the train from crossing Austrian soil, forcing the sealed car to take a more roundabout route. Winston Churchill later wrote that it was as if Lenin was a "plague bacillus." Indeed he was.

He arrived in St. Petersburg on April 16, where he was welcomed by Josef Stalin, a band and a large crowd waving red banners. He immediately took charge of the *Bolsheviks,* the most radical of the revolutionary groups. The goal of the Bolsheviks was total power—they had no intention of allowing the people a voice in the government. Of course they didn't tell the people that. Instead they stressed the Communist principle that all property and wealth should be taken from those who owned it and divided up among the ordinary people. Their slogan was "Peace, Bread and Land."

The Communists Take Power

As Lenin and his Bolsheviks plotted the final destruction of freedom in Russia, Pope Benedict XV continued working tirelessly for peace. On May 5 he offered an agonized prayer to the Blessed Mother, begging her to bring peace to her warring children. On May 13 she came in person to answer the prayer, appearing to three shepherd children (Lucia, Jacinta and Francisco) in Fatima, Portugal. Her message was prayer and penance, but at this point only the three children were listening.

On May 18 Marxists were admitted to the Russian government. On June 13 Mary appeared at Fatima for the second time. In late June Kerensky's disintegrating army was ordered forward. On July 8 the Russian army was totally wiped out, and Germany was able to send more divisions to the western front. On July 13 Mary told the children to tell the world that prayers must be offered for the conversion of Russia. "If they listen to my request," she said, "Russia will be converted and there will be peace. If not, she will scatter her errors throughout the world, provoking wars and persecutions of the Church."

On July 31 at 3:15 A.M., the Flanders Offensive began. Tanks were used, but they could make only one mile per hour, many got stuck, and not one reached its destination. The Germans had reinforced their position, and the Allies suffered heavy losses. If a few units did break through the German barbed wire and machine gun fire, they were quickly surrounded. The rain came down, and slogging through the mud was like moving in slow motion. By the end of August, the Flanders Offensive had produced 74,000 Allied casualties.

On August 13 the three children were unable to go to the Cova da Iria, site of the apparitions, because the anti-Catholic mayor had arrested them and tried to frighten them into denying that they had seen the Mother of God. On August 16 Pope Benedict XV offered a specific peace plan, but no one paid any attention.

On September 13 Mary appeared once again and promised a great miracle in October. The British attacks continued, as did the appalling casualty rates. The rain poured down all over Europe, on the soldiers drowning in the mud in Flanders, and on the thousands of people making their way to Fatima to see the promised miracle. Shell shock became an increasingly serious problem as men simply could not face another day of horror.

On October 13 at Fatima, the rain ceased. While the children knelt in ecstasy listening to the Mother of God, the sun danced and spun in the sky and appeared as if it were about to plummet to the earth. Thousands saw the miracle, including many skeptics who had come to Fatima simply to scoff when the miracle did not take place as they believed it would not, and including people up to twenty miles away who had not expected or planned to see any kind of miracle. Mary had given evidence that the apparitions were real. It remained to be seen how many people would heed her message of prayer and penance for world peace and the conversion of Russia.

On October 25 the rain still fell on Flanders, and the attackers made one yard per minute, losing 12,000 men. On November 6 the offensive at last died out. The Allies had transformed what had been a small bulge in the German lines into a larger one, which only served the purpose of giving the Germans good target practice. The longest gain was 9,000 yards, the average gain four miles. The Allies had not come close to the coast and had suffered half a million casualties. On April 9, 1918, the Germans counterattacked and in hours wiped out the whole gain.

In Russia the final revolution took place on November 7 (though it was October by the calendar the Russians used and is therefore called the *October Revolution*). The Bolsheviks seized the railroad stations, banks, power station, bridges and telephone exchange. Most of the soldiers stationed in St. Petersburg supported the Bolsheviks. By evening only the Winter Palace, the former residence of the Tsars, remained under Kerensky's control. At 9:00 P.M. the Bolsheviks started shelling the palace. By 1:00 A.M., the Red Guards were in the building. They broke into the rooms where the government leaders were hiding and took them prisoners.

On November 8 representatives of the Communist Party, also called Soviets, met. With Lenin dominating the meeting, they voted an end to the war, approved the seizure of all private property without paying for it, and elected Lenin head of the government. By November 18 the Communists were in complete control.

Although opposition forces (called "Whites") fought the Communists in several parts of the country, Lenin acted as if he had the full support of the people. He ordered the seizure of all private property and took over all industries. He declared that the government had no debts. He set up new courts. He confiscated all church lands and said that divorce was legal and could be granted for any reason at all. Lenin reinstituted the death penalty and began to arrest his rivals.

The situation of the ordinary people had not changed for the better. Food was still scarce. Crime was out of control. When elections were held for a Constituent Assembly, the Bolsheviks obtained only 24 per cent of the vote. Clearly the people did not want a Communist government.

Lenin went back on all his promises about representative government. He tried to sabotage the Constituent Assembly. When it finally met in spite of his attempts to postpone it, the Bolsheviks disrupted the proceedings. The government arrested more of its enemies and seized the printing presses of anti-Bolshevik newspapers. Finally the delegates were driven away.

On March 13, 1918, Lenin signed the Treaty of Brest-Litovsk with the Germans, giving away large tracts of Russian territory. On June 12, 1918, the royal family was brutally murdered.

Mary's July prophecy came true. The evil of Communism has spread throughout the world, bringing untold suffering to millions of people, a series of wars and persecutions of Christians and of others as great as any the world has ever known.

The End of the War

In the spring of 1918, the Germans tried a last great offensive in an attempt to win the war before the Americans arrived. But though the German troops smashed through the Allied lines, all they gained was the ruined land that had been fought over for almost four years. The exhausted soldiers could not make the final decisive breakthrough.

Then in the summer of 1918, 600,000 American soldiers began arriving in Europe. On August 8 the Allied troops smashed the German line. On September 12 the Americans won another resounding victory. Bulgaria, Turkey and Austria soon afterwards surrendered. The Hapsburg Empire was convulsed by revolution, and Charles and his family were forced to flee. In Germany a rebellion broke out, caused mainly by the food shortages which the English blockade had produced. The sailors in the German fleet mutinied. On November 9 Kaiser Wilhelm and the crown prince fled to Holland, and a republic was proclaimed in Berlin. On November 11 an armistice was signed and all fighting ceased. World War I was over. In four years over eight and a half million men had died and another 21,000,000 had been wounded.

World War I was an unnecessary war, fought for no good reason. But its effects on the future course of history were very great. The young men of Europe had been slaughtered by the millions. Europe was exhausted and disillusioned. Three ruling families (Hapsburg, Romanov, Hohenzollern) had been overthrown, and revolution had spread throughout Europe. The United States, virtually untouched by the war, was now a world power. And, most importantly, a Communist dictatorship had been established in Russia.

Review Questions

1. What were the main characteristics of England in the early years of the 20th century?
2. What were the main results of the Dreyfus Case in France?
3. What were the main characteristics of Germany in the early years of the 20th century?
4. Which countries coveted Austrian land?
5. Name the two Popes who succeeded Leo XIII. What was Modernism?
6. What was the anarchist movement?
7. How did Alexander II reform Russia? Who assassinated him? How did his son react to the assassination?

8. What probably led Lenin to become a Communist?
9. Summarize the characters of Nicholas II and Alexandra. What effect did their son's illness have on them?
10. What were the results of the Russo-Japanese War and Bloody Sunday in Russia?
11. How did Rasputin become part of the royal household? What were the effects of Alexandra's trust of him?
12. Summarize the events surrounding the assassination of Franz Ferdinand. Who was responsible?
13. List the steps that led to the involvement of all the nations of Europe in the war.
14. What was the Schlieffen Plan? Why did it fail? What were the results of its failure?
15. Describe the sinking of the Lusitania. Why did this event not bring the U.S. into the war?
16. Why did Italy come into the war? What were the consequences of its involvement?
17. What was the purpose of the Gallipoli invasion? Why did it fail?
18. What were the results of Nicholas' decision to take command at the front?
19. List the mistakes of the Battle of the Somme. What were the results of this battle?
20. Who succeeded Franz Josef? How did he differ from other leaders?
21. Describe the assassination of Rasputin.
22. Summarize the events that led to Nicholas' abdication. What mistake did his successor make?
23. What was the Sixtus Affair? Why did it fail?
24. What was the Nivelle Offensive? What were its results?
25. Summarize the events of 1917 that led to the Communist take-over of Russia.
26. Summarize the events at Fatima. What prophecies did the Blessed Mother make? Describe the October miracle.
27. What happened during the Flanders Campaign?
28. Why did the U.S. come into the war?
29. Summarize the events of 1918.
30. What were the results of World War I?

Projects

1. Prepare a map of World War I, showing the most important battles.
2. Imagine that you were a servant with the royal family during the time of the Russian Revolution and write a diary of your experiences.
3. Imagine that you are a soldier in the trenches during World War I. Write a letter home telling how you feel and what you are doing.
4. Give a detailed report on United States participation in World War I.

Chapter Twenty Eight
The World Between Wars

IN JANUARY 1919 the victorious nations of World War I met in the luxurious Hall of Mirrors at Louis XIV's Versailles Palace to prepare a peace settlement. They looked out over a devastated Europe. The destruction was not so much of property—except along the front in Belgium and France—but of human life. Millions of the young men of Germany, Austria, France, England and Russia had been killed or wounded. The survivors were discouraged, depressed and vengeful. England and France refused to accept any responsibility for the war, either its occurrence or the destruction it caused, though either of those nations could have prevented the spread of war or brought it to an early end if they had been willing to act unselfishly. Their selfishness would continue in the peace negotiations, the results of which would play a large part in causing the next great war.

The Versailles Treaty

The United States did not share the general mood of the European delegates. Because it had been almost untouched by the evils of the war, and yet had played a major role in the Allied victory, the United States was optimistic and self-confident. It had emerged for the first time as a major world power. President Woodrow Wilson was a respected figure.

Wilson attended the Versailles Conference as the personal representative of the United States, joining President Clemenceau of France and Prime Minister Lloyd George of Great Britain. Wilson was different from his companions. They were practical men: they wanted to get revenge on Germany and prevent its ever being a major power in Europe for the foreseeable future by weakening it to the greatest extent possible. Wilson, on the other hand, thought that he could prevent all future wars (World War I had been referred to in the United States as "the war to end all wars") by imposing the American view of government on the rest of the world. Wilson was strongly opposed to any form of government which was not elected. When Charles of Austria tried to communicate with Wilson to discuss peace negotiations, Wilson refused to have anything to do with the Austrian Emperor because he had not been elected to office. Wilson had even thought at first that the overthrow of the Russian Tsar was a fortunate occurrence because Nicholas had not been democratically elected.

Before the war had ended, Wilson had published *Fourteen Points*, a list of the conditions he thought should be included in any peace treaty. One of these was "self-determination"—the notion that people of different nationality groups should all have their own nations. He therefore supported the liberal revolutionaries who wanted to split the Austrian Empire into small countries, and he set out to re-draw the map of Europe. Unfortunately, Wilson was woefully ignorant of both European history and European geography. He united the Serbs and the Croats—who had a similar language—into the country of Yugoslavia though the Serbs and the Croats intensely disliked each other and had very little in common (for example, the Croats were Catholic and the Serbs Greek Orthodox). The Czechs and Slovaks were yoked into Czechoslovakia, though they had no more love for each other, or historic association, than the Serbs and the Croats. Wilson gave Austria's South Tyrol to Italy because the Italians showed him a false map marking the South Tyrol as part of "historic" Italy. Emperor Charles was driven from his homeland; with his wife and children, he took refuge in Switzerland, watching in dismay as the Empire which had stood for six and a half centuries was torn into tiny pieces.

Besides supporting "self-determination," Wilson's other great goal was to establish the League of Nations, an international organization which he believed would settle all disagreements between nations and thereby guarantee world peace. Lloyd George and Clemenceau were too realistic to believe that the League would really work, but they supported it in exchange for Wilson's grudging support of their revenge on Germany.

The German delegates were treated as criminals, confined to a hotel surrounded by barbed wire and patrolled by sentinels. They were not consulted on the peace treaty, but simply told that they must either sign the treaty or have the war resumed. Ninety minutes before Allied troops were to invade Germany, the German government agreed to a treaty which one delegate summed up thus: "The Allies could have expressed the whole thing more simply in one clause—'*Germany gives up her existence.*'"

The main punishments inflicted upon Germany by the *Versailles Treaty* were as follows: 1) Had to return Alsace and Lorraine to France. 2) Had to pay huge amounts of money, called *reparations,* to the victorious nations, the first installment of $5 billion due in five years. 3) Was limited to an army of 100,000 men. 4) Had to destroy its tanks and airplanes. 5) Could have no large guns and only a limited number of smaller ones. 6) Could have only six warships and had to hand over a quarter of its fishing fleet. 7) Had to allow the Allies to occupy the Rhineland (territory between France and Germany) for 15 years and then could not station any of its own soldiers there.

One good provision of the Versailles Treaty was that Poland was brought back into existence with its territory coming from Germany, Austria and Russia. Unfortunately, though, in order to give Poland an outlet to the sea, the *Polish Corridor* was cut through Germany. This meant that a strip of German land was artificially attached to Poland and that part of Germany (East Prussia) was separated from the rest.

The Versailles Treaty had two primary effects, neither of which was expected by the signers but both of which should have been foreseen, if the men involved had been less selfish and more concerned for Europe. The first was that the Germans were bitter and resentful. Perhaps Germany did bear primary responsibility for the war and should have been required to make some reparations. But the severity of the penalties placed upon Germany were far out of proportion to the guilt of that nation. This bitterness would be one of the direct causes of World War II.

Secondly, the destruction of the Austrian Empire left an emptiness in central Europe. For hundreds of years, the Hapsburgs had protected the small nationality groups within their Empire, so that they could not be conquered by larger nations. These groups had been able to keep their own customs and traditions and in large part manage their own affairs. But after World War I, the Hapsburg Empire was destroyed and new, smaller nations created and given independence. Without the Hapsburgs to protect them, their independence lasted only 20 years. First the Nazis conquered them, and then the Communists. Since 1989 they are "free," but a terrible series of wars developed in the former Yugoslavia.

One man could have saved Austria from this fate: the deposed Emperor Charles. He made two separate attempts to regain the throne in Hungary to be used as a base for restoring Hapsburg authority over central

Europe. But men who should have been Charles' supporters deceived and betrayed him. Though Charles, accompanied by Zita, tried a daring airplane trip into Hungary and rallied loyalist troops behind him, one of his own generals deliberately allowed Hungarian government troops to move into a key strategic position and Charles' attempt to regain his throne was foiled. He and his family were once again driven into exile, this time to the island of Madeira, where the unhealthful climate and miserable circumstances in which the former Emperor was forced to live brought about his premature death of pneumonia in 1922 at the age of 35. But his life had been so holy that the Church began investigations into the possible canonization of the last Hapsburg Emperor.

As for the League of Nations, Woodrow Wilson's great dream, it never amounted to anything. When Wilson returned to the United States, Congress refused to allow the U.S. to join. Wilson went on a tour of the country to get public support for the League, but this so exhausted him that he had a stroke and died not long after his term as President ended. The U.S. never did join the League, and that organization was unable to keep peace in the world.

The Soviet Union

In Russia, now renamed the Union of Soviet Socialist Republics, or Soviet Union, the Communist Party under Lenin tightened its grip. But it rapidly became apparent that Communism could not produce prosperity. Farmers refused to grow more crops than the minimum they needed, since any surplus belonged to the government. Workers, who found that the Communists had lied when they promised them a share in the ownership of factories, went on strike. Manufacturing rapidly declined. In 1921 the production of iron, for example, was only three percent of what it had been before World War I.

Lenin knew he could not remain in power if he did not improve the economy. So in 1922 he announced the *New Economic Policy,* allowing some freedom of ownership in manufacturing and farming. He also encouraged foreign capitalists to invest money in Russia and to build factories. Many capitalists from Europe and America did so. Gradually the economy improved. But before the improvement could be fully felt, five million Russians died of starvation—proof of the inability of Communism to feed its people.

Though Lenin did temporarily relax economic control, he did not relax anything else. He directed many of his attacks toward family life in

Russia. Marriage had no significance. A couple could get married simply by signing a government register and could get divorced the same way. Abortion on demand was allowed. Children were indoctrinated in Communism and encouraged to spy on their parents and to denounce them to Communist authorities.

Lenin also hated religion. The religious instruction of children was prohibited. Religious literature was banned. Parochial schools, seminaries and monasteries were closed. Church lands and religious objects were confiscated. Bishops and priests were arrested and many were killed.

Lenin organized the Communist International, which spread Communism through the world. Communist parties were formed in almost every nation with the aim of overthrowing governments and establishing Communism.

In January 1924 Lenin died, possibly murdered by Josef Stalin, who took over as dictator. In 1928 Stalin inaugurated the first of a series of *Five Year Plans* to industrialize the Soviet Union. All the peasants who weren't forced to work in factories were placed on *collective farms*, where the land was owned by the government. Some of the men who had owned small plots of land, especially the kulaks, refused to cooperate with this collectivization. Stalin ordered them rounded up at machine gun point and transported to the Arctic regions, where most of them died.

Stalin also wanted to protect his power. He began a series of *purges.* Any Communist whom he distrusted was arrested, tried and executed. Since the victims of the purges were Communists and therefore responsible for much of the misery now afflicting Russia, they deserved to be punished. But Stalin had no right to punish them. His only purpose was to gain the power to commit even greater evils.

What would your life have been like if you had lived under Stalin (who ruled until his death in 1953)? Your school would have taught only Communist doctrine and never permitted you even to consider any other point of view. You would have been taught to spy on your parents and report on them to the police. When you became old enough to work, the government would choose your job. You could not own your own home but would share an apartment with several families. You could own few things—you would never own a car, for example. To buy anything, you would stand in line, sometimes for hours, for poor quality goods. Your fellow workers would spy on you and you on them. If you criticized the government, you could be arrested without warning and tried in a court where you had no chance to prove your innocence. Afterwards you could be sent to a slave labor camp in Siberia. But even if that didn't happen, you would have no political or religious rights. You would be a slave of the government.

The Rise of Fascism

After the war there was a strong feeling that the liberal, democratic, parliamentary system just didn't work. There were many reasons for this belief: 1) The liberal democracies of England and France had helped plunge Europe into a miserable war. 2) Between the wars many parliamentary democracies had unstable governments. In Spain and Italy, for example, governments would rise and fall so fast that hardly anyone could keep track of them. 3) People realized that elections (even in stable countries like the U.S.) can lead to political corruption and power for the wealthy. 4) Many of the post-war liberal governments were unable to keep order or to stabilize the economy. Therefore, people in Europe were looking for strong governments. They didn't care much whether they had elections and parliaments or not—they wanted order.

In many countries this need was met by *fascism*. Fascism means government without elections or a parliament, with one strong man as head of state. Fascism promised order and stability, and fascist movements appeared in many countries.

Fascism in itself is neither good nor evil. Everything depends on the man who comes to power. A fascist government can be pro-Christian. Portugal was ruled wisely by a fascist government led by Antonio Salazar from 1932 until he died in 1971. In Romania, the fascist and deeply Christian Legion of the Archangel Michael, which required its members to be willing to die for Christ, provided strong opposition to liberalism and Communism.

Too often, though, the strong man ruler can become power-hungry and despotic. Such was the case in Italy. In 1919 Benito Mussolini formed the Italian Fascist Party (which took its name from the fasces, an ancient Roman symbol for power), nicknamed the Blackshirts for their uniforms. In 1921 Communist and Fascist riots in Florence marked the beginning of civil war between the two factions. In 1922 Fascists drove out the Communist government in Bologna and seized Milan. Then in October they marched on Rome, occupying the city. On October 31, the king called on Mussolini to form a government and granted him dictatorial powers. In 1923 Mussolini put through new election laws which made it easier for him to get total power. In 1924 the Fascist Party won the elections, with the help of some manipulation and force.

At first Mussolini was popular. He established order, increased industrial production, thereby ending unemployment, and gave the Italians pride in their country. He increased his popularity with the 1929 *Lateran Treaty,* granting the Pope his own independent territory, Vatican City, and ending the Pope's status as Prisoner of the Vatican. Gradually, though, Mussolini's rule became increasingly despotic, and Pope Pius XI wrote an encyclical condemning the Fascists for their pagan values.

The Rise of Hitler

The Versailles Treaty left enormous resentment in Germany, which had lost 70,000 square kilometers of territory and 6,000,000 inhabitants and was charged with reparations totaling 132 billion gold marks. The first government after the overthrow of the monarchy was socialist and could barely keep order. The Communist Party gained followers and stirred up violence in the streets. The January 1919 elections set up the Weimar Republic, a weak, liberal government. The constitution included a clause which permitted the chancellor to rule by decree (without consulting parliament) "if public order and security are seriously disturbed or endangered..." Food was scarce and jobs scarcer. Runaway inflation destroyed the savings of the middle and upper classes.

In September 1919 Adolf Hitler joined the small German Workers Party in Munich. He was a good organizer and speaker and built up the party, changing its name to National Socialist German Workers Party, or Nazi for short. The Nazi beliefs were militaristic, nationalistic, pagan, anti-semitic, and anti-Catholic. In October 1923 the Nazis attempted to take over the government of Bavaria in the Munich Beer Hall Putsch. The attempt was thwarted, and Hitler was put into jail, where he remained for 264 days. While in jail, he wrote *Mein Kampf (My Struggle),* outlining the situation then faced by Germany and his political philosophy and strategy.

When he was released from prison, Hitler began rebuilding the Nazi Party. Gradually the Nazis made gains in the elections. Hitler used modern campaigning techniques: films, records, radio, leaflets, airplanes. Between elections, the Nazis stirred up violence against the Communists, because support for the Nazis increased as disorder increased, since the Nazis promised a strong and orderly government. The main support for the Nazis came from the middle classes, sick of the inflation of the Weimar Republic, tired of instability and disorder, and resentful of the heavy punishments inflicted upon Germany after World War I. Hitler was a powerful speaker and told the Germans what they wanted to hear: that Germany was the greatest nation in the world, that the Germans were the "master race," that Germany had been unfairly treated and should get revenge.

After the November 1932 election, in which the Nazis elected 196 deputies to the Reichstag (Germany's parliament), far from a majority, Hitler demanded of President Hindenburg that he be appointed Chancellor (the main position of power in the government) as the price of Nazi cooperation. Hindenburg gave in to Hitler, but the Nazis still didn't have the majority in the Reichstag that they needed to impose their will on the country.

On February 27, 1933, the Reichstag building burned down. A young Communist was convicted of arson and executed. Evidence has since shown that he was put up to it by the Nazis, who wanted to discredit the Communists. They succeeded. In the March 1933 election the Nazis went up to 288 deputies. Then Hitler ordered the arrest of the 81 Communist deputies. Thus the Nazis now had a majority. They proceeded to pass the *Enabling Act*, which invoked the clause in the constitution allowing the chancellor to rule by decree, by a vote of 444-94, with various other parties in the Reichstag joining in voting for it. Hitler now had essentially dictatorial powers, which he had obtained legally in accord with the constitution, a fact not often realized.

In August 1934 Hindenburg died, and Hitler merged the posts of president and chancellor. He changed the oath of allegiance taken by army officers. No longer would they swear allegiance to Germany but to Hitler personally. In an election held to ratify his assumption of total power, Hitler won by a vote of 39,000,000 to 4,300,000. Hitler was now in complete control, with the vast majority of the people behind him.

In 1937 Pope Pius XI wrote an encyclical called *Mit Brennender Sorge* (*With Burning Sorrow*), condemning Nazism. Hitler stated that he would bring the rest of Europe under his control and then turn on his last and greatest enemy: the Catholic Church.

The Spanish Civil War

When the Carlists, rightful kings of Spain, were defeated, Spain brought upon itself more suffering than it could have realized. During the first third of the twentieth century, the government was unstable and the people unhappy. In 1931 the weak, liberal King Alfonso XIII abdicated. The atheist Azana came into power. He closed Catholic schools, expelled the Jesuits from Spain, and took religious symbols off the walls of Spanish public buildings. Spain divided into two groups: the Nationalists or traditionalists, and the Republicans or revolutionaries. On the Nationalist side were the Catholic Church, most of the army, the Falange (a fascist party, which tended toward violence as a solution to problems but was strongly anti-Communist), the Carlists, and the CEDA (a moderate traditionalist party). On the Republican side were the socialists, the Communists, the anarchists, and the Syndicalists (a liberal group).

In 1933 the CEDA won the election, but scandals were uncovered which discredited the party. In 1936 the Popular Front, a combination of the leftist groups, won the elections. Under the leadership of Largo Caballero, they began attacking the Church, confiscating all religious property. Many priests and nuns were murdered with the connivance of the government. On one occasion, the leftists put a statue of the Sacred Heart before a firing squad.

As the attacks on the Church increased and the government became clearly Communist, a group of generals in the army began planning a rising against the Popular Front, or Reds as the traditionalists called them. On July 13, 1936, Calvo Sotelo, a leader of the traditionalists, was murdered by the government police. Two generals, Emilio Mola and Francisco Franco, thereupon set the date for a rising of the army against the government. On July 18, Franco issued a proclamation calling for the re-establishment of authority in Spain.

The greatest support for the rising came from the province of Navarra, a stronghold of the Carlists, where the *requetes*—the military arm of the Carlists—had been holding training sessions. Franco sent a call to Navarra for 600 men to fight the government. In just one day, 40,000 men answered the call. Throughout the Civil War 100,000 requetes were in the field at all times, fighting for the Church, for Spain and for their families. The uprising came to be called the *Cruzada*, or Crusade, because it was a holy war against Christ's enemies.

Franco and the Nationalists received aid from Nazi Germany and Mussoloni's Italy. German planes fought on the Nationalist side, and about 14,000 Italian and 7,000 German troops were involved. Franco has been severely criticized for accepting aid from Hitler. But Franco personally had no use for Hitler or Nazism. For example, when World War II broke out, Hitler held a meeting with Franco to persuade him to occupy Gibraltar, taking it away from the British and allowing the Germans to use it as a naval base to block off the Mediterranean Sea. After the meeting, Hitler said, "I would rather have all of my teeth pulled than talk to that man again." Needless to say, Hitler didn't get Gibraltar. But Franco needed to get arms and weapons from somewhere and the Germans and Italians were the only ones who would aid him.

The Republicans received arms, technicians, trainers and officers from Communist Russia, in return for two-thirds of the entire gold reserve of Spain (about $300 million). There were also the Communist International Brigades, volunteers under Communist leadership from various other countries, such as the Abraham Lincoln Brigade from the U.S. There were 20,000 troops in these Brigades in Spain in 1936 alone. The Communist involvement was made most obvious in the treatment of nuns, priests and brothers in areas held by the Republicans and in the acts of sacrilege against Catholic churches.

The war lasted for almost three years, but the battle which best symbolizes the issues of the war and how they were resolved was fought in the first three months: the *Siege of the Alcazar* in Toledo.

Toledo is an ancient city about 40 miles from Madrid. Ferdinand and Isabel had once made it their capital, and had built a great church there. The Moslems had built a fort on one of Toledo's hills, and Charles V later made the fort into a royal palace. The fort was known as the Alcazar.

When Franco issued his proclamation, the military garrison in Toledo was commanded by Colonel Jose Moscardo, a strong traditionalist. When he received a government order to send the ammunition from Toledo's munitions factory to Madrid, he delayed as long as he could, then on July 21 issued a declaration of war. The Republican troops invaded the town. Moscardo, his troops and some civilians retreated into the Alcazar where they prepared to withstand the enemy. Altogether, 1760 people were in the fort, including 211 children.

The Communists thought they could force Moscardo to surrender. On July 23 Communist leader Cabello telephoned Moscardo, saying: "I give you ten minutes to surrender the Alcazar. If you don't, I'll shoot your son Luis who is standing here beside me." Moscardo's face did not betray his feeling. "I believe you," he said.

Cabello said: "And so that you can see it's true, he will speak to you."

Luis was given the phone. Moscardo said: "What is happening, my boy?"

"Nothing," Luis answered. "They say they are going to shoot me if the Alcazar does not surrender. But don't worry about me."

"If it is true," replied Moscardo, "commend your soul to God, shout 'Viva Espana' and die like a hero. Good-bye, my son, a kiss."

"Good-bye, Papa, a very big kiss."

Then Moscardo told Cabello: "You might as well forget the ten minutes. The Alcazar will never surrender!"

As the siege went on, food supplies became lower and lower. Finally they were forced to kill and eat their horses to avoid starvation. On August 1 the Communists began a heavy bombardment of the walls. On August 4, 170 heavy shells hit the walls, on August 15, 200. By August 29, most of the north wall had been destroyed. On September 8 they again asked Moscardo to surrender. He refused and heavier bombing was ordered. Seeing the Alcazar still standing, one of the Republican leaders said, "If we had a few—just a few—like that on our side, this war would soon be over."

The Republicans then began digging a mine under the Alcazar in an attempt to blow it up. The defenders in the Alcazar could hear the digging but could do nothing because of a layer of bedrock over the mine. They evacuated everyone from the area of the mine and prayed. The Republicans announced that the mine would be exploded on the morning of September 18, and reporters from all over the world came to watch what they thought would be the fall of the Alcazar. At 6:31 A.M. the mine went off with an explosion so loud it could be heard in Madrid, 40 miles away. But because of the defenders' precautions, no one was killed. Ironically, the rubble from the explosion helped to make a new barricade protecting the Alcazar. Communist troops attacked again and again but were driven off. By 10:20 A.M. the attack had ended.

On September 25 the Nationalist troops were nearing Toledo. Franco decided to postpone his attack on Madrid to bring relief to the brave defenders of the Alcazar. On September 27 another mine was exploded, but the attack was again fought off. In the evening the Nationalists arrived and the Alcazar was saved. Ninety-two soldiers had been killed, but not a single woman or child was lost—and two babies were born during the siege.

Knowledge of the courage of the defenders of the Alcazar spread rapidly throughout Spain. It symbolized the determination of the Spanish traditionalists to fight to the death for the Church, for their country, for all the values they loved. When Franco finally marched into Madrid in March 1939 and the Republicans surrendered, the Nationalist victory was due to the kind of spirit that had inspired the men and women in the Alcazar.

After the war, Franco was again condemned because he would not enter World War II on the Allied side. But after three years of bloodshed, the last thing Spain needed was another war. After World War II, the civilized world turned against Spain and refused to provide any trade or aid.

During the post-war famine, nuns literally starved to death in their convents. But somehow Spain survived. Franco brought peace, order and prosperity to Spain and kept that peace, order and prosperity for over 35 years.

The Spanish Civil War is one of the most important events of the twentieth century. The Communists suffered a decisive defeat after having apparently achieved a complete victory. The rest of Europe, however, was not as fortunate as Spain. The Spanish had defeated atheism and dictatorship. The rest of Europe had yet to suffer from these evils. Just a few months after Spain defeated its Communist enemy, Hitler unleashed his Nazi army on Europe and World War II began.

Review Questions

1. What were the main motives of Clemenceau, Lloyd George and Wilson at the Versailles Conference?
2. How did Wilson redraw the map of Europe. What were the consequences?
3. How was Germany punished by the Versailles Treaty?
4. What were the two primary effects of the Versailles Treaty?
5. How did Charles try to regain his throne? What happened as a result?
6. What was the New Economic Policy? Why did Lenin have to develop it? How did Lenin try to destroy traditional values in Russia? How, probably, did Lenin die?
7. Describe Stalin's rule of the Soviet Union.
8. Why were Europeans dissatisfied with parliamentary democracies after World War I?
9. What is fascism? Give two examples of good fascism.
10. How did Mussoloni come to power in Italy? What did he do to gain support? What was the Lateran Treaty?
11. How did Hitler come to power in Germany? Name the encyclical condemning Nazism.
12. Describe the steps leading up to the outbreak of the Spanish Civil War. What were the two sides in the war? What role was played by the Carlists?
13. What foreign assistance did each side receive? Refute the charge that Franco was pro-Nazi because he received aid from Hitler.
14. Re-tell the story of the Siege of the Alcazar.
15. Why did the Nationalists win the Civil War? What did their victory mean for Spain?

Projects

1. Draw a map of Europe before World War I and a map of Europe after the Versailles Treaty.
2. Do a report on the League of Nations.
3. Do report on life in Russia under Stalin.
4. Imagine that you were in the Alcazar during the siege. Write a diary of your experiences.

Chapter Twenty Nine
World War II

FROM THE MOMENT he took power in 1933, Adolf Hitler knew exactly what he wanted. He would use any methods necessary, no matter how immoral. He began by violating the Versailles Treaty, secretly building up his army and navy. On March 16, 1935, Hitler openly announced that Germany would have an army of one-half million men, yet England and France did nothing. On March 7, 1936, Hitler's troops occupied the Rhineland, also forbidden by the Versailles Treaty. The German generals were prepared to withdraw at the slightest sign of French opposition, but the French did nothing. On November 1, 1936, Hitler and Mussolini signed a treaty of mutual defense. Mussolini said that Germany and Italy would be an "axis" around which the rest of Europe would revolve, and henceforth the two countries were known as the *Axis Powers*. In just four years Hitler had developed Germany into a mighty military machine and proved the weakness of the countries who should have opposed him. On November 5, 1937, Hitler told his General Staff (the leaders of the armed forces) to prepare for all-out war.

Bloodless Conquest

His first goal—which he had outlined in *Mein Kampf,* though apparently no one really believed it—was to unite all German-speaking peoples under his domination. Austria was target #1. By a combination of terrorism within Austria and threats of war, Hitler forced the Austrian Prime Minister, Schuschnigg, to sign a document giving Nazis control over the Austrian government. But Hitler wanted total military domination of the center of the old Hapsburg Empire, and he simply needed an excuse to get it. Schuschnigg provided the excuse by calling for an election to determine whether the people wanted an independent Austria or a Nazi Austria. Calling this a violation of all their agreements and an aggression against Germany, Hitler sent his troops over the border on March 13, 1938. It happened so fast that hardly a shot needed to be fired. Neither England nor France took any action, and Germany absorbed Austria.

Target #2 was Czechoslovakia, which had been carved out of the Hapsburg Empire by the Versailles Treaty. Czechoslovakia included many nationalities: Czechs, Hungarians, Slovaks. But Hitler's main concern were the three and a quarter million Germans who lived in the *Sudetenland*. He began denouncing the "oppression" of the Germans by the Czechs. In May 1938 Hitler sent his troops to the Czech border, announcing to his generals, "It is my unalterable decision to smash Czechoslovakia by military action in the near future." Great Britain and France were finally getting nervous, but those countries were afraid of doing anything that might plunge Europe into another bloody conflict like World War I.

Finally the British Prime Minister Neville Chamberlain flew to Germany several times to confer with Hitler. At the first conference he agreed that the Sudetenland should be governed by Germany. At the second he agreed that the German army could immediately march into the Sudetenland. The Czechs had been persuaded to go along with the first surrender, but at the second they balked and began mobilizing their troops. Europe was in a state of fear and suspense, with everyone assuming that general war was now inevitable. But once again Chamberlain flew to Germany, meeting Hitler at Munich. Finally on September 30 Chamberlain and the Czechs agreed that German troops could march into the Sudetenland on October 1. In return Hitler solemnly promised Chamberlain that he had no further ambitions in Europe and would demand no more territory. Chamberlain returned to London, announcing that the Munich conference had won "peace in our time." This policy of giving in to dictators is known as *appeasement.*

Czechoslovakia's independence lasted just five and a half more months. With the Sudetenland occupied Czechoslovakia was helpless against Germany. On March 15, 1939 Hitler's army occupied the rest of the country, as Hitler announced that he was protecting the people against a tyrannical government. England and France did nothing.

The War Begins

Target #3 was Poland. Hitler demanded the city of Danzig, which was German-speaking, and a highway and railway line across the Polish Corridor. In March 1939 Chamberlain, outraged by the conquest of Czechoslovakia and at last realizing that Hitler had no intention of abiding by any agreement or compromise, announced that his government would guarantee Poland's independence.

On August 23 Germany and the U.S.S.R. concluded the *Ribbentrop Pact,* an agreement that neither country would go to war against the other. This was a stab in the back to England and France, who had counted on Stalin's opposition to Nazism. But the pact was made for temporary expediency by both sides, especially Germany. Both Stalin and Hitler were evil dictators who had no respect for human life and were responsible for the deaths of millions of innocent people. England and France should have expected that the two men would come to an agreement. In return for promising to stay out of any war with Germany, Stalin was guaranteed part of Poland.

On September 1, 1939, Hitler sent his army across the Polish border in a *Blitzkrieg* (lightning war), with planes, tanks and fast-moving men. Hitler's army was so advanced and the Polish army so outdated that the Poles didn't have a chance, though they fought heroically. When Poland was almost beaten, the Soviets moved in for their share, getting half of Poland almost without firing a shot. The Communists proceeded to murder 10,000 Polish army officers in the *Katyn Forest Massacre* and to deport thousands of Poles to slave labor camps.

England and France declared war on September 3, though they gave no military assistance to the Poles. After the surrender of Poland, nothing happened for several months, except for some sea engagements as Britain blockaded the German ports. This inaction is known as the *Sitzkrieg* or phony war. But when the Blitzkrieg struck again, it proved as powerful as before. On April 9 Denmark was overrun, and a few days later, Norway, though the Norwegians put up heroic resistance. In May paratroopers conquered Holland in five days. On May 28 Belgium surrendered. At this point the German army had trapped the British troops and could have moved in to wipe them out. But Hitler was still hoping to negotiate a peace with Great Britain so that he could turn his attention elsewhere. He sent his commanding generals a secret message ordering them temporarily to hold their positions and not move in on the British army.

As Hitler sent his message, he was unaware that the British were reading it at almost the same time as the German generals. In 1939 British secret agents had smuggled out of Poland one of Germany's new code machines, which the Germans called Enigma and the British *Ultra*. Ultra was highly sophisticated, and Ultra codes would have been almost impossible to decipher. But with one of the machines in their possession, the British Intelligence Service was able to unravel the German codes. Throughout the war the British Prime Minister, Winston Churchill, and the top commanders of the Allied forces against Germany were able to read German secret messages and to know where, when and how the Germans were going to attack. Knowledge of Ultra was limited to the highest levels. Lower officers, ordinary soldiers and civilians had no more knowledge than did the Germans that the codes had been broken. Ultra was the best kept secret of the war. In fact, the Ultra secret was not revealed until 1974.

But knowledge of the German plans did not mean that the British troops were out of danger. The British government called upon civilians to supply boats to evacuate the troops from the port of *Dunkirk* on the Belgian coast. British civilians came across the English Channel manning every kind of boat—from regular navy craft to small sailboats. In four days, they evacuated 194,620 men. This heroic response by the British people saved their army.

On June 5 the Germans launched a massive attack on France. After World War I France had built a series of fortifications called the Maginot Line, which was supposedly unbreakable. But Hitler's new mechanized army ran around the line as if it weren't there. German troops occupied Paris on June 14 and hoisted the Swastika on the Eiffel Tower. On June 10 Italy attacked France, though the country was already hopelessly beaten, in order to get a share of the spoils. On June 21 Hitler met with Marshal Petain, the new premier of France, to sign the surrender treaty. Hitler insisted that the signing take place in the same railway car on the exact spot where Germany had been forced to surrender after World War I. Hitler was determined to enjoy revenge to the fullest. Petain was allowed to govern the south and southeast part of France in return for allying with Germany. Petain went along with this in order to avoid the further shedding of blood. Frenchmen who rejected this policy formed the French *Resistance Movement*, which carried on guerrilla warfare against the Nazi occupation government and Petain. Similar underground resistance movements were formed in other Nazi-occupied countries.

The Axis powers now dominated the continent of Europe, except for a few neutral countries. As at the time of Napoleon, Great Britain stood alone. Hitler tried to persuade the British government to negotiate a peace treaty, but Churchill refused absolutely, saying that Britain would fight to the death.

The Battle of Britain

Like Napoleon, Hitler began planning an invasion of Britain, which he called Operation Sea Lion. He relied on his *Luftwaffe* (Air Force) to soften up Britain for the invasion, much as Napoleon had relied on his fleet. In August 1940 the Luftwaffe began bombing British military bases, inaugurating an air war with the Royal Air Force (RAF) known as the *Battle of Britain.* Hermann Goering, head of the Luftwaffe, predicted that Germany would need two to four weeks to destroy the greatly outnumbered RAF. But he did not take into account Ultra and the heroism of the RAF pilots.

From the beginning of the Battle of Britain, Ultra signals told the British high command how many planes Goering was sending, where they were coming from and (usually) what were their targets. They also knew that Goering's strategy was to get as many RAF Spitfire planes into the air as possible so that the German Messerschmitt fighter planes could take them out of action. So the RAF commanders sent up only limited numbers of planes, thereby upsetting Goering's strategy.

From August 24 to September 6, the Germans sent over an average of a thousand airplanes a day. During this time the RAF lost 455 Spitfires and a quarter of its pilots. But then Goering made a serious tactical mistake. From attacking military targets with the goal of drawing the fighter planes into action so that they could be destroyed, he switched to the massive night bombing of London, in retaliation for an RAF bombing of Berlin. For 57 consecutive nights the bombs rained down, as Londoners hid in bomb shelters and subway tunnels. Much of the city went up in flames during the *Blitz,* as it was called. But London's sufferings gave the RAF time to get more planes into shape and to train more pilots.

Then on September 15, the Luftwaffe mounted a great daylight assault on the battered English capital. Two hundred bombers and 600 fighters flew over England. Squadron after squadron of the RAF went into the air. All day the battle raged. During the height of the battle, the Prime Minister himself came to Air Force headquarters. Churchill looked over the charts and asked: "How many reserves have we?" Air Vice Marshal Park replied: "There are none." Every single RAF squadron was in the air; no reserves were left on the ground. But the invaders were driven back.

The crippled German squadrons returned to their bases on the continent. Though no one fully realized it at the time, the Battle of Britain had been won.

Eventually even Goering had to admit that Britain was not to be conquered, and the air war died down. Said Winston Churchill of the brave men of the RAF, who with the help of Ultra had saved England: "Never has so much been owed by so many to so few."

The Invasion of Russia

After Napoleon failed to defeat England, he attacked Russia. Now Hitler did the same thing. He had intended to keep the Ribbentrop Pact only as long as it suited him to do so, and in the fall of 1940, he made up his mind that the time to break the treaty had come. He was fortified in this decision by Russian aggression during the summer. In June, the Soviet Union had taken over Estonia, Latvia and Lithuania, three small countries on the border of the U.S.S.R. The residents of these countries were not Russian, and Stalin began a vicious persecution of them. The hardest hit was Lithuania, a Catholic country where the Soviet persecution attacked the Church. Also, on June 27 the Soviet Union took over part of Rumania. This was getting too close to Germany for Hitler's comfort, so he and his generals began preparing an invasion plan of Russia, with the code name of *Operation Barbarossa.*

In the meantime, things had not been going well for the Axis powers on other fronts. Mussolini's troops had met disaster in Egypt and Greece because the Italians were poor fighters. And Spain's Franco absolutely refused to help Hitler in his conquests of the Mediterranean lands. Then a revolt in Yugoslavia overthrew a pro-Nazi government. Hitler was so furious that he postponed Barbarossa four weeks in order to teach Yugoslavia a lesson. On April 6, 1941 the Germany army smashed through Greece and into Yugoslavia in a movement known as "Operation Punishment." The Nazis wiped out the capital city of Belgrade. Yugoslavia was utterly defeated, satisfying Hitler's desire for revenge, but the delay in Barbarossa was to have deadly consequences for Germany.

As the Russian secret agents brought in information that pointed to a German invasion, Stalin refused to believe it. Surprisingly, there is evidence to show that he trusted Hitler's assurances that Germany still regarded the Soviet Union as a friend. He should have known better.

On June 22, 1941, a three-pronged German attack smashed into the Soviet Union, with armies heading for Moscow in the center, Leningrad in the north and Ukraine in the south. For the first two weeks, the Germans were successful, largely because the attack had caught the Soviet government by surprise. But the Russians were fierce fighters and had many more troops than the Germans had suspected. The Germans were fighting along a thousand-mile front and had spread themselves too thin. In the north they besieged Leningrad, in the south they won a major victory at Kiev, but in the center the weather came to the aid of the Russians. The first snows came on October 6, slowing down the tanks and supply convoys. Nevertheless by the end of November, the Germans were within 30 miles of Moscow. On December 1 they mounted an all-out attack. But the superb Russian troops aided by the freezing weather held the city. By January the Germans were retreating for the first time in the war.

Hitler was furious, blaming his generals for the defeat. He therefore took over total control of the army and began directing the war personally, though he was hundreds of miles away. He absolutely forbade the German armies to retreat any further. This led to even more casualties—by February 28 a million men had been killed or wounded. The Germans were bogged down in the snow and mud of Russia. Nevertheless the army held together—it did not fall apart as had Napoleon's—giving the Germans hope that in the spring they could successfully counterattack.

War in the Pacific

Germany and Italy were not the only Axis powers. On November 27, 1936 Germany had signed a treaty of alliance with Japan. Just as Hitler wanted to establish a German-controlled "New Order" in Europe, so Japan wanted to dominate a "Co-Prosperity Sphere" in Asia. Japan had an outstanding navy and was simply waiting for a favorable opportunity to begin its conquest of the Pacific.

On October 16, 1941 a new prime minister named Tojo came into power in Japan. He ordered preparations for a surprise attack on the United States, regarded as Japan's primary rival in the Pacific. On November 24 a Japanese carrier task force sailed for Pearl Harbor, Hawaii, the chief U.S. naval base in the Pacific. Though relations between the U.S. and Japan had been getting steadily worse, the U.S. military in Hawaii did not know an attack was coming. On December 6 a U.S. Navy intelligence report listed most of the Japanese ships in their home ports, including all the ships of the task force. On December 7 at 7:30 A.M., the Japanese planes began bombing the U.S. fleet in Pearl Harbor, taking the Americans totally by surprise, sinking five battleships and three cruisers, destroying 177 aircraft and killing 3,000. On

December 8, the U.S. declared war on Japan. On December 11 Germany declared war on the U.S., one of Hitler's most serious mistakes because it brought America into the war against Germany. On both fronts, Pacific and European, America came into the war determined to win.

Japan moved rapidly through Asia and the Pacific. On December 13 they took Guam, on December 20 Wake Island. On December 25 they took Hong Kong from the British, in January 1942 the Netherlands East Indies. On February 15 they invaded Singapore from the north in a land operation. The British couldn't even put up a defense, because all their artillery was pointed in the wrong direction—toward the sea, from where they had been sure any attack would come. On March 9 the Japanese took Java, on May 6 the Philippines. The U.S. forces there had been under the command of General Douglas MacArthur, who promised the Filipinos: "I shall return." MacArthur was supreme commander of all Allied forces in the southwest Pacific, and would eventually keep his promise.

During all this time the Japanese appeared invincible as the U.S. recovered from Pearl Harbor and geared up for war. But on May 7 the U.S. fleet repulsed the Japanese in the Battle of the Coral Sea, thereby heading off an invasion of Australia. Then came the turning point of the Pacific war: the Battle of Midway, June 4-7, 1942.

The Japanese had a powerful fleet of carriers with their best Zeroes (fighter planes) and best pilots, and the fleet steamed toward Midway Island. They believed that most of the American carriers were far away or damaged. But the U.S. had broken the Japanese code. Admiral Raymond Spruance sailed toward Midway. The fleet included the carrier *Yorktown,* one of the ships the Japanese believed out of action. Fourteen hundred men working around the clock had repaired the ship in 48 hours, though the job was supposed to take ninety days.

Nevertheless the American fleet was outnumbered, and as the battle began the American planes were shot down at an alarming rate while inflicting little damage. Three torpedo squadrons were sent out, but only four planes returned.

But the torpedo squadrons had forced the Japanese fleet out of position and left them unprepared for the next attack. Fifty-four dive bombers from the carriers *Yorktown* and *Enterprise* sank three of the big Japanese carriers; later a fourth went under. The Japanese admiral had to turn back. This was one of the greatest U.S. naval victories of the war. The Japanese momentum was stopped. The Japanese had lost their best ships, their best planes, their best pilots; they were never able to make good the losses.

Two months later the American counter-offensive against Japan began when the U.S. Marines landed on Guadalcanal in the Solomon Islands, a south Pacific group which the Japanese had conquered. The Marines hung on with superb courage against a series of fierce assaults, while control of the sea shifted from American to Japanese with each nightfall. No less than six tremendous naval battles were fought in the Solomon Islands during the next three months. So many warships of both sides were sunk off Guadalcanal that the waters there were named "Ironbottom Bay." Finally on November 15, 1942 the American battleship *Washington*, with her sister battleship and all her escort destroyers sunk or crippled, won the decisive battle and assured the Marines' victory.

Germany Begins to Falter

In the early months of 1942 in Europe, the position of Hitler still looked very strong. The Axis Powers controlled Europe. General Erwin Rommel and his Afrika Korps of tanks were pushing through North Africa toward Egypt. German troops were deep within Russia. The Allies were still on the defensive.

Then on November 19 the Soviets launched an attack, surrounding the German Sixth Army in Stalingrad (in south Russia). The German General Von Paulus begged Hitler to let the army break out of Stalingrad and join another army moving up. Hitler refused to allow them to move an inch. The winter set in. The Germans did not have enough food, medicine or winter clothing. The Soviet army offered surrender terms. Hitler refused to accept them: the army must fight to the last man and to the last bullet. On January 10 the Russians began a heavy artillery bombardment. The Germans fought heroically but hopelessly. The Russian troops moved in relentlessly, finally forcing a German surrender (against Hitler's orders) at the end of January. Only 91,000 were left out of an army that had numbered 285,000 two months earlier. These men were marched to prison camps in Siberia, and only 5,000 ever saw Germany again.

In the meantime General Rommel in Africa was within 60 miles of the Nile but could go no farther. Thanks to Ultra, the Allies were able to bomb German ships so that Rommel could not get supplies. When Rommel launched a major attack on August 31, the British commander, General Montgomery, knew the exact number of Rommel's men, tanks, guns and aircraft and where he was going to attack. Without the element of surprise, Rommel did not have a chance. On October 21 at the Battle of El Alamein, Montgomery was able, thanks to Ultra, to make a breakthrough thrust through the weakest point of Rommel's forces. El Alamein was the first major ground battle the British had won. On November 8, combined British and American troops invaded Axis-held North Africa under the command of General Dwight D. Eisenhower. The Allied troops were now on the offensive.

Though Hitler still shouted in his speeches about total victory, the noose was slowly tightening. On July 10, 1943 the Allies landed in Sicily; on July 25 Mussolini was overthrown. On September 3 the Allies landed on the mainland of Italy. The battle up the boot of Italy was long and bloody, at least partly because the Allied generals made a number of costly mistakes.

In the meantime the Allied high command planned an invasion of France. They set up a "phantom army" in England at Kent to fool the Germans into thinking that the invasion would strike at Pas de Calais instead of at Normandy. Ultra told the Allies that their ruse had worked. Ultra also told them that the Germans did not expect the attack to take place in the first week of June because of the bad weather. Their armies were totally unprepared. Therefore Eisenhower ordered the attack in spite of the weather. On June 6, 1944—*D Day*—the Allied troops poured ashore on the beaches of Normandy and pushed deep into France. On June 20, Russia also launched an offensive, moving into Europe from the east.

A small group of Germans now decided that defeat was inevitable and therefore the best thing they could do for the country they loved was to assassinate Hitler, take over the government and negotiate a peace treaty with England and America, thereby freeing their armies to fight the Communist forces. This was not the first opposition to Hitler. The Kreisau Circle, a group of young Christians, had met regularly to plan for Germany of the future so that evils such as Nazism would not recur, but they were arrested and killed. Admiral Canaris, chief of German intelligence, used his high position to work against Hitler secretly and saved the lives of some intended victims of concentration camps. But none of the anti-Hitler groups had the really strong leadership they needed.

The leadership finally came from a Bavarian Catholic, Count Klaus von Stauffenberg, a brilliant young colonel in the German army who had lost an eye and a hand in the war. The assassination attempt was scheduled for July 20 when Stauffenberg was to be with Hitler at Regensberg. He carefully prepared a time bomb in his briefcase, carried it into the conference room, and put the briefcase by a table leg near Hitler's chair. The bomb was set to go off in ten minutes. As the time ticked away, Stauffenberg invented an excuse to leave the room. After he left, another German officer got up to look at some papers which Hitler was discussing. The briefcase was in his way. He moved it to the other side of a thick oak table leg. When the bomb went off, causing great damage, Hitler was protected by the oak. He was wounded but still alive.

Nevertheless, the plot might still have succeeded overall, if Stauffenberg's friends in Berlin had moved at once to seize the government. But they did not. They wandered around the city, waiting for definite word that Hitler was dead. Stauffenberg flew back to Berlin, sure that Hitler was dead and expecting the city to be in the hands of his friends. He found that nothing whatever had been done.

Stauffenberg and the others were arrested and brutally killed. No other serious attempts occurred to take over the government, largely because of the policy announced by Britain and America: the Allied governments would not negotiate a peace treaty with any German government but insisted on unconditional surrender. The Hitler regime had still another year to live, at the cost of great suffering for the people of Europe.

Victory in Europe

The Allied offensive went on. General George Patton, a daring tank commander, won victory after victory in France and Belgium. American and British pilots began the deadly policy of *saturation bombing*—wiping out the homes and working places of German civilians as a means of terrorizing Germany into ending the war.

But Hitler had one more card to play. He intended to gamble everything in the west on one massive offensive, hoping that a resounding German victory would convince the Allies to stop fighting. The German general in command, von Rundstedt, did not use Ultra machines to send his messages, relying instead on more old-fashioned methods such as field telephones. As a result the December 12 attack caught the Allies totally by surprise. General Eisenhower should have known better. The Germans launched their offensive through the Ardennes Forest, the same place where offensives had been launched in the Franco-Prussian War and World War I. The Battle of the Bulge, as it was known, was one of the bloodiest of the war. But after the initial surprise, the Allies were able to stop the offensive and push the Germans back. The Germans suffered 120,000 casualties, the Americans 56,000. But the Americans were able to make good their losses. The Germans had nothing left.

On the Eastern Front, the Russians were driving toward Germany. The Communist leaders had another goal besides defeating Germany. They intended to ensure Soviet domination of Eastern Europe after the war. In Hungary, Czechoslovakia, Poland, Yugoslavia, Rumania and Bulgaria, Communists were actively at work. In most of these countries anti-Communist movements opposed any attempt to replace one tyranny (Nazism) with another (Communism). The fate of these countries depended largely on Great Britain and America. British Prime Minister Churchill and American President Franklin Roosevelt agreed to give Stalin a free hand in Eastern Europe in exchange for his continued cooperation with them. As a result, the brave anti-Communist movements were crushed. The Communists established themselves in power by brutality and terror every bit as ruthless as that of the Nazis.

By April 15, 1945, Berlin alone remained under Nazi control. The sound of the Russian guns could be heard in the distance. Hitler and a few companions retired to an underground bunker. Hitler could not face the prospect of defeat. On April 30 he shot himself. He had been Chancellor of Germany for twelve years and three days, after having proclaimed a Thousand Year Reich (empire). The Reich lasted one more week. At 2:41 on May 7, what was left of the German High Command surrendered unconditionally to General Eisenhower.

Victory in the Pacific

In the meantime, Japan had been steadily driven back in the Pacific after the Battle of Midway and the hard-fought struggle for Guadalcanal. Finally the islands of Saipan, Tinian and Guam were taken, close enough to be used as bases to bomb the Japanese homeland. On June 16, 1944 the American bombing of Japan began; on June 19 and 20 the Japanese aircraft carriers struck back. In the Battle of the Philippine Sea, the Japanese lost 40 ships and 405 aircraft, and their naval air force was never again a threat in the war.

On October 20, 1944 General MacArthur kept his promise to the American and Filipino people by returning to the Philippines in command of a mighty American landing force. Four days later what was left of the Japanese navy challenged the landings. Since they now had almost no carrier planes, the Japanese admirals cleverly used their empty carriers as decoys to draw the invincible American carriers far away from the landing beaches. Then the Japanese attacked with their battleships and cruisers. Only a handful of planes and three small destroyers remained to protect the American landing force. In the all-day Battle of Leyte Gulf, this tiny force fought magnificently. All three U.S. destroyers were sunk. But the Japanese admiral could not believe that so few Americans would have dared to counter-attack him unless they had strong support close by. He turned back and sailed for home, and the Philippines were regained.

In February and March 1945 the U.S. Marines fought a bloody battle for Iwo Jima island. At a cost of almost 20,000 casualties, the Marines took the island and left a deathless memory when they raised the American flag atop Mount Suribachi. This scene is commemorated in the U.S. Marine Memorial in Arlington, Virginia. In April 1945 the Americans took Okinawa, giving them another air base, this one just 325 miles from Japan.

Some members of the Japanese government now wished to arrange peace terms with the Americans. But the Americans would not discuss any terms, insisting on unconditional surrender. This the Japanese refused, and the fighting went on.

Because of the unconditional surrender policy, it appeared that the war must end with an American invasion of Japan, fighting the Japanese yard by yard for their homeland. But President Harry Truman, who had taken office after Franklin D. Roosevelt died in April, had been advised that the most devastating weapon in all history had been developed by the United States: the atomic bomb. This seemed a sure way to force Japan to surrender. After agonizing over the morality of using a weapon which would inevitably incinerate tens of thousands of innocent civilians, Truman ordered a note to be sent to the Japanese demanding unconditional surrender, and adding "the alternative is prompt and utter destruction." The note made no mention of the atomic bomb or where and when this destruction would be visited upon the people.

On August 6, 1945 the atomic bomb was dropped on Hiroshima, killing more than 100,000 people, mostly civilians. An accurate count could never be made because of the total destruction. Near "ground zero" the bomb killed with such incredible power that nothing was left of the bodies of the people whom its shock wave struck but their outlines traced on concrete.

On the same day, the Soviet Union declared war on Japan to seize territory with little cost to itself, proceeding to overrun Manchuria. The Japanese government met to decide what to do. Before they reached a decision, a second atomic bomb was dropped August 9 on Nagasaki, the most Catholic city in Japan, with the same horrible results. Emperor Hirohito, who like most emperors in Japanese history had always been a figurehead rather than a real ruler, for once exerted his authority and ordered the Japanese surrender on the sole condition that he would be allowed to keep his title as emperor. The United States accepted his offer August 14, and on September 2 the Japanese signed the surrender document in the presence of General MacArthur on the U.S. battleship *Missouri* in Tokyo Bay. World War II was over.

The longest lasting result of World War II was the Communist take-over of Eastern Europe. Without the war and Allied agreements with Russia, the Communists almost certainly would not have been able to bring the people of Eastern Europe under their domination.

The Holocaust

One particularly horrifying aspect of the Nazi tyranny was the extermi-nation camps at Belsen, Dachau, Auschwitz and elsewhere, where millions of innocent people had been murdered. The primary victims were the Jews, whom Hitler regarded as subhuman and a threat to the purity of the German race. But many others were mercilessly killed, as well. In every country that Germany conquered, victims were rounded up. Some were forced to work until they could work no more and then killed, and others were killed upon arrival. The conditions were inhuman—little food, no medical care, inadequate shelter, torture. When the Allies reached some of the camps, the survivors were little more than living skeletons. But the brutality of the camps also brought out great heroism in many of the inmates as Christ and Satan warred for souls.

One story will illustrate both the evil and the good in the death camps. A Polish Franciscan priest named Maximilian Kolbe had been captured by the Nazis and imprisoned in Auschwitz, one of the worst of the death camps. Priests were given the hardest work and regularly lashed with horse-whips. The inmates were constantly hungry, and the winter cold ate into their bones. Father Maximilian was never heard to complain. In spite of threats of punishment, he heard confessions all night long.

Near the end of July 1941, the Germans found a prisoner missing in Father Maximilian's cellblock. The inmates were ordered to stand in the burning sun for hours with nothing to drink. Then the commandant an-nounced: "The fugitive has not been found. Ten of you will die for him in the starvation bunker." He went down the line, dragging out ten men to die. One of them cried: "Oh, my poor wife, my poor children, whom I will never see again." Suddenly Father Maximilian rushed to the commandant whispering to him, "I would like to die in place of the man who has a wife and children." The commandant could scarcely believe it. He hesitated. "All right. Go with them."

Father Maximilian and the other nine were thrown into the starvation bunker. From that moment on they were allowed nothing to eat or drink. But instead of the cries of anguish that usually came from the bunkers, the guards heard singing—hymns led by Father Maximilian. Finally, on the eve of the Assumption, only four prisoners were left. A guard entered, to inject the survivors with carbolic acid to kill them to make room for more victims. Father Maximilian stretched out his fleshless arm. He died in peace, his face shining with love for Christ. The man he saved lived to return to his family, and Father Kolbe has been canonized by the Church.

The Nazi extermination of Jews and others (sometimes referred to as the Holocaust) has given rise to an attack on the Catholic Church in general and Pope Pius XII in particular. The Pope is attacked for not explicitly condemning the Holocaust and thereby being in a way responsible for the deaths of millions of Jews.

But the facts of history show that the Pope was working against the Nazis and for the benefit of the Jews and that his decisions were beneficial to Christians and Jews alike, more beneficial in fact that an outright condemnation of the Holocaust.

Pope Pius XII was an experienced diplomat and did everything he could to forestall the war. After the invasion of Poland and the institution of persecution there, Pius XII wrote *Summi Pontificatus,* denouncing the deification of the state and recourse to arms. Heydrich forbade publication of the encyclical in Nazi-held territories. Pius XII also permitted Vatican Radio and *L'Osservatore Romano* (the official Vatican newspaper) to inform the world of Nazi atrocities in Poland. The persecution of the Church there was much worse than in Germany, and the Nazis wouldn't let Vatican officials conduct relief work in Poland.

In Germany, convents and monasteries were being closed, Catholic publications and organizations suppressed. The Nuncio in Berlin was forbidden permission to visit POW camps.

Thus we can clearly see that the Vatican and the Nazis were totally opposed to one another and that the Vatican made its assessment of Hitler clear. No explicit condemnation of persecution of Jews as such had been issued, but no objective observer could have any doubts as to where the Church stood.

But Pius XII was to do more than that. In his Christmas 1942 message, the Pope clearly condemned persecution based on race, and he condemned Nazi statism and the denial of individual worth. The Jews were not mentioned by name, but the message was clear. In April 1943 the Pope issued a message to the Slovak government condemning persecution of Jews specifically. In April 1944, Hungary, which was allied with the Axis, was told to round up Hungarian Jews. The Pope issued a strong statement condemning the action, and the Hungarian government refused to carry out the order.

But the Pope did far more than issue statements. When Adolf Eichmann ordered a death march of 20,000 Jews from Budapest to Theresienstadt for extermination, Cardinal Seredi and the Papal Nuncio organized relief vehicles to accompany marchers with food and medicine. They carried several thousand blank papal safe conduct passes and rescued about 2000 Jews. The Nuncio personally hid 200 Jews in his palace. Pius XII instructed churches, monasteries, and convents in Rome to take in Jews. These were extra-territorial property of the Vatican which the Italian police could not enter. Altogether, 55 monasteries and 100 convents in Rome were hiding Jews. Many Jews found refuge in the Vatican itself, including Dr. Zolli, the Chief Rabbi of Rome, who became a Catholic after the war. The Pope sent letters by hand to Italian bishops calling upon them to hide and rescue Jews. One of the main cities where this was done was Assisi, where the Franciscans coordinated hiding of Jews disguised as religious in cloisters, and printed false identity papers for them enabling them to escape past the American lines. In Italy, in fact, the majority of Jews were saved. The Pope also set up Delasem, an organization for assistance to foreign Jews. Four thousand received aid from this organization.

To put the Pope's actions in perspective, here is a statement by a Jewish leader, Pinchas E. Lapids, Israeli Consul in Italy: "The Catholic Church saved more Jewish lives during the war than all the other churches, religious institutions and rescue organizations put together. Its record stands in startling contrast to the achievements of the International Red Cross and the Western Democracies . . . The Holy See, the Nuncios and the entire Catholic Church saved some 400,000 Jews from certain death."

Thus Catholics need not be ashamed or apologetic, but, rather, proud of the Pope's stature as a moral leader.

Review Questions

1. List Hitler's violations of the Versailles Treaty.

2. Describe Hitler's two bloodless conquests.
3. What was the Ribbentrop Pact?
4. Describe the conquest of Poland, including the part played by the Soviet Union.
5. What was the Sitzkrieg? What countries did Hitler conquer immediately after the Sitzkrieg ended? Describe the rescue at Dunkirk.
6. What was Ultra? Summarize its significance throughout the entire war.
7. Describe the conquest of France and the terms Hitler made with Marshal Petain. What were the resistance forces?
8. Describe the Battle of Britain. Why did the British win?
9. Why did Hitler delay the invasion of Russia? Why was this a mistake?
10. Describe the initial months of the Russian campaign.
11. What happened at Pearl Harbor? What was the result?
12. What happened at Midway? Why is it called the turning point of the war?
13. Describe the battle at Guadalcanal.
14. What happened at Stalingrad? At El Alamein?
15. What was the first Allied offensive in Europe? The second?
16. What was D-Day? How were the Germans fooled?
17. What was the purpose of the Stauffenberg conspiracy? Why did it fail?
18. What was saturation bombing? What happened at the Battle of the Bulge?
19. What happened as the Russians moved toward Germany?
20. Describe the last days of the Third Reich.
21. What happened at the Battle of Leyte Gulf?
22. Why did the United States decide to drop the atomic bomb? Why was this decision not necessarily correct?
23. What happened after the atomic bombs were dropped?
24. What were the extermination camps? Tell the story of the martyrdom of Maximilian Kolbe.
25. Summarize the evidence that Pius XII was not indifferent to the fate of the Jews.

Projects

1. Prepare a series of maps of World War II, showing the various stages in the war and locating the most important battles both in Europe and the Pacific.

2. Choose one of the events of this chapter, do research on it, and write an account as if you had been an eyewitness. (Some suggestions: Battle of Britain, Battle of Stalingrad, Munich conference, Hitler's suicide, Stauffenberg's attempt to assassinate Hitler).

3. Prepare a mural on poster paper illustrating each phase of the Second World War, from Hitler's military buildup to the surrender of Japan.

4. Write a biography of one of the important figures from World War II.

Chapter Thirty
The Modern World

WORLD WAR II HAD ENDED in the searing heat of the atomic bomb and the fire in Hitler's bunker. But though much of Europe had been devastated, the prevailing mood was hopeful because of the apparent cordiality existing among the victorious Allied powers: the United States, Great Britain and the Soviet Union. No Versailles Conference was needed after World War II. Instead the "Big Three," as they were called, had worked out agreements at conferences during the war. The world looked forward to postwar cooperation as smooth as the cooperation during the war.

Postwar Europe

In February 1945, shortly before the war ended, U.S. President Franklin Roosevelt, British Prime Minister Winston Churchill and Soviet dictator Josef Stalin had met in the shabby, disease-ridden town of Yalta in southern Russia. Stalin was a clever and strong-willed man, able to exert great influence over Roosevelt, who at this time was quite ill, and even over Churchill, who normally was extremely strong-willed himself. Roosevelt was also under the influence of one of his advisers, Alger Hiss, who was later proved to be a member of the Communist Party.

At the *Yalta Conference* Roosevelt and Churchill agreed to give Russia a dominant influence over Poland and Eastern Europe, in return for Stalin's help in winning the war against Japan and for his support of the United Nations. It was not a very fair trade. Great Britain had originally gone to war against Germany to preserve Poland's independence. Now its independence was being given away, along with the freedom of other Eastern European peoples. At the same time, the Soviet Union was not needed to defeat Japan—in fact Stalin declared war against Japan only eight days before she surrendered. And though the U.S.S.R. joined the United Nations, that organization proved no more effective at keeping peace in the world than had the League of Nations and ended up as little more than a very expensive and highly-publicized joke.

After Germany surrendered, it was divided into four zones, one each occupied by Great Britain, France, the United States and the Soviet Union. Each of the four occupying powers was to prepare its zone for elections and a new government for all of Germany at an early date. But the Soviet leaders soon made it very clear that they had no intention of allowing Germany to be reunited. The Kremlin declared that their zone, which came to be known as East Germany, was an independent nation. In fact it was under Soviet domination. The other Allies held elections in their zones in 1946, and the Christian Democrat Party, under the leadership of Konrad Adenauer, won control of the government, eventually forming the German Federal Republic, or West Germany, as it was commonly known. Adenauer was an able leader and led devastated West Germany to renewed prosperity, as strong hostility grew up between West and East Germany.

Hopes for an early reunification of Germany collapsed in July 1948, when the Communists began the *Berlin Blockade.* The old German capital had also been divided into four occupation zones, even though it was in East German territory. The Communists halted all rail and road traffic into West Berlin, hoping to starve it into submission. But the U.S. refused to give in. Day after day, airplanes flew into the besieged city, bringing food, medicine and fuel. The Communists had no way of stopping the airlift, short of war, and eventually had to end the blockade, in May 1949. But this eliminated any hope for cooperation between the Soviet Union and the United States in Europe.

The Communists also attempted to extend their influence over Greece and Turkey in 1947 by starting civil wars in those two countries. But President Truman announced the *Truman Doctrine* (also known as *containment*) of supplying economic and military aid to countries threatened by Communist take-overs. Thanks to this help, the revolutionaries in both Greece and Turkey were defeated and the independence of those nations safeguarded.

The confrontation between the Western and Communist worlds came to be known as the *Cold War*. Though it did not involve actual shooting between the U.S. and the U.S.S.R., the U.S. government in general opposed Communism and tried to prevent the Soviet Union from increasing its power.

Postwar Asia

The Yalta Conference had also taken up the question of the territories conquered by Japan in Asia. Again to obtain Stalin's cooperation, the Soviet Union was promised control over many of these Asian territories, including Manchuria and North Korea. Stalin's goal was to guarantee a victory for the Chinese Communist forces seeking to control all of China.

In 1912 the old Chinese emperor had been overthrown, and men strongly influenced by western ideas of democracy had attempted to set up a liberal, parliamentary government. This proved unworkable and chaos soon resulted. Out of the chaos two leaders emerged: Mao Tse-tung, leading the Communists, and Chiang Kai-shek, a Christian anti-Communist who controlled the government (Nationalist) forces. In 1927 civil war broke out between the Communists and Nationalists, who fought each other for almost 25 years.

Throughout the late 1930s and during World War II, Chiang and his men fought valiantly against the Japanese. After Pearl Harbor, Chiang's spirited defense of China against Japan's aggression helped give the U.S. time to rebuild its shattered fleet. Mao and his Communists gave some help against Japan, but more often turned their guns against the Nationalists.

After the war and as a result of the Yalta Conference, the Soviet Union was in a position to pour aid into China for the Communists. Worn down by twenty years of fighting the Communists and the Japanese, Chiang needed U.S. help to carry on. But in the U.S., the climate of opinion was being turned against Chiang. Harry Dexter White, a Communist sympathizer who had an important position in the Treasury Department, undermined U.S. economic aid to Chiang. Some members of the State Department were strongly sympathetic to Mao and did everything they could to see that the U.S. gave as little support as possible to Chiang. Many articles and books were written condemning Chiang and praising Mao. As a result the U.S. gradually ceased its aid to Chiang and the Nationalists.

The situation of the Nationalists became steadily worse. In some battles their soldiers had only three or four cartridges each. Once, a division of soldiers coming to the front to relieve another division had to take the retiring soldiers' rifles because they had none of their own.

On January 21, 1949 Peking fell. In October 1949 the Communists proclaimed the People's Republic of China, with Mao as dictator. By the end of 1949, the Nationalists were driven to the island of Taiwan, where they set up the free Chinese government.

The Nationalist government was accused by its enemies in the U.S. of being undemocratic and unliberal. It probably was. But it was not cruel and oppressive and seems to have had the support of the people. The Communist government, once in power, slaughtered hundreds of thousands of people, outlawed the practice of religion, persecuted both native Christians and foreign missionaries, and set up a brutal dictatorship.

The Korean War

The Chinese Communists had total control of China by January 1950. In June the North Koreans, with weapons and ammunition supplied by the Soviet Union and Red China, launched an invasion of South Korea. Korea, an Asian peninsula, had been under Japan's control until the end of World War II. Then, like Germany, it was divided, with the Communists controlling North Korea and South Korea becoming independent, though closely allied to the United States. When North Korea launched its unprovoked attack on the South, it came as a complete surprise to everyone in the U.S. We had an unprepared, untrained army because our government had counted on peace. The soldiers sent first into Korea had been stationed on Japan, where they had but one week of training a year.

The U.S. Army was easily defeated by the North Koreans, who drove them back through Korea until they held only a small area around the southern port of Pusan (the Pusan Perimeter). At this point, the troop ships carrying the First Marine Division finally arrived. All the way over from the U.S., the Marines had been making bets as to whether they would get to Korea before the war had ended with a total U.S. defeat.

They were in time. Under the overall command of General Douglas MacArthur, the Marines launched an amphibious landing at Inchon in September. They outflanked the Communists and retook the capital city of Seoul, driving the Communists out of South Korea.

Then MacArthur made the biggest mistake of his long career. He overconfidently assumed that the war could quickly and easily be won and sent his troops racing into North Korea, where they spread themselves much too thinly. In December the Red Chinese came into the war, throwing their battle-tested troops against the greatly outnumbered Americans.

The First Marine Division found itself cut into five pieces, outnumbered ten to one.

But the Marines were not quitters. Fighting courageously against the bitter North Korean winter as well as against the Red Chinese armies, they fought their way out of the trap. One group marched two nights and a day through 24 degrees below zero weather to defeat a Red Chinese unit. The Marines evacuated their forces, bringing out all their wounded, with only 7,500 casualties as compared to 37,400 for the Communists. Four Red Chinese armies were completely eliminated as effective fighting forces by this one Marine division.

After this heroic march, the war settled down and neither side gained any significant new territory. Truce talks opened at Panmunjom on October 25, 1951, where it soon became obvious that both sides were willing to let the boundary between North and South Korea be where it had been when the war began. But the American negotiators insisted that prisoners of war on either side should not be forced to return to their homeland unless they wanted to go. The Red Chinese would not agree to this because a vast majority of the Chinese soldiers captured by the U.S. absolutely refused to return to Red China. At the same time, in spite of strenuous efforts to brainwash and propagandize U.S. soldiers, the Red Chinese were unable to persuade more than a handful of their prisoners to remain with them.

The U.S. would not back down on the prisoner-of-war issue. At last, in July 1953, the Communists gave in and signed the peace treaty. Most of the Chinese prisoners of war went to Taiwan.

The Korean War was a high point of the Cold War and represented that whole struggle. Like the Cold War, the Korean War began because the U.S. did not take seriously the Communist threat, but once it started the U.S. firmly opposed this aggression and fought the Communists to a standstill. This was also the result of the Cold War as a whole, as neither side significantly increased its territory or its influence.

Anti-Communism in the United States

Meanwhile, a series of events made it clear that Communism was also a threat within the United States. In 1948 a committee of the House of Representatives, called the House Un-American Activities Committee (HUAC), began a series of hearings on Communist espionage in the United States government, gradually uncovering the fact that a number of Communists or Communist sympathizers had held high positions in the

452

Roosevelt administration. The star witness was a man named Whittaker Chambers.

Himself a former Communist who had come to realize its evil and been converted to Christianity, Chambers revealed the names of several other Communists with whom he had been associated. One of the men he accused was Alger Hiss, who had been active at the Yalta Conference and was highly regarded by most important people in government, the universities and the media. Hiss absolutely denied ever having been a Communist. But Chambers' testimony could not be contradicted, and he clinched the case by producing the Pumpkin Papers—copies of secret documents which Hiss had made and which Chambers had temporarily hidden in a pumpkin. Hiss was eventually convicted for perjury and sentenced to prison. But Chambers had a larger goal than simply seeing Hiss in jail. He wanted to show the American people the evil of Communism and its drive to destroy all Christian values. His autobiography, *Witness*, was widely read and revealed to many people the true nature of Communism.

In 1949 came the exposure of an atom spy ring which had sold U.S. nuclear secrets to the Soviet Union. The Communists had learned of our discoveries in atomic weaponry almost as soon as we did, and were able to develop the atomic bomb much sooner than they otherwise would have.

It was clear, then, that the threat of Communism within the United States was very real. So when in 1950 a little known senator from Wisconsin, Joseph McCarthy, announced that large numbers of Communists were still in the government, many people believed him and supported his drive to expose these traitors.

McCarthy was an Irish-German Catholic who saw Communism not as an isolated evil but as part of the liberalism which had been the enemy of Christianity since the eighteenth century. But he was not an intellectual and tended to react emotionally, without always thinking clearly. Thus he gave his enemies an opening to attack him. Liberals in the press and the universities, who were not themselves Communists but had been friendly to those who were, launched a counterattack, accusing McCarthy of creating a "climate of fear" in the U.S., of trying to suppress free speech, of "character assassination." They coined a word, "McCarthyism," to mean any kind of attack on the character and decency of others. Yet by far the worst attacks were against McCarthy himself. And though his enemies said that he had made everyone in America afraid to speak out, they weren't the least bit afraid to call McCarthy a monster, insane, a threat to the United States.

At the Army-McCarthy hearings in 1954, the Army's lawyer, Joseph Welch, knew how to make McCarthy look as bad as possible. Welch distracted attention from the actual facts of Communist infiltration in the Army to McCarthy's own personality and the not always prudent way he handled investigations. Added to this were the hostile television commentators and newspaper stories. McCarthy never had a chance.

After the hearings, McCarthy's support went down. His own colleagues in the Senate turned against him, voting to censure (condemn) him. McCarthy was crushed. He had tried to do his best for his country but everyone turned against him. He went into a deep depression and took to drinking too much. He died on May 2, 1957, the victim of an irrational hatred which had not entirely disappeared even twenty years later.

The Hungarians Fight for Freedom

The destruction of McCarthy was a signal that anti-Communism was not as strong in the U.S. as it should have been. Nevertheless many people hoped that Dwight Eisenhower, elected President in 1952 and re-elected in 1956, might support a policy of liberation (helping to free countries from Communism) rather than mere containment (not letting them take over new countries). This hope was tested in a crucial situation in 1956.

The situation arose in Hungary, which had been brutally oppressed by the Communists since the end of World War II. But the Communists could not crush the Hungarian spirit. Eighty-five per cent Catholic, the Hungarians held fast to dreams of freedom, eager to fight their oppressors if given a chance.

The chance came on October 23, 1956. In the capital city of Budapest, Hungarians had been peacefully demonstrating in front of the radio station, protesting the station's refusal to broadcast their 16-point memorandum demanding governmental reform. The police opened fire with machine guns. The people exploded with all of the anger and frustration of the past ten years. Hungarians, soon to be named *Freedom Fighters*, toppled the gigantic statue of Stalin, captured the radio station, and cut the Soviet symbol out of Hungarian flags.

Erno Gero, First Secretary of the Hungarian Communist Party, was shocked when the army and the police both openly sided with the Freedom Fighters. He called in Soviet troops and at 5:00 A.M. on October 24, Hungarians in Budapest awakened to the rumble of tanks in the streets. To try to fool the Freedom Fighters into capitulating, Gero re-established the popular Imre Nagy as premier. But Nagy had no power, being surrounded by secret police with submachine guns.

For several days the Freedom Fighters held their own against unequal odds. They developed ingenious new methods of anti-tank warfare. Teenagers put bolts of silk, soaked in oil, in the streets. When the tanks were unable to move in the mess, they would run out and smear jam on the windshields. Colonel Pal Maleter, sent to break up a rebellion in the army barracks, was so impressed by the Freedom Fighters' convictions that he joined them.

The Communists retaliated savagely, firing into crowds of unarmed civilians. But the people only fought harder. In Moscow, Premier Khrushchev realized that continued fighting could spark uprisings in other East European countries. Gero was removed from office, Nagy was given permission to set up a new government, including non-Communists, and the Russian tanks began to withdraw.

The people danced in the streets. Nagy, though a Communist, was also a patriot. He saw this concession by the Kremlin as a chance to gain independence for Hungary. On October 30 he announced that he would hold free elections, which would have been Hungary's first under Communist rule. That evening, Maleter, grim and shaken, told Nagy: "I have to report that Soviet armored units are invading Hungary in large numbers ..."

Nagy refused to back down. The next day he prepared two declarations: that Hungary would leave the Warsaw Pact (the so-called treaty which gave the Soviet Union control over the Eastern European countries) and that Hungary would declare its neutrality. Knowing that Hungary alone couldn't withstand Communist pressure, he called on United Nations Secretary-General Dag Hammarskjold for assistance. But the U.N. paid no attention to Nagy's plea. Just the day before, French and English planes had bombed Suez in an action against Egypt, which had threatened to block off the Suez Canal. All the attention of the world turned to the Middle East, away from the valiant Hungarians struggling desperately for freedom.

At 4:00 A.M. on November 4, Russian tanks began an all-out attack. The Nagy government issued a frantic broadcast: "Please tell the world of the treacherous attack against our struggle for liberty. Our troops are already engaged in fighting. Help! Help! Help!" No one listened. The Russians issued an order: "Conquer or exterminate." The Hungarians rose to new heights of heroism. Thirty-two students formed a barricade around a statue of St. Imre, patron saint of Hungarian youth, which stood at an important street juncture. Armed only with sub-machine guns, Molotov cocktails and a few cans of gasoline, they held up two Soviet columns for eight hours, destroying five Russian tanks before the last boy died. Twenty men and women, armed only with stones and sticks, rushed an armored car after the Soviets in it killed a boy of six. Eight Soviet soldiers were left dead or badly wounded, and the armored car was wrecked. But the odds were impossibly unequal, and the cries for help went out to the West: "In the name of all honest Hungarians we appeal to all honest men in the world. Do you love liberty? So do we. Do you have wives and children? So have we. We have wounded who have given their blood for the sacred cause of liberty, but we have no bandages, no medicines. The last piece of bread has been eaten. In the name of all that is dear to you, we ask you to help." A special message went to President Eisenhower: "We ask for immediate intervention, immediate intervention."

Nothing whatever was done. Said Eisenhower: "Hungary couldn't be reached by any of the U.S. or U.N. units without traversing neutral territory. Unless the major nations of Europe would, without delay, ally themselves spontaneously with us (an unimaginable prospect) we could do nothing. Sending troops into Hungary through hostile or neutral territory would have involved us in a general war." All the U.N. could manage was a resolution calling on the Soviet Union to stop interfering in Hungary's affairs. It was, of course, ignored.

The Soviets leveled Budapest. At one of the last garrisons, the Kilian Barracks, only 40 Freedom Fighters remained by November 7. The Soviets promised them safe passage if they would surrender. Out they marched, heads held high: teenage boys, blood seeping through their bandages; two men on crutches made of old window frames; a girl helping a wounded man. As the gates banged shut behind them, the Soviet machine gunners clicked back their magazines. The Hungarians were massacred.

Hungary lost its finest men and women. Hundreds were killed, thousands more sent to slave labor camps in Siberia. Two hundred thousand fled to Austria, wading through icy swamps to escape. Nagy was arrested, after being promised safe passage, and executed. Janos Kadar was placed in power, taking orders directly from Moscow. The Hungarian uprising was totally and brutally crushed, and the world knew—whether or not the United States admitted it—that the U.S. could not be relied upon to help bring freedom to nations living under Communist rule.

From Containment to Detente

Having rejected a policy of liberation, the U.S. government soon began moving away even from containment, and the Communists began moving to increase the territory they controlled.

In January 1960, Cuba fell to the Communists. Cuban exiles attempted to regain their island's freedom in 1961, thinking they had U.S. support, but the support was inadequate; the attempt failed. Brazil, however, overthrew a pro-Communist government in 1964, and Chile overthrew the Communist government of Salvador Allende in 1973.

Also in 1961, the citizens of Berlin woke one August morning to find a concrete wall topped with barbed wire down the middle of their city. The Soviets had erected the *Berlin Wall* to prevent further escapes into West Germany. Later they built vicious and deadly traps all along the border between East and West Germany. The U.S. did nothing about this outrage. The West German government under the liberal Willy Brandt eventually recognized the independence of East Germany and renounced even the desire of reunification.

But perhaps the most tragic confrontation of Communists and anti-Communist forces at this time came in Vietnam. Communist guerrillas under the leadership of Ho Chi Minh (a lifelong Communist and a personal friend of Lenin, Stalin and Mao) had been active in the Indochina peninsula during and after World War II. The French, who had moved into Indochina during the days of imperialism, were finally forced to withdraw in 1954 when their fortress of Dienbienphu fell after a prolonged siege. At the Geneva conferences following the French defeat, Laos and Cambodia were given their independence and Vietnam was divided into the Communist North and the free South. Many observers expected South Vietnam soon to fall to Communism, but under the strong and able leadership of Ngo Dinh Diem, a committed Catholic, the South Vietnamese government and economy were stabilized, thousands of refugees from the North were successfully absorbed, and the Communist guerrillas (Viet Cong) were resisted. Diem received military aid and advisers from the United States, but all the fighting was done by South Vietnamese.

Realizing that Diem's government was not going to collapse, the Communists developed a new strategy. They began anti-Diem agitation, accusing him of being oppressive and undemocratic and of persecuting the Buddhists in South Vietnam. The American mass media gave publicity to this agitation, especially stressing Diem's refusal to hold elections, but without pointing out that Viet Cong terrorism in the countryside would make truly free elections impossible. Eventually Communist agitators persuaded some misguided Buddhist monks that the only way they could save their country from Diem was to commit public suicide by burning themselves to death as a protest. These suicides were given wide coverage in American newspapers and on television. Liberal advisers in the administration of U.S. President John Kennedy persuaded him that Diem must be ousted. U.S. officials in Vietnam encouraged discontented generals in the South Vietnamese army to overthrow Diem, which they did on November 2, 1963. In the course of the coup, Diem and his brother were murdered, after being promised safe conduct out of Vietnam.

Without Diem's firm hand, the South Vietnamese government fell into chaos. For the next two years, there was an average of one new government every two months. As Communists stepped up military activity, the South was increasingly unable to meet it effectively. Kennedy's successor, Lyndon Johnson (Kennedy had been himself assassinated November 22, 1963) ordered massive U.S. bombing of North Vietnam, and then in June 1965 U.S. ground troops arrived in South Vietnam. Soon there were half a million U.S. servicemen fighting in Vietnam.

In the U.S., opposition to involvement in the war erupted into violence especially on college and university campuses. Though the cause was certainly just—helping save the South Vietnamese from Communism—liberals in the press and on the campuses confused the issue and convinced large numbers of Americans that we had no business being in Vietnam. The mass media was even able to portray U.S. victories in early 1968 as defeats. The opposition became so violent that Johnson opened peace negotiations and began troop withdrawals, which were continued by his successor, Richard Nixon (elected in November 1968).

Nixon pursued a policy of *detente*, the idea that there are no significant differences between Communist countries and Western countries and that therefore they should cooperate wherever possible and no longer regard themselves as enemies. Nixon visited Communist China, the first U.S. President to grant legitimacy to the Peking government, and worked to end U.S. involvement in Vietnam as quickly as possible. His negotiators made the enormous concession of allowing North Vietnamese troops to remain in Vietnam after U.S. troops were withdrawn, a policy which almost guaranteed a Communist takeover.

The last U.S. combat troops were withdrawn in 1973. In 1975 the Communists launched a major offensive. U.S. government officials evacuated only about a quarter of the South Vietnamese who had worked with the Americans, thereby dooming those remaining to almost certain death. The Communists overran all of South Vietnam and soon had control of Laos and Cambodia as well, setting up brutal Communist dictatorships throughout the Indochinese peninsula. In Cambodia, the government of Pol Pot was responsible for the deaths of a quarter of the nation's population.

That same year, Angola and Mozambique (former Portuguese colonies in Africa) came under Communist control, as the U.S., disillusioned and embittered by Vietnam, refused to give anti-Communist freedom fighters any aid. Communists also solidified their control over Ethiopia. Their only failure in 1975 was in Portugal, where massive popular opposition arose to a Communist government which had seized power in the country of Fatima. On the anniversary of the July 13 apparition, thousands of Portuguese came to Fatima to beg Our Lady's intercession for their country. That same day, anti-Communist uprisings erupted. They continued throughout the summer, without any organized leadership except the spiritual inspiration provided by Francisco Maria da Silva, the Archbishop of Braga. By September the Communists had been forced out of the government and Portugal was saved.

But that failure, though an important one, did not stop the Communists. In 1979 they invaded Afghanistan and in that same year set up a Marxist government in the Central American country of Nicaragua. It was not until the mid-1980's, under President Reagan, that the U.S. began reversing its policy of detente to give aid to the freedom fighters resisting Communism around the world.

The Counter-Revolution against Communism

The utter failure of the Communist economic system to feed its people, the inability of a command economy to adapt to the computer age, the successes of the freedom fighters against Communist regimes, particularly in Afghanistan, and the consequent drains on the Soviet economy and military morale, all led Mikhail Gorbachev, who took over as General Secretary of the Communist Party in 1986, to announce his policies of glasnost (openness) and perestroika (restructuring). When this tiny crack was opened in the prison door, the satellite states of Eastern Europe did not hesitate to push the door open wide and march right through. Gorbachev chose to let them go, and the people of Eastern Europe knew a degree of freedom for the first time since World War II.

It is no accident that the counter-revolution against Communism began in Poland, the most Catholic of Eastern European countries and the home of Pope John Paul II. In 1980 the Pope had supported the Catholic labor union movement, Solidarity, led by Lech Walesa, even letting it be known privately that if Soviet tanks invaded Poland to crush Solidarity, the Pope would return to his homeland to be with his people. A Communist-backed attempt to assassinate the Pope failed on May 13, 1981, but in December of that year President Jaruzelski imposed martial law and arrested Walesa. Solidarity appeared to be crushed and freedom dead in Poland.

But the Polish economy did not improve, Solidarity stayed alive underground, and Pope John Paul II continued to speak out in favor of freedom and human rights. In January 1989, knowing that Gorbachev was not going to bail Poland out of its problems, President Jaruzelski opened negotiations with Solidarity leader Lech Walesa on re-legalization of Solidarity, granting full legalization in March and promising free elections. Solidarity and its supporters won the elections in a landslide, and Communism was out of power in Poland.

While it is difficult to know exactly what is transpiring in the former U.S.S.R., other Eastern European countries and the "republics" of the Soviet Union itself soon began following the road to freedom. The Berlin Wall was destroyed in November 1989; Czechoslovakia held "free" elections in December 1989; Hungary held its elections in March 1990. In the U.S.S.R. the republics of the Union of Soviet Socialist Republics began one by one declaring sovereignty. On June 12, 1991, Boris Yeltsin, who stood for independence for all the republics, a free market economy, and a democratic political system, was elected President of the Russian Republic. Communist hardliners attempted a coup in August 1991, but Yeltsin's leadership inspired resistance to the coup and it failed miserably. On December 25, 1991 the hammer and sickle flag was lowered for the last time from above the Kremlin. The name of Russia's second largest city was changed from Leningrad back to St. Petersburg. However, Communists still retain positions of power, and the political, social and economic situation in the former Soviet Union remains unsettled.

The legacy of atheism and suffering left by Communism will be with the people of Eastern Europe and the former Soviet Union for years if not decades to come. There is also the grave problem of secularism and materialism entering from the West. But after decades of slavery, the dark shadow of Communism appears at last to be lifting from these people.

The Second Vatican Council

In 1907 Pope St. Pius X had written the encyclical *Pascendi*, which condemned Modernism, that heresy which denied the historical reliability of Scripture and therefore the fact of the Incarnation, denied the role of the supernatural in our lives, and denied the existence of absolute, unchanging truth. The Pope's efforts against Modernism were largely successful, and the heresy disappeared from public view. For the next 50 years, as the Western world seemed to go up in flames, with large numbers of people rejecting a Christian world view to pursue false ideologies such as Nazism and Communism, or simply to take refuge in materialism, the Church was strong and united. Under Pius XI and Pius XII, the Church taught clearly and unmistakably on doctrinal and moral issues, and the Catholic people, clergy and laity alike, seemed to stand firmly with the Popes.

Pope Pius XII died in 1958. His successor was John XXIII. John shocked and surprised the Church and the world by calling an ecumenical council, Vatican Council II, the first since Vatican Council I in 1869-1870. He said that the teaching of Vatican II would be "predominantly pastoral." Few people could imagine why the Council had been called. Earlier councils had been called in response to major heresies or great crises in the Church, but the Church at the time seemed stronger than ever.

But though the supernatural strength of the Church is always infinite, because it is the strength of Christ, the worldly strength of the Church at this time was more apparent than real, as events would soon demonstrate. Though Modernism had been condemned in 1907, Modernism had not died. Gradually Modernists had gained key posts in seminaries, universities and diocesan offices throughout Europe and the United States. They had to teach their beliefs subtly and carefully, but over the years many people were unwittingly corrupted by some portion of Modernism. Even those who were not themselves affected by Modernism had no idea of how strong it still was. The outward strength of the Church led them to be complacent, unprepared to face a Modernist challenge, should one emerge.

The first session of Vatican Council II opened on October 11, 1962 and ended December 7. On June 3, 1963, Pope John XXIII died after a long, painful struggle with cancer. His successor was Pope Paul VI, who continued the Council with three more sessions: September 29–December 4, 1963; September 14–November 21, 1964; September 14–December 7, 1965. Many Modernists had succeeded in getting appointed as advisers to the Council Fathers. But because the Holy Spirit protects ecumenical councils when they are in union with the Pope, the Council documents contain no explicitly Modernist statements, although some statements have been seen as ambiguous. All of the Vatican II documents can be understood in accord with traditional Catholic doctrine, presenting Catholic teaching and calling upon all Catholics in the modern world to profess openly their

Faith and to use the graces of God to help bring that world closer to Christ.

Having failed to get the Council to teach Modernism, the Modernists tried another strategy. They were able to get their views into the Western press, which played up Modernist ideas as the "spirit of Vatican II" and totally ignored the actual teaching of the documents. In the United States and Western Europe, the Modernist views were the ones most often heard. Many orthodox clergy and religious did not realize that the Modernists were attacking unchangeable Catholic teachings and they did not study the Vatican II documents themselves, so they could not counter the threat. Modernist ideas spread like wildfire, leaving the ordinary people either misled into accepting Modernism or confused as to what the Church was really teaching. The concept that anything "pre-Vatican II" was now outdated became common. Some orthodox Catholics realized what was going on but over-reacted, some rejecting the Council altogether and others even rejecting the authority of the Pope to make any changes whatsoever in Church practices. Thus there were few in the West who really profited from the Council.

During the years after the Council, the non-Western world saw a phenomenal growth in converts and vocations. In Africa, for example, the Catholic population increased from 29 to 66 million from 1965-1985, with a consequent increase in vocations. Similar increases came in South Korea, Poland, and Central and South America. As the Western world turned from God, the non-Western world turned toward Him.

Pope Paul VI saw what was happening. He himself lamented that "the smoke of Satan" seemed to have entered the Church, but he chose not to take any direct action against the Modernist resurgence, perhaps for fear that in the confusion then existing, many people might be driven out of the Church by disciplinary action against a few. He chose instead to uphold orthodoxy through clear teaching, most notably the *Credo of the People of God,* which firmly restated fundamental Catholic doctrine, and the encyclical *Humanae Vitae (On Human Life),* which stressed the value of human life, the beauty of Christian marriage, and the instrinsic evil of contraception.

Because of both of these decisions—to teach clearly but not to discipline—the Pope was attacked on all sides. Liberals attacked him for his teachings, especially *Humanae Vitae,* openly encouraging disobedience to his moral teachings. On the other side, he was himself accused of being a Modernist because he did not take disciplinary actions against the Modernists and silence them and/or remove them from positions of authority. Thus, Pope Paul VI may have had a special vocation of suffering:

to endure the attacks against him and to offer them to God for the good of the Church.

Paul VI died in August 1978. His immediate successor, John Paul I, reigned only a month. He was succeeded by the first non-Italian Pope since the 16th century: Cardinal Karol Wojtyla of Poland, who took the name John Paul II. John Paul II continued the strong moral teaching of his predecessors, began to discipline Modernist leaders and traveled around the world so that Catholics and non-Catholics alike could see and hear the Supreme Pontiff. It is almost ironic that he be a Pope from a Communist country, since Communism has represented the greatest external threat to the Church in the twentieth century.

Throughout the Western world, the loss of moral and religious beliefs could be seen: the acceptance of divorce, the legalization of abortion, the increase of acceptance of immorality, the decline in the numbers of believing Christians and so on. This moral decline was the logical result of events which began with the sundering of Christendom in the sixteenth century. We have traced these events throughout the seventeenth, eighteenth and nineteenth centuries, and now see their culmination in the moral corruption of the late twentieth century. But the Church, founded by Christ on the Rock of St. Peter, holds firm to doctrinal and moral truth. Only in the Holy Catholic Church can the answers to the problems of the modern world be found.

Review Questions

1. What happened at the Yalta Conference?
2. What happened in Germany immediately after the war? What did this reveal about the possibility of postwar cooperation?
3. What was the Truman Doctrine (containment)? What was the Cold War?
4. Describe the fall of China to the Communists.
5. Summarize the main events of the Korean War. What was its significance?
6. What was the significance of the Hiss-Chambers case? What did McCarthy try to do? What happened to him?
7. What happened during the Hungarian fight for freedom? What role did the U.S. play? What did this reveal about U.S. policies?
8. What gains did the Communists make in 1960 and 1961?

9. What kind of leader was Diem? How did the Communists undermine his authority? Describe his overthrow.
10. What were the short-term and long-term results of the overthrow of Diem?
11. Why did the U.S. decide to withdraw from Vietnam? What were the results of this withdrawal?
12. What other gains did the Communists make in 1975 and shortly thereafter?
13. Where did the Communists fail? Why?
14. What were perestroika and glasnost?
15. List three reasons why Gorbachev announced the policies of perestroika and glasnost.
16. Explain the role of Pope John Paul II in the liberation of Poland from Communism.
17. Explain the steps by which Poland's liberation was achieved.
18. List the steps that brought about the end of the Communist regime in the Soviet Union.
19. Summarize the history of Modernism up to the calling of Vatican Council II.
20. Who called the Council? Why was this a surprise?
21. Describe the Council documents. How did the Modernists subvert the Council?
22. Give evidence since the Council of the flowering of the Faith in the non-Western world.
23. Describe the pontificate of Pope Paul VI.
24. Describe the pontificate of Pope John Paul II.
25. How does the Church stand in contrast to the modern world?

Projects

1. Do research and then act out an event from this chapter. (Some suggestions: Yalta Conference, Whittaker Chambers-Alger Hiss confrontation, Army-McCarthy hearings.)
2. Write an eyewitness account of one of the events of this chapter.
3. Read one of the documents of Vatican II and summarize its contents.
4. Read an encyclical by Pope Paul VI or Pope John Paul II and summarize its contents.

Epilogue
History and the Future

As WE SAID IN THE FIRST CHAPTER, history is the story of events which have made a difference to the world. The writing of history requires the passage of time, so that the effect of events can be judged. Therefore, we cannot comment on current events because it is not yet possible to make historical judgments on these events.

But we can look to the future, using the knowledge we have gained of the past. Though public life in many of the countries of the world has become anti-Christian, though politics are a matter of power rather than of justice, though wars have become much more destructive of innocent persons than ever before, yet hope remains. Christianity grows rapidly in Africa, the Popes issue strong statements on doctrinal and moral questions, orthodox lay people begin initiatives in education, pro-life and other areas. The West is declining, but other areas of the world may be rising to take its place. Or new sources of strength may be found in the countries that have been the centers of Christian civilization for so long. Through it all, Christ the King, the Lord of History, will be bringing members of His Kingdom on earth to perfection. We may not always be able to understand how this is happening, but we know that it will.

So we come to the end of a story which began four thousand years ago in the plains of Sumeria when God spoke to Abraham. We have seen empires and conquerors come and go. We have seen great villains: Rameses II, Nero, Attila, Cecil, Richelieu, Robespierre, Napoleon, Lenin, Hitler, Ho Chi Minh. We have seen great heroes: Abraham, Moses, the early martyrs, Pope Leo the Great, St. Patrick, Charlemagne, Queen Isabel, Charles V, Philip II, Maria Teresa, the men and women of the Alcazar, the Hungarian Freedom Fighters. The struggle between good and evil has gone on continually; and though we know that good will triumph overall, we can never be sure of the outcome of any individual battle. But through it all, one institution has survived every crisis, weathered every storm: the Catholic Church. Nothing else comes close to equaling its record. And probably the only safe prediction that can be made about the future is that the Church will continue to survive and provide the means of salvation until history is completed and Christ comes in glory at the end of the world.

Project

Make a mural illustrating the most important events in history from Abraham to the present.

Bibliography

Auclair, Marcelle. *Teresa of Avila.* Doubleday, Garden City, N.Y., 1953.

Bradford, Ernle. *The Great Siege.* Harcourt, Brace, New York, 1961.

Brandi, Karl. *The Emperor Charles V.* Humanities Press, Atlantic Highlands, N.J., 1939.

Brook-Shepherd, Gordon. *The Last Hasburg.* London, 1968.

Carroll, Warren H. *The Building of Christendom.* Christendom College Press, Front Royal, Virginia, 1987.

_____. *The Founding of Christendom.* Christendom College Press, Front Royal, Virginia, 1985.

_____. *1917: Red Banners, White Mantle.* Christendom College Press, Front Royal, Virginia, 1981.

Catholic Encyclopedia. Encyclopedia Press, New York, 1912.

Chamberlin, E. R. *Marguerite of Navarre.* Dial, New York, 1974.

Chambers, Whittaker. *Witness.* Random House, New York, 1952.

Crankshaw, Edward. *The Fall of the House of Habsburg.* Viking, New York, 1963.

_____. *The Habsburgs.* Viking, New York, 1971.

_____. *Maria Theresa.* Viking, New York, 1969.

_____. *The Shadow of the Winter Palace.* Viking, New York, 1976.

Cowden-Guido, Richard. *Report from the Synod.* Trinity, Manassas, Virginia, 1986.

Cronin, Vincent. *Louis and Antoinette.* Morrow, New York, 1975.

_____. *Pearl to India.* Dutton, New York, 1959.

_____. *The Wise Man from the West.* Doubleday, Garden City, N.Y., 1957.

Daniel-Rops, Henri. *Cathedral and Crusade.* Doubleday, Garden City, N.Y., 1963.

_____. *The Catholic Reformation.* Doubleday, Garden City, N.Y., 1964.

_____. *The Church in the Dark Ages.* Doubleday, Garden City, N.Y., 1962.

_____. *The Church of Apostles and Martyrs.* Doubleday, Garden City, 1962.

_____. *The Protestant Reformation.* Doubleday, Garden City, N.Y., 1963.

Dirvin, Joseph. *Saint Catherine Labouré of the Miraculous Medal.* Farrar, Straus and Cudahy, New York, 1958.

Eberhardt, Newman. *A Summary of Catholic History.* Herder, St. Louis, 1960.

Fraser, Antonia. *Mary, Queen of Scots.* Greenwich House, New York, 1969.

—————. *Royal Charles.* Knopf, New York, 1979.

Gillingham, John. *Richard the Lionheart.* Times Books, New York, 1978.

Hales, E. E. Y. *Pio Nono.* Kenedy, New York, 1954.

—————. *Revolution and Papacy.* University of Notre Dame, Notre Dame, Indiana, 1966.

Pratt, Fletcher. *The Battles that Changed History.* Hanover House, Garden City, N.Y., 1956.

Heller, John. *Report on the Shroud of Turin.* Houghton Mifflin, Boston, 1983.

Hollis, Christopher and Ronald Brownrigg. *Holy Places.* Praeger, New York, 1969.

Howarth, David. *The Voyage of the Armada.* Viking, New York, 1981.

Hughes, David. *The Star of Bethlehem.* Pocket Books, New York, 1979.

Jarrett, Bede. *Life of St. Dominic.* Doubleday, Garden City, N.Y., 1964.

Kubek, Anthony. *How the Far East Was Lost.* Regnery, Chicago, 1963.

Longford, Elizabeth. *Wellington: The Years of the Sword.* Harper & Row, New York, 1969.

Loomis, Stanley. *The Fatal Friendship.* Doubleday, Garden City, N.Y., 1972.

—————. *Paris in the Terror.* Lippincott, Philadelphia, 1964.

Mann, Horace. *The Lives of the Popes in the Middle Ages.* Kegan Paul, Trench, Trubner & Co., London, 1932.

Massie, Robert. *Nicholas and Alexandra.* New York, 1967.

Mattingly, Garret. *Catherine of Aragon.* Vintage Books, New York, 1941.

Mirus, Jeffrey A., ed. *Reasons for Hope.* Christendom College Press, Front Royal, Virginia, 1982.

Morison, Samuel Eliot. *Admiral of the Ocean Sea.* Little, Brown, Boston, 1942.

—————. *Coral Sea, Midway and Submarine Actions.* Little, Brown, Boston, 1958.

—————. *Leyte.* Little, Brown, Boston, 1958.

Pastor, Ludwig. *History of the Popes.* Kegan Paul, Trench, Trubner & Co., London, 1923.

Pearlman, Moshe. *The Maccabees.* New York, 1963.

Purcell, Mary. *The First Jesuit*. Doubleday, Garden City, N.Y., 1956.
Renault, Gilbert. *The Caravels of Christ*. Putnam, New York, 1959.
Ricciotti, Guiseppe. *The Age of Martyrs*. Bruce, Milwaukee, 1959.
Shirer, William L. *The Rise and Fall of the Third Reich*. Fawcett Crest,
    New York, 1960.
Thomas, Hugh. *The Spanish Civil War*. Harper & Row, New York, 1961.
Todd, James Henthorn, trans. *The War of the Gaedhil with the Gaill, or The
    Invasions of Ireland by the Danes and other Norsemen*. Longmans,
    Green, London, 1867.
Tuchman, Barbara. *The Guns of August*. Dell, New York, 1962.
Walsh, William Thomas. *Isabella of Spain*. McBride, New York, 1930.
──────────. *Philip II*. Sheed and Ward, New York, 1937.
──────────. *Saint Peter the Apostle*. Macmillan, New York, 1948.
Waugh, Evelyn. *Edmund Campion*. Doubleday, Garden City, N.Y., 1956.
Wedgwood, C. V. *The King's Peace*. Collier Books, New York, 1955.
──────────. *The Thirty Years War*. Doubleday, Garden City, N.Y., 1961.
Weider, Ben and David Hapgood. *The Murder of Napoleon*. Berkley
    Books, New York, 1983.
Wilson, Ian. *The Shroud of Turin*. Doubleday, Garden City, N.Y., 1978.
Winston, Richard. *Thomas Becket*. Knopf, New York, 1967.

Index

Great Catholic History Texts For High School and Up!!

About The Author

Anne W. Carroll is the founder and director of Seton School in Manassas, Virginia, where she has spent the last 20 years developing and teaching an authentically Catholic curriculum at the junior and senior high school levels.

Holding an M.A. in English, Mrs. Carroll has taught many subjects over the years and has a special love for history. She uses *Christ the King—Lord of History* for a two-year history curriculum covered in the freshman and sophomore years.

Mrs. Carroll resides in Manassas, Virginia with her husband, Warren H. Carroll, noted Catholic historian and founder of Christendom College.